A Practical Introduction to Data Structures and Algorithm Analysis
Java Edition

Clifford A. Shaffer

Department of Computer Science
Virginia Tech

An Alan R. Apt Book

PRENTICE HALL, Upper Saddle River, New Jersey 07458

Library of Congress Cataloging-in-Publication Data

Shaffer, Clifford, A.
    A Practical Introduction to Data Structures and Algorithm Analysis, Java Edition
        p. cm.
    "An Alan R. Apt book"
    Includes bibliographical references and index.
    ISBN: 0-13-660911-2
CIP Data available

Publisher: **ALAN APT**
Editor: **LAURA STEELE**
Production editor: **EDWARD DEFELIPPIS**
Editor-in-chief: **MARCIA HORTON**
Managing editor: **BAYANI MENDOZA DE LEON**
Assistant Vice President of Production and Manufacturing: **DAVID W. RICCARDI**
Art director: **HEATHER SCOTT**
Cover designer:
Copy editor: **TRULY DONOVAN**
Manufacturing buyer: **JULIA MEEHAN**
Editorial Assistant: **KATE KAIBNI**

Printed in the United States of America

10 9 8 7 6 5 4

ISBN   0-13-660911-2

Prentice-Hall International (UK) Limited, *London*
Prentice-Hall of Australia Pty. Limited, *Sydney*
Prentice-Hall of Canada, Inc., *Toronto*
Prentice-Hall Hispanoamericana, S. A., *Mexico*
Prentice-Hall of India Private Limited, *New Delhi*
Prentice-Hall of Japan, Inc., *Tokyo*
Pearson Education Asia Pte. Ltd., *Singapore*
Editora Prentice-Hall do Brasil, Ltda., *Rio de Janeiro*

Contents

Preface

We study data structures so that we can learn to write more efficient programs. But why must programs be efficient when new computers are faster every year? The reason is that our ambitions grow with our capabilities. Instead of rendering efficiency needs obsolete, the modern revolution in computing power and storage capability merely raises the efficiency stakes as we computerize more complex tasks.

The quest for program efficiency need not and should not conflict with sound design and clear coding. Creating efficient programs has little to do with "programming tricks," but rather is based on good organization of information and good algorithms. A programmer who has not mastered the basic principles of clear design will not likely write efficient programs. Conversely, clear programs require clear data organization and clear algorithms. Most computer science curricula recognize that good programming skills begin with a strong emphasis on fundamental software engineering principles. Then, once a programmer has learned the principles of clear program design and implementation, the next step is to study the effects of data organization and algorithms on program efficiency.

Approach: Many techniques for representing data are described in this book. These techniques are presented within the context of the following principles:

1. Each data structure and each algorithm has costs and benefits. Practitioners need a thorough understanding of how to assess costs and benefits to be able to adapt to new design challenges. This requires an understanding of the principles of algorithm analysis, and also an appreciation of the significant effects of the physical medium employed (e.g., data stored on disk versus main memory).

2. Related to costs and benefits is the notion of tradeoffs. For example, it is quite common to reduce time requirements at the expense of an increase in space requirements, or vice versa. Programmers face tradeoff issues regularly in all phases of software design and implementation, so the concept must become deeply ingrained.

3. Programmers should know enough about common practice to avoid reinventing the wheel. Thus, students need to learn the commonly used data structures and related algorithms.

4. Data structures follow needs. Students must learn to assess application needs first, then find a data structure with matching capabilities. To do this requires competence in principles 1, 2, and 3.

Organization: Data structures and algorithms textbooks tend to fall into one of two categories: teaching texts or encyclopedias. Books that attempt to do both usually fail at both. This book is intended as a teaching text. I believe it is more important for a practitioner to understand the principles required to select or design the data structure that will best solve some problem than it is to memorize a lot of textbook implementations. Hence, I have designed this as a teaching text that covers most standard data structures, but not all. A few data structures that are not widely adopted are used to illustrate important principles. Some relatively new data structures that should become widely used in the future are included.

This book is intended for a single semester course at the undergraduate level, or for self-study by technical professionals. Readers should have programming experience, typically two semesters or the equivalent of a structured programming language such as Pascal or **C**. Prerequisite mathematical techniques are reviewed in Chapter 2; readers who are already familiar with induction proofs and recursion will have an advantage.

While this book is designed for a one semester course, there is more material here than can properly be covered in one semester. This is deliberate, and provides some flexibility to the instructor. A sophomore level class where students have little background in basic data structures or analysis might cover Chapters 1-12 in detail, as well as selected topics from Chapter 13. That is how I use the book for my own sophomore level class. Students with greater background might cover Chapter 1, skip most of Chapter 2 except for reference, briefly cover Chapters 3 and 4 (but pay attention to Section 4.1.3), and then cover the remaining chapters in detail. Again, only certain topics from Chapter 13 might be covered, depending on the programming assignments selected by the instructor.

Chapter 13 is intended in part as a source for larger programming exercises. I recommend that all students taking a data structures course be required to implement some advanced tree structure, or another dynamic structure of comparable difficulty such as the Skip List or sparse matrix representations of Chapter 12. None of these data structures are significantly more difficult to implement than the Binary Search Tree, and any of them should be within a student's ability after completing Chapter 5.

While I have attempted to arrange the presentation in an order that makes sense, instructors should feel free to re-arrange the topics as they see fit. Once the reader has mastered Chapters 1-6, the remaining material has relatively few dependencies. Clearly, external sorting depends on understanding internal sorting and disk files. Section 6.2 on the UNION/FIND algorithm is used in Kruskal's Minimum-Cost Spanning Tree algorithm. Section 10.2 on self-organizing lists mentions the buffer replacement schemes covered in Section 9.3. Chapter 14 draws on examples from throughout the book. Section 15.3 relies on knowledge of graphs. Otherwise, most topics depend only on material presented earlier within the same chapter.

Use of Java: The programming examples are written in Java™. As with any programming language, Java has both advantages and disadvantages. Java is a small language. There usually is only one way to do something, and this has the happy tendency of encouraging a programmer toward clarity when used correctly. In this respect, it is superior to **C** or **C++**. Java serves nicely for defining and using most traditional data structures such as lists and trees. On the other hand, Java is quite poor when used to do file processing, being both cumbersome and inefficient. It is also a poor language when fine control of memory is required. As an example, applications requiring memory management, such as those discussed in Section 12.4, are difficult to write in Java. Since I wish to stick to a single language throughout the text, like any programmer I must take the bad along with the good. The most important issue is to get the ideas across, whether or not those ideas are natural to a particular language of discourse. Most programmers will use a variety of programming languages throughout their career, and the concepts described in this book should prove useful in a variety of circumstances.

I do not wish to discourage those unfamiliar with Java from reading this book. I have attempted to make the examples as clear as possible while maintaining the advantages of Java. Java is used here strictly as a tool to illustrate data structures concepts. Fortunately, Java is an easy language for **C** or Pascal programmers to read with a minimal amount of study of the syntax related to object-oriented programming. In particular, I make use of Java's support for hiding implementation details, including features such as classes, private class members, and interfaces. These features of the language support the crucial concept of separating logical design, as embodied in the abstract data type, from physical implementation as embodied in the data structure.

I make no attempt to teach Java within the text. An Appendix is provided that describes the Java syntax and concepts necessary to understand the program examples. I also provide the actual Java code used in the text through anonymous FTP.

Inheritance, a key feature of object-oriented programming, is used only sparingly in the code examples. Inheritance is an important tool that helps programmers avoid duplication, and thus minimize bugs. From a pedagogical standpoint, however, inheritance often makes code examples harder to understand since it tends to spread the description for one logical unit among several classes. Thus, some of my class definitions for objects such as tree or list nodes do not take full advantage of possible inheritance from earlier code examples. This does not mean that a programmer should do likewise. Avoiding code duplication and minimizing errors are important goals. Treat the programming examples as illustrations of data structure principles, but do not copy them directly into your own programs.

My Java implementations serve to provide concrete illustrations of data structure principles. They are not meant to be a series of commercial-quality Java class implementations. The code examples provide less parameter checking than is sound programming practice for commercial programmers. Some parameter checking is included in the form of calls to functions in class **Assert**. These functions are modeled after the **C** standard library function **assert**. Method **Assert.notFalse** takes a Boolean expression. If this expression evaluates to **false**, then the program terminates immediately. Method **Assert.notNull** takes a reference to class **Object**, and terminates the program if the value of the reference is **null**. (To be precise, these functions throw an **IllegalArgumentException**, which typically results in terminating the program unless the programmer takes action to handle the exception.) Terminating a program when a function receives a bad parameter is generally considered undesirable in real programs, but is quite adequate for understanding how a data structure is meant to operate. In real programming applications, Java's exception handling features should be used to deal with input data errors.

I make a distinction in the text between "Java implementations" and "pseudocode." Code labeled as a Java implementation has actually been compiled and tested on one or more Java compilers. Pseudocode examples often conform closely to Java syntax, but typically contain one or more lines of higher level description. Pseudocode is used where I perceived a greater pedagogical advantage to a simpler, but less precise, description.

Most chapters end with a section entitled "Further Reading." These sections are not comprehensive lists of references on the topics presented. Rather, I include books and articles that, in my opinion, may prove exceptionally informative or entertaining to the reader. In some cases I include references to works that should become familiar to any well-rounded computer scientist.

Exercises and Projects: Proper use of data structures cannot be learned simply by reading a book. You must practice by implementing real programs, constantly comparing different techniques to see what really works best in a given situation. At the same time, students should also work problems to develop their analytical abilities. I provide over 300 exercises and suggestions for programming projects. I urge readers to take advantage of them.

Contacting the Author and Supplementary Materials: A book such as this is sure to contain errors and have room for improvement. I welcome bug reports and constructive criticism. I can be reached by electronic mail via the Internet at **shaffer@cs.vt.edu**. Alternatively, comments can be mailed to:

> Cliff Shaffer
> Department of Computer Science
> Virginia Tech
> Blacksburg, VA 24061

A set of LaTeX-based transparency masters for use in conjunction with this book can be obtained via anonymous FTP at **ftp.prenhall.com** in directory

`pub/esm/computer_science.s-041/shaffer/ds/supplements/transparencies`

The Java code examples are also available from this site at

`pub/esm/computer_science.s-041/shaffer/ds/code`

Online WWW pages for Virginia Tech's sophomore level data structures class can be found at URL

http://ei.cs.vt.edu/~cs2604

as can information about SWAN, a data structure visualization and graphical debugging tool.

This book was typeset by the author with LaTeX, a macro package for TeX. The bibliography was prepared using BibTeX. The index was prepared using `makeindex`. The figures were mostly drawn with `Xfig`. Figures 3.1 and 10.5 were partially created using Mathematica.

Acknowledgments: It takes a lot of help from a lot of people to make a book. I wish to acknowledge a few of those who helped to make this book possible. I apologize for the inevitable omissions. My department head, Jack Carroll, provided unwavering moral support of this project. Virginia Tech helped make this whole thing possible through sabbatical research leave during Fall 1994, enabling me to get this project off the ground. Mike Keenan, Lenny Heath, and Jeff Shaffer provided valuable input on early versions of the chapters. I especially wish to thank Lenny Heath for many years of stimulating discussions about algorithms and analysis (and how to teach both to students). Thanks to Layne Watson for his help with Mathematica, and to Bo Begole, Philip Isenhour, Jeff Nielsen, and Craig Struble for much technical assistance. Thanks to Steve Edwards, Mark Abrams and Dennis Kafura for answering lots of silly questions about C++ and Java.

I am truly indebted to the many reviewers of this manuscript. Reviewers include: J. David Bezek (University of Evansville), Douglas Campbell (Brigham Young University), Karen Davis (University of Cincinnati), Vijay Kumar Garg (University of Texas – Austin), Jim Miller (University of Kansas), Bruce Maxim (University of Michigan – Dearborn), Jeff Parker (Agile Networks/Harvard), Dana Richards (George Mason University), Jack Tan (University of Houston), and Lixin Tao (Concordia University). Without their help, this book would contain many more technical errors and many fewer insights.

Without the hard work of many people at Prentice Hall, none of this would be possible. Authors simply do not create printer-ready books on their own. Foremost thanks go to Laura Steele and Alan Apt, my editors. My production editors, Kathleen Caren for the C++ version, and Ed DeFelippis for the Java version, kept everything moving smoothly during that horrible rush at the end. Thanks to Bill Zobrist and Bruce Gregory (I think) for getting me into this in the first place. Others at Prentice Hall who helped me along the way include Truly Donovan, Linda Behrens and Phyllis Bregman.

I am sure I owe thanks to many others at Prentice Hall for their help in ways that I am not even aware of.

I wish to express my appreciation to Hanan Samet for teaching me about data structures. I learned much of the philosophy presented here from him as well, though he is not responsible for any problems with the result. Thanks to my wife, Terry, for her love and support. Finally, and most importantly, to all of the data structures students over the years who have taught me what is important and what should be skipped in a data structures course, and the many new insights they have provided. This book is dedicated to them.

Clifford A. Shaffer
Blacksburg, Virginia
1997

Part I

Preliminaries

1

Data Structures and Algorithms

Representing information is fundamental to computer science. The primary purpose of most computer programs is to store and retrieve information rather than to perform calculations. To be practical in terms of storage requirements and running time, such programs must organize their information in a way that supports efficient processing. For this reason, the study of data structures and the algorithms that manipulate them is at the heart of computer science.

1.1 A Philosophy of Data Structures

1.1.1 The Need for Data Structures

You might think that with ever more powerful computers, program efficiency is becoming less important. However, more powerful computers encourage us to attempt more complex problems. More complex problems demand more computation, making the need for efficient programs even greater. As tasks become more complex they become less like our everyday experience. Today's computer scientists must be trained to have a thorough understanding of the principles behind efficient program design, since their ordinary life experiences often do not apply when designing programs.

In the most general sense, a data structure is any data representation and its associated operations. Viewed as a data representation, even an integer or floating point number stored on the computer is a simple data structure. More typically, a data structure is meant to be an organization or structuring for a collection of data items. A sorted list of integers stored in an array is an example of such a structuring.

3

Given sufficient space to store a collection of data items, it is always possible to search for specified items within the collection, print or otherwise process the data items in any desired order, or modify the value of any particular data item. Thus, it is possible to perform all necessary operations on any data structure. However, the choice of data structure can make the difference between a program running in a few seconds and one requiring many days.

It should go without saying that people write programs to solve problems. However, it is crucial to keep this truism in mind when selecting a data structure to solve a particular problem. Only by first analyzing the problem to determine the performance goals that must be achieved can there be any hope of selecting the right data structure for the job. A surprising number of program designers ignore this analysis step, and apply a data structure that they are familiar with but which is inappropriate to the problem. The result is typically a slow program. Conversely, there is no sense in adopting a complex representation to "improve" a program that can meet its performance goals when implemented using a simpler design.

Definition 1.1 A solution is said to be **efficient** if it solves the problem within the required **resource constraints**. Examples of resource constraints include the total space available to store the data – possibly divided into separate main memory and disk space constraints – and the time allowed to perform each subtask. A solution may also be called efficient if it requires fewer resources than known alternatives. The **cost** of a solution is the amount of resources that the solution consumes. Most often, cost is measured in terms of one key resource such as time, with the implied assumption that the solution meets the other resource constraints.

When selecting a data structure to solve a problem, you should follow these steps:

1. Analyze your problem to determine the resource constraints that any solution must meet.

2. Determine the basic operations that must be supported and quantify the resource constraints for each operation. Examples of basic operations include inserting a data item into the data structure, deleting a data item from the data structure, and finding a specified data item.

3. Select the data structure that best meets these requirements.

This three-step approach to selecting a data structure operationalizes a data-centered view to design. The first concern is for the data and the operations to be performed on them, the next concern is the representation for those data, and the final concern is the implementation of that representation.

Resource constraints on certain key operations, such as search, inserting data records, and deleting data records, normally drive the data structure selection process. Many issues relating to the relative importance of these operations are addressed by the following three questions, which you should ask yourself whenever you must choose a data structure:

- Are all data items inserted into the data structure at the beginning, or are insertions interspersed with other operations?

- Can data items be deleted?

- Are all data items processed in some well-defined order, or is random access allowed?

Typically, interspersing insertions with other operations, allowing deletion, and supporting random access to data items all require more complex rep-resentations.

1.1.2 Costs and Benefits

Each data structure has associated costs and benefits. It is generally incorrect to say that one data structure is better than another for use in all situations. For nearly every data structure and algorithm presented in this book, you will see examples of where it is the best choice. Some of the examples will be surprising.

A data structure requires a certain amount of space for each data item it stores, a certain amount of time to perform a single basic operation, and a certain amount of programming effort. Each problem has constraints on available space and time. Each solution to a problem makes use of the basic operations in some relative proportion, and the data structure selection process must account for this. Only after a careful analysis of your problem's characteristics can you determine the best data structure for the task.

> **Example 1.1** A database system to support a bank's customer account records is being designed. It must be possible for customer accounts to be added and deleted, and for the customer to get account

information and make deposits and withdrawals. Customers are willing to wait a few minutes while accounts are created or deleted, but are not willing to wait more than a few seconds for an individual account transaction such as a money deposit or withdrawal.

The bank provides an automated teller machine (ATM) for customer access to account balances, and to do deposits and withdrawals. These ATM transactions do not modify the database significantly (for simplicity, assume that if money is added or removed, this transaction simply changes the value stored in an account record). Adding a new account to the database is allowed to take several minutes (the typical customer opens accounts infrequently, waiting in the bank manager's office while it happens). Deleting an account has no time constraint, since from the customer's point of view all that matters is that all the money be returned (equivalent to a withdrawal). From the bank's point of view, the account record might be removed from the database system after business hours.

A data structure that is inefficient for deletion, but highly efficient for search and moderately efficient for insertion, should meet the resource constraints imposed by this problem. Records are accessible by account number (sometimes called an "exact match" search). One data structure that meets these requirements is the hash table described in Chapter 10.4. Hash tables allow for extremely fast exact match search. Records can be modified quickly when the modification does not affect their length. Hash tables also support efficient insertion of new records. While deletions can also be supported efficiently, too many deletions lead to some degradation in performance for the remaining operations. However, the hash table can be reorganized periodically to restore the system to peak efficiency. Such reorganization can occur off-line so as not to affect ATM transactions.

1.1.3 Goals of This Book

This book has three primary goals. The first is to teach the commonly used data structures. These form a programmer's basic data structure "toolkit." For many problems, a data structure in the toolkit is the ideal choice.

The second goal is to teach the idea of tradeoffs and reinforce the concept that there are costs and benefits associated with every data structure. This is done by presenting the various data structures and showing their costs and benefits when applied to sample problems.

The third goal is to teach how to measure the effectiveness of a data structure or algorithm. Only through such measurement can you determine which data structure in your toolkit is most appropriate for a new problem. The techniques presented also allow you to judge the merits of new data structures that you or others might invent.

1.2 Abstract Data Types and Data Structures

The previous section presented the terms "data item" and "data structure" without properly defining them. This section presents terminology and motivates the design process embodied in the three-step approach to selecting a data structure.

Definition 1.2 A **type** is a collection of values. For example, the Boolean type consists of the values **true** and **false**. The integers also form a type. A **data type** is a type together with a collection of operations to manipulate the type. For example, an integer variable is a member of the integer data type. Addition is an example of an operation on the integer data type. A **data item** is a piece of information or a record whose value is drawn from a type. A data item is said to be a **member** of a data type. An integer is a **simple data item** because it contains no subparts. A bank account record may contain several pieces of information such as name, address, account number, and account balance. Such a record is an example of an **aggregate data item**.

There is an important distinction to be made between the description of a data type and its implementation in a computer program. For example, there are the two traditional data structures for implementing the list data type: the linked list and the array-based list. The list data type is therefore implemented by one of a choice of data structures: a linked list or an array. Even the term "array" is ambiguous in that it can refer either to a data type or an implementation. "Array" is commonly used in computer programming to mean a contiguous block of memory locations, where each memory location stores one fixed-length data item. By this meaning, an array is a particular data structure. However, array can also mean a data type composed of a homogeneous collection of data items, each data item identified by a particular index number. From this perspective, it is possible to implement arrays in many different ways. For example, Section 12.3 describes the data structure used to implement a sparse matrix, a large two-dimensional array that stores only a relatively few non-zero values. This implementation is quite different from the traditional array of contiguous memory locations.

Definition 1.3 An **abstract data type** (ADT) defines a data type solely in terms of a type and a set of operations on that type. Each operation is defined by its inputs and outputs. An ADT definition does not specify *how* the data type is implemented. These details are properly hidden from the user of the ADT. The process of hiding implementation details is known as **encapsulation**. A **data structure** is the physical implementation of an ADT. Each operation associated with the ADT is implemented by one or more subroutines. The term "data structure" often refers to data stored in a computer's main memory. The related term **file structure** often refers to the organization of data on peripheral storage, such as a disk drive or magnetic tape.

Example 1.2 The mathematical concept of an integer, along with operations that manipulate integers, form an ADT. The Java `int` variable type is a physical representation of the abstract integer. Unfortunately, the `int` variable representation is not completely true to the abstract integer, as there are limitations on the range of values an `int` variable may store. If these limitations prove unacceptable, then some other implementation for the ADT "integer" must be devised.

Example 1.3 An ADT for a list of integers might include the following operations:

- Insert a new integer at the end of the list.
- Print the integers in order as they appear in the list.
- Return `true` if a particular integer is in the list.
- Delete the integer at a particular position in the list.

From this description, the input and output of each operation should be clear, but the implementation for lists has not been specified.

Example 1.4 When operating a car, the primary activities are steering, accelerating and braking. On nearly all passenger cars, you steer by turning the steering wheel, accelerate by pushing the gas pedal, and brake by pushing the brake pedal. This design for cars can be viewed as an ADT with operations "steer," "accelerate" and "brake." Two cars may implement these operations in radically different ways, yet most drivers can operate many different cars since the ADT presents a uniform method of operation.

The concept of an ADT is one instance of an important principle that must be understood by any successful computer scientist: managing complexity through abstraction. A central theme of computer science is complexity and techniques for handling it. Humans deal with complexity by assigning a label to an assembly of objects or concepts, and then manipulating the label in place of the assembly. Cognitive psychologists call such a label a **metaphor**. A particular label may be related to other pieces of information or other labels. This collection may in turn be given a label, forming a hierarchy of concepts and labels. This hierarchy of labels allows us to focus on important issues while ignoring unnecessary details.

> **Example 1.5** We apply the label "hard drive" to a collection of hardware that manipulates data on a particular type of storage device, and we use the label "CPU" for the hardware that controls execution of computer instructions. These and other labels are gathered together under the label "computer." Since even small home computers have millions of components, some form of abstraction is necessary before you can comprehend how a computer operates.

Imagine a complex computer program that implements and manipulates an ADT. The ADT is implemented in one part of the program by a particular data structure. While designing those parts of the program that use the ADT, we can think in terms of operations on the data type without concern for the data structure's implementation. Without this ability to simplify our thinking about a complex program, we would have no hope of understanding or implementing it.

> **Definition 1.4** Data items have both a **logical** and a **physical** form. The definition of the data item by an ADT is its logical form. The implementation of the data item within a data structure is its physical form.

> **Example 1.6** A particular Java environment may provide a library of functions for manipulating lists of integers. The logical form of the list is defined by the collection of functions, their inputs, and their

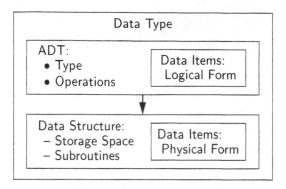

Figure 1.1 The relationship between data items, abstract data types, and data structures. The ADT defines the logical form of the data type. The data structure implements the physical form of the data type.

outputs (in other words, an ADT). Internally, a variety of physical implementations for lists of integers is possible. Several are described in Section 4.1.

Figure 1.1 illustrates this relationship between logical and physical forms for data items.

Some sections of this book focus on physical implementations for a given data structure. Other sections use the logical ADT for the data type in the context of a higher level task. To help separate the logical ADT for a data type from its physical implementation as a data structure, the program examples used in this book are written in Java. As an object-oriented programming language, Java provides many features to support encapsulation. The program examples are meant to be understandable by anyone who has experience with a structured programming language such as Pascal or **C**. If you have problems reading the examples due to unfamiliarity with Java, be sure to read the Appendix carefully. The Appendix introduces the Java syntax and concepts used in the book. While it is not sufficient to teach you how to write programs in Java, the Appendix should be sufficient to let you understand the Java examples. Readers already familiar with Java can safely ignore the Appendix.

1.3 Problems, Algorithms, and Programs

While this is a book mainly concerned with data structures and related algorithms, programmers deal constantly with problems, algorithms, and computer programs. These are three distinct concepts.

Problems: As your intuition would suggest, a **problem** is a task to be performed. It is best thought of in terms of inputs and matching outputs. A problem definition should not include any constraints on *how* the problem is to be solved – the solution method should be developed only after the problem is precisely defined and thoroughly understood. However, a problem definition should include constraints on the resources that may be consumed by any acceptable solution. For any problem to be solved by a computer, there are always such constraints, whether stated or implied. For example, any computer program may use only the main memory and disk space available, and it must run in a "reasonable" amount of time.

Problems can be viewed as functions in the mathematical sense.

Definition 1.5 A **function** is a matching between inputs (the **domain**) and outputs (the **range**). An input to a function may be a single value or a collection of information. The values making up an input are called the **parameters** of the function. Different inputs are permitted to generate the same output. However, any particular input must always result in the same output every time the function is computed using that input.

This concept of all problems being functions might not match your intuition for the behavior of computer programs. You might know of programs to which you can give the same value on two separate occasions, and two different outputs will result. For example, if you type "date" on many computers, you will get the current date. Naturally the date will be different on different days, even though the same command is given. However, there is obviously more to the input for the date program than the command that you type to run the program. The date program computes a function. In other words, on any particular day there can only be a single answer returned by a properly running date program on a completely specified input. For all computer programs, the output is completely determined by the program's full set of inputs. Even a "random number generator" is completely determined by its inputs (although some random number generating systems appear to get around this by accepting a random input from a physical process beyond the user's control). The relationship between programs and functions is explored further in Section 15.4.

Algorithms: An **algorithm** is a method or a process followed to solve a problem. If the problem is viewed as a function, then an algorithm takes the input and transforms it to the output. A problem can be solved by many different algorithms. A given algorithm solves only one problem (i.e., computes a particular function). This book covers many problems, and for several of these problems I present more than one algorithm. For the important problem of sorting I present nearly a dozen algorithms!

The advantage of knowing several solutions to a problem is that different solutions may be more efficient for specific variations of the problem, or for different inputs to the same problem. For example, one sorting algorithm may be the best for sorting small sets of numbers, another might be the best for sorting large sets of numbers, and a third might be the best for sorting variable length strings.

By definition, an algorithm possesses several properties. Something can only be called an algorithm to solve a particular problem if it has all of these properties:

1. It must be *correct*. In other words, it must compute the desired function, converting each input to the correct output.

2. It is composed of a series of *concrete steps*. Concrete means that the action described by that step is completely understood – and doable – by the person or machine that must perform the algorithm. Each step must also be performable in a finite amount of time. Thus, the algorithm gives us a "recipe" for solving the problem by doing a series of steps, where each such step is within our capacity to perform. The ability to perform a step may depend on who or what is intended to execute the recipe. For example, the steps of a cookie recipe in a cookbook might be considered sufficiently concrete for instructing a human cook, but not for programming an automated cookie-making factory.

3. There can be *no ambiguity* as to which step will be performed next. Often it is the next step of the algorithm description. Selection (e.g., the `if` and `switch` statements in Java) is normally a part of any language for describing algorithms. Selection allows a choice for which step will be performed next, but the selection process is unambiguous.

4. It must be composed of a *finite* number of steps. If the description for the algorithm were made up of an infinite number of steps, we could never hope to write it down, nor implement it as a computer program. Most languages for describing algorithms (including English or "pseudocode") provide some way to perform repeated actions, known as iteration. Examples of iteration include the `while` and `for` loop

constructs of Java. Iteration allows for short descriptions, with the number of steps actually performed controlled by the input.

5. It must *terminate.* In other words, it may not go into an infinite loop.

Programs: We often think of a **computer program** as an instance, or concrete representation, of an algorithm in some programming language. In this book, nearly all of the algorithms are presented in terms of programs, or parts of programs. Naturally, there are many programs that are instances of the same algorithm, since any modern computer programming language can be used to implement any algorithm (although some programming languages can make life easier for the programmer). To simplify presentation throughout the remainder of the text, I often use the terms "algorithm" and "program" interchangeably, despite the fact that they are really separate concepts. By definition, an algorithm must provide sufficient detail that it can be converted into a program when needed.

The requirement that an algorithm must terminate means that not all computer programs are algorithms. Your operating system is one such program. However, you can think of the various tasks for an operating system (each with associated inputs and outputs) as individual problems, each solved by specific algorithms implemented by a part of the operating system program, and each one of which terminates once its output is produced.

Definition 1.6 A **problem** is a function or a mapping of inputs to outputs. An **algorithm** is a recipe for solving a problem whose steps are concrete and unambiguous. The algorithm must be correct, of finite length, and must terminate for all inputs. A **program** is an instantiation of an algorithm in a computer programming language.

1.4   Algorithm Efficiency

There are often many approaches to solving a problem. How do we choose between them? At the heart of computer program design are two (sometimes conflicting) goals:

1. To design an algorithm that is easy to understand, code, and debug.

2. To design an algorithm that makes efficient use of the computer's resources.

Ideally, the resulting program is true to both of these goals. Sometimes we say that such a program is "elegant." While the algorithms and program code examples presented here attempt to be elegant in this sense, it is not the purpose of this book to explicitly treat issues related to goal (1). These are primarily concerns of the discipline of Software Engineering. Rather, this book is mostly about issues relating to goal (2).

How do we measure efficiency? Chapter 3 describes a method for evaluating the efficiency of an algorithm or computer program, called **algorithm analysis**. Algorithm analysis also allows you to measure the inherent difficulty of a problem. The remaining chapters use algorithm analysis techniques whenever an algorithm is presented. This allows you to see how each algorithm compares to other algorithms for solving the same problem in terms of its efficiency.

1.5   Further Reading

The first authoritative work on data structures and algorithms was the series of books *The Art of Computer Programming* by Donald E. Knuth, with Volumes 1 and 3 being most relevant to the study of data structures [Knu73, Knu81]. A modern encyclopedic approach to data structures and algorithms that should be easy to understand once you have mastered this book is *Algorithms* by Robert Sedgewick [Sed88]. For an excellent and highly readable (but more advanced) teaching introduction to algorithms, their design, and their analysis, see *Introduction to Algorithms: A Creative Approach* by Udi Manber [Man89]. For an advanced, encyclopedic approach, see *Introduction to Algorithms* by Cormen, Leiserson, and Rivest [CLR90].

For a gentle introduction to ADTs and program specification, see *Abstract Data Types: Their Specification, Representation, and Use* by Thomas, Robinson, and Emms [TRE88].

The claim that all modern programming languages can implement any algorithm (stated more precisely, any function that is computable by one programming language is computable by any programming language with certain standard capabilities) is a key result from computability theory. For an introduction to this field see Lewis and Papadimitriou, *Elements of the Theory of Computation* [LP81].

Much of computer science is devoted to problem solving – indeed, this is what attracts many people to the field. *How to Solve It* by George Pólya [Pól57] is considered to be the classic work on how to improve your problem-solving abilities. Another recommended book is *Conceptual Block-busting* by James L. Adams [Ada79].

See *The Origin of Consciousness in the Breakdown of the Bicameral Mind* by Julian Jaynes [Jay90] for a good discussion on how humans use the concept of metaphor to handle complexity.

On a more pragmatic level, most people study data structures to write better programs. If you expect your program to work correctly and efficiently, it must first be understandable to yourself and your co-workers. See Kernighan and Plauger's *The Elements of Programming Style* [KP78] for how to develop good coding and documentation style. For an excellent (and entertaining!) introduction to the difficulties involved with writing large programs, see *The Mythical Man-Month: Essays on Software Engineering* by Frederick P. Brooks [Bro75].

Finally, if you want to be a successful Java programmer, you need good reference manuals close at hand. A good, gentle introduction to the basics of the language is *On to Java* [WN96] by Winston and Narasimhan. David Flanagan's *Java in a Nutshell* [Fla96] provides a good reference for those familiar with the basics of the language.

1.6 Exercises

The exercises for this chapter are different from those for the rest of the book in that most of them are answered in the following chapters. However, you should *not* look up the answers in other parts of the book. The purpose of these exercises is to make you think about some of the issues to be covered later on. Answer them to the best of your ability with your current knowledge.

1.1 Think of a program you have used that is unacceptably slow. Identify the specific operations that make the program slow. Identify other basic operations that the program performs quickly enough.

1.2 Most programming languages have a built-in integer data type. Normally this representation has a fixed size, thus placing a limit on how large a value may be stored in an integer variable. Describe a representation for integers that has no size restriction (other than the limits of the computer's available main memory), and thus no limit on how large an integer may be stored. Briefly show how your representation can be used to implement the operations of addition, multiplication, and exponentiation.

1.3 Define an ADT for character strings. Your ADT should consist of typical functions that can be performed on strings, with each function defined in terms of its input and output.

1.4 Define an ADT for a list of integers. Your ADT should consist of the functions that can be performed on lists, with each function defined in terms of its input and output.

1.5 Define an ADT for a set of integers (remember that a set may not contain duplicates). Your ADT should consist of the functions that can be performed on sets, with each function defined in terms of its input and output.

1.6 Briefly describe how integer variables are typically represented on a computer. (Look up one's complement and two's complement arithmetic in an introductory computer science textbook if you are not familiar with these.) Why does this representation for integers qualify as a data structure as defined in Definition 1.3?

1.7 Define an ADT for a two-dimensional array of integers. Specify precisely the basic operations that may be performed on such arrays. Next, imagine an application that stores an array with 1000 rows and 1000 columns, where less than 10,000 of the array values are non-zero. Describe two different implementations for such arrays that would be more space efficient than a standard two-dimensional array implementation requiring one million positions.

1.8 Does every problem have an algorithm?

1.9 Consider the design for a spelling checker program meant to run on a home computer. The spelling checker should be able to handle a document of less than twenty pages quickly. Assume that the spelling checker comes with a dictionary of about 20,000 words in ASCII format. What primitive operations must be implemented on the dictionary, and what is a reasonable time constraint for each operation?

1.10 Imagine that you have been hired to design a database service containing information about cities and towns in the United States. There are many thousands of cities and towns, and the database program should allow users to find information about a particular place by name. Users should also be able to find all places that match a particular value or range of values for attributes such as location or population. Describe the basic capabilities of the system in terms of what operations the user should see, and state a reasonable time constraint for each operation.

1.11 Imagine that you are given an array of records that are sorted with respect to some key field contained in each record. Give two different algorithms for searching the array to find the record with a specified key value. Which one do you consider "better" and why?

1.12 How would you go about comparing two proposed algorithms for sorting an array of integers? In particular,

(a) What would be appropriate measures of cost to use as a basis for comparing the two sorting algorithms?

(b) What tests would you use to determine how the two algorithms perform under these cost measures?

1.13 A common problem for compilers and text editors is to determine if the parentheses (or other brackets) in a string are balanced and properly nested. For example, the string "((())()())()" contains properly nested pairs of parentheses, but the string ")()(" does not; and the string "())" does not contain properly matching parentheses.

(a) Give an algorithm that returns **true** if a string contains properly nested and balanced parentheses, and **false** if otherwise. *Hint*: At no time while scanning a legal string from left to right will you have encountered more right parentheses than left parentheses.

(b) Give an algorithm that returns the position in the string of the first offending parenthesis if the string is not properly nested and balanced. That is, if an excess right parenthesis is found, return its position; if there are too many left parentheses, return the position of the first excess left parenthesis. Return -1 if the string is properly balanced and nested.

1.14 A graph consists of a set of objects (called vertices) and a set of edges, where each edge connects two vertices. Any given pair of vertices can be connected by only one edge. Describe at least two different ways to represent in a computer the connections defined by the vertices and edges of a graph, such that your representations can be used to determine whether there is an edge between a given pair of vertices.

1.15 Write down as many different approaches to sorting 1000 numbers as you can think of. Which one(s) are best?

2

Mathematical Preliminaries

This chapter presents mathematical notation, background information, and techniques used throughout the book. This material is provided primarily for review and reference. You may wish to study the relevant sections when you encounter unfamiliar notation or mathematical techniques in later chapters.

Section 2.7 on estimating may be unfamiliar to many readers. Estimating is not a mathematical technique, but rather a general engineering skill that you may not have encountered before. It is enormously useful to computer scientists doing design work, since any proposed solution whose estimated resource requirements fall well outside the problem's resource constraints can be discarded immediately.

2.1 Sets

The concept of a set in the mathematical sense has wide application in computer science.

Definition 2.1 A **set** is a collection of distinguishable **members** or **elements**. The members are typically drawn from some larger population known as the **base type**. Each member of a set is either a **primitive element** of the base type or is a set itself. There is no concept of duplication in a set. Each value from the base type is either in the set or not in the set.

For example, a set named **R** may be composed of the integers 3, 4, and 5. In this case, **R**'s members are 3, 4, and 5, and the base type is integer. Depending on the base type of the set, members often have a linear order.

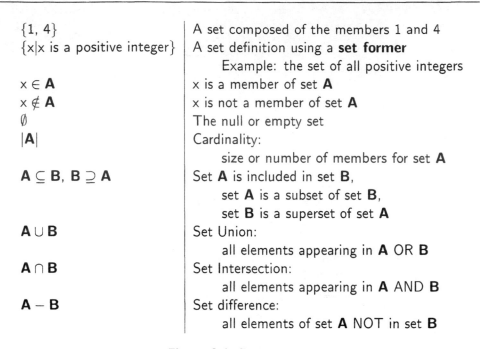

$\{1, 4\}$	A set composed of the members 1 and 4
$\{x \mid x$ is a positive integer$\}$	A set definition using a **set former**
	Example: the set of all positive integers
$x \in \mathbf{A}$	x is a member of set $\mathbf{A}$
$x \notin \mathbf{A}$	x is not a member of set $\mathbf{A}$
$\emptyset$	The null or empty set
$\|\mathbf{A}\|$	Cardinality:
	size or number of members for set $\mathbf{A}$
$\mathbf{A} \subseteq \mathbf{B}, \mathbf{B} \supseteq \mathbf{A}$	Set $\mathbf{A}$ is included in set $\mathbf{B}$,
	set $\mathbf{A}$ is a subset of set $\mathbf{B}$,
	set $\mathbf{B}$ is a superset of set $\mathbf{A}$
$\mathbf{A} \cup \mathbf{B}$	Set Union:
	all elements appearing in $\mathbf{A}$ OR $\mathbf{B}$
$\mathbf{A} \cap \mathbf{B}$	Set Intersection:
	all elements appearing in $\mathbf{A}$ AND $\mathbf{B}$
$\mathbf{A} - \mathbf{B}$	Set difference:
	all elements of set $\mathbf{A}$ NOT in set $\mathbf{B}$

Figure 2.1 Set notation.

Definition 2.2 A **linear order** has the following properties:

1. For any elements a and b in set $\mathbf{S}$, exactly one of $a < b$, $a = b$, or $b < a$ is true.

2. For all elements a, b, and c in set $\mathbf{S}$, if $a < b$ and $b < c$, then $a < c$. This is known as the property of **transitivity**.

Examples of base types with a linear order include integers, characters, and real numbers. In contrast, if the set is composed of fruit then there is no commonly accepted standard on the relative ordering of, say, apples and oranges. Sometimes an order is imposed artificially, perhaps through use of an enumerated type supported by some programming languages.

Figure 2.1 shows the symbols commonly used to express sets and their relationships. Here are some examples of this notation in use. First define two sets, $\mathbf{R}$ and $\mathbf{S}$.

$$\mathbf{R} = \{2, 3, 5\}, \qquad \mathbf{S} = \{5, 10\}.$$

$|\mathbf{R}| = 3$ (since $\mathbf{R}$ has three members) and $|\mathbf{S}| = 2$ (since $\mathbf{S}$ has two members). The union of $\mathbf{R}$ and $\mathbf{S}$, written $\mathbf{R} \cup \mathbf{S}$, is the set of elements in either $\mathbf{R}$ or $\mathbf{S}$, which is $\{2, 3, 5, 10\}$. The intersection of **R** and **S**, written **R** $\cap$ **S**, is the set of elements that appear in both **R** and **S**, which is $\{5\}$. The set difference of **R** and **S**, written **R** $-$ **S**, is the set of elements that occur in **R** but not in **S**, which is $\{2, 3\}$. Note that **R** $\cup$ **S** = **S** $\cup$ **R** and that **R** $\cap$ **S** = **S** $\cap$ **R**, but in general **R** $-$ **S** $\neq$ **S** $-$ **R**. In this example, **S** $-$ **R** = $\{10\}$.

A concept related to sets is that of a sequence.

Definition 2.3 A **finite sequence** of length n is a function f whose domain is the set $\{0, 1, ..., n - 1\}$. The implication of this definition is that unlike a set,

   (i) the elements of the sequence have an order (the 0th member, 1st member, and so on), and

   (ii) a sequence may contain duplicates that are distinct members of the sequence (since $f(i)$ can be equal to $f(j)$).

2.2   Miscellaneous Notation

Units of measure: Following the IEEE recommended standard for notation, "B" will be used as an abbreviation for bytes, "b" for bits, "MB" for megabytes (2^{20} bytes), "KB" for kilobytes ($2^{10} = 1024$ bytes), and "ms" for milliseconds (a millisecond is one one-thousandth of a second). Spaces are never placed between the number and the unit abbreviation when a power of two is intended. Thus a disk drive of size 540 megabytes (where a megabyte is intended as 2^{20} bytes) will be written as "540MB." Spaces are used when a decimal value is intended. An amount of 2000 bits would therefore be written "2 Kb" while "2Kb" represents 2048 bits. 2000 milliseconds is written as 2000 ms. Note that in this book large amounts of storage are nearly always measured in powers of two and times in powers of ten.

Factorial function: The **factorial** function, written $n!$ for n an integer greater than 0, is the product of the numbers between 1 and n, inclusive. Thus, $5! = 1 \cdot 2 \cdot 3 \cdot 4 \cdot 5 = 120$. As a special case, $0! = 1$. The factorial function grows quickly as n becomes larger. Since computing the factorial function directly is a time consuming process, it is sometimes useful to have an equation that provides a good approximation. Stirling's approximation states that $n! \approx \sqrt{2\pi n}(\frac{n}{e})^n$, where $e \approx 2.71828$ (e is the base for the system of natural logarithms).[1]

---

[1]The symbol "$\approx$" means "approximately equal."

Permutations: A **permutation** of a sequence is simply the members of the sequence arranged in some order. For example, a permutation of the numbers 1 through n would be those numbers arranged in any order. If the sequence contains n distinct members, then there are $n!$ different permutations for the sequence. This is because there are n choices for the first member in the permutation; for each choice of first member there are $n - 1$ choices for the second member, and so on. Sometimes one would like to obtain a **random permutation** for a sequence, that is, any one of the $n!$ possible permutations selected in such a way that each permutation has equal probability of being selected. A simple Java function for generating a random permutation is as follows. Here, the n values of the sequence are stored in positions 0 through $n - 1$ of array **A**, function `swap(A, i, j)` exchanges elements i and j in array **A**, and `DSutil.random(n)` returns an integer value in the range 0 to $n - 1$.

```
static void permute(Object[] A) {
  for (int i = A.length; i > 0; i--) // for each i
    swap(A, i-1, DSutil.random(i)); //   swap A[i-1] with
}                                    //   a random element
```

Boolean variables: A **Boolean variable** is a variable (of type `boolean` in Java) that takes on one of the two values `true` and `false`. These two values are often associated with the values 1 and 0, respectively, although there is no reason why this needs to be the case. It is poor programming practice to rely on the correspondence between 0 and `false` (in fact, Java will not allow this).

Floor and ceiling: The **floor** of x (written $\lfloor x \rfloor$) takes real value x and returns the greatest integer $\leq x$. For example, $\lfloor 3.4 \rfloor = 3$, as does $\lfloor 3.0 \rfloor$. The **ceiling** of x (written $\lceil x \rceil$) takes real value x and returns the least integer $\geq x$. For example, $\lceil 3.4 \rceil = 4$, as does $\lceil 4.0 \rceil$. In Java, the equivalent library functions are `Math.floor` and `Math.ceil`.

Modulus operator: The **modulus** (or **mod**) function returns the remainder of an integer division. Sometimes written $n \bmod m$ in mathematical expressions, the syntax for the Java modulus operator is **n % m**. From the definition of remainder, $n \bmod m$ is the integer r such that $n = qm + r$ for q an integer, and $0 \leq r < m$. Alternatively, the modulus is $n - m \lfloor n/m \rfloor$. The result of $n \bmod m$ must be between 0 and $m - 1$. For example, $5 \bmod 3 = 2$; $25 \bmod 3 = 1$, $5 \bmod 7 = 5$, $5 \bmod 5 = 0$, and $-3 \bmod 5 = 2$. Note that this last example gives the answer based on the mathematical definition of the modulus. In some programming languages, the actual result of the modulus operator in a program when either of the operands is negative is not reliable in the sense that different compilers may give different answers. In this book, all operands to the modulus operator are positive.

2.3   Logarithms

A **logarithm** of base b for value y is the power to which you must raise b to get y. Normally, this is written as $\log_b y = x$. Thus, we can say

$$\log_b y = x \iff b^x = y \iff b^{\log_b y} = y,$$

where $\iff$ means "is equivalent to."

Logarithms are used frequently by programmers. Here are two typical uses. First, many programs require an encoding for a collection of objects. What is the minimum number of bits needed to represent n code values? The answer is $\lceil \log_2 n \rceil$ bits. For example, if you have 1000 codes to store, you will require at least $\lceil \log_2 1000 \rceil = 10$ bits to have 1000 different codes (with 10 bits there are actually 1024 distinct code values available). The second common use of logarithms is in the analysis of algorithms that work by breaking a problem into smaller subproblems. One such algorithm is the binary search for a given value within a list ordered by value. Binary search first looks at the middle element and determines if the value being searched for is in the upper half or the lower half of the list. The algorithm then continues splitting the appropriate sublist in half until the desired value is found. (Binary search is described in more detail in Section 3.5.) How many times can a list of size n be split in half until only one element remains in the final sublist? The answer is $\log_2 n$ times.

In this book, nearly all logarithms used are of base two. This is because data structures and algorithms most often divide things in half, or store codes with binary bits. Whenever you see the notation $\log n$ in this book, it means $\log_2 n$. If any base for the logarithm other than two is intended, then the base is shown explicitly.

Logarithms have the following properties, for any positive values of m, n, and r, and any positive integers a and b.

1. $\log nm = \log n + \log m$.

2. $\log n/m = \log n - \log m$.

3. $\log n^r = r \log n$.

4. $\log_a n = \log_b n / \log_b a$.

The first two properties state that the logarithm of two numbers multiplied (or divided) can be found by adding (or subtracting) the logarithms of the two numbers.[2] Property (3) is simply an extension of property (1). Property (4) tells us that, for variable n and any two integer constants a and b, $\log_a n$ and $\log_b n$ differ by the constant factor $\log_b a$, regardless of the value of n. Most analyses in this book are of a type that ignores constant factors in costs. Property (4) says that such analyses need not be concerned with the base of the logarithm, since this can change the total cost only by a constant factor.

When discussing logarithms, exponents often lead to confusion. Property (3) tells us that $\log n^2 = 2 \log n$. How do we indicate the square of the logarithm (as opposed to the logarithm of n^2)? This could be written as $(\log n)^2$, but it is traditional to use $\log^2 n$. Alternatively, we might want to take the logarithm of the logarithm of n. This is written $\log \log n$.

2.4 Recursion

An algorithm is **recursive** if it calls itself to do part of its work. For this approach to be successful, the "call to itself" must be on a smaller problem then the one originally attempted. In general, a recursive algorithm must have two parts: the **base case**, which handles a simple input that can be solved without resorting to a recursive call, and the recursive part which contains one or more recursive calls to the algorithm where the parameters are in some sense "closer" to the base case than those of the original call. Here is a recursive Java function to compute the factorial of n. A trace of this function's execution for a small value of n is presented in Section 4.2.4.

```
static long fact(int n) { // Must have n < 21 to fit in long
  Assert.notFalse((n >= 0) && (n < 21), "Input out of range");
  if (n <= 1)  return 1;  // Base case: return base solution
  return n * fact(n-1);   // Recursive call for n > 1
}
```

---

[2]These properties form the basis of the slide rule. Adding two numbers can be viewed as joining two lengths together and measuring their combined length. Multiplication is not so easily done. However, if the numbers are first converted to the lengths of their logarithms, then those lengths can be added and the inverse logarithm of the resulting length gives the answer for the multiplication (this is simply logarithm property (1)). A slide rule measures the length of the logarithm for the numbers, lets you slide bars representing these lengths to add up the total length, and finally converts this total length to the correct numeric answer by taking the inverse of the logarithm for the result.

The first two lines of the function constitute the base cases. If $n \leq 1$, then one of the base cases computes a solution for the problem.[3] Otherwise, `fact` "punts" – it calls a function that knows how to find the factorial of $n - 1$. Of course, function `fact` itself is capable of doing this! The design for recursive algorithms can always be approached in this way. First write the base cases. Then think about solving the problem by combining the results of one or more smaller – but similar – subproblems. If the algorithm you write is correct, then certainly you can rely on it (recursively) to solve the smaller subproblems. What could be simpler?

Recursion has no counterpart in everyday problem solving. The concept can be difficult to grasp since it requires you to think about problems in a new way. To use recursion effectively, it is necessary to train yourself to stop analyzing the recursive process beyond the recursive call. The subproblems will take care of themselves.

The recursive version of the factorial function may seem unnecessarily complicated to you since the same effect can be achieved by using a `while` loop. Here is another example of recursion, based on a famous puzzle called "Towers of Hanoi." The natural Java implementation has multiple recursive calls, and cannot be rewritten easily using `while` loops.

The Towers of Hanoi puzzle begins with three poles and n rings, where all rings start on the leftmost pole (labeled pole 1). The rings each have a different size, and are stacked in order of decreasing size with the largest ring at the bottom as shown in Figure 2.2.a. The problem is to move the rings from the leftmost pole to the rightmost pole (labeled pole 3) in a series of steps. At each step the top ring on some pole is moved to another pole. There is one limitation on where rings may be moved: A ring can never be moved on top of a smaller ring.

How can you solve this problem? It is easy if you don't think too hard about the details. Instead, consider that all rings are to be moved from pole 1 to pole 3. It is not possible to do this without first moving the bottom (largest) ring to pole 3. To do so, pole 3 must be empty, and only the bottom ring can be on pole 1. The remaining $n - 1$ rings must be stacked up in order on pole 2, as shown in Figure 2.2.b. How can you do this? Assume that a function X is available to solve the problem of moving

---

[3]Function `Assert.notFalse` is modeled after the `assert` function of the standard **C** library. Its input parameter is a Boolean expression. If this expression evaluates to `false`, then `Assert.notFalse` makes the program terminate. If this expression evaluates to `true`, `Assert.notFalse` does nothing. Function `Assert.notNull` operates in a similar manner on an `Object` reference.

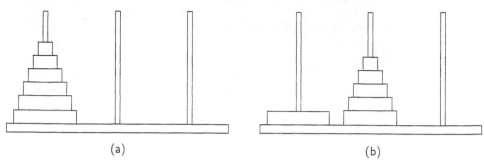

(a)   (b)

Figure 2.2 Towers of Hanoi example. (a) The initial conditions for a problem with six rings. (b) A necessary intermediate step on the road to a solution.

the top $n - 1$ rings from pole 1 to pole 2. Then move the bottom ring from pole 1 to pole 3. Finally, again use function X to move the remaining $n - 1$ rings from pole 2 to pole 3. In both cases, "function X" is simply the Towers of Hanoi function called on a smaller version of the problem.

The secret to success is relying on the Towers of Hanoi algorithm to do the work for you. You need not be concerned about the gory details of *how* the Towers of Hanoi subproblem will be solved. That will take care of itself provided that two things are done. First, there must be a base case (what to do if there is only one ring) so that the recursive process will not go on forever. Second, the recursive call to Towers of Hanoi can only be used to solve a smaller problem, and then only one of the proper form (one that meets the original definition for the Towers of Hanoi problem, assuming appropriate renaming of the poles).

Here is a Java implementation for the recursive Towers of Hanoi algorithm. Function `move(start, goal)` takes the top ring from pole `start` and "moves" it to pole `goal`. If the `move` function were to print the values of its parameters, then the result of calling TOH would be a list of ring-moving instructions that solves the problem.

```
static void TOH(int n, Pole start, Pole goal, Pole temp) {
  if (n == 0) return;         // Base case
  TOH(n-1, start, temp, goal); // Recursive call: n-1 rings
  move(start, goal);          // Move bottom disk to goal
  TOH(n-1, temp, goal, start); // Recursive call: n-1 rings
}
```

Those who are unfamiliar with recursion may find it hard to accept that it is used primarily as a tool for designing or describing a simple algorithm.

A recursive algorithm usually does not yield the most efficient computer program for solving the problem since recursion involves function calls, which are typically more expensive than other alternatives such as a `while` loop. However, the recursive approach usually provides an algorithm that is reasonably efficient in the sense discussed in Chapter 3. (But not always! See Exercise 2.3.) If necessary, the clear, recursive solution can later be modified to yield a faster implementation. This topic is discussed further in Section 4.2.4.

2.5 Summations and Recurrences

Most programs contain loop constructs. When analyzing running time costs for programs with loops, we may need to add up the costs for each time the loop is executed. This is an example of a **summation**. Summations are simply the sum for some function over a range of parameter values. Summations are typically written with the following "Sigma" notation:

$$\sum_{i=1}^{n} f(i).$$

This notation indicates that we are summing the value of $f(i)$ over some range of (integer) values. The parameter to the expression and its initial value are indicated below the $\sum$ symbol. Here, the notation $i = 1$ indicates that the parameter is i and that it begins with the value 1. At the top of the $\sum$ symbol is the expression n. This indicates the maximum value for the parameter i. Thus, this notation means to sum the values of $f(i)$ as i ranges from 1 through n. This can also be written

$$f(1) + f(2) + \cdots + f(n-1) + f(n).$$

Within a sentence, Sigma notation is typeset as $\sum_{i=1}^{n} f(i)$.

Given a summation, you typically wish to replace it with an equation that directly computes the summation. Such an equation is known as a **closed form solution**. For example, the summation $\sum_{i=1}^{n} 1$ is simply the expression "1" summed n times (remember that i ranges from 1 to n). Since the sum of n 1s is n, the closed form solution for this summation is n. The following is a list of summations that appear in this book, along with their closed form solutions.

$$\sum_{i=1}^{n} i \quad = \quad \frac{n(n+1)}{2}. \tag{2.1}$$

$$\sum_{i=1}^{n} i^2 = \frac{2n^3 + 3n^2 + n}{6}. \qquad (2.2)$$

$$\sum_{i=1}^{\log n} n = n \log n. \qquad (2.3)$$

$$\sum_{i=0}^{\infty} a^i = \frac{1}{1-a} \text{ for } 0 < a < 1. \qquad (2.4)$$

As special cases to Equation 2.4,

$$\sum_{i=1}^{n} \frac{1}{2^i} = 1 - \frac{1}{2^n}, \qquad (2.5)$$

and

$$\sum_{i=0}^{n} a^i = \frac{a^{n+1} - 1}{a - 1} \text{ for } a > 1. \qquad (2.6)$$

In another variation,

$$\sum_{i=1}^{n} \frac{i}{2^i} = 2 - \frac{n+2}{2^n}. \qquad (2.7)$$

As a special case to Equation 2.6,

$$\sum_{i=0}^{n} 2^i = 2^{n+1} - 1. \qquad (2.8)$$

As a corollary to Equation 2.8,

$$\sum_{i=0}^{\log n} 2^i = 2^{\log n + 1} - 1 = 2n - 1. \qquad (2.9)$$

Finally, the sum of reciprocals from 1 to n, called the **Harmonic Series** and written $\mathcal{H}_n$, has an approximate closed form solution as follows:

$$\mathcal{H}_n = \sum_{i=1}^{n} \frac{1}{i}; \quad \log_e n < \mathcal{H}_n < 1 + \log_e n. \qquad (2.10)$$

Most of these equalities can be proved easily by mathematical induction (see Section 2.6.2). Unfortunately, induction does not help us derive a closed form solution. Techniques for deriving closed form solutions are discussed in Section 14.1. Knowledge of such techniques is not required to understand data structures or algorithm analysis.

The running time for a recursive algorithm is most easily expressed by a recursive expression since the total time for the recursive algorithm includes the time to run the recursive call. A **recurrence relation** defines a function by means of an expression that includes one or more (smaller) instances of itself. Some classic examples include the recursive definition for the factorial function:

$$n! = (n-1)! \cdot n, \quad 1! = 0! = 1.$$

and the Fibonacci sequence:

$$\text{Fib}(n) = \text{Fib}(n-1) + \text{Fib}(n-2); \quad \text{Fib}(1) = \text{Fib}(2) = 1.$$

From this definition we see that the first seven numbers of the Fibonacci sequence are

$$1, 1, 2, 3, 5, 8, \text{ and } 13.$$

Notice that this definition contains two parts: the general definition for $\text{Fib}(n)$ and the base cases for $\text{Fib}(1)$ and $\text{Fib}(2)$. Likewise, the definition for factorial contains a recursive part and base cases.

Recurrence relations are often used to model the cost of recursive functions. For example, the number of moves required by the Towers of Hanoi algorithm for n disks is $\mathbf{T}(n) = 2\mathbf{T}(n-1)+1$, since to solve the problem, we must solve the problem for $n-1$ disks, make a move, then solve the problem again for $n-1$ disks.

As with summations, we typically wish to replace the recurrence relation with a closed form solution. Recurrence relations are infrequently used in this book, and their closed form solutions will be supplied at the time of use. Techniques to find closed form solutions for recurrence relations are discussed in Section 14.2. Knowledge of such techniques is not required to understand data structures or algorithm analysis.

2.6 Mathematical Proof Techniques

This section briefly introduces the two proof techniques most commonly used in this book: Proof by Contradiction and Proof by Mathematical Induction.

2.6.1 Proof by Contradiction

The simplest way to *disprove* a theorem or statement is to find a counterexample to the theorem. Unfortunately, no number of examples supporting a theorem is sufficient to prove that the theorem is correct. However, there is an approach that is vaguely similar to disproof by counterexample, called Proof by Contradiction. To prove a theorem by contradiction, we first *assume* that the theorem is *false*. We then find a logical contradiction stemming from this assumption. If the logic used to find the contradiction is correct, then the only way to resolve the contradiction is to recognize that the assumption that the theorem is false must be incorrect, that is, to conclude that the theorem must be true.

Example 2.1 Here is a simple proof by contradiction.

Theorem 2.1 *There is no largest integer.*

Proof: Proof by contradiction.

Step 1. Contrary assumption: Assume that there *is* a largest integer. Call it B (for "biggest").

Step 2. Show this assumption leads to a contradiction: Consider $C = B+1$. C is an integer since it is the sum of two integers. Also, $C > B$. Thus, we have reached a contradiction. The only flaw in our reasoning is the initial assumption that the theorem is false. Thus, we conclude that the theorem is correct.   □

2.6.2   Proof by Mathematical Induction

Mathematical induction is much like recursion, and is applicable to a wide variety of theorems. Induction also provides a useful way to think about algorithm design, since it encourages you to think about solving a problem by building up from simple subproblems.

Let **T** be a theorem to prove, and express **T** in terms of a positive integer parameter n. Mathematical induction states that **T** is true for any value of parameter n (for $n \geq c$, where c is some small constant) if the following two conditions are true:

1. **Base Case:** **T** holds for $n = c$, and

2. **Induction Step:** If **T** holds for $n - 1$, then **T** holds for n.

Proving the base case is usually easy, typically requiring that some small value such as 1 be substituted for n in the theorem and applying simple algebra or logic as necessary to verify the theorem. Proving the induction step is sometimes easy, and sometimes difficult. An alternative formulation of the induction step is known as **strong induction**. The induction step for strong induction is:

2a. Induction Step: If **T** holds for all k, $c \le k < n$, then **T** holds for n.

Proving either variant of the induction step (in conjunction with verifying the base case) yields a satisfactory proof by mathematical induction.

The two conditions that make up the induction proof combine to demonstrate that **T** holds for $n = 2$ as an extension of the fact that **T** holds for $n = 1$. This fact, combined again with condition (2) or (2a), indicates that **T** also holds for $n = 3$, and so on. Thus, **T** holds for all values of n once the two conditions have been proved.

What makes mathematical induction so powerful (and so mystifying to most people at first) is that we can take advantage of the *assumption* that **T** holds for all values less than n to help us prove that **T** holds for n. This is known as the **induction hypothesis**. Having this assumption to work with makes the induction step easier to prove than tackling the original theorem itself.

Note the similarities between recursion and induction. Both are anchored on one or more base cases. A recursive function relies on the ability to call itself to get the answer for smaller instances of the problem. Likewise, induction proofs rely on the truth of the induction hypothesis to prove the theorem.

Example 2.2 Here is a sample proof by mathematical induction.

Theorem 2.2 *The sum of the first n numbers is* $n(n + 1)/2$.

Proof: The proof is by mathematical induction.

1. **Check the base case.** For $n = 1$, the sum is simply 1. The formula states that for $n = 1$, $1(1 + 1)/2 = 1$. Thus, the formula is correct for the base case.

2. **State the induction hypothesis.** The induction hypothesis is
$$\sum_{i=1}^{n-1} i = \frac{(n-1)((n-1)+1)}{2} = \frac{(n-1)(n)}{2}.$$

3. **Use the assumption from the induction hypothesis for $n - 1$ to show that the result is true for n.** The induction hypothesis states that $\sum_{i=1}^{n-1} i = (n-1)(n)/2$, and since $\sum_{i=1}^{n} i =$

$\sum_{i=1}^{n-1} i + n$, we have

$$\sum_{i=1}^{n} i = \sum_{i=1}^{n-1} i + n = \frac{(n-1)(n)}{2} + n = \frac{n^2 - n + 2n}{2} = \frac{n(n+1)}{2}.$$

Thus, by mathematical induction, $\sum_{i=1}^{n} i = n(n+1)/2$.   □

Example 2.3 Here is another simple proof by induction that illustrates choosing the proper variable for induction. We wish to prove by induction that the sum of the first n positive odd numbers is n^2. First we need a way to describe the nth odd number, which is simply $2n - 1$. This also allows us to cast the theorem as a summation.

Theorem 2.3 $\sum_{i=1}^{n}(2i - 1) = n^2$.

Proof: The base case of $n = 1$ yields $1 = 1^2$, which is true. The induction hypothesis is

$$\sum_{i=1}^{n-1}(2i - 1) = (n - 1)^2.$$

We now use the induction hypothesis to show that the theorem holds true for n. The sum of the first n odd numbers is simply the sum of the first $n - 1$ odd numbers plus the nth odd number.

$$\begin{aligned}
\sum_{i=1}^{n}(2i - 1) &= (\sum_{i=1}^{n-1}(2i - 1)) + 2n - 1 \\
&= (n - 1)^2 + 2n - 1 \\
&= n^2 - 2n + 1 + 2n - 1 \\
&= n^2.
\end{aligned}$$

Thus, by mathematical induction, $\sum_{i=1}^{n}(2i - 1) = n^2$.   □

Example 2.4 This next example uses induction without involving summations. It also illustrates a more flexible definition of base cases.

Theorem 2.4 *2¢ and 5¢ stamps can be used to form any denomination (for denominations ≥ 4).*

Proof: Note that the theorem defines the problem for denominations ≥ 4 because it does not hold for the values 1 and 3. Using 4 as the base case, a 4¢ denomination can be made from two 2¢ stamps. The induction hypothesis is that a denomination of size $n - 1$ can be made from some combination of 2¢ and 5¢ stamps. We now use the induction hypothesis to show how to derive denominations of size n. Either the makeup for denomination $n - 1$ includes a 5¢ stamp, or it does not. If so, then replace that 5¢ stamp with three 2¢ stamps. If not, then the makeup must have included at least two 2¢ stamps (since it is at least of size 4 and contains only 2¢ stamps). In this case, replace two of the 2¢ stamps with a single 5¢ stamp. In either case, we now have a denomination of size n made up of 2¢ and 5¢ stamps. Thus, by mathematical induction, the theorem is correct. □

Example 2.5 Here is an example using strong induction.

Theorem 2.5 *For* n > 1, n *is divisible by some prime number.*

Proof: For the base case, choose $n = 2$. Two is divisible by the prime number 2. The induction hypothesis is that *any* value a, $2 \leq a < n$, is divisible by some prime number. There are now two cases to consider when proving the theorem for n. If n is a prime number, then n is divisible by itself. If n is not a prime number, then $n = a \times b$ for a and b, both integers less than n but greater than 1. The induction hypothesis tells us that a is divisible by some prime number. That same prime number must also divide n. Thus, by mathematical induction, the theorem is correct. □

Example 2.6 Our final example of mathematical induction proves a theorem from geometry. It also illustrates a technique of induction proof where we take n objects and remove an arbitrary object to use the induction hypothesis.

Define a **two-coloring** for a set of regions as a way of assigning one of two colors to each region such that no two regions sharing a side have the same color. For example, a chessboard is two-colored. Figure 2.3 shows a two-coloring for the plane with three lines. We will assume that the two colors to be used are black and white.

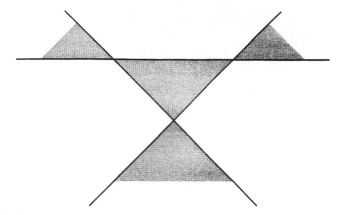

Figure 2.3 A two-coloring for the regions formed by three lines in the plane.

Theorem 2.6 *The set of regions formed by* n *infinite lines in the plane can be two-colored.*

Proof: Consider the base case of a single infinite line in the plane. This splits the plane into two regions. One region is colored black and the other white, which yields a valid two-coloring. The induction hypothesis is that the set of regions formed by $n-1$ infinite lines can be two-colored. To prove the theorem for n, consider the set of regions formed by the $n-1$ lines remaining when any one of the n lines is removed. By the induction hypothesis, this set of regions can be two-colored. Now, put the nth line back. This splits the plane into two half-planes, each of which (independently) has a valid two-coloring. Unfortunately, the regions newly split by the nth line violate the rule for a two-coloring. Take all regions on one side of the nth line and reverse their coloring. Those regions split by the nth line are now properly two-colored, since the part of the region to one side of the line is now black and the region to the other side is now white. Thus, by mathematical induction, the entire plane is two-colored. $\square$

2.7 Estimating

One of the most useful life skills that you can gain from your computer science training is how to perform quick estimates for solving a problem. This is sometimes known as "back of the napkin" or "back of the envelope" calculation. Both nicknames suggest that only a rough estimate is produced.

Estimation techniques are a regular part of an engineering curriculum, but are often neglected in computer science. Estimation techniques are no substitute for rigorous detailed analysis of a problem, but they can serve to indicate when a rigorous analysis is warranted: If the estimate indicates that the solution is unworkable, then further analysis is probably unnecessary.

Estimating can be formalized by the following three-step process:

1. Determine the major parameters that affect the problem.

2. Derive an equation that relates the parameters to the problem.

3. Select values for the parameters, and apply the equation to yield an estimated solution.

When doing estimations, a good way to reassure yourself that the estimate is reasonable is to do it in two different ways. In general, if you want to know what comes out of a system, you can either try to estimate that directly, or you can estimate what goes into the system (assuming that what goes in must later come out). If both approaches (independently) give similar answers, then this should build confidence in the estimate.

Be sure when estimating that your units match; for example, do not add feet and pounds. Verify that the result is in the correct units. Always keep in mind that the output of a calculation is only as good as its input. The more uncertain your valuation for the input parameters in step 3, the more uncertain the output value. However, back of the envelope calculations are often only meant to get an answer within an order of magnitude, or perhaps within a factor of two. Before doing an estimate, you should decide on acceptable error bounds, such as within 10%, within a factor of two, and so forth. Once you are confident that an estimate falls within your error bounds, leave it alone! Do not try to get a more precise estimate than necessary for your purpose.

Example 2.7 Here is an example of back of the envelope calculation. How many library bookcases does it take to store books containing one million pages? I estimate that a 500 page book requires about one inch on the library shelf, yielding about 200 feet of shelf space for one million pages. If a shelf is about 4 feet wide, then 50 shelves are required. If a bookcase contains 5 shelves, this yields about 10 big library bookcases. To reach this conclusion, I made estimates for the number of pages per inch, the width of a library shelf, and the number of shelves in a library bookcase. None of my estimates are likely to be precise, but I feel confident that my answer is correct to within a factor of two. (After writing this, I went to the library and looked at some real bookcases. They were only about 3 feet wide, but typically had 7 shelves for a total of 21 shelf-feet. So I was correct to within 10% on bookcase capacity, far better than I expected or needed.)

Example 2.8 Another estimation example from everyday life: Is it more economical to buy a car that gets 20 miles per gallon, or one that gets 30 miles per gallon but costs $1,000 more? The typical car is driven about 12,000 miles per year. If gasoline costs $1/gallon, then the yearly gas bill is $600 for the less efficient car and $400 for the more efficient car. If we ignore issues such as the payback that would be received if we invested $1,000 in a bank, it would take 5 years to make up the difference in price. At this point, the buyer must decide if price is the only criterion and if a 5-year payback time is acceptable. Naturally, a person who drives more will make up the difference more quickly, and changes in gasoline prices will also greatly affect the outcome.

2.8 Further Reading

Most of the topics covered in this chapter are considered part of Discrete Mathematics. An introduction to this field is *Discrete Mathematics with Applications, 2nd Edition* by Susanna S. Epp [Epp95]. An advanced treatment of many mathematical topics useful to computer scientists is *Concrete Mathematics: A Foundation for Computer Science* by Graham, Knuth, and Patashnik [GKP89].

See "Technically Speaking" from the February 1995 issue of *IEEE Spectrum* [Sel95] for a discussion on the standard for indicating units of computer storage used in this book.

Udi Manber's *Introduction to Algorithms* [Man89] makes extensive use of mathematical induction as a technique for developing algorithms.

For more information on recursion, see *Thinking Recursively* by Eric S. Roberts [Rob86]. To learn recursion properly, it is worth your while to learn the programming language LISP, even if you never intend to write a LISP program. In particular, Friedman and Felleisen's *The Little LISPer* [FF89] is designed to teach you how to think recursively as well as teach you LISP. This book is entertaining reading as well.

A good book on writing mathematical proofs is Daniel Solow's *How to Read and Do Proofs* [Sol90]. Also see *How to Write a Proof* by Leslie Lamport [Lam93].

For more about back of the envelope calculation, see two Programming Pearls by John Louis Bentley entitled *The Back of the Envelope* and *The Envelope is Back* [Ben84, Ben86a, Ben86b, Ben88]. *Genius: The Life and Science of Richard Feynman* by James Gleick [Gle92] gives insight into how important back of the envelope calculation was to the developers of the atomic bomb, and to modern theoretical physics in general.

2.9 Exercises

2.1 Rewrite the factorial function of Section 2.4 without using recursion.

2.2 Rewrite the **for** loop for the random permutation generator of Section 2.2 as a recursive function.

2.3 Here is a simple recursive fuction to compute the Fibonacci sequence:

```
static long fibr(int n) { // Recursive Fibonacci generator
  Assert.notFalse((n>0) && (n<02), "Parameter out of range");
  if ((n == 1) || (n == 2)) return 1; // Base case
  return fibr(n-1) + fibr(n-2);      // Recursive call
}
```

This algorithm turns out to be very slow, calling **Fibr** a total of more than Fib(n) times. Contrast this with the following iterative algorithm:

```
static long fibi(int n) {    // Iterative Fibonacci generator
  Assert.notFalse((n>0) && (n<92), "Parameter out of range");
  long curr, prev;
  if ((n == 1) || (n == 2)) return 1;
  curr = prev = 1;             // curr holds current Fib value
  for (int i=3; i<=n; i++) { // Compute next value
    curr = prev + curr;
    prev = curr - prev;       // prev holds previous Fib value
  }
  return curr;
}
```

Function **Fibi** executes the **for** loop $n - 2$ times. Explain why **Fibr** is so much slower than **Fibi**.

2.4 Write a recursive function to solve a generalization of the Towers of Hanoi problem where each ring may begin on any pole so long as no ring sits on top of a smaller ring.

2.5 Prove by contradiction that the number of primes is infinite.

2.6 Prove that $\sqrt{2}$ is irrational.

2.7 Explain why

$$\sum_{i=1}^{n} i = \sum_{i=1}^{n}(n - i + 1) = \sum_{i=0}^{n-1}(n - i).$$

2.8 Prove Equation 2.2 using mathematical induction.

2.9 Prove Equation 2.5 using mathematical induction.

2.10 Prove Equation 2.8 using mathematical induction.

2.11 Prove that the sum of the first n even numbers is $n^2 + n$

    (a) indirectly by using the proof of Example 2.3 for odd numbers.

    (b) directly by mathematical induction.

2.12 Prove that $\mathrm{Fib}(n) < (\frac{5}{3})^n$.

2.13 Prove, for $n \geq 1$, that

$$\sum_{i=1}^{n} i^3 = \frac{n^2(n + 1)^2}{4}.$$

2.14 The following theorem is called the **Pigeonhole Principle**.

    Theorem 2.7 *When* n + 1 *pigeons roost in* n *holes, there must be some hole containing at least two pigeons.*

    (a) Prove the Pigeonhole Principle using proof by contradiction.

    (b) Prove the Pigeonhole Principle using mathematical induction.

2.15 Assume that an n-bit integer (represented by standard binary notation) takes any value in the range 0 to $2^n - 1$ with equal probability.

    (a) For each bit position, what is the probability of its value being 1 and what is the probability of its value being 0?

    (b) What is the average number of "1" bits for an n-bit random number?

    (c) What is the expected value for the position of the leftmost "1" bit? In other words, how many positions on average must we examine when moving from left to right before encountering a "1" bit? Show the appropriate summation.

2.16 What is the total volume of your body in liters (or, if you prefer, gallons)?

2.17 An art historian has a database of 20,000 full-screen color images.

    (a) About how much space will this require? How many CD-ROMs would be required to store the database? (A CD-ROM holds about 600MB of data). Be sure to explain all assumptions you made to derive your answer.

    (b) Now, assume that you have access to a good image compression technique that can store the images in only 1/10 of the space required for an uncompressed image. Will the entire database fit onto a single CD-ROM if the images are compressed?

2.18 How many cubic miles of water flow out of the mouth of the Mississippi River each day? DO NOT look up the answer or any supplemental facts. Be sure to describe all assumptions made in arriving at your answer.

2.19 When buying a home mortgage, you often have the option of paying some money in advance (called "discount points") to get a lower interest rate. Assume that you have the choice between two 15-year mortgages: one at 8%, and the other at $7\frac{3}{4}$% with an up-front charge of 1% of the mortgage value. How long would it take to recover the 1% charge when you take the mortgage at the lower rate? As a second, more precise estimate, how long would it take to recover the charge plus the interest you would have received if you had invested the equivalent of the 1% charge in the bank at 5% interest while paying the higher rate? DO NOT use a calculator to help you answer this question.

2.20 Here are some questions that test your working knowledge of how fast computers operate. Is disk drive access time normally measured in milliseconds (thousandths of a second) or microseconds (millionths of a second)? Does your RAM memory access a word in more or less than one microsecond? How many instructions can your CPU execute in one year if the machine is left running all the time? DO NOT use paper or a calculator to derive your answers.

2.21 Does your home contain enough books to total one million pages? How many total pages are stored in your school library building?

2.22 How many words are in this book?

2.23 How many hours are one million seconds? How many days? Answer these questions doing all arithmetic in your head.

2.24 How many cities and towns are there in the United States?

2.25 A man begins a car trip to visit his in-laws. The total distance is 60 miles, and he starts off at a speed of 60 miles per hour. After driving exactly 1 mile, he loses some of his enthusiasm for the journey, and (instantaneously) slows down to 59 miles per hour. After traveling another mile, he again slows to 58 miles per hour. This continues, progressively slowing by 1 mile per hour for each mile traveled until the trip is complete.

   (a) How long does it take the man to reach his in-laws?

   (b) How long would the trip take in the continuous case where the speed smoothly diminishes with the distance yet to travel?

3

Algorithm Analysis

This chapter introduces the basics of algorithm analysis. Algorithm analysis is a methodology for estimating the resource consumption of an algorithm. It allows us to compare the relative costs of two or more algorithms for solving the same problem. Algorithm analysis also gives algorithm designers a tool for estimating whether a proposed solution is likely to meet the resource constraints for a problem. After reading this chapter, you should understand

- the concept of a **growth rate**, the rate at which the cost of an algorithm grows as the size of its input grows;

- the concept of upper and lower bounds for a growth rate, and how to estimate these bounds for a simple program, algorithm, or problem; and

- the difference between the cost of an algorithm (or program) and the cost of a problem.

The chapter concludes with a brief discussion of the practical difficulties encountered when empirically measuring the cost of a program, and some principles for code tuning to improve program efficiency.

3.1 Introduction

How do you compare two algorithms for solving some problem in terms of efficiency? One way is to implement both algorithms as computer programs and then run them on a suitable range of inputs, measuring how much of the resources in question each program uses. This approach is often unsatisfactory for four reasons. First, there is the effort involved in programming and testing two algorithms when at best you only want to keep one. Second, when empirically comparing two algorithms there is always the chance that one of the programs was "better written" than the other, and that the relative qualities of the underlying algorithms are not truly represented by their implementations. Third, the choice of empirical test cases might unfairly favor one algorithm. Fourth, you could find that even the better of the two algorithms does not fall within your resource budget – you must begin the entire process again with yet another program implementing a new algorithm.

These problems can often be avoided by using a technique called **asymptotic algorithm analysis**, or simply **algorithm analysis**. Algorithm analysis measures the efficiency of an algorithm, or its implementation as a program, as the input size becomes large. It is actually an estimating technique, and does not tell us anything about the relative merits of two programs where one is always "slightly faster" than the other. However, asymptotic algorithm analysis has proved useful to computer scientists who must determine if a particular algorithm is worth considering for implementation.

The critical resource for a program is most often its running time. However, you cannot pay attention to running time alone. You must also be concerned with other factors such as the space required to run the program (both main memory and disk space). Typically you will analyze the *time* required for an *algorithm* (or the instantiation of an algorithm in the form of a program), and the *space* required for a *data structure.*

Many factors affect the running time of a program. Some relate to the environment in which the program is compiled and run. Such factors include the speed of the computer's CPU, bus, and peripheral hardware. Competition with other users for the computer's resources can make a program slow to a crawl. The programming language and the quality of code generated by a particular compiler can have a significant effect. The "coding efficiency" of the programmer who converts the algorithm to a program can have a tremendous impact as well.

If you need to get a program working within time and space constraints on a particular computer, all of these factors can be relevant. Yet, none of these factors address the differences between two algorithms or data structures. To be fair, programs derived from two algorithms for solving the same problem should both be compiled with the same compiler and run on the same computer under the same conditions. As much as possible, the same amount of care should be taken in the programming effort devoted to each program to make the implementations "equally efficient." In this sense, all of the factors mentioned above should cancel out of the comparison since they apply to both algorithms equally.

If you truly wish to understand the running time of an algorithm, there are other factors that are more appropriate to consider than machine speed, programming language, compiler, and so forth. Ideally we would measure the running time of the algorithm under standard benchmark conditions. However, we have no way to calculate the running time reliably other than to run an implementation of the algorithm on some computer. The only alternative is to use some other measure as a proxy for running time.

Of primary consideration when estimating an algorithm's performance is the number of **basic operations** required by the algorithm to process an input of a certain **size**. The terms "basic operations" and "size" are both rather vague and depend on the algorithm being analyzed. Size is often the number of inputs processed. For example, when comparing sorting algorithms, the size of the problem is typically measured by the number of records to be sorted. A basic operation must have the property that its time to complete does not depend on the particular values of its operands. Adding or comparing two integer variables are examples of basic operations in most programming languages. Summing the contents of an array containing n integers is not, since the cost depends on the value of n (i.e., the size of the input).

Example 3.1 Consider a simple algorithm to solve the problem of finding the largest value in an array of n integers. The algorithm looks at each number in turn, saving the largest value seen so far. This algorithm is called the *largest value sequential search*, and is illustrated by the following Java function:

```
static int largest(int[] array) {    // Find largest value
  int currLargest = 0;               // Store largest value
  for (int i=0; i<array.length; i++) // For each array element
   if (array[i] > currLargest)       //   if this is largest
     currLargest = array[i];         //     remember it
  return currLargest;                // Return largest value
}
```

Here, the size of the problem is n, the number of integers stored in **array**. The basic operation is to "examine" a single integer, by comparing it to a variable that stores the largest integer seen so far.

It is reasonable to assume that it takes a fixed amount of time to examine one integer in the array, regardless of the value of that integer or its position in the array.

Since the most important factor affecting running time is normally size of the input, for a given input size n we often express the time **T** to run the algorithm as a function of n, written as **T**(n). Note that we always assume **T**(n) is a non-negative value.

Let us call c the amount of time required to examine a value in function `largest`. Included in c is the time to increment variable i (since this must be done for each value in the array), as well as the actual assignment when a larger value is found. We do not care right now what the precise value of c may be. Nor are we concerned with the little bit of extra time taken before executing the loop to initialize `largest` – we just want a reasonable approximation for the time taken to execute the algorithm. The total time to run `largest` is therefore approximately cn, since we must look at n values with each "examine" step costing c time. We say that function `largest` (and the largest value sequential search algorithm in general) has a running time expressed by the equation

$$\mathbf{T}(n) = cn.$$

This equation describes the growth rate for the running time of the largest value sequential search algorithm.

Example 3.2 The running time of a statement that assigns the first value of an integer array to a variable is simply the time required to copy the value of the first array value. We can assume this assignment takes a constant amount of time regardless of the value. Let us call c_1 the amount of time necessary to copy an integer. No matter how large the array on a typical computer (given reasonable conditions for memory and array size), the time to copy the value from the first position of the array is always c_1. Thus, the equation for this algorithm is simply

$$\mathbf{T}(n) = c_1,$$

indicating that the size of the input n has no effect on the running time. This is called a **constant** running time.

Example 3.3 Consider the following Java code:

```
sum = 0;
for (i=1; i<=n; i++)
   for (j=1; j<=n; j++)
      sum++;
```

What is the running time for this code fragment? Clearly it takes longer to run when n is larger. The basic operation in this example is the increment operation for variable sum. We can assume that incrementing takes constant time; call this time c_2. (As explained later in this chapter, we can ignore the time required to initialize sum, and to increment the loop counters i and j. In practice, these costs can safely be bundled into time c_2.) The total number of increment operations is n^2. Thus, we say that the running time is

$$\mathbf{T}(n) - c_2 n^2.$$

The concept of growth rate is extremely important. It is what allows us to compare the running time of two algorithms without actually writing two programs and running them on the same computer.

Figure 3.1 shows a graph for five equations, each meant to describe the running time for a particular program or algorithm. A variety of growth rates representative of those for typical algorithms are shown. The two equations labeled $10n$ and $20n$ are graphed by straight lines. A growth rate of cn (for c any positive constant) is often referred to as a **linear** growth rate or running time. This means that as the value of n grows, the running time of the algorithm grows in the same proportion. Doubling the value of n roughly doubles the running time. An algorithm whose running-time equation has a high-order term containing a factor of n^2 is said to have a **quadratic** growth rate. In Figure 3.1, the line labeled $2n^2$ represents a quadratic growth rate. The line labeled 2^n represents an **exponential** growth rate. This name comes from the fact that n appears in the exponent.

As you can see from Figure 3.1, the difference between an algorithm whose running time has equation $\mathbf{T}(n) = 10n$ and another with equation $\mathbf{T}(n) = 2n^2$ is tremendous. For $n > 5$, the algorithm with running time $\mathbf{T}(n) = 2n^2$ is much slower. This is despite the fact that $10n$ has a greater constant factor than $2n^2$. Comparing the two curves marked $20n$ and $2n^2$ shows that changing the constant factor for one of the equations only shifts

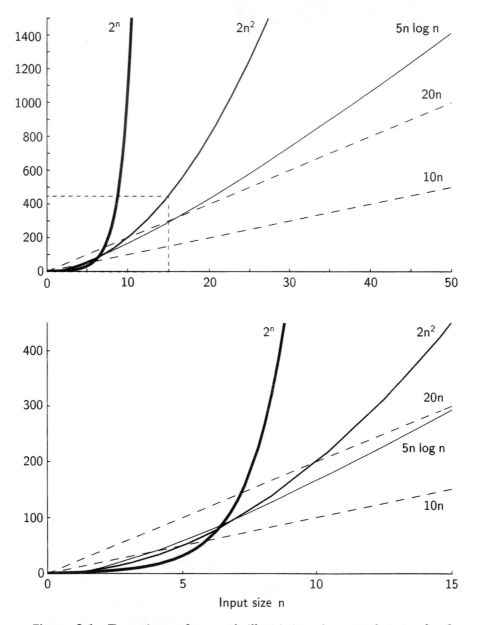

Figure 3.1 Two views of a graph illustrating the growth rates for five equations. The bottom view shows in detail the lower left portion of the top view. The horizontal axis represents input size. The vertical axis can represent time, space, or any other measure of cost.

the point at which the two curves cross. For $n > 10$, the algorithm with equation $\mathbf{T}(n) = 2n^2$ is slower than the algorithm with equation $\mathbf{T}(n) = 20n$. This graph also shows that the equation $\mathbf{T}(n) = 5n \log n$ grows somewhat more quickly than both $\mathbf{T}(n) = 10n$ and $\mathbf{T}(n) = 20n$, but not nearly so quickly as the equation $\mathbf{T}(n) = 2n^2$. For any integer constants $a, b > 1$, n^a grows faster than either $\log^b n$ or $\log n^b$. Finally, an algorithm with equation $\mathbf{T}(n) = 2^n$ is prohibitively expensive for even modest values of n. Note that for any constants $a, b \geq 1$, a^n grows faster than n^b.

3.2   Best, Worst, and Average Cases

For some algorithms, different inputs of a given size can require different amounts of time. For example, consider the problem of searching an array of size n to find the position with a particular value K (assume that K occurs exactly once in the array). The *sequential search* algorithm begins at the first position in the array and looks at each value in turn until K is found. Once K is found, the algorithm stops. This is different from the largest value sequential search algorithm of Example 3.1, which always examines every array value.

There is a wide range of possible running times for the sequential search algorithm. The first value in the array could be K, and so only one value is examined. In this case the running time is short. This is the **best case** for this algorithm – it is not possible for sequential search to look at less than one value. Alternatively, if the last position in the array contains K, then the running time is relatively long, since the algorithm must examine n values. This is the **worst case** for this algorithm – sequential search never looks at more than n values. If we implement sequential search as a program and run it many times on many arrays of size n, or search for many different values of K within the same array, we expect the algorithm on average to go halfway through the array before finding the value we seek. On average, the algorithm examines about $n/2$ values. We call this the **average-case** running time for this algorithm.

When analyzing an algorithm, should we study the best, worst, or average case? Normally we are not interested in the best case, since this might happen only rarely and generally is too optimistic for a fair characterization of the algorithm's running time. In other words, analysis based on the best case is not likely to be representative of the behavior of the algorithm. However, there are rare instances where a best-case analysis is useful – in particular, when the best case has high probability of occurring. In Chapter 8 you will see an example where taking advantage of the best-case running time for one sorting algorithm makes a second more efficient.

How about the worst case? The advantage to analyzing the worst case is that you know for certain that the algorithm must perform at least that well. This is especially important for real-time applications, such as for the computers that monitor an air traffic control system. Here, it would not be acceptable to use an algorithm that can handle n planes quickly enough *most of the time*, but which fails to perform quickly enough when all n airplanes are coming from the same direction.

For other applications – particularly when a program is run many times on many inputs – worst-case analysis might not be a representative measure of the algorithm's performance. Often we prefer to know the average-case running time. This means that we would like to know the *typical* behavior of the algorithm on inputs of size n. Unfortunately, average-case analysis is not always possible. Average-case analysis first requires that we understand how data are distributed. For example, it was stated previously that the sequential search algorithm on average examines half of the array values. This was based on the assumption that K is equally likely to appear in any position in the array. If this assumption is not correct, then the algorithm does *not* necessarily examine half of the array values in the average case. See Section 10.2 for further discussion regarding the effects of data distribution on the sequential search algorithm.

The characteristics of a data distribution have a significant effect on many search algorithms, such as those based on hashing (Section 10.4) and search trees (e.g., see Section 5.5). Incorrect assumptions about data distribution can have disastrous consequences on a program's space or time performance. On the other hand, unusual data distributions can also be used to advantage, as shown in Section 10.2.

In summary, for real-time applications we are likely to prefer a worst-case analysis of an algorithm. Otherwise, we often desire an average-case analysis if we know enough about the distribution of our input to compute the average case. If not, then we must resort to worst-case analysis.

3.3   A Faster Computer, or a Faster Algorithm?

Imagine that you have a problem to solve, and you know of an algorithm whose running time is proportional to n^2. Unfortunately, the resulting program takes ten times too long to run. If you replace your current computer with a new one that is ten times faster, will the n^2 algorithm become acceptable? If the problem size remains the same, then perhaps the faster computer will allow you to get your work done quickly enough even with an algorithm having a high growth rate. But a funny thing happens to most people who get a faster computer. They don't run the same problem faster – they run a bigger problem! Say that on your old computer you were content to sort 10,000 numbers because that could be done by the computer during your lunch break. On your new computer you might hope to sort 100,000 numbers in the same time. You won't be back from lunch any sooner, so you are better off solving a larger problem. And since the new machine is ten times faster, you would like to sort ten times as many numbers.

If your algorithm's growth rate is linear (i.e., if the equation that describes the running time on n numbers is $\mathbf{T}(n) = cn$ for some constant c), then 100,000 numbers on the new machine will be sorted in the same time as 10,000 numbers on the old machine. If the algorithm's growth rate is greater than cn (e.g., $c_1 n^2$), then you will *not* be able to do a problem ten times the size in the same amount of time on a machine that is ten times faster.

How much larger a problem can be solved in a given amount of time by a faster computer? Assume that the new machine is ten times faster than the old. Say that the old machine could solve a problem of size n in an hour. What is the largest problem that the new machine can solve in one hour? Figure 3.2 shows how large a problem can be solved on the two machines for the five running-time functions from Figure 3.1.

This table illustrates many important points. The first two equations are both linear; only the value of the constant factor has changed. In both cases, the machine that is ten times faster gives an increase in problem size by a factor of ten. In other words, while the value of the constant does affect the absolute size of the problem that can be solved in a fixed amount of time, it *does not* affect the improvement in problem size gained by a faster computer. This relationship holds true regardless of the algorithm's growth rate: Constant factors never affect the relative improvement gained by a faster computer.

An algorithm with time equation $\mathbf{T}(n) = 2n^2$ does not receive nearly so great an improvement from the faster machine as an algorithm with linear growth rate. Instead of an improvement by a factor of ten, the improvement is only the square root of that: $\sqrt{10} \approx 3.16$. Thus, the algorithm with higher growth rate receives less of a benefit from a faster computer *and* allows only a smaller problem to be solved.

T(n)	n	n'	Change	n'/n
10n	1,000	10,000	$n' = 10n$	10
20n	500	5,000	$n' = 10n$	10
5n log n	250	1,842	$\sqrt{10}n < n' < 10n$	7.37
$2n^2$	70	223	$n' = \sqrt{10}n$	3.16
2^n	13	16	$n' = n + 3$	--

Figure 3.2 The increase in problem size that can be run in a fixed period of time on a computer that is ten times faster. The first column lists the right-hand sides for each of the five growth rate equations of Figure 3.1. For the purpose of this example, arbitrarily assume that the old machine can run 10,000 basic operations in one hour. The second column shows the maximum value for n that can be run in 10,000 basic operations on the old machine. The third column shows the value for n', the new maximum size for the problem that can be run in the same time on the new machine that is ten times faster. Variable n' is the greatest size for the problem that can run in 100,000 basic operations. The fourth column shows how the size of n changed to become n' on the new machine. The fifth column shows the increase in the problem size as the ratio of n' to n.

The algorithm with growth rate $\mathbf{T}(n) = 5n \log n$ improves by a greater amount than the one with quadratic growth rate, but not by as great an amount as the algorithms with linear growth rates.

Note that something special happens in the case of the algorithm whose running time grows exponentially. In Figure 3.1, the curve for the algorithm whose time is proportional to 2^n goes up very quickly. In Figure 3.2, the increase in problem size on the machine ten times as fast is shown to be about $n + 3$ (to be precise, it is $n + \log_2 10$). The increase in problem size for an algorithm with exponential growth rate is by a constant addition, not by a multiplicative factor. Since the old value of n was 13, the new problem size is 16. If next year you buy another computer ten times faster yet, then the new computer (100 times faster than the original computer) will only run a problem of size 19. If you had a second program with exponential growth rate for which the original computer could run a problem of size 1000 in an hour, than a machine ten times faster can run a problem only of size 1003 in an hour! Thus, an exponential growth rate is radically different than the other growth rates shown in Figure 3.2. The significance of this difference is explored in Chapter 15.

Instead of buying a faster computer, consider what happens if you replace an algorithm whose running time is proportional to n^2 with a new algorithm whose running time is proportional to $n \log n$. In the graph of Figure 3.1, a fixed amount of time would appear as a horizontal line. If the line for the amount of time available to solve your problem is above the point at which the curves for the two growth rates in question meet, then the algorithm whose running time grows less quickly is faster. An algorithm with running time $\mathbf{T}(n) = n^2$ requires $1024 \times 1024 = 1,048,576$ time steps for an input of size $n = 1024$. An algorithm with running time $\mathbf{T}(n) = n \log n$ requires $1024 \times 10 = 10,240$ time steps for an input of size $n = 1024$, which is an improvement of much more than a factor of ten when compared to the algorithm with running time $\mathbf{T}(n) = n^2$. Since $n^2 > 10n \log n$ whenever $n > 58$, if the typical problem size is larger than 58 for this example then you would be much better off changing algorithms instead of buying a computer ten times faster. Furthermore, when you do buy a faster computer, an algorithm with a slower growth rate provides a greater benefit in terms of larger problem size that can run in a certain time on the new computer.

3.4 Asymptotic Analysis

Despite the larger constant for the curve labeled $10n$ in Figure 3.1, the curve labeled $2n^2$ crosses it at the relatively small value of $n = 5$. What if we double the value of the constant in front of the linear equation? As shown in the graph, the curve labeled $20n$ is surpassed by the curve labeled $2n^2$ once $n = 10$. The additional factor of two for the linear growth rate does not much matter; it only doubles the x-coordinate for the intersection point. In general, changes to a constant factor in either equation only shift *where* the two curves cross, not *whether* the two curves cross.

When you buy a faster computer or a faster compiler, the new problem size that can be run in a given amount of time is larger by the same factor, regardless of the constant on the running-time equation. The time curves for two algorithms with different growth rates still cross, regardless of their running-time equation constants. For these reasons, we usually ignore the constants when we want an estimate of the running time or other resource requirements of an algorithm. This simplifies the analysis and keeps us thinking about the most important aspect: the growth rate. This is called **asymptotic algorithm analysis**. To be precise, asymptotic analysis refers to the study of an algorithm as the input size "gets big" or reaches a limit (in the calculus sense). However, it has proved to be so useful to ignore all constant factors that asymptotic analysis is used for most algorithm comparisons.

It is not always reasonable to ignore the constants. When comparing algorithms meant to run on small values of n, the constant can have a large effect. For example, if the problem is to sort a collection of exactly five numbers, then an algorithm designed for sorting thousands of numbers is probably not appropriate, even if its asymptotic analysis indicates good performance. There are rare cases where the constants for two algorithms under comparison can differ by a factor of 1000 or more, making the one with lower growth rate impractical for most purposes due to its large constant. Asymptotic analysis is a form of "back of the envelope" estimation for algorithm resource consumption. It provides a simplified model of the running time or other resource needs of an algorithm. This simplification usually helps you understand the behavior of your algorithms. Just be aware of the limitations to asymptotic analysis in the rare case where the constant is important.

3.4.1 Upper Bounds

Several terms are used to describe the running-time equation for an algorithm. These terms – and their associated symbols – indicate precisely what aspect of the algorithm's behavior is being described. One is the **upper bound** for the running time of the algorithm. It indicates the upper or highest growth rate that the algorithm can have.

The upper bound is not the same as the worst case for a given input of size n. Rather, it is the upper bound for the growth rate expressed as an equation. Thus, to make any statement about the upper bound of an algorithm, we must be making it about some class of inputs of size n. We measure this upper bound nearly always on the best-case, average-case or worst-case inputs. Thus, we cannot say, "this algorithm has an upper bound to its growth rate of n^2." We must say something like, "this algorithm has an upper bound to its growth rate of n^2 *in the average case.*"

Since the phrase "has an upper bound to its growth rate of $f(n)$" is long and often used when discussing algorithms, we adopt a special notation, called **big-Oh notation**. If the upper bound for an algorithm's growth rate (for, say, the worst case) is $f(n)$, then we would write that this algorithm is "in the set $O(f(n))$" (or just "in $O(f(n))$") in the worst case. For example, if n^2 grows as fast as $\mathbf{T}(n)$ (the running time of our algorithm) for the worst-case input, we would say the algorithm is "in $O(n^2)$ in the worst case."

The following is a precise definition of what is meant by an upper bound. Here, $\mathbf{T}(n)$ represents the true running time of the algorithm, and $f(n)$ is some expression for the upper bound.

> **Definition 3.1** For $\mathbf{T}(n)$ a non-negatively valued function, $\mathbf{T}(n)$ is in the set $O(f(n))$ if there exist two positive constants c and n_0 such that $\mathbf{T}(n) \leq cf(n)$ for all $n > n_0$.

Constant n_0 is the smallest value of n for which the claim of an upper bound holds true. Usually n_0 is small, such as 1, but does not need to be. You must also be able to pick some constant c, but it is irrelevant what the value for c actually is. In other words, the definition says that for *all* inputs of the type in question (such as the worst case for all inputs of size n) that are large enough (i.e., $n > n_0$), the algorithm *always* executes in less than $cf(n)$ steps for some constant c.

> **Example 3.4** Consider the sequential search algorithm for finding a specified value in an array. If visiting and testing one value in the array requires c_s steps where c_s is a positive number, then in the average case $\mathbf{T}(n) = c_s n/2$. For all values of $n > 1$, $c_s n/2 \leq c_s n$. Therefore, by the definition, $\mathbf{T}(n)$ is in $O(n)$ for $n_0 = 1$ and $c = c_s$.

> **Example 3.5** For a particular algorithm, $\mathbf{T}(n) = c_1 n^2 + c_2 n$ in the average case where c_1 and c_2 are positive numbers. Then, $c_1 n^2 + c_2 n \leq c_1 n^2 + c_2 n^2 \leq (c_1 + c_2)n^2$ for all $n > 1$. So, $\mathbf{T}(n) \leq cn^2$ for $c = c_1 + c_2$, and $n_0 = 1$. Therefore, $\mathbf{T}(n)$ is in $O(n^2)$ by the definition.

> **Example 3.6** Assigning the first position of an array to a variable takes constant time regardless of the size of the array. Thus, $\mathbf{T}(n) = c$ (for the best, worst, and average cases). We could say in this case that $\mathbf{T}(n)$ is in $O(c)$. However, it is traditional to say that an algorithm whose running time has a constant upper bound is in $O(1)$.

Just knowing that something is in $O(f(n))$ says only how bad things can get. Perhaps things are not nearly so bad. Since we know sequential search is in $O(n)$ in the worst case, it is also true to say that sequential search is in $O(n^2)$. But sequential search is practical for large n, in a way that is not true for some other algorithms in $O(n^2)$. We always seek to define the running time of an algorithm with the tightest (lowest) possible upper bound. Thus, we prefer to say that sequential search is in $O(n)$. This also explains why the phrase "is in $O(f(n))$" or the notation "$\in O(f(n))$" is used instead of "is $O(f(n))$" or "$= O(f(n))$." There is no strict equality to the use of big-Oh notation. $O(n)$ is in $O(n^2)$, but $O(n^2)$ is not in $O(n)$.

3.4.2 Lower Bounds

Big-Oh notation describes an upper bound. In other words, big-Oh notation states a claim about the greatest amount of some resource (usually time) that is required by an algorithm for some class of inputs of size n (typically measured for the worst input, the average of all possible inputs, or the best input).

Similar notation is used to describe the least amount of a resource that an algorithm needs for some class of input. Like big-Oh notation, this is a measure of the algorithm's growth rate. Like big-Oh notation, it works for any resource, but we most often measure the least amount of time required. And again, like big-Oh notation, we are measuring the resource required for some particular class of inputs: the worst-, average-, or best-case input of size n.

The lower bound for an algorithm (or a problem, as explained later) is denoted by the symbol Ω, pronounced "big-Omega" or just "Omega." The following definition for Ω is symmetric with the definition of big-Oh:

Definition 3.2 For $\mathbf{T}(n)$ a non-negatively valued function, $\mathbf{T}(n)$ is in the set $\Omega(g(n))$ if there exist two positive constants c and n_0 such that $\mathbf{T}(n) \geq cg(n)$ for all $n > n_0$.

Example 3.7 Assume $\mathbf{T}(n) = c_1 n^2 + c_2 n$ for c_1 and $c_2 > 0$. Then,

$$c_1 n^2 + c_2 n \geq c_1 n^2$$

for all $n > 1$. So, $\mathbf{T}(n) \geq cn^2$ for $c = c_1$ and $n_0 = 1$. Therefore, $\mathbf{T}(n)$ is in $\Omega(n^2)$ by the definition.

It is true that the equation of Example 3.7 is in $\Omega(n)$. However, as with big-Oh notation, we wish to get the "tightest" (for Ω notation,[1] the largest) bound possible. Thus, we prefer to say that this running time is in $\Omega(n^2)$.

---
[1] An alternative (non-equivalent) definition for Ω is as follows:

Definition 3.3 $\mathbf{T}(n)$ is in the set $\Omega(g(n))$ if there exists a positive constant c such that $\mathbf{T}(n) \geq cg(n)$ for an infinite number of values for n.

Roughly, this definition says that for an "interesting" number of cases, the algorithm takes at least $cg(n)$ time. Note that this definition is *not* symmetric with the definition of big-Oh. For $g(n)$ to be a lower bound, this definition *does not* require that $\mathbf{T}(n) \geq cg(n)$ for

Recall the sequential search algorithm to find a value K within an array of numbers. In the average and worst cases this algorithm is in $\Omega(n)$, since in both the average and worst cases we must examine *at least cn* values (where c is $1/2$ in the average case and 1 in the worst case).

3.4.3 Θ Notation

The definitions for big-Oh and Ω give us ways to describe the upper bound for an algorithm (if we can find an equation for the maximum cost of a particular class of inputs of size n) and the lower bound for an algorithm (if we can find an equation for the minimum cost for a particular class of inputs of size n). When the upper and lower bounds are the same within a constant factor, we indicate this by using Θ (big-Theta) notation. An algorithm is said to be $\Theta(h(n))$ if it is in $O(h(n))$ *and* it is in $\Omega(h(n))$. Note that we drop the word "in" for Θ notation, since there is a strict equality for two equations with the same Θ. In other words, if $f(n)$ is $\Theta(g(n))$, then $g(n)$ is $\Theta(f(n))$.

Since the sequential search algorithm is both in $O(n)$ and in $\Omega(n)$ in the average case, we say it is $\Theta(n)$ in the average case.

---

all values of n greater than some constant. It only requires that this happen often enough, in particular that it happen for an infinite number of values for n. The motivation for this alternate definition can be found in the following example.

Example 3.8 Assume a particular algorithm has the following behavior:

$$\mathbf{T}(n) = \begin{cases} n & \text{for all odd } n \geq 1. \\ n^2/100 & \text{for all even } n \geq 0. \end{cases}$$

From this definition, $n^2/100 \geq \frac{1}{100}n^2$ for all even $n \geq 0$. So, $\mathbf{T}(n) \geq cn^2$ for an infinite number of values of n (i.e., for all even n) for $c = 1/100$. Therefore, $\mathbf{T}(n)$ is in $\Omega(n^2)$ by the definition.

For the equation of Example 3.8 it is true that all inputs of size n take at least cn time. But an infinite number of inputs of size n take cn^2 time, so we would like to say that the algorithm is in $\Omega(n^2)$. Unfortunately, Definition 3.2 will yield a lower bound of $\Omega(n)$ since it is not possible to pick constants c and n_0 such that $\mathbf{T}(n) \geq cn^2$ for all $n > n_0$. Definition 3.3 does result in a lower bound of $\Omega(n^2)$ for this algorithm, which seems to fit common sense more closely. Fortunately, few real algorithms or computer programs display the pathological behavior of this example. Definition 3.2 generally yields the expected result.

As you can see from this discussion, asymptotic bounds notation is not a law of nature. It is merely a powerful notational tool created by mathematicians and refined by computer scientists to describe the behavior of algorithms.

Given an arithmetic expression describing the time requirement for an algorithm, the upper and lower bounds always meet. That is because in some sense we have a perfect analysis for the algorithm, embodied by the running-time equation. For many algorithms (or their instantiations as programs), it is easy to come up with the equation that defines their runtime behavior. Most algorithms presented in this book are well-understood and we can almost always give a Θ analysis for them. However, Chapter 15 discusses a whole class of algorithms for which we have no Θ analysis, just some unsatisfying big-Oh and Ω analyses. Exercise 3.11 presents a short, simple program for which nobody currently knows the true upper or lower bounds. Thus, while we prefer to use Θ notation when we know enough about an algorithm, limitations on our ability to analyze certain algorithms may require use of big-Oh or Ω notations.

3.4.4 Simplifying Rules

Once you determine the running-time equation for an algorithm, it really is a simple matter to derive the big-Oh, Ω, and Θ expressions from the equation. You do not need to resort to the formal definitions of asymptotic analysis. Instead, you can use the following rules to determine the simplest form.

Definition 3.4 Four asymptotic analysis simplification rules.

   1. If $f(n)$ is in $O(g(n))$ and $g(n)$ is in $O(h(n))$, then $f(n)$ is in $O(h(n))$.

   2. If $f(n)$ is in $O(kg(n))$ for any constant $k > 0$, then $f(n)$ is in $O(g(n))$.

   3. If $f_1(n)$ is in $O(g_1(n))$ and $f_2(n)$ is in $O(g_2(n))$, then $f_1(n) + f_2(n)$ is in $O(\max(g_1(n), g_2(n)))$.

   4. If $f_1(n)$ is in $O(g_1(n))$ and $f_2(n)$ is in $O(g_2(n))$, then $f_1(n)f_2(n)$ is in $O(g_1(n)g_2(n))$.

The first rule says that if some function $g(n)$ is an upper bound for your cost function, then any upper bound for $g(n)$ is also an upper bound for your cost function. A similar property holds true for Ω notation: If $g(n)$ is a lower bound for your cost function, then any lower bound for $g(n)$ is also a lower bound for your cost function. Likewise for Θ notation.

The significance of rule (2) is that you can ignore any multiplicative constants in your equations when using big-Oh notation. This rule also holds true for Ω and Θ notations.

Rule (3) says that given two parts of a program run in sequence (whether two statements or two sections of code), you need consider only the more expensive part. This rule applies to Ω and Θ notations as well. For both, you need consider only the more expensive part.

Rule (4) is used to analyze simple loops in programs. If some action is repeated some number of times, and each repetition has the same cost, then the total cost is the cost of the action multiplied by the number of times that the action takes place. This rule applies to Ω and Θ notations as well.

Taking the first three rules collectively, you can ignore all constants and all lower-order terms to determine the asymptotic growth rate for any cost function. The advantages and dangers of ignoring constants were discussed near the beginning of this section. Ignoring lower-order terms is reasonable when performing an asymptotic analysis. The higher-order terms soon swamp the lower-order terms in their contribution to the total cost as n becomes larger. Thus, if $\mathbf{T}(n) = 3n^4 + 2n^2$, then $\mathbf{T}(n)$ is in $\mathrm{O}(n^4)$; the n^2 term contributes relatively little to the total cost.

Throughout the rest of this book, these simplification rules are used when discussing the cost for a program or algorithm.

3.5 Calculating the Running Time of a Program

This section presents the analysis for several simple code fragments.

Example 3.9 We begin with an analysis of a simple assignment statement to an integer variable.

```
a = b;
```

Since the assignment statement takes constant time, it is $\Theta(1)$.

Example 3.10 Consider a simple `for` loop.

```
sum = 0;
for (i=1; i<=n; i++)
   sum += n;
```

The first line is $\Theta(1)$. The `for` loop is repeated n times. The third line takes constant time so, by simplification rule (4) of Section 3.4.4, the total cost for executing the two lines making up the `for` loop is $\Theta(n)$. By rule (3), the cost of the entire code fragment is also $\Theta(n)$.

Example 3.11 We now analyze a code fragment with several **for** loops, some of which are nested.

```
sum = 0;
for (j=1; j<=n; j++)      // First for loop
    for (i=1; i<=j; i++)  //   is a double loop
        sum++;
for (k=0; k<n; k++)       // Second for loop
    A[k] = k;
```

This code fragment has three separate statements: the first assignment statement and the two **for** loops. Again the assignment statement takes constant time; call it c_1. The second **for** loop is just like the one in Example 3.10, and takes $c_2 n = \Theta(n)$ time.

The first **for** loop is a double loop and requires a special technique. We work from the inside of the loop outwards. The expression **sum++** requires constant time; call it c_3. Since the inner **for** loop is executed j times, by rule (4) it has cost $c_3 j$. The outer **for** loop is executed n times, but each time the cost of the inner loop is different since it costs $c_3 j$ with j changing each time. You should see that for the first execution of the outer loop, j is 1. For the second execution of the outer loop, j is 2. Each time through the outer loop, j becomes one greater, until the last time through the loop when $j = n$. Thus, the total cost of the loop is c_3 times the sum of the numbers 1 through n. From Equation 2.1, we know that

$$\sum_{j=1}^{n} j = \frac{n(n+1)}{2},$$

which is $\Theta(n^2)$. By rule (3), $\Theta(c_1 + c_2 n + c_3 n^2)$ is simply $\Theta(n^2)$.

Example 3.12 Compare the asymptotic analysis for the following two code fragments:

```
sum1 = 0;
for (i=1; i<=n; i++)      // First double loop
    for (j=1; j<=n; j++)  //   do n times
        sum1++;

sum2 = 0;
for (i=1; i<=n; i++)      // Second double loop
    for (j=1; j<=i; j++)  //   do i times
        sum2++;
```

In the first double loop, the inner **for** loop always executes n times. Since the outer loop executes n times, it should be obvious that the statement **sum++** is executed precisely n^2 times. The second loop is similar to the one analyzed in the previous example, with cost $\sum_{j=1}^{n} j$. This is approximately $\frac{1}{2}n^2$. Thus, both double loops cost $\Theta(n^2)$, though the second requires about half the time of the first.

Example 3.13 Not all doubly nested **for** loops are $\Theta(n^2)$. The following pair of nested loops illustrates this fact:

```
sum1 = 0;
for (k=1; k<=n; k*=2)
   for (j=1; j<=n; j++)
      sum1++;

sum2 = 0;
for (k=1; k<=n; k*=2)
   for (j=1; j<=k; j++)
      sum2++;
```

The first code fragment has its outer **for** loop executed $\log n$ times since on each iteration k is multiplied by two until it reaches n. Since the inner loop always executes n times, the total cost for the first code fragment can be expressed as $\sum_{i=0}^{\log n} n$. Note that a variable substitution takes place here to create the summation, with $k = 2^i$. From Equation 2.3, the solution for this summation is $\Theta(n \log n)$. In the second code fragment, the outer loop is also executed $\log n$ times. The inner loop has cost k, which doubles each time. The summation can be expressed as $\sum_{i=0}^{\log n} 2^i$ where n is assumed to be a power of two and again $k = 2^i$. From Equation 2.9, we know that this summation is simply $\Theta(n)$.

What about other control statements? **While** loops are analyzed in a manner similar to **for** loops. The cost of an **if** statement in the worst case is the greater of the costs for the **then** and **else** clauses. This is also true for the average case, assuming that the size of n does not affect the probability of executing one of the clauses (which is usually, but not necessarily, true). For **switch** statements, the worst-case cost is that of the most expensive branch. For subroutine calls, simply add the cost of executing the subroutine.

Unfortunately, determining the execution time of a recursive subroutine can be particularly difficult. The running time for a recursive subroutine is typically best expressed by a recurrence relation. For example, the recursive factorial function `rfact` of Section 2.4 calls itself with a value one less than its input value. The result of this recursive call is then multiplied by the input value, which takes constant time. Thus, the cost of the factorial function is a constant plus the time to execute the recursive call on the smaller input. This running time can be expressed as

$$\mathbf{T}(n) = \mathbf{T}(n-1) + c.$$

The closed form solution for this recurrence relation is $\Theta(n)$.

There are rare situations in which the probability for executing the various branches of an `if` or `switch` statement are functions of the input size. For example, for input of size n, the `then` clause of an `if` statement might be executed with probability $1/n$. An example would be an `if` statement that executes the `then` clause only for the smallest of n values. To perform an average-case analysis for such programs, we cannot simply count the cost of the `if` statement as being the cost of the more expensive branch. In such situations, the technique of amortized analysis (see Section 14.3) can come to the rescue.

The final example of algorithm analysis for this section will compare two algorithms for performing search in an array. Earlier, we determined that the running time for sequential search on an array where the search value K is equally likely to appear in any location is $\Theta(n)$ in both the average and worst cases. We would like to compare this running time to that required to perform a **binary search** on an array whose values are stored in order from lowest to highest.

Binary search begins by examining the value in the middle position of the array; call this position mid and the corresponding value k_{mid}. If $k_{mid} = K$, then processing can stop immediately. This is unlikely to be the case, however. Fortunately, knowing the middle value provides useful information that can help guide the search process. In particular, if $k_{mid} > K$, then you know that the value K cannot appear in the array at any position greater than mid. Thus, you can eliminate future search in the upper half of the array. Conversely, if $k_{mid} < K$, then you know that you can ignore all positions in the array less than mid. Either way, half of the positions are eliminated from further consideration. Binary search next looks at the middle position in that part of the array where value K may exist. The value at this position again allows us to eliminate half of the remaining positions from consideration. Repeating this process, you will find the desired value (or determine

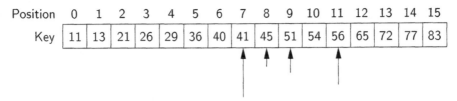

Figure 3.3 An illustration of binary search on a sorted array of 16 positions. Consider a search for the position with value $K = 45$. Binary search first checks the value at position 7. Since $41 < K$, the desired value cannot appear in any position below 7 in the array. Next, binary search checks the value at position 11. Since $56 > K$, the desired value (if it exists) must be between positions 7 and 11. Position 9 is checked next. Again, its value is too great. The final search is at position 8, which contains the desired value. Thus, function `binary` returns position 8. Alternatively, if K were 44 then the same series of record accesses would be made. After checking position 8, `binary` would return UNSUCCESSFUL.

that it is not in the array) in at most $\log n$ comparisons. Figure 3.3 illustrates the binary search method. Here is a Java implementation for binary search:

```
static int binary(int K, int[] array, int left, int right) {
  // Return position of the element in array (if any) with value K
  int l = left-1;
  int r = right+1;      // l and r are beyond the bounds of array
  while (l+1 != r) {    // Stop when l and r meet
    int i = (l+r)/2;    // Look at middle of remaining subarray
    if (K < array[i]) r = i;      // In left half
    if (K -- array[i]) return i; // Found it
    if (K > array[i]) l = i;      // In right half
  }
  return UNSUCCESSFUL; // Search value not in array
}
```

Function `binary` is designed to find the (single) occurrence of K and return its position. A special value is returned if K does not appear in the array. This algorithm can be modified to implement variations such as returning the position of the first occurrence of K in the array if multiple occurrences are allowed, and returning the position of the greatest value less than K when K is not in the array.

Comparing sequential search to binary search, we see that as n grows large, the $\Theta(n)$ running time for sequential search in the average and worst cases quickly becomes much greater than the $\Theta(\log n)$ running time for binary search. Taken in isolation, binary search appears to be much more efficient than sequential search. Note however that the running time for sequential search will be roughly the same regardless of whether or not the array values are stored in order. In contrast, binary search requires that the array values be ordered from lowest to highest. Depending on the context in which binary search is to be used, this requirement for a sorted array could be detrimental to the running time of a complete program, since maintaining a sorted array generally leads to greater cost when inserting new elements into the array. This is an example of a tradeoff between the advantage of binary search during search and the disadvantage related to maintaining a sorted array. Only in the context of the complete problem to be solved can we know whether the advantage outweighs the disadvantage.

3.6   Analyzing Problems

You normally use the techniques of "algorithm" analysis to analyze an algorithm, or the instantiation of an algorithm as a program. However, you can also use these same techniques to analyze the cost of a problem. It makes sense to say that the upper bound for a problem cannot be worse than the upper bound for the best algorithm that we know for that problem. But what does it mean to give a lower bound for a problem? It is much easier to show that an algorithm (or program) is in $\Omega(f(n))$ than it is to show that a problem is in $\Omega(f(n))$. For a problem to be in $\Omega(f(n))$ means that *every* algorithm that solves the problem is in $\Omega(f(n))$, even algorithms that we have not thought of!

So far all of our examples of algorithm analysis give "obvious" results, with big-Oh always matching Ω. To understand how big-Oh, Ω, and Θ notations are properly used to describe our understanding of a problem or an algorithm, it is best to consider an example where you do not already know a lot about the problem.

Let us look ahead to analyzing the problem of sorting to see how this process works. What is the least possible cost for any sorting algorithm in the worst case? The algorithm must certainly read the n items to be sorted and print them out again in sorted order. Thus, any sorting algorithm must take at least cn time just to read the input and print the result. For many problems, this observation that n inputs must be read leads to an easy $\Omega(n)$ lower bound.

In your previous study of computer science, you have probably seen an example of a sorting algorithm whose running time is in $O(n^2)$ in the worst case. The simple Bubble Sort and Insertion Sort algorithms typically given as examples in a first year programming course have running times in $O(n^2)$.

Thus, the problem of sorting can be said to have an upper bound in $O(n^2)$. How do we close the gap between $\Omega(n)$ and $O(n^2)$? Can there be a better sorting algorithm? If you can think of no algorithm whose worst-case growth rate is better than $O(n^2)$, and if you have discovered no analysis technique to show that the least cost for the problem of sorting in the worst case is greater than $\Omega(n)$, then you cannot know for sure whether or not there is a better algorithm.

Chapter 8 presents sorting algorithms whose running time is in $O(n \log n)$ for the worst case. This greatly narrows the gap. We now have a lower bound in $\Omega(n)$ and an upper bound in $O(n \log n)$. Should we search for a faster algorithm? Many have tried, without success. Fortunately (or perhaps unfortunately?), Chapter 8 also includes a proof that any sorting algorithm must have running time in $\Omega(n \log n)$ in the worst case.[2] This proof is one of the most important results in the field of algorithm analysis, and it means that no sorting algorithm can possibly run faster than $cn \log n$ for all inputs of size n. Thus, we can conclude that the problem of sorting is $\Theta(n \log n)$ in the worst case, since the upper and lower bounds have met.

3.7 Multiple Parameters

Sometimes the proper analysis of an algorithm requires multiple parameters to describe the cost. To illustrate the concept, consider an algorithm to compute the rank ordering for counts of all pixel values in a picture. Pictures are often represented by a two-dimensional array, and a pixel is simply one cell in the array. The value of a pixel is the color or intensity of the picture for that pixel. Assume that each pixel can take any integer value in the range 0 to $C - 1$. The problem is to find the number of pixels of each color value and then sort the color values with respect to the number of times each value appears in the picture. Assume that the picture is a rectangle with P pixels. A pseudocode algorithm to solve the problem follows:

```
for (i=0; i<C; i++)     // Initialize count
    count[i] = 0;
for (i=0; i<P; i++)     // Look at all of the pixels
    count[value(i)]++;  // Increment proper pixel value count
sort(count);            // Sort pixel value counts
```

---

[2]While it is fortunate to have the proof, it is unfortunate that sorting is $\Theta(n \log n)$ rather than $\Theta(n)$!

In this example, `count` is an array of size C that stores the number of pixels for each color value. Function `value(i)` returns the color value for pixel i.

The time for the first `for` loop (which initializes `count`) is based on the number of colors, C. The time for the second loop (which determines the number of pixels with each color) is $\Theta(P)$. The time for the final line, the call to `sort`, depends on the cost of the sorting algorithm used. From the discussion of the previous section, we can assume that the sorting algorithm has cost $\Theta(P \log P)$ if P items are sorted, thus yielding $\Theta(P \log P)$ as the total algorithm cost.

Is this a good representation for the cost of this algorithm? What is actually being sorted? It is not the pixels, but rather the colors. What if C is much smaller than P? Then the estimate of $\Theta(P \log P)$ is pessimistic, because much fewer than P items are being sorted. Instead, we should use P as our analysis variable for steps that look at each pixel, and C as our analysis variable for steps that look at colors. Then we get $\Theta(C)$ for the initialization loop, $\Theta(P)$ for the pixel count loop, and $\Theta(C \log C)$ for the sorting operation. This yields a total cost of $\Theta(P + C \log C)$.

Why can we not simply use the value of C for input size and say that the cost of the algorithm is $\Theta(C \log C)$? Because, C is typically much less than P. For example, a picture could have 1000×1000 pixels, but only have a range of 256 possible colors. So, P is one million, which is much larger than $C \log C$. But, if P is smaller, or C larger (even if it is still less than P), then $C \log C$ can become the larger quantity. Thus, neither variable should be ignored.

3.8   Space Bounds

Besides time, space is the other computing resource that is commonly of concern to programmers. Just as computers have become much faster over the years, they have also received greater allotments of memory. Even so, the amount of available disk space or main memory can be significant constraints for algorithm designers.

The analysis techniques used to measure space requirements are similar to those used to measure time requirements. However, while time requirements are normally measured for an algorithm that manipulates a particular data structure, space requirements are normally determined for the data structure itself. The concepts of asymptotic analysis for growth rates on input size apply completely to measuring space requirements.

Example 3.14 What are the space requirements for an array of n integers? If each integer requires c bytes, then the array requires cn bytes, which is $\Theta(n)$.

Example 3.15 Imagine that we want to keep track of friendships between n people. We can do this with an array of size $n \times n$. Each row of the array represents the friends of an individual, with the columns indicating who is a friend. For example, if person i knows person j, then we place a mark in column j of row i in the array. Likewise, we should also place a mark in column i of row j since we will assume that friendship works both ways. For n people, the total size of the array is $\Theta(n^2)$.

A data structure's primary purpose is to store data in a way that allows efficient access to those data. To provide efficient access, it may be necessary to store additional information about where the data are within the data structure. For example, each node of a linked list must store a pointer to the next value on the list. All such information stored in addition to the actual data values is referred to as **overhead**. Ideally, overhead should be kept to a minimum while allowing maximum access. The need to maintain a balance between these opposing goals in what makes the study of data structures so interesting.

Definition 3.5 One important principle of algorithm design is often referred to as the **space/time tradeoff** principle. The space/time tradeoff principle says that one can often achieve a reduction in time if one is willing to sacrifice space or vice versa.

Many programs can be modified to reduce storage requirements by "packing" or encoding information. "Unpacking" or decoding the information requires additional time. Thus, the resulting program uses less space but runs slower. Conversely, many programs can be modified to pre-store results or reorganize information to allow faster running time at the expense of greater storage requirements. Typically, the changes in time and space are both by a constant factor.

The space/time tradeoff principle is illustrated by storing a set of 32 Boolean flags. You could store the flags in 32 integer values, one for each flag. Java defines an `int` to be 4 bytes in size, so this representation would require a total of 128 bytes. You can also take advantage of Java's ability to do computation on single-byte `byte` variables and store the 32 flags using 32 bytes. Since a Boolean variable can take on only one of two values, it would be most space efficient to store the 32 flags packed into a single 32-bit (4-byte) `int` variable.[3] Unfortunately, on most computers it takes longer to set or extract a bit value from within an `int` than it does to get or set the value of a `byte` or `int` variable. On my computer, the fastest implementation is to store the 32 flags using 32 `byte` variables. It takes roughly the same time to set a value in an `int` or `boolean` variable, but it takes about twice as long to set or extract a bit within a 32-bit `int` variable using bitwise operators. On your computer, the relative times may vary, but it is likely to take longer to set a bit field value than to set the value for one of the basic variable types. Thus, as an implementor you have the choice to optimize either space or time. Note that in each of these implementations, n Boolean flags require $\Theta(n)$ space. The difference is only a matter of a constant factor.

Another example of a space/time tradeoff is the **lookup table**. A lookup table pre-stores the value of a function that would otherwise be computed each time it is needed. For example, 12! is the greatest value for the factorial function that can be stored in a 32-bit `int` value. If you are writing a program that often computes factorials, it is likely to be much more time efficient to simply pre-compute the 12 storable values in a table. Whenever the program needs the value of $n!$ for $n \leq 12$, it can simply check the lookup table. (If $n > 12$, the value is too large to store as a `int` variable anyway.) Compared to the time required to compute factorials, it may be well worth the small amount of additional space needed to store the lookup table.

Lookup tables can also store approximations for an expensive function such as sine or cosine. If you compute this function only for exact degrees or are willing to approximate the answer with the value for the nearest degree, then a lookup table storing the computation for exact degrees can be used instead of repeatedly computing the sine function. Note that initially building the lookup table requires a certain amount of time. Your application must use the lookup table often enough to make this initialization worthwhile.

The next example of space/time tradeoff is typical of what a programmer might encounter when trying to optimize space. Here is a simple code fragment for sorting a set of records, where each record has a key field which is used as the sort key. The function `x.key()` returns the key value for record x. There are n records, and the keys are a permutation of the num-

---

[3]Ideally, the 32 flags could be stored using an array of 32 `boolean` variables. Unfortunately, most Java virtual machines implement the logical 1-bit `boolean` type with a 1-byte physical representation.

bers from 0 to $n-1$ (that is, there are no repeated keys). This is an example of a Binsort, which is discussed in Section 8.7. Binsort assigns each record to an array position corresponding to its key value.

```
for (i=0; i<n; i++)
  B[A[i].key()] = A[i];
```

This is efficient and requires $\Theta(n)$ time. However, it also requires two arrays of size n. Next is a code fragment that places the permutation in order, but does so within the same array (thus it is an example of an "in place" sort):

```
for (i=0; i<n; i++)
  while (A[i].key() != i) // Swap element A[i] with A[A[i].key()]
    DSutil.swap(A, i, A[i].key());
```

Function `swap(A, i, j)` exchanges elements i and j in array A. It may not be obvious that the second code fragment actually sorts the records. To see that this does work, notice that each pass through the for loop will at least move the record with key value i to its correct position in the array, and that `A[i].key()` must be greater than or equal to i. A total of at most n swap operations take place, since a record cannot be moved out of its correct position once it has been placed there, and each swap operation places at least one record in its correct position. Thus, this code fragment has cost $\Theta(n)$. However, it requires more time to run than the first code fragment. On my computer the second version takes between two and three times as long to run as the first, but it only requires half the space.

A second principle for the relationship between a program's space and time requirements applies to programs that process information stored on disk, as discussed in Chapter 9 and thereafter. Strangely enough, the disk-based space/time tradeoff principle is almost the reverse of the space/time tradeoff principle for programs using main memory.

Definition 3.6 The **disk-based space/time tradeoff** principle states that the smaller you can make your disk storage requirements, the faster your program will run. This is because the time to read information from disk is enormous compared to computation time, so almost any amount of additional computation needed to unpack the data is going to be less than the disk-reading time saved by reducing the storage requirements.

Naturally this principle does not hold true in all cases, but it is good to keep in mind when designing programs that process information stored on disk.

A True Story

A few years ago, one of my graduate students had a big problem. His thesis work involved several intricate operations on a large database. He was now working on the final step. "Dr. Shaffer," he said, "I am running this program and it seems to be taking a long time." After examining the algorithm we realized that its running time was $\Theta(n^2)$, and that it would likely take one to two weeks to complete. Even if we could keep the computer running uninterrupted for that long, he was hoping to complete his thesis and graduate before then. Fortunately, we realized that there was a fairly easy way to convert the algorithm so that its running time was $\Theta(n \log n)$. By the next day he had modified the program. It ran in only a few hours, and he finished his thesis on time.

3.9 Some Practical Considerations

In practice, there is not such a big difference in running time between an algorithm whose growth rate is $\Theta(n)$ and another whose growth rate is $\Theta(n \log n)$. There is, however, an enormous difference in running time between algorithms with growth rates of $\Theta(n \log n)$ and $\Theta(n^2)$. As you shall see during the course of your study of common data structures and algorithms, it is not unusual that a problem whose obvious solution requires $\Theta(n^2)$ time also has a solution that requires $\Theta(n \log n)$ time. Examples include sorting and searching, two of the most important computer problems.

While not nearly so important as changing an algorithm to reduce its growth rate, "code tuning" can also lead to dramatic improvements in running time. Code tuning is the art of hand-optimizing a program to run faster or require less storage. For many programs, code tuning can reduce running time by a factor of ten, or cut the storage requirements by a factor of two or more. I once tuned a critical function in a program – without changing its basic algorithm – to achieve a factor of 200 speedup. To get this speedup, however, I did make major changes in the representation of the information, converting from a symbolic coding scheme to a numeric coding scheme on which I was able to do direct computation.

Here are some suggestions for ways to go about speeding up your programs by code tuning.

The most important thing to realize is that most statements in a program do not have much effect on the running time of that program. There are normally just a few key subroutines, possibly even key lines of code within the key subroutines, that account for most of the running time. There is little point to cutting in half the running time of a subroutine that accounts for only 1% of the total. Focus your attention on those parts of the program that have the most impact.

When tuning code, it is important to gather good timing statistics. Many compilers and operating systems include profilers and other special tools to help gather information on both time and space usage. These are invaluable when trying to make a program more efficient.

Be careful not to use tricks that make the program unreadable. Most code tuning is simply cleaning up a carelessly written program, not taking a clear program and adding tricks. In particular, you should develop an appreciation for the capabilities of modern compilers to make extremely good optimizations of expressions. "Optimization of expressions" here means a rearrangement of arithmetic or logical expressions to run more efficiently. Be careful not to damage the compiler's ability to do such optimizations for you in an effort to optimize the expression yourself. Always check that your "optimizations" really do improve the program by running the program before and after the change on a suitable benchmark set of input. Many times I have been wrong about the positive effects of code tuning in my own programs. Most often I am wrong when I try to optimize an expression. It is hard to do better than the compiler.

It could happen that you have the need to compare two different programs to see which is "better" at performing some task. Be warned that comparative timing of programs is a difficult business, often subject to experimental errors arising from uncontrolled factors (system load, the language or compiler used, etc.). The most important point is not to be biased in favor of one of the programs. If you are biased, this is certain to be reflected in the timings. One look at competing software or hardware vendors' advertisements should convince you of this. The most common pitfall when writing two programs to compare their performance is that one receives more code-tuning effort than the other. As mentioned above, code tuning can often reduce running time by a factor of ten. If the running times for two programs differ by a constant factor regardless of input size (i.e., their growth rates are the same), then differences in code tuning can easily account for any difference in running time.

The greatest time and space improvements come from a better data structure or algorithm. The final thought for this chapter is:

First tune the algorithm, then tune the code.

3.10   Further Reading

Pioneering works on algorithm analysis include *The Art of Computer Programming* by Donald E. Knuth [Knu73, Knu81], and *The Design and Analysis of Computer Algorithms* by Aho, Hopcroft, and Ullman [AHU74]. Definition 3.3 for Ω comes from [AHU83]. The use of the notation "$\mathbf{T}(n)$ is in $O(f(n))$" rather than the more commonly used "$\mathbf{T}(n) = O(f(n))$" I derive from Brassard and Bratley [BB88], though certainly this usage predates them. A good book to read for further information on algorithm analysis techniques is *Compared to What?* by Gregory J.E. Rawlins [Raw92].

Bentley [Ben88] describes one problem in Numerical Analysis for which, since 1945, the complexity of the best known algorithm has decreased from $O(n^7)$ to $O(n^3)$. For a problem of size $n = 64$, this is roughly equivalent to the speedup achieved from all advances in computer hardware during the same time period.

While the most important aspect of program efficiency is the algorithm, much improvement can be gained from efficient coding of a program. As cited by Frederick P. Brooks in *The Mythical Man-Month* [Bro75], an efficient programmer can often produce programs that run five times faster than an inefficient programmer, even when neither takes special efforts to speed up their code. For excellent and enjoyable essays on improving your coding efficiency, and ways to speed up your code when it really matters, see the books of Jon Bentley [Ben82, Ben86a, Ben88].

As an interesting aside, writing a correct binary search algorithm is not easy. Knuth [Knu81] notes that while the first binary search was published in 1946, the first bug-free algorithm was not published until 1962! See Section 6.2.1 of [Knu81] for a discussion. Bentley ("Writing Correct Programs" in [Ben86a]) has found that 90% of computer professionals cannot write a bug-free binary search in two hours.

3.11   Exercises

3.1 For the five expressions of Figure 3.1, state for which values of n each expression is most efficient.

3.2 Graph the following expressions. For each expression, state for which values of n that expression is the most efficient.

$$4n^2 \qquad \log_3 n \qquad 3^n \qquad 20n \qquad 2 \qquad \log_2 n \qquad n^{2/3}$$

3.3 Arrange the following expressions by growth rate from slowest to fastest.

$$4n^2 \qquad \log_3 n \qquad 3^n \qquad 20n \qquad 2 \qquad \log_2 n \qquad n^{2/3}$$

Where does $n!$ fit into this ordering?

3.4 **(a)** Suppose that a particular algorithm has time complexity $\mathbf{T}(n) = 3 \times 2^n$, and that executing an implementation of it on a particular machine takes T seconds for n inputs. Now suppose that we are presented with a machine that is 64 times as fast. How many inputs could we process on the new machine in T seconds?

(b) Suppose that another algorithm has time complexity $\mathbf{T}(n) = n^2$, and that executing an implementation of it on a particular machine takes T seconds for n inputs. Now suppose that we are presented with a machine that is 64 times as fast. How many inputs could we process on the new machine in T seconds?

(c) A third algorithm has time complexity $\mathbf{T}(n) = 8n$. Executing an implementation of it on a particular machine takes T seconds for n inputs. Given a new machine that is 64 times as fast, how many inputs could we process in T seconds?

3.5 Hardware vendor XYZ Corp. claims that their latest computer will run 100 times faster than that of their competitor, Prunes, Inc. If the Prunes, Inc. computer can execute a program on input of size n in one hour, what size input can XYZ's computer execute in one hour for each algorithm with the following growth rate equations?

$$n \qquad n^2 \qquad n^3 \qquad 2^n$$

3.6 Using the definitions of big-Oh and Ω, find the upper and lower bounds for the following expressions. Be sure to state appropriate values for c and n_0.

(a) $c_1 n$

(b) $c_2 n^3 + c_3$

(c) $c_4 n \log n + c_5 n$

(d) $c_6 2^n + c_7 n^6$

3.7 Does every algorithm have a Θ running-time equation? In other words, are the upper and lower bounds for the running time (on any specified class of inputs) always the same?

3.8 For each of the following pairs of functions, either $f(n)$ is in $O(g(n))$, $f(n)$ is in $\Omega(g(n))$, or $f(n) = \Theta(g(n))$. For each pair, determine which relationship is correct. Briefly explain your answer.

   (a) $f(n) = \log n^2$; $g(n) = \log n + 5$.
   (b) $f(n) = \sqrt{n}$; $g(n) = \log n^2$.
   (c) $f(n) = \log^2 n$; $g(n) = \log n$.
   (d) $f(n) = n$; $g(n) = log^2 n$.
   (e) $f(n) = n \log n + n$; $g(n) = \log n$.
   (f) $f(n) = 10$; $g(n) = \log 10$.
   (g) $f(n) = 2^n$; $g(n) = 10n^2$.
   (h) $f(n) = 2^n$; $g(n) = 3^n$.

3.9 Determine Θ for the following code fragments in the average case. Assume that all variables are of type `int`.

   (a)
```
a = b + c;
d = a + e;
```

   (b)
```
sum = 0;
for (i=0; i<3; i++)
    for (j=0; j<n; j++)
        sum++;
```

   (c)
```
sum=0;
for (i=0; i<n*n; i++)
    sum++;
```

   (d) Assume array **A** contains n values.

```
for (i=0; i<n; i++) {
  for (j=0; j<n; j++)
    A[i] = DSutil.random(n); // random takes constant time
  sort(A, n);                // sort takes n log n time
}
```

   (e) Assume array **A** contains a random permutation of the values from 0 to $n - 1$.

```
sum3 = 0;
for (i=0; i<n; i++)
  for (j=0; A[j]!=i; j++)
    sum3++;
```

(f)
```
sum = 0;
if (EVEN(n))
  for (i=0; i<n; i++)
    sum++;
else
  sum = sum + n;
```

3.10 **Theorem 3.1** $\log n! = \Theta(n \log n)$.

The easiest way to prove this theorem is to prove the upper and lower bounds separately.

(a) Prove that $\log n!$ is in $\Omega(n \log n)$.

(b) Prove that $\log n!$ is in $O(n \log n)$.

3.11 Give the best *lower* bound that you can for the following code fragment, as a function of the initial value of n.

```
while (n > 1)
  if (ODD(n))
    n = 3 * n + 1;
  else
    n = n / 2;
```

Do you think that the upper bound is likely to be the same as the answer you gave for the lower bound?

3.12 Does every problem for which there exists some algorithm have a Θ running-time equation? In other words, for every problem, and for any specified class of inputs, is there some algorithm whose upper bound is equal to the problem's lower bound?

3.13 Given an array storing numbers ordered by value, modify the binary search routine to return the position of the first number with value K in the situation where K can appear multiple times in the array. Be sure that your algorithm is $\Theta(\log n)$, that is, do *not* resort to sequential search once an occurrence of K is found.

3.14 Given an array storing numbers ordered by value, modify the binary search routine to return the position of the number with the greatest value less than K when K itself does not appear in the array. Return **ERROR** if the least value in the array is greater than K.

3.15 Design an algorithm to assemble a jigsaw puzzle. Assume that each piece has four sides, and that each piece's final orientation is known (top, bottom, etc.). Assume that you have available a function

```
bool compare(Piece a, Piece b, Side ad)
```

that can tell, in constant time, whether piece a connects to piece b on a's side ad and b's opposite side bd. The input to your algorithm should consist of a $n \times m$ array of random pieces, along with dimensions n and m. The algorithm should put the pieces in their correct positions in the array. Your algorithm should be as efficient as possible in the asymptotic sense. Write a summation for the running time of your algorithm on n pieces, and then derive a closed-form solution for the summation.

3.16 Prove that if an algorithm is $\Theta(f(n))$ in the average case then it is $\Omega(f(n))$ in the worst case.

3.12   Projects

3.1 Repeat on your computer the experiment from Section 3.8 regarding the space/time tradeoff for Boolean flags. Compare the time required to access values stored alternatively as a `byte`, a `boolean`, an `int`, or a single bit field within an `int` variable. There are two things to be careful of when writing your program. First, be sure that your program does enough variable accesses to make meaningful measurements – a single access is much smaller than the measurement rate for all four methods. Second, be sure that your program spends as much time as possible doing variable accesses rather than other things such as calling timing functions or incrementing `for` loop counters.

3.2 Implement sequential search and binary search algorithms on your computer. Run timings for each algorithm on arrays of size $n = 10^i$ for i ranging from 1 to as large a value as your computer's memory and compiler will allow. For both algorithms, store the values 0 through $n - 1$ in order in the array, and use a variety of random search values in the range 0 to $n - 1$ on each size n. Graph the resulting times.

Part II

Fundamental Data Structures

4

Lists, Stacks, and Queues

This chapter describes representations for lists and two important restricted forms of list, the stack and the queue. We begin in Section 4.1 by defining an ADT for lists. Then two implementations for the list ADT – the static array-based list and the dynamic linked list using pointers – are covered in detail and their relative merits discussed. Sections 4.2 and 4.3 cover stacks and queues, respectively. Java implementations for each of these data structures are presented.

4.1 Lists

A **list** is a finite, ordered sequence of data items known as **elements**. "Ordered" in this definition means that each element has a **position** in the list. In other words, there is a first element in the list, a second element, and so on. Each list element also has a data type. In the simple list implementations discussed in this chapter, all elements of the list have the same data type, although there is no conceptual objection to lists whose elements have differing data types if the application requires it (see Section 12.2). The operations defined as part of the list ADT do not depend on the elemental data type. For example, the list ADT can be used for lists of integers, lists of characters, etc.

A list is said to be **empty** when it contains no elements. The number of elements currently stored is called the **length** of the list. The beginning of the list is called the **head**, the end of the list is called the **tail**. There may or may not be some relationship between the value of an element and its position in the list. For example, **sorted lists** have their elements positioned in ascending order of value, while **unsorted lists** have no particular relationship between element values and positions. This chapter will consider only unsorted lists. Chapters 8 and 10 will treat the problems of how to create and search sorted lists efficiently.

When presenting the contents of a list, our notation will be to enclose the list elements in parentheses and separate them by commas. For example, the list

$$(a_0, a_1, ..., a_{n-1})$$

contains n elements. The subscript indicates an element's position within the list.[1] For all $i > 0$, the element with subscript i immediately follows the element with subscript $i - 1$. Using this notation, the empty list would appear as ( ).

Before selecting a list implementation, a program designer should first consider what basic operations the implementation must support. Our common intuition about lists tells us that a list should be able to grow and shrink in size. We should be able to insert and remove elements from anywhere in the list. We should be able to gain access to any element's value, either to read it or to change it. We must be able to create and clear (or reinitialize) lists. It is also convenient to access the next or previous element from the "current" one.

The next step is to define the ADT for a list object in terms of a set of operations on that object. In Java, an object is implemented as a class. This section describes the intent of each list operation, but not how operations are implemented. Two complete implementations are presented later, both of which use the same list ADT to define their operations, but which are considerably different in approach. Figure 4.1 shows the public face of the list ADT in the form of a Java interface. This is all the knowledge that a Java programmer needs to use a particular list implementation. Figure 4.1 assumes that the list elements are references to type **Object**. When a list is created, the actual data type of the elements may be whatever is convenient for the application, such as a simple **Integer**, or a more complicated structure defined by the user.

The descriptions for several member functions in Figure 4.1 mention a "current" position. For example, member **setFirst** sets the current position to be the first element on the list, while members **next** and **prev** move the

---

[1]To be consistent with Java array usage, the first position on the list is denoted as 0, not 1. Thus, if there are n elements in the list, they are given positions 0 through $n - 1$. This may seem unusual to readers familiar with a language such as Pascal, but it is much less confusing to adopt this notation consistently, rather than to change numbering schemes within certain program examples.

```
interface List {              // List ADT
public void clear();          // Remove all Objects from list
public void insert(Object item);  // Insert Object at curr position
public void append(Object item);  // Insert Object at tail of list
public Object remove();       // Remove/return current Object
public void setFirst();       // Set current to first position
public void next();           // Move current to next position
public void prev();           // Move current to prev position
public int length();          // Return current length of list
public void setPos(int pos);  // Set current to specified pos
public void setValue(Object val); // Set current Object's value
public Object currValue();    // Return value of current Object
public boolean isEmpty();     // Return true if list is empty
public boolean isInList();    // True if current is within list
public void print();          // Print all of list's elements
} // interface List
```

Figure 4.1 The interface for the list class, showing the member functions.

current position to the next and previous elements, respectively. The intention is that any implementation for this ADT support the concept of a current position.

The first member function of the `List` interface is the `clear` function. This function clears all elements from an existing list, returning the list to its initial (empty) state. Member `insert` inserts a value at the current position. This function allows new elements to be inserted at any position within the list. For example, if the list contains (12, 32, 15) and the current position is set to indicate element 32, then calling `insert` with value 99 will change the list to be (12, 99, 32, 15).

Member `append` places an element at the end of the list. Member `remove` removes the current element from the list. Member `setFirst` sets the current position indicator to be the first element on the list. Members `next` and `prev` set the current position indicator to the next element and the previous element, respectively. Member `length` returns the current number of elements in the list. Member `setPos(i)` sets the current position to be the ith element on the list (with 0 being the position of the beginning element of the list). Member `setValue` replaces the value of the current element. Member `currValue` returns the value of the current element. Note that initialized lists and cleared lists have no elements, thus they can have no current element. It is not permitted to call `currValue` or `setValue` on an empty list. Any list implementation should detect such misuses of a list object.

Member `isEmpty` returns `true` if the list is empty, and `false` otherwise. Member `isInList` returns `true` if the current position actually indicates a position within the list (rather than being off the end of the list, or being associated with an empty list). This is useful when processing every element on the list by order of position, as shown in the following code fragment.

```
for (MyList.setFirst(); MyList.isInList(); MyList.next())
  DoSomething(MyList.currValue());
```

Finally, member **print** prints out the contents of the list.

The list class declaration presented here is just one of many possible interpretations for lists. Figure 4.1 provides most of the operations that one naturally expects to perform on lists, and serves to illustrate the issues relevant to implementing the list data structure. As an example of using the list ADT, we can create a function to find the next occurrence (starting from the current position) of an element with a particular key value. The **find** function needs no knowledge about the list implementation. However, the **find** function must know something about the type of an element stored on the list. As with many of the data structures presented in this book, we will assume that the data objects stored on the list support interface **Elem**, defined as follows.

```
interface Elem {                    // Interface for generic element type
  public abstract int key();  // Key used for search and ordering
} // interface Elem
```

Interface **Elem** simply ensures that the element type support member function **key**, which returns an integer value to be used as a search key. Within the bounds of this restriction, the list elements can be of any type.

Here is the **find** function, which finds the first occurrence of an element with key value K within the list, and sets the list's current position to that element. Member **find** returns **true** if a record with key value K is found, and **false** otherwise. If K does not appear in the list, the list position is set so that **isInList** will return **false**. Note that the list is searched beginning with the current position.

```
// Starting at current position,
// find Elem with the next occurrence of key value K in List L
public static Elem find(List L, int K) {
  while (L.isInList())
    if (((Elem)L.currValue()).key() == K)
      return (Elem)L.currValue();
    else L.next();
  return null;
}
```

4.1.1 Array-Based List Implementation

There are two standard approaches to implementing lists, the **array-based** or **sequential** list, and the **linked** list. This section discusses the array-based approach. The linked list is presented in Section 4.1.2. Time and space efficiency comparisons for the two are discussed in Section 4.1.3.

The array-based list implementation uses an array to store the elements of the list. This implies that an array of some fixed size will be allocated, so the size of the array must be known when the list object is created. Since each list object may have a differently sized array, this size must be remembered by each list object. At any given time the list actually holds some number of elements that may be less than the maximum allowed by the array. This actual number of elements currently in the list must also be remembered by the list object.

The array-based list implementation stores the elements of the list in contiguous array positions. Array positions correspond to list positions. In other words, element i of the list is stored in array cell i. The head of the list is always at position 0. This makes random access to any element in the list quite easy. Given some position in the list, the value of the element in that position can be accessed directly. Thus, access to any element using the setPos function followed by the currValue function takes $\Theta(1)$ time.

Since the array-based list implementation is defined to store list elements in contiguous cells of the array, the insert, append, and remove functions must maintain this property. Inserting or removing elements at the tail of the list is easy, and the append operation takes $\Theta(1)$ time. However, if we wish to insert an element at the head of the list, all elements currently in the list must shift one position toward the tail to make room, as illustrated by Figure 4.2. This process takes $\Theta(n)$ time if there are n elements already in the list. If we wish to insert at position i within a list of n elements, then $n - i$ elements must shift toward the tail. Removing an element from the head of the list is similar in that all elements in the array must shift toward the head by one position to fill in the gap. To remove the element at position i, $n - i - 1$ elements must shift toward the head. In the average case, insertion or removal requires moving half of the elements, which is $\Theta(n)$.

Figure 4.3 shows the class declaration for the array-based list implementation, called AList. Note that this class implements the List interface, which means that it implements each of the members defined by List. Class AList has four data members. These are the array that holds the list elements (listArray), the maximum size for the list (msize), the actual

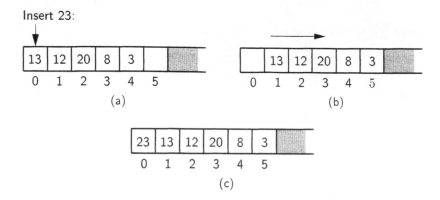

Figure 4.2 Inserting an element at the head of an array-based list requires shifting all existing elements in the array by one position toward the tail. (a) A list containing five elements before inserting an element with value 23. (b) The list after shifting all existing elements one position to the right. (c) The list after 23 has been inserted in array position 0. Shading indicates the unused part of the array.

current size (`numInList`), and the position of the current element in the array (`curr`). Since these variables are declared to be `private`, they may only be accessed by functions that are members of the class.

The first two member functions of the `AList` class implementation are its constructors. Constructors control initialization when the list is created. The first constructor takes no parameter, while the second takes an integer parameter indicating the maximum size of the list. This will be the size of `listArray`. In the case where a list is created without a maximum size being specified, the value `defaultSize` is used to fix the size of `listArray`. Both constructors call a private member function named `setup` to do the actual initialization, including allocating space for `listArray` and initializing the other data members.

The remaining member functions implement the other functions specified by the `List` interface.

4.1.2 Linked Lists

The second traditional approach to implementing lists makes use of pointers and is usually called a **linked list**. The linked list is **dynamic**, that is, it allocates memory for new list elements as needed.

A linked list is made up of a series of objects, called the **nodes** of the list. Since a list node is a distinct object (as opposed to simply a cell in an

```
class AList implements List {    // Array-based list implementation

private static final int defaultSize = 10; // Default array size

private int msize;              // Maximum size of list
private int numInList;          // Actual number of Objects in list
private int curr;               // Position of current Object
private Object[] listArray;     // Array holding list Objects

AList() { setup(defaultSize); } // Constructor: use default size

AList(int sz) { setup(sz); }    // Constructor: user-specified size

private void setup(int sz) {    // Do actual initialization work
  msize = sz;
  numInList = curr = 0;
  listArray = new Object[sz];    // Create listArray
}

public void clear()             // Remove all Objects from list
{ numInList = curr = 0; }       // Simply reinitialize values

public void insert(Object it) { // Insert Object at current position
  Assert.notFalse(numInList < msize, "List is full");
  Assert.notFalse((curr >= 0) && (curr <= numInList),
                  "Bad value for curr");
  for (int i=numInList; i>curr; i--) // Shift Objects to make room
    listArray[i] = listArray[i-1];
  listArray[curr] = it;
  numInList++;                  // Increment list size
}

public void append(Object it) { // Insert Object at tail of list
  Assert.notFalse(numInList < msize, "List is full");
  listArray[numInList++] = it;  // Increment list size
}

public Object remove() {        // Remove and return current Object
  Assert.notFalse(!isEmpty(), "Can't delete from empty list");
  Assert.notFalse(isInList(), "No current element");
  Object it = listArray[curr];  // Hold removed Object
  for(int i=curr; i<numInList-1; i++) // Shift elements down
    listArray[i] = listArray[i+1];
  numInList--;                  // Decrement list size
  return it;
}

public void setFirst() { curr = 0; } // Set curr to first position
```

Figure 4.3 Implementation for the array-based list class.

```java
public void prev() { curr--; }  // Move curr to previous position

public void next() { curr++; }  // Move curr to next position

public int length()             // Return length of list
{ return numInList; }

public void setPos(int pos)     // Set curr to specified position
{ curr = pos; }

public void setValue(Object it) { // Set current Object's value
  Assert.notFalse(isInList(), "No current element");
  listArray[curr] = it;
}

public Object currValue() {     // Return current Object's value
  Assert.notFalse(isInList(), "No current element");
  return listArray[curr];
}

public boolean isEmpty()        // Return true if list is empty
{ return numInList == 0; }

public boolean isInList()       // True if curr is within list
{ return (curr >= 0) && (curr < numInList); }

public void print() {           // Print all list's Objects
  if (isEmpty()) System.out.println("()");
  else {
    System.out.print("( ");
    for (setFirst(); isInList(); next())
      System.out.print(currValue() + " ");
    System.out.println(")");
  }
}
} // class Alist
```

Figure 4.3 (continued)

```
class Link {                    // A singly linked list node
  private Object element;    // Object for this node
  private Link next;          // Pointer to next node in list
  Link(Object it, Link nextval)          // Constructor 1
    { element = it;  next = nextval; }    //  Given Object
  Link(Link nextval) { next = nextval; } // Constructor 2
  Link next() { return next; }
  Link setNext(Link nextval) { return next = nextval; }
  Object element() { return element; }
  Object setElement(Object it) { return element = it; }
} // class Link
```

Figure 4.4 A simple linked list node class definition.

array), it is good practice to make a separate list node class. An additional benefit to creating a list node class is that it can be reused by the linked implementations for the stack and queue data structures presented later in this chapter. Figure 4.4 shows the complete definition for list nodes, called the Link class. Objects in the Link class contain an element field to store the element value, and a next field to store a pointer to the next node on the list. The list built from such nodes is called a **singly linked list**, since each list node has a single pointer to the next node on the list.

The Link class is quite simple. There are two forms for its constructor, one for which an initial element value is supplied and one for which no element value is given. The remaining functions allow users of the class to get access to the two (private) data members. Users of the class are allowed to get the value and set the value of the next and element fields. While this allows users of the Link class to set these values in any way, in principle this is a better approach than making the data members public. The reason is that the "set" access functions can be written to control what changes will be permitted. Note that the Link class need not be visible to users of the list implementation. The Link class really belongs to the linked list implementation and is not part of the List class public interface. If desired, Java's **package** capability can be used to restrict users of the linked list from access to the Link objects.

Figure 4.5 shows the implementation for the linked list class, named LList. Again, it implements the List interface.

A list object stores a pointer to the first (head) node and a pointer to the last (tail) node. The current position is represented by a pointer to a list node, rather than with an index into the list array.

Figure 4.6(a) shows a graphical depiction for a linked list storing four integers. The value stored in a pointer variable is indicated by an arrow

```
class LList implements List {  // Linked list class
private Link head;             // Pointer to list header
private Link tail;             // Pointer to last Object in list
protected Link curr;           // Pointer to current Object

LList(int sz) { setup(); }     // Constructor -- Ignore sz
LList() { setup(); }           // Constructor

private void setup()           // Do initialization
{ tail = head = curr = new Link(null); } // Create header node

public void clear() {          // Remove all Objects from list
  head.setNext(null);          // Drop access to rest of links
  curr = tail = head;          // Reinitialize
}

// Insert Object at current position
public void insert(Object it) {
  Assert.notNull(curr, "No current element");
  curr.setNext(new Link(it, curr.next()));
  if (tail == curr)            // Appended new Object
    tail = curr.next();
}

// Insert Object at end of list
public void append(Object it) {
  tail.setNext(new Link(it, null));
  tail = tail.next();
}

public Object remove() {       // Remove and return current Object
  if (!isInList()) return null;
  Object it = curr.next().element();   // Remember value
  if (tail == curr.next()) tail = curr; // Removed last: set tail
  curr.setNext(curr.next().next());    // Remove from list
  return it;                   // Return value removed
}

public void setFirst()         // Set curr to first position
{ curr = head; }

public void next()             // Move curr to next position
{ if (curr != null) curr = curr.next(); }
```

Figure 4.5 Implementation for the linked list version of the List class.

```
public void prev() {             // Move curr to previous position
  if ((curr == null) || (curr == head)) // No previous Object
    { curr = null;  return; }            //   so just return
  Link temp = head;              // Start at front of list
  while ((temp != null) && (temp.next() != curr))
        temp = temp.next();
  curr = temp;                   // Found previous link
}

public int length() {            // Return current length of list
  int cnt = 0;
  for (Link temp = head.next(); temp != null; temp = temp.next())
     cnt++;                      // Count the number of Objects
  return cnt;
}

public void setPos(int pos) { // Set curr to specified position
  curr = head;
  for(int i=0; (curr!=null) && (i<pos); i++)
    curr = curr.next();
}

public void setValue(Object it) // Set current Object's value
{ Assert.notFalse(isInList());  curr.next().setElement(it); }

public Object currValue() {    // Return value of current Object
  if (!isInList()) return null;
  return curr.next().element();
}

public boolean isEmpty()       // Return true if list is empty
{ return head.next() == null; }

public boolean isInList()      // True if curr is within list
  { return (curr != null) && (curr.next() != null); }

public void print() {          // Print out the list's elements
  if (isEmpty()) System.out.println("()");
  else {
    System.out.print("( ");
        for (setFirst(); isInList(); next())
          System.out.print(currValue() + " ");
    System.out.println(")");
  }
}
} // class LList
```

Figure 4.5 (continued)

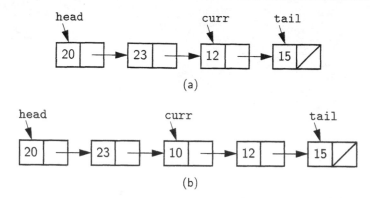

Figure 4.6 Illustration of a linked list implementation with `curr` pointing directly to the current list node. (a) Linked list prior to inserting element with value 10. (b) Desired effect of inserting element with value 10.

"pointing" to something. Java uses the special symbol `null` for a pointer value that points nowhere, such as for the last element's `next` field. `null` pointers are indicated graphically by a diagonal slash through a pointer variable's box.

Figure 4.6(a) shows the list's `curr` pointer pointing directly to the current list node. At first this seems to be the obvious implementation. However, consider what happens if we wish to insert a new node into the list at this position. The value 10 is to be inserted at the current position of the linked list in Figure 4.6(a), with the goal being the linked list shown in Figure 4.6(b). Recall that by our definition for `insert`, the new element is inserted at the current position on the list. This definition seems reasonable and presents no problem for the array-based implementation. However, there is a problem with the linked list implementation as shown in Figure 4.6(a). To "splice" the list node containing the new element into the list, the list node storing 23 must have its `next` pointer changed to point to the new node. Unfortunately, there is no convenient access to the node preceding the one pointed to by `curr`.

One (expensive) solution would be to work from the head of the list until the list node preceding the current node is found. A more reasonable solution would be to copy the value of the new element into the current node, and then place the old current element value into a new list node that follows the current node. This will get everything in the right place at the cost of an unnecessary copy. Unfortunately, this solution fails due to a similar problem that arises when trying to remove the last node in the list. For example, if `curr` pointed to the node with value 15 in Figure 4.6(a), and we wished to

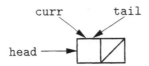

Figure 4.7 Initial state of a linked list when using a header node.

delete it, there is no way to avoid making a change to the node containing value 12.

Another alternative is to have **curr** point to the node *preceding* the one containing the current element. In other words, if the node labeled 12 in Figure 4.6(a) is the current one, then **curr** should actually point to the node labeled 23. This makes insertion fairly easy.

This new definition for current position leads to a new problem. If there is only one element in the list, then there is no preceding element for **curr** to point at. Thus, lists with no elements or one element present special cases. Another special case arises any time we wish the current position to be at the first element. All such special cases require additional code in the list implementation, increasing both code complexity and the chance of introducing a programming bug. Note that equivalent special cases would arise if **curr** was defined to point directly to the current node.

These special cases can be eliminated by implementing linked lists with a special **header node** as the first node of the list. This header node is a list node like any other, but its value is ignored and it is not considered to be an actual element of the list. The header node saves coding effort since we no longer need to consider special cases for empty lists, lists of one node, or the current element being at the head of the list. The cost of this simplification is the space for the header node. The savings come in reduced code complexity. Additional savings come in smaller code size since statements to handle the special cases are omitted. In practice, this typically saves more space than that required for the header node, depending on the number of lists created. Figure 4.7 shows the state of an initialized or empty list when using a header node. Figure 4.8 shows the insertion example of Figure 4.6 using a header node and the convention that **curr** points to the node preceding the actual current node.

An additional benefit comes from defining the current element to be in the node following the node pointed to by **curr**. Now, we can insert a new element at any position in the list. Consider again the naive implementation in which **curr** points directly to the current element. Since we define **insert** as inserting a new element at the current position, under this definition there

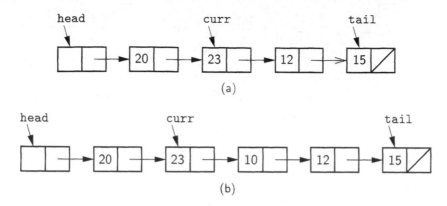

Figure 4.8 Insertion using a header node and revised definition for `curr`.
(a) Linked list before insertion. The current node is the one containing 12.
(b) Linked list after inserting the node containing 10.

is no way to add an element at the end of the list with `insert`. If `curr` points
to the last element, then an insert will place the new element in the next-
to-last position. However, our revised definition for `curr` allows `insert` to
place a new node at the end of the list whenever `curr` points to the last
existing node. If `curr` points to the header node, then an insert will place
the new element at the beginning of the list.

Implementation for most member functions of the `list` class is straightforward. However, `insert` and `remove` should be studied carefully.

Inserting a new element at the current position within the list is a three-
step process. First, the new list node is created and the value being inserted
is stored into it. Second, the `next` field of the new list node is assigned to
point to the current list node. Third, the `next` field of the node *preceding*
the current node is assigned to point to the newly inserted node. Since
`curr` already points to the node preceding the node storing the current list
element, this is easily done. The following line in the `insert` function of
Figure 4.5 actually does all three of these steps.

```
curr.setNext(new Link(it, curr.next()));
```

Operator **new** creates the new link node, and function "`curr.setNext()`"
sets the current node's **next** field to point at it. Operator **new** calls the
constructor for the **Link** class, which takes two parameters. The first is the
value for the element, called `it`. The second is the value to be placed in
the list node's **next** field, in this case the value returned by the function

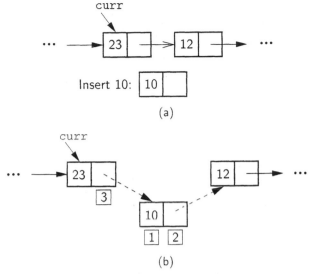

Figure 4.9 The linked list insertion process. (a) The linked list before insertion. (b) The linked list after insertion. $\boxed{1}$ marks the **element** field of the new link node. $\boxed{2}$ marks the **next** field of the new link node, which is set to point to what used to be the current node in the list (the node with value 12). $\boxed{3}$ marks the **next** field of the node that precedes the current node in the list. It used to point to the node containing 12, now it points to the new node containing 10.

call "**curr.next()**." Figure 4.9 illustrates this three-step process. Insertion requires $\Theta(1)$ time.

Removing a node from the linked list requires only that the appropriate pointer be redirected around the node to be deleted. The following line from the **remove** function of Figure 4.5 does precisely this.

```
curr.setNext(curr.next().next());    // Remove from list
```

However, we must be careful not to "lose" the element being removed, since we wish to return it. Thus, temporary pointer **it** is first assigned to point to the element being removed. Figure 4.10 illustrates the **remove** function. Removing the current element requires $\Theta(1)$ time.

Member **next** simply moves **curr** one position toward the tail of the list, which takes $\Theta(1)$ time. Member **prev** moves **curr** one position toward the head of the list, but its implementation is more difficult. In a singly linked list, there is no pointer to the previous node. Thus, the only alternative is to march down the list from the beginning until we reach the current node

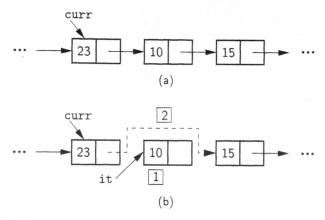

Figure 4.10 The linked list removal process. (a) The linked list before removing the node with value 10. (b) The linked list after removal. $\boxed{1}$ marks the list node being removed – it is set to point to the element. $\boxed{2}$ marks the **next** field of the preceding list node, which is set to point to the node following the one being deleted.

(being sure always to remember the node before it, since that is what we really want). This takes $\Theta(n)$ time in the average case. Implementation of member **setPos** is similar in that finding the ith position requires marching down i positions from the head of the list, taking $\Theta(i)$ time. Implementations for the remaining operations are straightforward.

Freelists

The Java free-store management operator **new** is relatively expensive to use. This is also true for the equivalent functions in **C**, **C++**, Pascal, and many other programming languages. The problem is that free-store routines must handle requests to and from free store with no particular pattern, as well as requests of vastly different sizes. In Java, there is the additional expense involved with running the "garbage collector," which is responsible for finding and returning to free store any space that is no longer used by the program. Until a few years ago, many **C** and Pascal compilers did not properly implement their free-store functions. Some would fail under certain patterns of usage, others would become unreasonably slow. In some extreme cases, the function meant to return memory to free storage was not implemented at all! Instead the compiler would simply discard any returned storage.

Most compilers today provide reasonable implementations for their free-store functions. However, the general nature of free-store managers makes them inefficient. The conditions under which list nodes are created and deleted in a linked-list implementation allow the Link class programmer to provide simple but efficient memory management routines in place of the system-level free-store operators. Instead of making repeated calls to **new** or relying on the garbage collector to gather space from nodes that have been removed, the Link class can handle its own **freelist**. A freelist holds those list nodes that are not currently being used. When a node is deleted from a linked list, it is placed at the head of the freelist. When a new element is to be added to a linked list, the freelist is checked to see if a list node is available. If so, the node is taken from the freelist. If the freelist is empty, the standard **new** operator can still be called.

Freelists are particularly useful for linked lists that periodically grow and then shrink. The freelist will never grow larger than the largest size so far of the linked list. Requests for new nodes (after the list has shrunk) can be handled by the freelist.

The freelist itself is accessed by a static data member called **freelist**. When a data member is declared "static," a single copy of that data member is shared by all objects of the class. In this case, all Link objects will reference the same copy of the freelist variable.

Our approach to implementing freelists is to add two new functions to the Link class implementation, called **get** and **release**. The freelist version of the Link class is shown in Figure 4.11. To use the new functions, the LList implementation of Figure 4.5 must be modified to call them. The modified **insert**, **append**, and **remove** functions are shown in Figure 4.12. Note that function **get** is declared **static**. This is because it is not meant to be called on a particular Link object. Instead, the modified **insert** function references get as "Link.get()."

The freelist functions **get** and **release** both run in $\Theta(1)$ time, except in the case where the freelist is exhausted and the **new** operator must be called.

4.1.3 Comparison of List Implementations

Now that you have seen two substantially different implementations for lists, it is natural to ask which is better. If you must implement a list for some particular task, which implementation should you choose?

Array-based lists have the disadvantage that their size must be predetermined so that the array can be allocated. Array-based lists cannot grow beyond their predetermined size. Also, whenever the list contains only a few elements, a substantial amount of space may be tied up in a largely empty array. Linked lists have the advantage that they only need space for the

```
class Link {  // Singly linked list node with freelist
  private Object element; // Object for this Link
  private Link next;       // Pointer to next Link in list
  Link(Object it, Link nextval)        // Constructor 1
  { element = it;  next = nextval; }    //  Given Object
  Link(Link nextval) { next = nextval; } // Constructor 2
  Link next() { return next; }
  Link setNext(Link nextval) { return next = nextval; }
  Object element() { return element; }
  Object setElement(Object it) { return element = it; }

  // Extensions to support freelists
  static Link freelist = null;     // Freelist for the class

  static Link get(Object it, Link nextval) { // Get new link
    if (freelist == null)
      return new Link(it, nextval); // Get from free store
    Link temp = freelist;          // Get from freelist
    freelist = freelist.next();
    temp.setElement(it);
    temp.setNext(nextval);
    return temp;
  }

  void release() {    // Return Link to freelist
    element = null;   // Drop reference to the element
    next = freelist;
    freelist = this;
  }
} // class Link
```

Figure 4.11 Implementation for the Link class with a freelist. Methods get and release have been added, along with a static freelist variable.

objects actually on the list. There is no limit to the number of elements on a linked list, so long as there is free-store memory available. The amount of space required by a linked list is $\Theta(n)$, while the space required by the array-based list implementation is $\Omega(n)$, but can be greater.

Array-based lists have the advantage that there is no wasted space for an individual element. Linked lists require that a pointer be added to every list node. If the element size is small, then the overhead for links can be a significant fraction of the total storage. When the array for the array-based list is completely filled, there is no storage overhead. In this situation, the array-based list is more space efficient by a constant factor.

A simple formula can be used to determine whether the array-based list or linked list implementation will be more space efficient in a particular situation. Call n the number of elements currently in the list, P the size of a

```
// Insert Object at current position
public void insert(Object it) {
  Assert.notNull(curr, "No current element");
  curr.setNext(Link.get(it, curr.next())); // Get Link
  if (tail == curr)                // Appended new Object
    tail = curr.next();
}

public void append(Object it) { // Insert Object at tail of list
  tail.setNext(Link.get(it, null));        // Get Link
  tail = tail.next();
}

public Object remove() {              // Remove and return current Elem
  Assert.notFalse(isInList(), "No current element");
  Object it = curr.next().element();    // Remember value
  if (tail == curr.next()) tail = curr; // Removed last: set tail
  Link tempptr = curr.next();
  curr.setNext(curr.next().next());      // Remove from list
  tempptr.release();                     // Release Link
  return it;                             // Return value removed
}
```

Figure 4.12 Implementation for the insert, append, and remove members of the LList class with a freelist. Note calls to Link.get() and Link.release().

pointer in storage units (typically four bytes), E the size of a data element in storage units (this could be anything, from one bit for a Boolean variable on up), and D the maximum number of list elements that can be stored in the array. The amount of space required for the array-based list is DE, regardless of the number of elements actually stored in the list at any given time. The amount of space required for the linked list is $n(P + E)$. The smaller of these expressions for a given value n determines the more space efficient implementation for n elements. In general, the linked implementation requires less space than the array-based implementation when relatively few elements are in the list. Conversely, the array-based implementation becomes more space efficient when the array is close to full. Using these equations, we can solve for n to determine the break-even point beyond which the array-based implementation is more space efficient. This occurs when $n > DE/(P + E)$. If $P = E$ (e.g., a four-byte **long** element and a four-byte pointer), then the break-even point is at $D/2$.

As a rule of thumb, linked lists are better when implementing lists whose number of elements varies widely or is unknown. Array-based lists are generally more space efficient when the user knows in advance approximately how large the list will become.

Array-based lists are faster for random access by position. Positions can easily be adjusted forwards or backwards by **next** and **prev**. These operations always take $\Theta(1)$ time. In contrast, singly linked lists have no explicit access to the previous element, and access by position requires that we march down the list from the front to the specified position. Both of these operations require $\Theta(n)$ time in the average and worst cases.

Given a pointer to a suitable location in the list, the **insert** and **remove** functions for linked lists require only $\Theta(1)$ time. Array-based lists must shift the remainder of the list up or down within the array. This requires $\Theta(n)$ time in the average and worst cases. For many applications, the time to insert and delete elements dominates all other operations. For this reason alone, linked lists are often preferred to array-based lists.

When implementing the array-based list, an implementor could use a Java **Vector** object instead of a simple array. The difference is that a Java **Vector** implements a data structure known as a **dynamic array**. A dynamic array grows and shrinks depending on the number of elements that are actually stored. In this way, the programmer can get around the limitation on the standard array that its size cannot be changed once the list has been created. This also means that space need not be allocated to the **Vector** until it is used. The disadvantage of this approach is that it takes time to deal with space adjustments on the **Vector**. Each time the **Vector** grows in size, its contents must be copied. A good implementation of the **Vector** class will grow and shrink the array in such a way as to keep the overall cost for a series of insert/delete operations relatively inexpensive. To analyze the cost of using a **Vector** we need to use a technique known as **amortized analysis**, which is covered in Section 14.3.

4.1.4 Element Implementations

Both the array-based and linked list implementations as presented store a reference to an **Object**. For larger elements, this is desirable, since it minimizes the cost of making a copy of the element to store on the list, and also allows multiple list elements to refer to the same object if desired. Not only might this save space, but it also means that a modification to an element's value is automatically reflected at all locations where it is referenced.

By having each list element be a reference to an **Object**, we are storing a pointer with each list element. Of course, each of these pointers requires space of its own. If elements are never duplicated, then this additional space

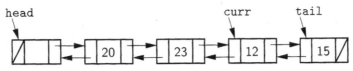

Figure 4.13 A doubly linked list.

is certain to add unnecessary overhead. For small objects such as an `int` variable, the amount of overhead involved is significant.

Whether it is more advantageous to use pointers to elements or not depends on the intended application. In general, the larger the elements and the more they are duplicated, the more likely that pointers to elements is the better approach.

A second issue faced by implementors of a list class (or any other data structure that stores a collection of user-defined data elements) is whether the elements stored are all required to be of the same type. This is known as **homogeneity** in a data structure. In some applications, the user would like to define the class of the data element that is stored on a given list, but then never permit objects of a different class to be stored on that same list. There are a number of techniques that implementors of a list class can use to ensure that the element type for a given list remains fixed, while still permitting different lists to store different element types. One approach is to store an object of the appropriate type in the header node of the list (perhaps an object of the appropriate type is supplied as a parameter to the list constructor), and then check that all insert operations on the list use the proper element type. Another approach is to check at each `insert` operation that the element being inserted is of the same type as that of the first list element.

4.1.5 Doubly Linked Lists

The singly linked list presented in Section 4.1.2 allows for direct access from a list node only to the next node in the list. A **doubly linked list** is designed to allow convenient access from a list node to the next node and also to the preceding node on the list. The doubly linked list node accomplishes this in the obvious way by storing two pointers: one to the node following it (as in the singly linked list), and a second pointer to the node preceding it. Figure 4.13 illustrates the doubly linked list concept.

The doubly linked list is useful primarily because it is easier to implement than a singly linked list. We could allow `curr` to point directly to the current node in the doubly linked list since the `prev` pointer allows access

```
class DLink {                  // A doubly-linked list node
  private Object element;      // Object for this node
  private DLink next;          // Pointer to next node in list
  private DLink prev;          // Pointer to previous node in list
  DLink(Object it, DLink n, DLink p)              // Constructor 1
  { element = it;  next = n; prev = p; }          //  Given Object
  DLink(DLink n, DLink p) { next = n;  prev = p; } // Constructor 2
  DLink next() { return next; }
  DLink setNext(DLink nextval) { return next = nextval; }
  DLink prev() { return prev; }
  DLink setPrev(DLink prevval) { return prev = prevval; }
  Object element() { return element; }
  Object setElement(Object it) { return element = it; }
} // class Dlink
```

Figure 4.14 Doubly linked list node implementation.

to the previous node in the list. However, we will maintain the convention of having **curr** point to the node preceding the node containing the current element for two reasons: (1) to avoid a special case when inserting into an empty list, and (2) to allow nodes to be inserted at any position in the list. If **curr** pointed directly to the current node, **insert** could not be used to insert a node at the end of the list.

Whether a list implementation is doubly or singly linked should be hidden from the **List** class user. Figure 4.14 shows the complete implementation for a **Link** class to be used with doubly linked lists. Figure 4.16 shows the implementation for the **insert**, **append**, **remove**, and **prev** doubly linked list member functions. The remaining member functions for the doubly linked list class are unmodified from Figure 4.5. Again, the doubly-linked list implementation implements the **List** interface.

The **insert** function is conceptually simple for doubly linked lists. Figure 4.15 shows the list before and after insertion of a node with value 10. The following three lines of code from Figure 4.16 do the actual work.

```
curr.setNext(new Link(it, curr.next(), curr));
if (curr.next().next() != null)
  curr.next().next().setPrev(curr.next());
```

The three parameters to the **new** operator allow the list node class constructor to set the **element**, **next**, and **prev** fields, respectively, for the new link node. The **new** operator returns a pointer to the newly created node. Variable **curr**'s **next** field is then set to point to the new node. The final step is to change the **prev** field of the node following the newly inserted node. The **if** statement is included to ensure that such a node really exists (i.e., that we are not inserting at the end of the list).

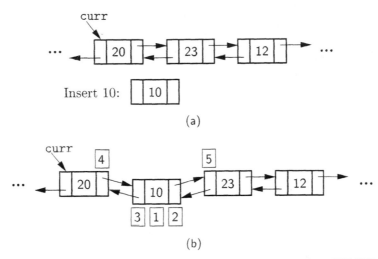

(a)

(b)

Figure 4.15 Insertion for doubly-linked lists. The boxes labeled 1, 2, and 3 correspond to assignments done by the linked-list node constructor. Box 4 marks the assignment to curr->next. Box 5 marks the assignment to the **prev** pointer of the node following the newly inserted node.

The **List** class append function from Figure 4.16 is even simpler because there is no following node to be concerned with. Here is the crucial code.

```
tail.setNext(new Link(it, null, tail));
tail = tail.next();
```

Again, the **Link** class constructor sets the **element**, **next**, and **prev** fields of the node when the **new** operator is executed. Since the new node will be placed at the end of the list, its **next** field is initialized to **null**. The **next** field of the last node already on the list (pointed to by **tail**) is set to point to the new node. Finally, **tail** is set to point to the appended node.

Function **remove** (illustrated by Figure 4.17) is also straightforward. First, variable **it** is set to point to the element being removed. The following four lines then adjust the pointers.

```
if (curr.next().next() != null)
  curr.next().next().setPrev(curr);
else tail = curr;  // Removed last Object: set tail
curr.setNext(curr.next().next());  // Remove from list
```

The first two lines set the **prev** field of the node following the one being deleted. But this can only happen if there *is* a following node. If not, then **tail** must point to the node being deleted, and so is adjusted on the third

```
// Insert Object at current position
public void insert(Object it) {
  Assert.notNull(curr, "No current element");
  curr.setNext(new DLink(it, curr.next(), curr));
  if (curr.next().next() != null)
    curr.next().next().setPrev(curr.next());
  if (tail == curr)              // Appended new Object
    tail = tail.next();
}

public void append(Object it) { // Insert Object at tail of list
  tail.setNext(new DLink(it, null, tail));
  tail = tail.next();
}

public Object remove() {         // Remove and return current Object
  Assert.notFalse(isInList(), "No current element");
  Object it = curr.next().element(); // Remember Object
  if (curr.next().next() != null)
    curr.next().next().setPrev(curr);
  else tail = curr;  // Removed last Object: set tail
  curr.setNext(curr.next().next()); // Remove from list
  return it;                     // Return value removed
}

public void prev()               // Move curr to previous position
{ if (curr != null) curr = curr.prev(); }
```

Figure 4.16 Implementations for doubly linked list class `insert`, `append`, `remove`, and `prev` member functions.

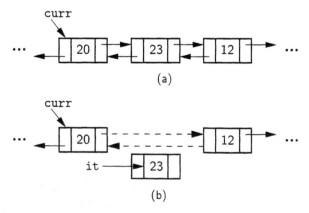

(a)

(b)

Figure 4.17 Doubly linked list removal. Pointer `it` is set to point to the current element. Then the nodes to either side of the node being removed have their pointers adjusted.

line. Finally, the **next** field of the node preceding the one being deleted is adjusted. The final step of function **remove** is to return the value of the deleted element.

The only disadvantage of the doubly linked list as compared to the singly linked list is the additional space used. The doubly linked list requires two pointers per node, and in the implementation presented it requires twice as much overhead as the singly linked list. There is a space-saving technique that can be employed in some programming languages[2] to eliminate the additional space requirement, though it will complicate the implementation and be somewhat slower. Thus, the technique is an example of a space/time tradeoff. It is based on the following properties of the exclusive-or (XOR) function (where ˆ represents the exclusive-or operator).

$$(L\,\hat{}\,R)\,\hat{}\,R \;=\; L$$
$$(L\,\hat{}\,R)\,\hat{}\,L \;=\; R$$

In other words, given two values XORed together, either can be recovered by XORing the other to the combination. Thus, the doubly linked list can be implemented by storing the XOR of the two pointer values in the space required by a single pointer field. Of course, to recover one of the values requires that the other be supplied. A pointer to the first node in the list, along with the value of one of its two link fields, will allow access to all of the remaining nodes of the list in order. This is because the pointer to the node must be the same as the value of the following node's **prev** pointer. It is possible to move down the list breaking apart the XORed link fields as though you were opening a zipper.

The principle behind this technique is worth remembering, since it has many applications. For example, it is widely used in computer graphics. A region of the computer screen can be highlighted by XORing the outline of a box around it. XORing the box outline a second time restores the original contents of the screen. A second example is illustrated by the following code fragment to swap the contents of two variables without using a temporary variable (at the cost of three XOR operations).

```
a = a ^ b;
b = a ^ b;  // Now b contains the original value of a
a = a ^ b;  // Now a contains the original value of b
```

---

[2]Java does not support this technique, since it does not allow arithmetic operations on pointers.

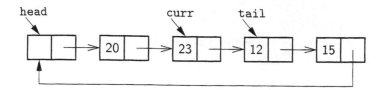

Figure 4.18 A circular singly linked list.

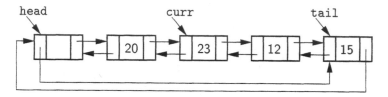

Figure 4.19 A circular doubly linked list.

4.1.6   Circular Linked Lists

Some applications do not require that there be a particular first or last list element. In such cases, it may be convenient to allow access from the last element to the first. In the normal linked list, the **next** field of the last element stores the value **null**. By instead storing a pointer to the first element in the list, a **circular list** is created. With this implementation, a **tail** pointer is no longer needed. Figure 4.18 illustrates a circular singly linked list. Figure 4.19 illustrates a circular doubly linked list. The primary danger with such implementations is that list processing operations may go into an infinite loop since there is no obvious end to the list. However, the **head** pointer can be used as a marker to determine when list processing has worked full circle through the list.

4.2   Stacks

The **stack** is a restricted variant of the list in which elements may be inserted or removed from only one end. While this restriction makes stacks less flexible, it also makes stacks both efficient and easy to implement. Many applications require only the limited form of insert and remove operations that stacks provide. In such cases, it is more efficient to use the simpler stack data structure rather than the more general list. For example, the freelist of Section 4.1.2 is really a stack.

Despite their restrictions, stacks have many uses. Thus, a special vocabulary for stacks has developed. Accountants used the notion of a stack long before the invention of the computer. They called the stack a "LIFO" list, which stands for "Last-In, First-Out." Note that one implication of the LIFO policy is that stacks store and remove elements in reverse order of their arrival.

It is traditional to call the accessible element of the stack the **top** element. Elements are not said to be inserted; instead they are **pushed** onto the stack. When removed, an element is said to be **popped** from the stack.

As with lists, there are many variations on stack implementation. The two approaches presented here are **array-based** and **linked stacks**, which are analogous to array-based and linked lists, respectively.

4.2.1 Array-Based Stacks

Figure 4.20 shows a complete implementation for the array-based stack class. As with the array-based list implementation, `listArray` must be declared of fixed size when the stack is created. In the stack constructor, `sz` serves to indicate this size. Member `top` acts somewhat like a current position value while indicating the number of elements currently in the stack. However, the "current" position is always at the top of the stack, so a separate member to keep track of the current position is not useful for stacks.

The array based stack implementation is essentially a simplified version of the array-based list. The only important decision to be made is which end of the array should represent the top of the stack. One choice is to make the top be at position 0 in the array. In terms of list functions, all `insert` and `remove` operations would then be on the element in position 0. This implementation is inefficient, since now every `push` (`insert`) or `pop` (`remove`) operation will require that all elements currently in the stack be shifted one position in the array, for a cost of $\Theta(n)$ if there are n elements. The other choice is have the top element be at position $n-1$ when there are n elements in the stack. In other words, as elements are pushed onto the stack, they are appended to the tail of the list. Member `pop` removes the tail element. In this case, the cost for each `push` or `pop` operation is only $\Theta(1)$.

For the implementation of Figure 4.20, `top` is defined to be the array index for the first free position in the stack. Thus, an empty stack has `top` set to 0, the first available free position in the array.[3] Members `push` and `pop` simply place an element into or remove an element from the array position

---

[3] Alternatively, `top` could have been defined to be the index for the top element in the stack, rather than the first free position. If this had been done, the empty list would initialize `top` as -1.

```
class AStack implements Stack {      // Array based stack class

  private static final int defaultSize = 10;

  private int size;                  // Maximum size of stack
  private int top;                   // Index for top Object
  private Object [] listarray;       // Array holding stack Objects

  AStack() { setup(defaultSize); }
  AStack(int sz) { setup(sz); }

  public void setup(int sz)
  { size = sz;  top = 0; listarray = new Object[sz]; }

  public void clear()                // Remove all Objects from stack
    { top = 0; }

  public void push(Object it) {      // Push Object onto stack
    Assert.notFalse(top < size, "Stack overflow");
       listarray[top++] = it;
  }

  public Object pop() {              // Pop Object from top of stack
    Assert.notFalse(!isEmpty(), "Empty stack");
       return listarray[--top];
  }

  public Object topValue() {         // Return value of top Object
    Assert.notFalse(!isEmpty(), "Empty stack");
       return listarray[top-1];
  }

  public boolean isEmpty()           // Return true if stack is empty
    { return top == 0; }
} // class AStack
```

Figure 4.20 Array-based stack class implementation.

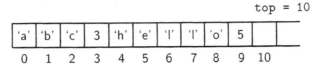

Figure 4.21 An array-based stack storing variable-length strings. Each position stores either one character or the length of the string immediately to the left of it in the stack.

indicated by **top**. Since **top** is assumed to be at the first free position, **push** first inserts its value into the top position and then increments **top**. Likewise, **pop** first decrements **top** and then removes the top element.

The array-based implementation can easily be modified to support elements of varying size, such as character strings. Assume in this case that the stack array is broken into equal-sized storage units such as **byte** or **int**, and that each element fits into a certain number of these storage units. If the value for the size of the largest possible element can be stored in a single storage unit, then the size of each element can be stored in the topmost storage unit for that element. The **push** operation would store an element requiring i storage units in the i positions beginning with the current value of **top**, and store the size in the position i storage units above **top**. The value of **top** would then be reset above the newly inserted element. The **pop** operation need only look at the size value stored in position **top** − 1, and then pop off the appropriate number of units. Figure 4.21 illustrates an array-based stack storing variable-length strings.

4.2.2 Linked Stacks

The linked stack implementation is a simplified version of the linked list implementation. The freelist of Section 4.1.2 is an example of a linked stack. Elements are inserted and removed only from the head of the list. The header node is not used because no special case code is required for lists of zero or one elements. Figure 4.22 shows the complete class implementation for the linked stack. The only data member is **top**, a pointer to the first (top) link node of the stack.

Member **push** first modifies the **next** field of the newly created link node to point to the top of the stack and then sets **top** to point to the new link node. Member **pop** is also quite simple. The variable **it** is set to point to the top element. The stack is updated by setting **top** to point to the next element in the stack. The original top element value is then returned as the value of the **pop** function.

```
class LStack implements Stack {          // Linked stack class
  private Link top;                      // Pointer to list header

  public LStack() { setup(); }           // Constructor
  public LStack(int sz) { setup(); }     // Constructor: ignore sz

  private void setup() { top = null; }   // Initialize stack

  public void clear() { top = null; }    // Remove Objects from stack

  public void push(Object it)            // Push Object onto stack
  { top = new Link(it, top); }

  public Object pop() {                  // Pop Object at top of stack
    Assert.notFalse(!isEmpty(), "Empty stack");
    Object it = top.element();
    top = top.next();
    return it;
  }

  public Object topValue()               // Get value of top Object
  { Assert.notFalse(!isEmpty(), "No top value");
    return top.element(); }

  public boolean isEmpty()               // Return true if empty stack
  { return top == null; }
} // class LStack
```

Figure 4.22 Linked stack class implementation.

4.2.3 Comparison of Array-Based and Linked Stacks

All operations for the array-based and linked stack implementations take constant time. The only basis for comparison is the total space required. The analysis is similar to that done for list implementations. The array-based stack must declare a fixed-size array initially, and some of that space is wasted whenever the stack is not full. The linked stack can shrink and grow, but requires the overhead of a link field for every element.

When multiple stacks are to be implemented, it is possible to take advantage of the one-way growth of the array-based stack. This can be done by using a single array to store two stacks. One stack grows inward from each end as illustrated by Figure 4.23, hopefully leading to less wasted space. However, this only works well when the space requirements of the two stacks are inversely correlated. In other words, ideally when one stack grows, the other will shrink. This is particularly effective when elements are taken from one stack and given to the other. If instead both stacks grow at the same time, then the free space in the middle of the array will be exhausted quickly.

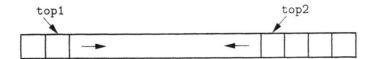

top1   top2

Figure 4.23 Two stacks housed in a single array, both growing toward the middle.

4.2.4 Implementing Recursion

Perhaps the most common application for stacks is not even visible to its users. This is the implementation of subroutine calls in most programming languages. A subroutine call is normally implemented by placing necessary information about the subroutine (including the return address, parameters, and local variables) onto a stack. This information is called an **activation record**. Further subroutine calls add to the stack. Each return from a subroutine pops one activation record off the stack. Figure 4.24 illustrates the implementation of the recursive factorial function of Section 2.4 from the runtime environment's point of view.

Since an activation record must be created and placed onto the stack, each subroutine call is a relatively expensive operation. While recursion is often used to make implementation easy and clear, sometimes you may want to eliminate the overhead imposed by the recursive function calls. Where possible, the most efficient way to do this is to replace the recursive function with an iterative version, as can easily be done for the factorial function.

Unfortunately, it is not always possible to replace recursion with iteration. Sometimes recursion, or some imitation of it, is necessary when implementing algorithms that require multiple branching, such as in the Towers of Hanoi algorithm or when traversing a binary tree. The Mergesort and Quicksort algorithms of Chapter 8 are also examples in which recursion is required. Fortunately, it is always possible to imitate recursion with a stack.

As a simple example of replacing recursion with a stack, consider the following non-recursive version of the factorial function.

```
static long fact(int n) { // Must have n < 21 to fit in long
  Assert.notFalse((n >= 0) && (n < 21), "Input out of range");
  Stack S = new AStack(n-1); // Make stack just big enough
  while (n > 1) S.push(new Integer(n--));
  long result = 1;
  while (!S.isEmpty())
    result = result * ((Integer)S.pop()).longValue();
  return result;
}
```

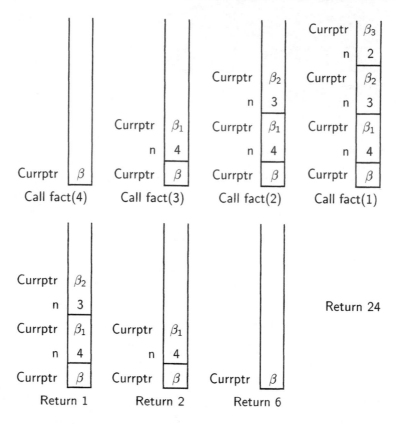

Figure 4.24 Implementing recursion with a stack. β values indicate the address of the program instruction to return to after completing the current function call. On each recursive function call to `rfact` (from Section 2.4), both the return address and the current value of n must be saved. Each return from `rfact` pops the top activation record off the stack.

Here, we simply push successively smaller values of n onto the stack until the base case is reached, then repeatedly pop off the stored values and multiply them into the result.[4]

In practice, an iterative form of the factorial function would be both simpler and faster than this version. However, let us now turn to a non-recursive version of the Towers of Hanoi function, which cannot be done iteratively. The problem is that the TOH function shown in Figure 2.2 makes

---

[4]Note that the `Stack` class stores an element of type `Object`. Thus, a simple (base type) `int` variable cannot be used here, since the element must be of a true class type. Instead, the elements stored are of type `Integer`, with the necessary explicit conversion from type `int` and to type `long` being used.

two recursive calls, one to move $n-1$ rings off the bottom ring, and another to move these $n-1$ rings back to the goal pole. We can eliminate the recursion by using a stack to store a representation of the three operations that TOH must perform: two recursive calls and a move operation. To do so, we must first come up with a representation of the various operations, implemented as a class whose objects will be stored on the stack. Here is such a class.

```
class TOHobj {
  public int op;
  public int num;
  public Pole start, goal, temp;

  TOHobj(int o, int n, Pole s, Pole g, Pole t) // TOH
  { op = o; num = n; start = s; goal = g; temp = t; }

  TOHobj(int o, Pole s, Pole g)                // MOVE
  { op = o; start = s; goal = g; }
}
```

Class TOHobj stores five fields: an operation field (indicating either a move or a new TOH operation), the number of rings, and the three poles. Note that the move operation actually only needs to store information about two poles. Thus, there are two constructors: one to store the state when imitating a recursive call, and one to store the state for a move operation. The non-recursive version of TOH can now be presented.

```
static final int MOVE = 1;       // Move operation indicator
static final int TOH = 2;        // TOH operation indicator

static void TOH(int n, Pole start, Pole goal, Pole temp) {
  Stack S = new AStack(2*n+1);   // Make stack just big enough
  S.push(new TOHobj(TOH, n, start, goal, temp)); // Initial form
  while (!S.isEmpty()) {
    TOHobj it = (TOHobj)S.pop(); // Grab next task
    if (it.op == MOVE)           // Do a move
      move(it.start, it.goal);
    else if (it.num > 0) {       // Imitate three statements in TOH
                                 // recursive solution (in reverse)
      S.push(new TOHobj(TOH, it.num-1, it.temp, it.goal, it.start));
      S.push(new TOHobj(MOVE, it.start, it.goal));  // A move to do
      S.push(new TOHobj(TOH, it.num-1, it.start, it.temp, it.goal));
    }
  }
}
```

We first define two constant values, TOH and MOVE, to indicate the operations to be performed. Note that an array-based stack is used, since we know that the stack will need to store exactly $2n + 1$ elements. The new version of TOH begins by placing on the stack a description of the initial problem of n rings. The rest of the function is simply a while loop that pops the stack, and executes the appropriate operation. In the case of a TOH operation (for $n > 0$), we store on the stack representations for the three operations executed by the recursive version. However, these operations must be place on the stack in reverse order, so that they will be popped off in the correct order.

Some "naturally recursive" applications lend themselves to efficient implementation with a stack, since the amount of information needed to describe a subproblem is small. For example, Figure 8.9 in Section 8.4 shows a stack-based implementation for Quicksort.

4.3 Queues

Like the stack, the **queue** is a form of restricted list. Queue elements may only be inserted at the back (called an **enqueue** operation) and removed from the front (called a **dequeue** operation). Queues operate like standing in line at a movie theater.[5] If nobody cheats, then newcomers go to the back of the line. The person at the front of the line is the next to be served. Note that queues store their contents in order of arrival. Accountants have used queues since long before the existence of computers. They call a queue a "FIFO" list, which stands for "First-In, First-Out." This section presents two implementations: the array-based queue and the linked queue.

4.3.1 Array-Based Queues

The array-based queue is somewhat tricky to implement effectively: A simple conversion of the array-based list implementation is not efficient.

Assume that there are n elements in the queue. The array-based list implementation requires that all elements of the list be stored in the first n positions of the array. If we choose the rear element of the queue to be in position 0, then **dequeue** operations require only $\Theta(1)$ time since the front element of the queue (the one being removed) is the last element of the list. However, **enqueue** operations will require $\Theta(n)$ time, since the

---

[5]In Great Britain, a line of people is called a "queue," and getting into line to wait for service is called "queuing up."

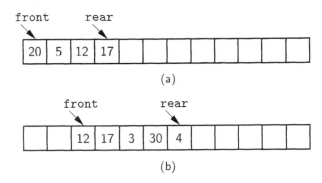

Figure 4.25 After repeated use, elements in the array-based queue will drift to the back of the array. (a) The queue after the initial four numbers 20, 5, 12, and 17 have been inserted. (b) The queue after elements 20 and 5 are deleted, following which 3, 30, and 4 are inserted.

n elements currently in the queue must each be shifted one position in the array. If instead we chose the rear element of the queue to be in position $n-1$, then an **enqueue** operation is equivalent to an append operation on a list. This requires only $\Theta(1)$ time. But now, a **dequeue** operation requires $\Theta(n)$ time, since all of the elements must be shifted down by one position to retain the property that the remaining $n-1$ queue elements reside in the first $n-1$ positions of the array.

A far more efficient implementation can be obtained by relaxing the requirement that all elements of the queue must be in the first n positions of the array. We will still require the elements to be in contiguous array positions, but the contents of the queue will be permitted to drift within the array, as illustrated by Figure 4.25. Now, both the **enqueue** and the **dequeue** operations can be performed in $\Theta(1)$ time since no other elements in the queue need be moved.

This implementation raises a new problem, as illustrated by the following example. Assume that the front element of the queue is initially at position 0, and that elements are added to successively higher numbered positions in the array. When elements are removed from the queue, the front index increases. Over time, the entire queue will drift toward the higher numbered positions in the array. Once an element is inserted into the highest numbered position in the array, the queue has run out of space. This happens despite the fact that there may be free positions at the low end of the array where elements have previously been removed from the queue.

The "drifting queue" problem can be solved by pretending that the array is circular, and so allow the queue to continue directly from the highest num-

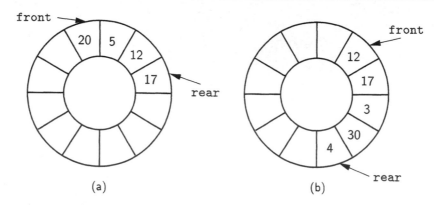

Figure 4.26 The circular queue with array positions increasing in the clockwise direction. (a) The queue after the initial four numbers 20, 5, 12, and 17 have been inserted. (b) The queue after elements 20 and 5 are deleted, following which 3, 30, and 4 are inserted.

bered position in the array to the lowest numbered position. This is easily implemented through use of the modulus operator. In this way, positions in the array are numbered from 0 through `size` − 1, and position `size` − 1 is defined to immediately precede position 0 (which is equivalent to position `size % size`). Figure 4.26 illustrates this solution.

There remains one more serious, though subtle, problem to the array-based queue implementation. How can we recognize when the queue is empty or full? Assume that `front` stores the array index for the front element in the queue, and `rear` stores the array index for the rear element. If both `front` and `rear` have the same position, then under this scheme there must be one element in the queue. Thus, an empty queue would be recognized by having `rear` be *one less* than `front` (taking into account the fact the queue is circular, so position `size` − 1 is actually considered to be one less than position 0). But what if the queue is completely full? In other words, what is the situation when a queue with n array positions available contains n elements? In this case, if the front element is in position 0, then the rear element is in position `size` − 1. But this means that the value for `rear` is one less than the value for `front` when the circular nature of the queue is taken into account. In other words, the full queue is indistinguishable from the empty queue!

You might think that the problem is in the assumption about `front` and `rear` being defined to store the array indices of the front and rear elements, respectively, and that some modification in this definition will allow a solution. Unfortunately, the problem cannot be remedied by a simple change to the definition for **front** and **rear**, because of the number of conditions or **states** that the queue can be in. Ignoring the actual position of the first element, and ignoring the actual values of the elements stored in the queue, how many different states are there? There can be no elements in the queue, one element, two, and so on. At most there can be n elements in the queue if there are n array positions. This means that there are $n + 1$ different states for the queue (0 through n elements are possible).

If the value of **front** is fixed, then $n + 1$ different values for **rear** are needed to distinguish among the $n+1$ states. However, there are only n possible values for **rear** unless we invent a special case for, say, empty queues. This is an example of the Pigeonhole Principle defined in Exercise 2.14. The pigeonhole principle states that, given n pigeonholes and $n+1$ pigeons, when all of the pigeons go into the holes we can be sure that at least one hole contains more than one pigeon. In similar manner, we can be sure that two of the $n + 1$ states are indistinguishable by their relative values of **front** and **rear**. We must seek some other way to distinguish full from empty queues.

One obvious solution is to track whether the queue is empty or not by keeping a count of the number of elements currently in the queue. This leaves n positions and n states. Another solution is to make the array of size $n + 1$ and only allow n elements to be stored. Which of these solutions to adopt is purely a matter of the implementor's taste in such affairs. My choice is to use an array of size $n + 1$.

Figure 4.27 presents an array-based queue class implementation. As usual, **listArray** is a pointer to the array that holds the queue elements, and as usual, the queue constructor allows an optional parameter to set the maximum size of the queue. The array as created is actually large enough to hold one element more than the queue will allow, so that empty and full queues can be distinguished. Member **size** is used to control the circular motion of the queue (it is the base for the modulus operator). Member **rear** is set to the position of the rear element. To slightly simplify the implementation, member **front** is set to the position *preceding* the front element. Thus, an empty queue will have **front** and **rear** equal. The advantage of this definition for **front** is that the dequeue operation will increment **front** before returning the element value.

In this implementation, the front of the queue is defined to be toward the lower numbered positions in the array (in the counter-clockwise direction in Figure 4.26), and the rear of the queue is defined to be toward the higher numbered positions. Thus, **enqueue** increments the rear pointer (modulus

```
class AQueue implements Queue {    // Array-based queue class
  private static final int defaultSize = 10;
  private int size;                 // Maximum size of queue
  private int front;                // Index prior to front item
  private int rear;                 // Index of rear item
  private Object [] listArray;      // Array holding Objects

  AQueue() { setup(defaultSize); } // Constructor: default size
  AQueue(int sz) { setup(sz); }    // Constructor: set size

  void setup(int sz)                // Initialize queue
  { size = sz+1;  front = rear = 0;  listArray = new Object[sz+1]; }

  public void clear()               // Remove all Objects from queue
  { front = rear = 0; }

  public void enqueue(Object it) { // Enqueue Object at rear
    Assert.notFalse(((rear+1) % size) != front, "Queue is full");
    rear = (rear+1) % size;         // Increment rear (in circle)
    listArray[rear] = it;
  }

  public Object dequeue() {         // Dequeue Object from front
    Assert.notFalse(!isEmpty(), "Queue is empty");
    front = (front+1) % size;       // Increment front
    return listArray[front];        // Return value
  }

  public Object firstValue() {      // Return value of front Object
    Assert.notFalse(!isEmpty(), "Queue is empty");
    return listArray[(front+1) % size];
  }

  public boolean isEmpty()          // Return true if queue is empty
  { return front == rear; }
} // class AQueue
```

Figure 4.27 Array-based queue class implementation.

size), and dequeue increments the front pointer. Implementation of all member functions is straightforward.

4.3.2   Linked Queues

The linked queue implementation is a straightforward adaptation of the linked list. Figure 4.28 shows the linked queue class declaration. Members front and rear are pointers to the front and rear queue elements, respectively. As with the linked stack implementation, no header link node is used.

The linked queue member functions are only slightly changed from their linked list counterparts. Since this implementation stores no header node, it must check for the special case of an empty queue resulting from the enqueue function. Essentially, enqueue simply places the new element in a link node at the end of the linked list (i.e., the node that rear points to), and then advances rear to point to the new link node. Member dequeue simply grabs the front element of the list and advances the front pointer.

4.3.3   Comparison of Array-Based and Linked Queues

All member functions for both the array-based and linked queue implementations require constant time. The space comparison issues are the same as for the equivalent stack implementations. Unlike the array-based stack implementation, there is no convenient way to store two queues in the same array, unless items are always transferred directly from one queue to the other. Variable-length records can be stored in the array-based queue in a manner similar to that described for array-based stacks.

4.4   Exercises

4.1 Assume a list contains the following elements:

$$(2, 23, 15, 5, 9).$$

Write a series of Java statements using the List interface to delete the element with value 15.

4.2 Section 4.1.3 states "the space required by the array-based list implementation is $\Omega(n)$, but can be greater." Explain why this is so.

4.3 Show the list resulting from each series of list operations using the ADT of Figure 4.1. Assume that lists L1 and L2 are empty at the beginning of each series. Show where the current element is in the list.

```
class LQueue implements Queue {        // Linked queue class
  private Link front;                  // Pointer to front node
  private Link rear;                   // Pointer to rear node

  public LQueue() { setup(); }         // Constructor
  public LQueue(int sz) { setup(); }   // Constuctor: Ignore sz

  private void setup()                 // Initialize queue
  { front = rear = null; }

  // Remove all Objects from queue
  public void clear() { front = rear = null; }

  // Enqueue Object at rear of queue
  public void enqueue(Object it) {
    if (rear != null) {                // Queue not empty: add to end
      rear.setNext(new Link(it, null));
      rear = rear.next();
    }
    else front = rear = new Link(it, null); // Empty queue
  }

  public Object dequeue() {            // Dequeue Object from front
    Assert.notFalse(!isEmpty());       // Must be something to dequeue
    Object it = front.element();       // Store dequeued Object
    front = front.next();              // Advance front
    if (front == null) rear = null;    // Dequeued last Object
    return it;                         // Return Object
  }

  public Object firstValue()           // Return value of top Object
  { Assert.notFalse(!isEmpty());  return front.element(); }

  public boolean isEmpty()             // Return true if queue is empty
  { return front == null; }
} // clases LQueue
```

Figure 4.28 Linked queue class implementation.

   (a)   `L1.append(10);`
            `L1.append(20);`
            `L1.append(15);`

   (b)   `L2.append(10);`
            `L2.append(20);`
            `L2.append(15);`
            `L2.setFirst();`
            `L2.insert(39);`
            `L2.next();`
            `L2.insert(12);`

4.4 Write a series of Java statements that use the list ADT to create a list capable of holding twenty elements and which actually stores the following list:

$$(2, 23, 15, 5, 9).$$

4.5 Section 4.1.3 presents an equation for determining the break-even point for the space requirements of two implementations of lists. The variables are D, E, P, and n. What are the dimensional units for each variable, and do both sides of the equation balance in terms of their dimensional units?

4.0 Use the space equation of Section 4.1.3 to determine the break-even point for an array-based list and linked list implementation when the size of a list element is eight bytes, the size of a pointer is four bytes and the size of the array is twenty elements.

4.7 Modify the code of Figure 4.5 to implement circular singly linked lists.

4.8 Modify the code of Figure 4.16 to implement circular doubly linked lists.

4.9 Using the list ADT of Figure 4.1, write a function to interchange the current element and the one immediately following it on a list.

4.10 Add to the code of Figure 4.5 a member function to reverse the order of the elements on the list. Your algorithm should run in $\Theta(n)$ time for a list of n elements.

4.11 Modify the code of Figure 4.20 to implement two stacks sharing the same array.

4.12 Section 4.3.1 defines **front** as the position preceding the front element. The reason for doing so is to allow the dequeue operation to increment **front** before returning the element value. Explain why this is an advantage over defining **front** to be the position of the front element.

4.13 Determine the size of a Java `long` variable and a pointer on your computer. Then calculate the break-even point beyond which the array-based list is more space efficient than the linked list for lists whose elements are of type `long`.

4.14 Modify the array-based queue definition of Figure 4.27 to use a separate Boolean member to keep track of whether the queue is empty, rather than require that one array position remain empty.

4.15 A **palindrome** is a string that reads the same forwards as backwards. Using only a fixed number of stacks and queues, the stack and queue ADT functions, and a fixed number of `int` and `char` variables, write an algorithm to determine if a string is a palindrome. Assume that the string is read from standard input one character at a time. The algorithm should output `true` or `false` as appropriate.

4.16 Let Q be a non-empty queue, and let S be an empty stack. Using only the stack and queue ADT functions and a single element variable X, write an algorithm to reverse the order of the elements in Q.

4.17 An unsorted array-based list of integers allows for constant time insert simply by adding a new integer at the end of the list. Unfortunately, searching for the integer with key value X requires time $\Theta(n)$ in the average case for a list of n integers. On the other hand, a sorted array-based list of n integers can be searched in $\Theta(\log n)$ time by using a binary search. However, inserting a new integer requires $\Theta(n)$ time since many integers may be shifted in the array. How might data be organized to support both insertion and search in $\Theta(\log n)$ time?

4.18 A common problem for compilers and text editors is to determine if the parentheses (or other brackets) in a string are balanced and properly nested. For example, the string "((())())()" contains properly nested pairs of parentheses, but the string ")()(" does not, and the string "())" does not contain properly matching parentheses.

(a) Give an algorithm that returns `true` if a string contains properly nested and balanced parentheses, and `false` otherwise. Use a stack to keep track of the number of left parentheses seen so far. *Hint*: At no time while scanning a legal string from left to right will you have encountered more right parentheses than left parentheses.

(b) Give an algorithm that returns the position in the string of the first offending parenthesis if the string is not properly nested and balanced. That is, if an excess right parenthesis is found, return its position; if there are too many left parentheses, return the position of the first excess left parenthesis. Return −1 if the string is properly balanced and nested. Use a stack to keep track of the number and positions of left parentheses seen so far.

4.5 Projects

4.1 Revise and implement the linked list implementation to support sorted lists, that is, lists whose element values are stored in order from lowest to highest. The first step is to modify the `List` interface, since certain member functions are no longer permitted. For example, it is not acceptable to insert an element at an arbitrary position in a sorted list.

4.2 The Java list implementations presented in Section 4.1 do not support homogeneity of list elements. Revise the `List` class ADT, and the array and linked list implementations, to allow the user of a list to indicate when a `List` object is created what class the elements must be. The `List` class member functions should then ensure that only elements of this class are inserted onto the list.

4.3 Use singly linked lists to implement integers of unlimited size. You should implement addition, subtraction, multiplication, and exponentiation operations. Limit exponents to be positive integers. What is the asymptotic running time of each of your operations, expressed in terms of the number of digits for the two operands of each function?

4.4 Implement a city database using unsorted lists. Each database record contains the name of the city (a string of arbitrary length) and the coordinates of the city expressed as integer x and y coordinates. Your database should allow records to be inserted, deleted by name or coordinate, and searched by name or coordinate. Another operation that should be supported is to print all records within a given distance of a specified point. Implement the database using an array-based list implementation, and then a linked list implementation. Collect running time statistics for each operation in both implementations. What are your conclusions about the relative advantages and disadvantages of the two implementations? Would storing records on the list in alphabetical order by city name speed any of the operations? Would keeping the list in alphabetical order slow any of the operations?

5

Binary Trees

The list representations of Chapter 4 have a fundamental limitation: Either search or insert can be made efficient, but not both at the same time. Tree structures provide both efficient access and update to collections of data. Binary trees in particular are widely used and relatively easy to implement. This chapter begins by presenting definitions and key properties of binary trees. Section 5.2 discusses how to access all nodes of the tree in an organized manner. Section 5.3 presents various methods for implementing binary trees. Sections 5.4 to 5.6 present binary trees for use in specific applications: Huffman coding trees for text compression, Binary Search Trees for searching, and heaps for implementing priority queues.

5.1 Definitions and Properties

Definition 5.1 A **binary tree** is made up of a finite set of elements called **nodes**. This set either is **empty**, or consists of a node called the **root** together with two binary trees, called the left and right **subtrees**, which are disjoint from each other and from the root. The roots of these subtrees are **children** of the root. There is an **edge** from a node to each of its children, and a node is said to be the **parent** of its children.

If n_1, n_2, ..., n_k is a sequence of nodes in the tree such that n_i is the parent of n_{i+1} for $1 \leq i < k$, then this sequence is called a **path** from n_1 to n_k. The **length** of the path is $k - 1$. If there is a path from node R to node M, then R is an **ancestor** of M, and M is a **descendant** of R. Thus, all nodes in the tree are descendants of the root of the tree, while the root is the ancestor of all nodes.

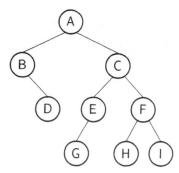

Figure 5.1 An example binary tree. Node A is the root. Nodes B and C are A's children. Nodes B and D together form a subtree. Node B has two children: Its left child is the empty tree and its right child is D. Nodes A, C, and E are ancestors of G. Nodes D, E, and F make up level 2 of the tree; node A is at level 0. The edges from A to C to E to G form a path of length 3. Nodes D, G, H, and I are leaves. Nodes A, B, C, E, and F are internal nodes. The depth of I is 3. The height of this tree is 4.

Definition 5.2 The **depth** of a node M in the tree is the length of the path from the root of the tree to M. The **height** of a tree is one more than the depth of the deepest node in the tree. All nodes of depth d are at **level** d in the tree. The root is at level 0, and its depth is 0.

A **leaf** node is any node that has two empty children. An **internal** node is any node that has at least one non-empty child.

Figure 5.1 illustrates Definitions 5.1 and 5.2. Figure 5.2 illustrates an important point regarding the structure of binary trees. Since *all* binary tree nodes have two children, the binary trees shown in Figures 5.2(a) and 5.2(b) are *not* the same.

Two restricted forms of binary tree are sufficiently important to warrant special names.

Definition 5.3 Each node in a **full** binary tree is either (1) an internal node with exactly two non-empty children or (2) a leaf. A **complete** binary tree has a restricted shape obtained by starting at the root and filling the tree by levels from left to right. In the complete binary tree of height d, all levels except possibly level $d - 1$ are completely full. The bottom level has all of its nodes filled in from the left side.

Figure 5.3 illustrates the differences between full and complete binary trees. There is no particular relationship between these two tree shapes; that

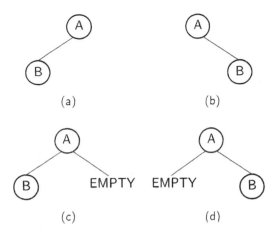

Figure 5.2 Two different binary trees. (a) A binary tree whose root has a non-empty left child. (b) A binary tree whose root has a non-empty right child. (c) The binary tree of (a) with the missing right child made explicit. (d) The binary tree of (b) with the missing left child made explicit.

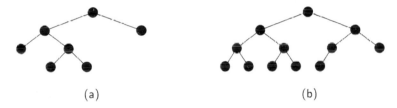

Figure 5.3 Examples of full and complete binary trees. (a) This tree is full (but not complete). (b) This tree is complete (but not full).

is, the tree of Figure 5.3(a) is full but not complete while the tree of Figure 5.3(b) is complete but not full.[1] The Huffman coding tree (Section 5.4) is an example of a full binary tree. The heap data structure (Section 5.6) is an example of a complete binary tree.

---

[1] While these definitions for full and complete binary tree are the ones most commonly used, they are not universal. Some textbooks may even reverse these definitions! Since the common meaning of the words "full" and "complete" are quite similar, there is little that you can do to distinguish between them other than to memorize the definitions. Here is a memory aid which you might find useful: "Complete" is a wider word than "full," and complete binary trees tend to be wider than full binary trees since each level of a complete binary tree is as wide as possible.

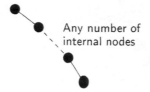

Figure 5.4 A tree containing n internal nodes and a single leaf.

5.1.1   The Full Binary Tree Theorem

Some binary tree implementations store data only at the leaf nodes, using the internal nodes only to provide structural information. More generally, binary tree implementations may require some amount of space for internal nodes, and a different amount for leaf nodes. Thus, to analyze the space required by such implementations, it is useful to know the minimum and maximum fraction of the nodes that are leaves in a tree containing n internal nodes.

Unfortunately, a binary tree of n internal nodes might have only one non-empty leaf. This occurs when the internal nodes are arranged in a chain ending in a single leaf as shown in Figure 5.4. In this case, the number of leaves is low because each internal node has only one non-empty child. To find an upper bound on the number of leaves for a tree of n internal nodes, note that the most nodes come when each internal node has two non-empty children, that is, when the tree is full. However, this observation does not tell what shape of tree will yield the highest percentage of non-empty leaves. It turns out not to matter, since all full binary trees of n internal nodes have the same number of leaves. This fact allows us to compute the space requirements for a full binary tree implementation whose leaves require a different amount of space from its internal nodes. The following theorem states the number of leaf nodes in all full binary trees with n internal nodes.

Theorem 5.1 Full Binary Tree Theorem: *The number of leaves in a non-empty full binary tree is one more than the number of internal nodes.*

Proof: The proof is by mathematical induction on n, the number of internal nodes. This is an example of an induction proof where we reduce from an arbitrary instance of size n to an instance of size $n - 1$ that meets the induction hypothesis.

- **Base Cases**: The non-empty tree with zero internal nodes has one leaf node. A full binary tree with one internal node has two leaf nodes. Thus, the base cases for $n = 0$ and $n = 1$ conform to the theorem.

- **Induction Hypothesis**: Assume that any full binary tree **T** containing $n - 1$ internal nodes has n leaves.

- **Induction Step**: Given tree **T** with n internal nodes, select an internal node I whose children are both leaf nodes. Remove both of I's children, making I a leaf node. Call the new tree **T'**. **T'** has $n - 1$ internal nodes. From the induction hypothesis, **T'** has n leaves. Now, return I's two children. We again have tree **T** with n internal nodes. How many leaves does **T** have? Since **T'** has n leaves, adding the two children yields $n + 2$. However, node I counted as one of the leaves in **T'**, and has now become an internal node. Thus, tree **T** has $n + 1$ leaf nodes and n internal nodes.

Therefore, by mathematical induction the theorem holds for all values of $n \geq 0$. □

When measuring the space requirements of a binary tree implementation, it is useful to know how many empty subtrees a tree will contain. A simple extension of the Full Binary Tree Theorem tells us exactly how many empty subtrees there are in *any binary tree*, whether full or not. There are two simple approaches to proving the following theorem, and both provide useful ways of thinking about binary trees.

Theorem 5.2 *The number of empty subtrees in a non-empty binary tree is one more than the number of nodes in the tree.*

Proof 1: Take an arbitrary binary tree **T** and replace every empty subtree with a leaf node. Call the new tree **T'**. All nodes originally in **T** will be internal nodes in **T'**. **T'** is a full binary tree, since every internal node of **T** now must have two children in **T'**, and each leaf node in **T** must have two children in **T'** (the leaves just added). The Full Binary Tree Theorem tells us that the number of leaves in a full binary tree is one more than the number of internal nodes. Thus, the number of new leaves that were added to create **T'** is one more than the number of nodes in **T**. But each of these new leaf nodes corresponds to an empty subtree in **T**. Thus, the number of empty subtrees in **T** is one more than the number of nodes in **T**. □

Proof 2: By definition, every node in binary tree **T** has two children, for a total of $2n$ children in a tree of n nodes. Every node except the root node has one parent, for a total of $n - 1$ parents. In other words, there are $n - 1$ non-empty children. Since the total number of children is $2n$, $n + 1$ of the children must be empty. □

5.1.2 A Binary Tree Node ADT

Before discussing applications for binary trees, we should consider what aspects of binary trees are likely to be generic to all applications. For example, we must be able to initialize a binary tree, or tell if the tree is empty. Some activities may be unique to the application. For example, we may wish to combine two binary trees by making their roots be the children of a new root node. Other activities are centered around the nodes. For example, we may need access to the left or right child of a node, or the parent of a node. We may need access to the node's data value.

Clearly there are activities that relate to nodes (e.g., reach the parent or a child), and activities that relate to trees (e.g., tree initialization). This indicates that nodes and trees should be separate classes in a Java implementation. For now, we concentrate on the class to implement binary tree nodes. This class will be used by various binary tree structures presented later in this chapter. Sample definitions for the binary tree class itself will be presented as part of the discussion on binary tree applications.

Figure 5.5 shows a Java interface for binary tree nodes, called `BinNode`. As with the `List` class implementations of Chapter 4, class `BinNode` is assumed to store a reference to type `Object`. When a binary tree is created, the actual data type of the elements may be whatever is convenient for the application. Member functions are provided that return the element value, return a pointer to the left child or right child of the node, set the element value, set the left or right child of the node, or indicate whether the node is a leaf.

5.2 Binary Tree Traversals

Often we wish to process a binary tree by "visiting" each of its nodes, each time performing a specific action such as printing the contents of the node. Any process for visiting the nodes in some order is called a **traversal**. Any traversal that lists every node in the tree exactly once is called an **enumeration** of the tree's nodes. Some applications do not require that the nodes be visited in any particular order so long as each node is visited precisely once. For other applications, nodes must be visited in a particular order. For example, we may wish to visit each node *before* we visit its children. This is called a **preorder traversal**. The preorder enumeration for the binary tree of Figure 5.1 is

ABDCEGFHI.

```
interface BinNode { // ADT for binary tree nodes
  // Return and set the element value
  public Object element();
  public Object setElement(Object v);

  // Return and set the left child
  public BinNode left();
  public BinNode setLeft(BinNode p);

  // Return and set the right child
  public BinNode right();
  public BinNode setRight(BinNode p);

  // Return true if this is a leaf node
  public boolean isLeaf();
} // interface BinNode
```

Figure 5.5 A binary tree node ADT.

Note that the first node printed is the root. Then all nodes of the left subtree are printed (in preorder) before any node of the right subtree.

Alternatively, we may wish to visit each node only *after* we visit its children (and their subtrees). This is called a **postorder traversal**. The postorder enumeration for the binary tree of Figure 5.1 is

DBGEHIFCA.

An **inorder traversal** first visits the left child (including its entire subtree), then visits the node, and finally visits the right child (including its entire subtree). The inorder enumeration for the binary tree of Figure 5.1 is

BDAGECHFI.

A traversal routine is easily written as a recursive function. Its input parameter is a pointer to a node R, with the initial call passing in a pointer to the root node of the tree. The traversal then visits R and its children (if any) in the desired order. For example, a preorder traversal specifies that R is visited before its children. This can easily be implemented in Java as follows.

```
void preorder(BinNode rt) // rt is the root of the subtree
{
  if (rt == null) return; // Empty subtree
  visit(rt);
  preorder(rt.left());
  preorder(rt.right());
}
```

Function `preorder` first checks that the tree is not empty (if it is, then the traversal is done and `preorder` simply returns). Otherwise, `preorder` makes a call to `visit`, which processes the root node (i.e., prints the value or performs some computation as required by the application). Function `preorder` is then called recursively on the left subtree, which will visit all nodes in that subtree. Finally, `preorder` is called on the right subtree, visiting all remaining nodes in the tree. Postorder and inorder traversals are similar. They simply change the order in which the node and its children are visited, as appropriate.

5.3   Binary Tree Implementations

This section begins with a pointer-based node implementation for binary trees. Then comes a discussion on techniques for determining the space requirements for a binary tree implementation. The section concludes with an introduction to the array implementation for complete binary trees.

5.3.1   Pointer-Based Node Implementations

By definition, all binary tree nodes have two children, though one or both children can be empty. Binary tree nodes normally contain a data value field; the space required to store a value depends on the application. The most common node implementation includes a value field and pointers to the children. Figure 5.6 shows a complete declaration for binary tree node class `BinNodePtr`.

BinNodePtr includes a data member of type `Object`, named `element`. Every `BinNode` also has two pointers, one to its left child and another to its right child. Besides constructor functions, `BinNodePtr` implements the functions required by the `BinNode` interface to set and return the element value, left child, and right child of the node, as well as a function to indicate if the current node is a leaf. Figure 5.7 shows a binary tree using the pointer-based implementation.

For certain applications it may be convenient to add a pointer to the node's parent, allowing easy upward movement in the tree. Using a parent pointer is somewhat analogous to adding a link to the previous node in a doubly linked list. In practice, the parent pointer is usually unnecessary and adds to the overhead.

An important decision in the design of a pointer-based node implementation is whether the same class definition will be used for leaves and internal

```
// Binary tree node with pointers to children
class BinNodePtr implements BinNode {
  private Object element; // Object for this node
  private BinNode left;    // Pointer to left child
  private BinNode right;   // Pointer to right child

  public BinNodePtr() {left = right = null; } // Constructor 1
  public BinNodePtr(Object val) {          // Constructor 2
    left = right = null;
    element = val;
  }

  public BinNodePtr(Object val, BinNode l, BinNode r) // Construct 3
  { left = l; right = r; element = val; }

  // Return and set the element value
  public Object element() { return element; }
  public Object setElement(Object v) { return element = v; }

  // Return and set the left child
  public BinNode left() { return left; }
  public BinNode setLeft(BinNode p) { return left = p; }

  // Return and set the right child
  public BinNode right() { return right; }
  public BinNode setRight(BinNode p) { return right = p; }

  public boolean isLeaf()  // Return true if this is a leaf node
  { return (left == null) && (right == null); }
} // class BinNodePtr
```

Figure 5.6 A binary tree node class declaration.

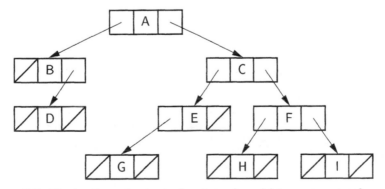

Figure 5.7 Illustration of a typical pointer-based binary tree implementation, where each node stores two child pointers and a value.

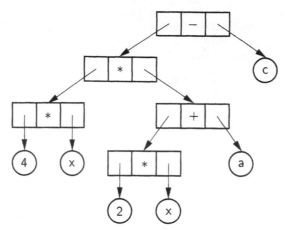

Figure 5.8 An expression tree for $4x(2x + a) - c$.

nodes. Some applications require data values only for the leaves. Other applications require one type of value for the leaves and another for the internal nodes. Examples include the binary trie of Section 13.1, the PR quadtree described in Section 13.3, and the expression tree introduced later in this section. By definition, only internal nodes have non-empty children, and so it is unnecessary to store pointers to the (non-existent) children of leaf nodes. Thus, it may save space to have separate implementations for internal and leaf nodes.

As an example of a tree that stores different information at the leaf and internal nodes, consider the expression tree illustrated by Figure 5.8. The expression tree represents an algebraic expression composed of binary operators such as addition, subtraction, multiplication, and division. The internal nodes of the tree store operators, while the leaves store operands. The tree of Figure 5.8 represents the expression $4x(2x + a) - c$. The storage requirements for a leaf are quite different from those of an internal node. Internal nodes store one of a small set of operators, so internal nodes could store either a small code identifying the operator or a single byte for the operator's character symbol. Leaves must store variable names or numbers. Thus, the leaf node value field must be considerably larger to handle the wider range of possible values. At the same time, leaf nodes need not store child pointers. Thus, separate leaf and internal node implementations should save space for this application.

Different types for leaf and internal nodes can be implemented in some programming languages such as Pascal and **C++** by using a variant record or union. However, not all languages (Java included) support unions. In addition, unions may be inefficient if the sizes for the leaf and internal node subtypes are very different, since the union requires that each node be large enough to store any one of these subtypes. A better approach is available in Java through the use of class inheritance. In this example, we will use our `BinNode` interface as the base class, and derive two separate subclasses to implement the leaf and internal nodes. Internal nodes (implemented by class `IntlNode`) store an operator value and child pointers of type `BinNode`; they do not distinguish their children's actual subclass. Leaf nodes (implemented by class `LeafNode`) store only a leaf node value. Whenever a node is examined, its version of `isLeaf` yields the node's subclass. Figure 5.9 presents a sample implementation.

The two derived classes `LeafNode` and `IntlNode` each contain implementations for `isLeaf`. Class `IntlNode` accesses its children through base class pointers (that is, pointers of type `BinNode`). Function `traverse` illustrates the use of these subclasses. When `traverse` calls "`rt.isLeaf()`," the Java runtime environment determines which subclass this particular instance of `rt` happens to be, and calls that subclass's version of `isLeaf`. Function `isLeaf` then indicates the actual node type. The other member functions of the derived subclasses are accessed in a similar way, since the runtime environment knows the type for a given object.

5.3.2 Space Requirements

This section presents techniques for calculating the amount of overhead required by a binary tree implementation. Recall that overhead is the amount of space necessary to maintain the data structure – in other words, any space not used to store data values. The amount of overhead depends on several factors including which nodes store data values (all nodes, or just the leaves), whether there is a parent pointer, and whether the tree is a full binary tree.

In a simple pointer-based implementation for the binary tree such as that of Figure 5.6, every node has two pointers to its children (even when the children are `null`). Theorem 5.2 tells us that about half of the pointers are "wasted" `null` values that serve only to indicate tree structure.

If only leaves store data values, then the fraction of total space devoted to overhead depends on whether the tree is full. If the tree is not full, then conceivably there may only be one leaf node at the end of a series of internal nodes. Thus, the overhead can be an arbitrarily high percentage for non-full binary trees. The overhead fraction drops as the tree becomes closer to full,

```
class LeafNode implements BinNode { // Leaf node subclass
  private String var;                 // Operand value

  public LeafNode(String val) { var = val; } // Constructor
  public Object element() { return var; }
  public Object setElement(Object v) { return var = (String)v; }
  public BinNode left() { return null; }
  public BinNode setLeft(BinNode p) { return null; }
  public BinNode right() { return null; }
  public BinNode setRight(BinNode p) { return null; }
  public boolean isLeaf() { return true; }
} // class LeafNode

class IntlNode implements BinNode { // Internal node subclass
  private BinNode left;               // Left child
  private BinNode right;              // Right child
  private Character opx;              // Operator value

  public IntlNode(Character op, BinNode l, BinNode r)
    { opx = op; left = l; right = r; } // Constructor
  public Object element() { return opx; }
  public Object setElement(Object v) { return opx = (Character)v; }
  public BinNode left() { return left; }
  public BinNode setLeft(BinNode p) { return left = p; }
  public BinNode right() { return right; }
  public BinNode setRight(BinNode p) { return right = p; }
  public boolean isLeaf() { return false; }
} // class IntlNode
static void traverse(BinNode rt) { // Preorder traversal
  if (rt == null) return;          // Nothing to visit
  if (rt.isLeaf())                 // Process leaf node
    VisitLeafNode(rt.element());
  else {                           // Processinternal node
    VisitInternalNode(rt.element());
    traverse(rt.left());
    traverse(rt.right());
  }
}
```

Figure 5.9 An implementation for separate internal and leaf node representations using Java class inheritance from the BinNode interface.

being the lowest if the tree is truly full. In this case, about one half of the nodes are internal, contributing to overhead.

A simple implementation storing two child pointers and a data value with every node requires total space amounting to $n(2p + d)$ for a tree of n nodes. Here, p stands for the amount of space required by a pointer, and d stands for the amount of space required by a data value. The total overhead space will be $2pn$ for the entire tree. Thus, the overhead fraction will be $2p/(2p + d)$. The actual value of this expression depends on the relative size of pointers and data fields. If we arbitrarily assume that $p = d$, then a full tree has about two thirds of its total space taken up in overhead. Great savings can be had by eliminating the pointers from leaf nodes in full binary trees. Since about half of the nodes are leaves and half internal nodes, and since only internal nodes now have overhead, the overhead fraction in this case will be approximately

$$\frac{\frac{n}{2}(2p)}{\frac{n}{2}(2p) + dn} = \frac{p}{p + d}.$$

If $p = d$, this means the overhead drops to about one half of the total space. However, if only leaf nodes store useful information, the overhead fraction for this implementation is actually three quarters of the total space, since half of the "data" space is unused.

A better implementation for an application requiring a full binary tree that stores data only at the leaf nodes is for the internal nodes to store two pointers and no data field while the leaf nodes store only a data field. Such an implementation requires $2pn + d(n + 1)$ units of space. If $p = d$, the overhead is about $2p/(2p + d) = 2/3$.

There is one serious flaw with this analysis. When using separate implementations for internal and leaf nodes, there must be a way to distinguish between the node types. When separate node types are implemented via Java subclasses, the runtime environment stores information with each object allowing it to determine the correct subclass to use when the isLeaf function is called. This means that a substantial amount of additional space is being stored with each node. Only one bit is truly necessary to distinguish the two possibilities. Some implementors find a spare bit within the node's value field in which to store the node type indicator. An alternative is to use a spare bit within a node pointer to indicate node type. This is often possible in languages that permit arithmetic operations on pointer variables, and where the compiler requires that structures and classes start on word boundaries, leaving the last bit of a pointer value always zero. Thus, this bit can be used to store the node-type flag, and is reset to zero before the pointer is dereferenced. (Java does not permit such arithmetic operations on pointers.) Another alternative when the leaf value field is smaller than a pointer is to replace the pointer to a leaf with the leaf's value. When space is limited, such techniques can make the difference between success and failure. In any other situation, such "bit packing" tricks should be avoided since they are often machine dependent at worst, and difficult to debug and understand at best.

5.3.3   Array Implementation for Complete Binary Trees

The previous section points out that a large fraction of the space in a binary tree implementation is devoted to tree structure overhead, not to storing useful data. This section presents a simple, compact implementation for complete binary trees. Recall that complete binary trees have all levels except the bottom filled out completely, and the bottom level has all of its nodes filled in from left to right. Thus, a complete binary tree of n nodes has only one possible shape. You might think that a complete binary tree is such an unusual occurrence that there is no reason to develop a special implementation for it. However, the complete binary tree has practical uses, the most important being the heap data structure discussed in Section 5.6. Heaps are often used to implement priority queues (Section 5.6) and for external sorting algorithms (Section 9.7).

Assume node positions in the complete binary tree are numbered consecutively, level by level, from left to right as shown in Figure 5.10(a). An array can store the tree's data values efficiently, placing each data value at the index corresponding to that node's position within the tree. Figure 5.10(b) lists the array indices for the children, parent, and siblings of each node in Figure 5.10(a). From Figure 5.10(b), you should see a pattern regarding the positions of a node's relatives within the array. Simple formulae can be derived for calculating the array index for each relative of a node from its index. No explicit pointers are necessary to reach a node's left or right child. This means there is no overhead to the array implementation if the array is selected to be of size n for a tree of n nodes.

The formulae for calculating the array indices of the various relatives of a node are as follows. The index of the node in question is r; n is the total number of nodes in the tree.

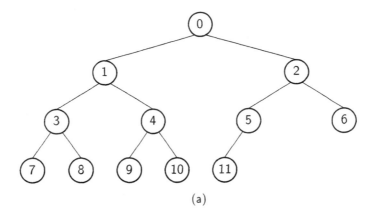

(a)

Node/Index	0	1	2	3	4	5	6	7	8	9	10	11
Parent	–	0	0	1	1	2	2	3	3	4	4	5
Left Child	1	3	5	7	9	11	–	–	–	–	–	–
Right Child	2	4	6	8	10	–	–	–	–	–	–	–
Left Sibling	–	–	1	–	3	–	5	–	7	–	9	–
Right Sibling	–	2	–	4	–	6	–	8	–	10	–	–

(b)

Figure 5.10 A complete binary tree and its array implementation. (a) The complete binary tree with twelve nodes. (b) The array indices for the relatives of each node. A dash indicates that the relative does not exist.

- $\text{Parent}(r) = (r - 1)/2$ if $0 < r < n$.
- $\text{Left child}(r) = 2r + 1$ if $2r + 1 < n$.
- $\text{Right child}(r) = 2r + 2$ if $2r + 2 < n$.
- $\text{Left sibling}(r) = r - 1$ if r is even and $0 < r < n$.
- $\text{Right sibling}(r) = r + 1$ if r is odd and $r + 1 < n$.

5.4 Huffman Coding Trees

The space/time tradeoff principle from Section 3.8 suggests that one can often gain an improvement in space requirements in exchange for a penalty in running time. There are many applications where this is a desirable tradeoff. A typical example is storing files on disk. If the files are not actively used, the owner may wish to compress them to save space. Later, they can be uncompressed for use, which costs some time, but only once.

We often represent a set of items in a computer program by assigning a unique code to each item. For example, the standard ASCII coding scheme assigns a unique eight-bit value to each character. It takes a certain minimum number of bits to provide unique codes for each character. For example, it takes $\lceil \log 128 \rceil$ or seven bits to provide the 128 unique codes needed to represent the 128 symbols of the ASCII character set.[2]

The requirement for $\lceil \log n \rceil$ bits to represent n unique code values assumes that all codes will be the same length. This is called a **fixed-length** coding scheme. ASCII coding is an example of a fixed-length coding scheme, since all characters require the same amount of space. If all characters were used equally often, then a fixed-length coding scheme is the most space efficient method. However, you are probably aware that not all characters are used equally often.

Figure 5.11 shows the relative frequencies of the letters of the alphabet as they appear in a representative sample of English documents. From this table we can see that the letter 'E' appears much more often than the letter 'Z' – about 60 times as often. In normal ASCII, the words "DEED" and "FUZZ" require the same amount of space (four bytes). It would seem that words such as "DEED," which are composed of relatively common letters, should be storable in less space than words such as "FUZZ," which are composed of relatively uncommon letters.

If some characters are used more frequently than others, is it possible to take advantage of this fact and somehow assign them shorter codes? The price could be that other characters require longer codes, but this may be worthwhile if such characters appear rarely enough. This concept is at the heart of file compression techniques in common use today. The next section presents one such approach to assigning **variable-length** codes, called Huffman coding. While it is not commonly used in its simplest form for file compression (there are better methods), Huffman coding gives the flavor of such coding schemes.

---

[2]The ASCII standard is eight bits, not seven, even though there are only 128 characters represented. The eighth bit is used either to check for transmission errors, or to support extended ASCII codes with an additional 128 characters.

Letter	Frequency	Letter	Frequency
A	77	N	67
B	17	O	67
C	32	P	20
D	42	Q	5
E	120	R	59
F	24	S	67
G	17	T	85
H	50	U	37
I	76	V	12
J	4	W	22
K	7	X	4
L	42	Y	22
M	24	Z	2

Figure 5.11 Relative frequencies for the 26 letters of the alphabet as they appear in a selected set of English documents. This table is derived from [Wel88], Appendix 2. "Frequency" represents the expected frequency of occurrence per 1,000 letters, ignoring case.

5.4.1 Building Huffman Coding Trees

Huffman coding assigns codes to characters such that the length of the code depends on the relative frequency or **weight** of the corresponding character. Thus, it is a variable-length code. If the estimated frequencies for letters matches the actual frequency found in an encoded message, then the length of that message will typically be less than if a fixed-length code had been used. The Huffman code for each letter is derived from a full binary tree called the **Huffman coding tree**, or simply the **Huffman tree**. Each leaf of the Huffman tree corresponds to a letter. The goal is to build a tree with the **minimum external path weight**. Define the **weighted path length** of a leaf to be its weight times its depth. The binary tree with minimum external path weight is the one with the minimum sum of weighted path lengths for the given set of leaves. A letter with high weight should have low depth, so that it will count the least against the total path length. As a result, another letter may be pushed deeper in the tree if it has less weight.

The process of building the Huffman tree is quite simple. First, order the letters in a list by ascending weight (i.e., frequency). Next, remove the first two letters (the ones with lowest weight) from the list, and assign them to leaves in what will become the Huffman tree. Assign these leaves as the

Letter	C	D	E	F	K	L	U	Z
Freq	32	42	120	24	7	42	37	2

Figure 5.12 The relative frequencies for eight selected letters.

children of an internal node whose weight is the sum of the weights for the two children. Take this sum and put it back on the list in the correct place necessary to preserve the order of the list. This process is repeated until only one item remains on the list, and a full Huffman tree has been built.

Figure 5.13 illustrates part of the Huffman tree construction process for the eight letters of Figure 5.12. Ranking D and L arbitrarily by alphabetical order, the letters are ordered by frequency as:

$$Z \quad K \quad F \quad C \quad U \quad D \quad L \quad E$$
$$2 \quad 7 \quad 24 \quad 32 \quad 37 \quad 42 \quad 42 \quad 120$$

We can view each of these letters as being in separate Huffman trees initially, with each tree composed of a single leaf node. These separate trees will eventually be joined into a single Huffman tree. Since the first two letters on the list are Z and K, they are selected to be the first leaves joined in the tree. They become the children of an internal node with weight 9. Thus, a tree whose root has weight 9 is placed back on the list, where it takes up the first position. The next step is to take values 9 and 24 off the list (corresponding to the partial tree with two leaf nodes built in the last step, and the partial tree storing the letter F, respectively) and join them together. The resulting root node has weight 33, and so this tree is placed on the list between the trees with values 32 (for letter C) and 37 (for letter U). This process continues until a tree whose root has weight 306 is built.

Figure 5.14 shows the Java class declarations for two classes. The first is `LettFreq` which stores a letter/frequency pair. The second class is for the Huffman tree itself. Each node of the Huffman tree stores a pointer to a `LettFreq` object. Figure 5.15 shows the Java code for the tree-building process.

Huffman tree building is an example of a **greedy algorithm**. At each step, the two subtrees with least weight are joined together. This makes the algorithm simple, but does it give the desired result? This section concludes with a proof that the Huffman tree indeed gives the most efficient arrangement for the set of letters.

The proof requires the following lemma.

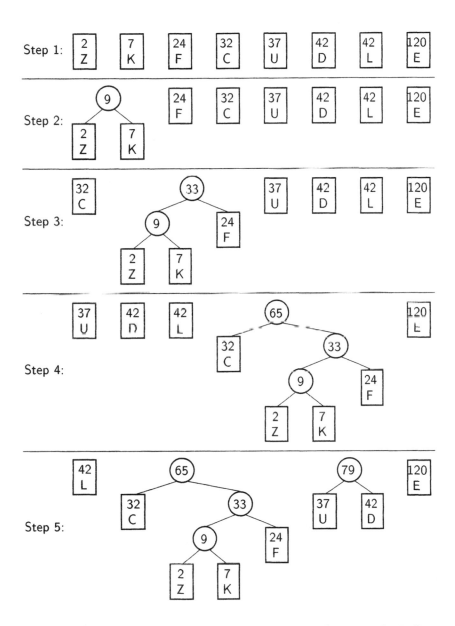

Figure 5.13 The first five steps of the building process for a sample Huffman tree.

```
class LettFreq {       // A letter/frequency pair
  private char lett;   // The letter
  private int freq;    // Frequency for the letter

  public LettFreq(int f, char l) { freq = f;  lett = l; }
  public LettFreq(int f) { freq = f; }
  public int weight() { return freq; }  // Return the weight
  public char letter() { return lett; } // Return the letter
} // class LettFreq

class HuffTree { // A Huffman coding tree
  private BinNode root;  // Root of the Huffman coding tree

  public HuffTree(LettFreq val)
  { root = new BinNodePtr(val); }
  public HuffTree(LettFreq val, HuffTree l, HuffTree r)
  { root = new BinNodePtr(val, l.root(), r.root()); }

  public BinNode root() { return root; }
  public int weight()      // Weight of tree is weight of root node
  { return ((LettFreq)root.element()).weight(); }
} // class HuffTree
```

Figure 5.14 Class declarations for the Huffman tree.

Lemma 5.1 *For any Huffman tree storing at least two letters, the two letters with least frequency are siblings whose depth is at least as deep as any other leaf nodes in the tree.*

Proof: Call the two letters with least frequency l_1 and l_2. They must be siblings since **buildTree** selects them in the first step of the construction process. Assume that l_1 and l_2 are not the deepest nodes in the tree. In this case, the Huffman tree must either look as shown in Figure 5.16, or in some sense be symmetrical to this. For this situation to occur, the parent of l_1 and l_2, labeled V, must have greater weight than the node labeled X. Otherwise, function **buildTree** would have selected node V in place of node X as the child of node U. However, this is impossible since l_1 and l_2 are the letters with least frequency.   □

Theorem 5.3 *The Huffman tree has the minimum external path weight for the given set of letters.*

Proof: The proof is by reducing induction on n, the number of letters.

```
// Build a Huffman tree from list hufflist
static HuffTree buildTree(List hufflist) {
  HuffTree temp1, temp2, temp3;
  LettFreq tempnode;

  for(hufflist.setPos(1); hufflist.isInList(); hufflist.setPos(1)) {
    // While at least two items left
    hufflist.setFirst();
    temp1 = (HuffTree)hufflist.remove();
    temp2 = (HuffTree)hufflist.remove();
    tempnode = new LettFreq(temp1.weight() + temp2.weight());
    temp3 = new HuffTree(tempnode, temp1, temp2);

    // return to the list in sorted order
    for (hufflist.setFirst(); hufflist.isInList(); hufflist.next())
      if (temp3.weight() <=
          ((HuffTree)(hufflist.currValue())).weight())
        { hufflist.insert(temp3); break; } // Put in list
    if (!hufflist.isInList())                 // It is heaviest value
      hufflist.append(temp3);
  }
  hufflist.setFirst();       // Tree now only element on list
  return (HuffTree)hufflist.remove(); // Return the tree
}
```

Figure 5.15 Implementation for Huffman tree construction. Function buildTree takes as input hufflist, the list of partial Huffman trees, which initially are single leaf nodes as shown in Step 1 of Figure 5.13. The body of function buildTree consists mainly of a for loop. Each time through the for loop, the first two partial trees are taken off the list and placed in variables temp1 and temp2. A new root node is created (temp3) and these two partial trees are set to be its children. Finally, temp3 is returned to hufflist.

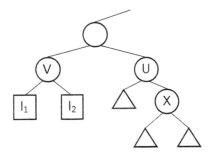

Figure 5.16 An impossible Huffman tree, showing the situation where the two nodes with least weight, l_1 and l_2, are not the deepest nodes in the tree. Triangles represent subtrees.

- **Base Case**: For $n = 2$, the Huffman tree must have the minimum external path weight since there are only two possible trees, each with identical weighted path lengths for the two leaves.

- **Induction Hypothesis**: Assume that a Huffman tree with $n - 1$ leaves has minimum external path length.

- **Induction Step**: Given a Huffman tree $\mathbf{T}$ with n leaves, $n \geq 2$, suppose that $w_1 \leq w_2 \leq \cdots \leq w_n$ where w_1 to w_n are the weights of the letters. Call V the parent of the letters with frequencies w_1 and w_2. From the lemma, we know that the nodes corresponding to the letters with frequencies w_1 and w_2 are as deep as any nodes in $\mathbf{T}$. Thus, we cannot reduce the external path length of $\mathbf{T}$ by replacing the children of V with deeper but more expensive nodes since they are already the deepest nodes in the tree. Call $\mathbf{T}'$ the Huffman tree that is identical to $\mathbf{T}$ except that node V is replaced with a leaf node V' whose weight is $w_1 + w_2$. By the induction hypothesis, $\mathbf{T}'$ has minimum external path length. Returning the children to V' restores tree $\mathbf{T}$, which must also have minimum external path length.

Thus, by mathematical induction, the theorem is correct. $\qquad\qquad\square$

5.4.2   Assigning and Using Huffman Codes

Once the Huffman tree has been constructed, it is an easy matter to assign codes to individual letters. Beginning at the root, we assign either a '0' or a '1' to each edge in the tree. '0' is assigned to edges connecting a node with its left child, and '1' to edges connecting a node with its right child. This process is illustrated by Figure 5.17. The Huffman code for a letter is simply a binary number determined by the path from the root to the leaf corresponding to that letter. Thus, the code for E is '0' since the path from the root to the leaf node for E takes a single left branch. The code for K is '111101' since the path to the node for K takes four right branches, then a left, and finally one last right. Figure 5.18 lists the codes for all eight letters.

Given codes for the letters, it is a simple matter to use these codes to encode a text message. We simply replace each letter in the string with its binary code. A lookup table can be used for this purpose. Using the code generated by our example Huffman tree, the word "DEED" is represented by the bit string "10100101" and the word "FUZZ" is represented by the bit string "111111100111100111100."

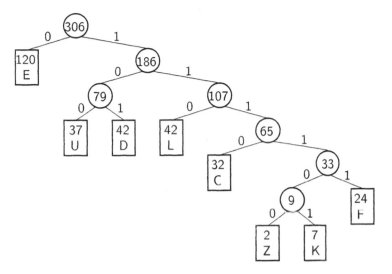

Figure 5.17 A Huffman tree for the letters of Figure 5.12.

Letter	Freq	Code	Bits
C	32	1110	4
D	42	101	3
E	120	0	1
Γ	24	11111	5
K	7	111101	6
L	42	110	3
U	37	100	3
Z	2	111100	6

Figure 5.18 The Huffman codes for the letters of Figure 5.12.

Decoding the message is done by looking at the bits in the coded string from left to right until a letter is decoded. This can be done by using the Huffman tree in a reverse process from that used to generate the codes. Decoding the bit string begins at the root of the tree. We take branches depending on the bit value – left for '0' and right for '1' – until reaching a leaf node. This leaf contains the first character in the message. We then process the next bit in the code from the root again to start the next character.

To decode the bit string "1011001110111101" we begin at the root of the tree and take a right branch for the first bit which is '1.' Since the next bit is a '0' we take a left branch. We then take another right branch (for the third bit '1'), arriving at the leaf node corresponding to the letter D. Thus,

the first letter of the coded word is D. We then begin again at the root of
the tree to process the fourth bit, which is a '1.' Taking a right branch,
then two left branches (for the next two bits which are '0'), we reach the leaf
node corresponding to the letter U. Thus, the second letter is U. In similar
manner we complete the decoding process to find that the last two letters
are C and K, spelling the word "DUCK."

A set of codes is said to meet the **prefix property** if no code in the set
is the prefix of another. The prefix property guarantees that there will be no
ambiguity in how a bit string is decoded. In other words, once we reach the
last bit of a code during the decoding process, we know which letter it is the
code for. Huffman codes certainly have the prefix property since any prefix
of a code will correspond to an internal node, while all codes correspond to
leaf nodes. For example, the code for F is '11111.' Taking five right branches
in the Huffman tree of Figure 5.17 brings us to the leaf node containing F.
We can be sure that no letter can have code '111' because this corresponds
to an internal node of the tree, and the tree-building process places letters
only at the leaf nodes.

How efficient is Huffman coding? In theory, it is an optimal coding
method whenever the true frequencies are known, and the frequency of a
letter is independent of the context of that letter in the message. In practice, the frequencies of letters do change depending on context. For example,
while E is the most commonly used letter of the alphabet in English documents, T is more common as the first letter of a word. This is why most
commercial compression utilities do not use Huffman coding as their primary
coding method.

Another factor that affects the compression efficiency of Huffman coding
is the relative frequencies of the letters. Some frequency patterns will save no
space as compared to fixed-length codes; others can result in great compression. In general, Huffman coding does better when there is large variation
in the frequencies of letters. In the particular case of the frequencies shown
in Figure 5.18, we can determine the expected savings from Huffman coding
if the actual frequencies of a coded message match the expected frequencies.

Since the sum of the frequencies in Figure 5.18 is 306 and E has frequency 120, we expect it to appear 120 times in a message containing 306 letters. An actual message may or may not meet this expectation. Letters D,
L, and U have code lengths of three, and together are expected to appear
121 times in 306 letters. Letter C has a code length of four, and is expected
to appear 32 times in 306 letters. Letter F has a code length of five, and

is expected to appear 24 times in 306 letters. Finally, letters K and Z have code lengths of six, and together are expected to appear only 9 times in 306 letters. The average expected cost per character is simply the sum of the cost for each character (c_i) times the probability of its occurring (p_i), or

$$c_1 p_1 + c_2 p_2 + \cdots + c_n p_n.$$

This can be reorganized as

$$\frac{c_1 f_1 + c_2 f_2 + \cdots + c_n f_n}{f_T}$$

where f_i is the frequency of letter i and f_T is the total for all letter frequencies. For this set of frequencies, the expected cost per letter is

$$[(1 \times 120) + (3 \times 121) + (4 \times 32) + (5 \times 24) + (6 \times 9)]/306 = 785/306 \approx 2.57$$

A fixed-length code for these eight characters would require $\log 8 = 3$ bits per letter as opposed to about 2.57 bits per letter for Huffman coding. Thus, Huffman coding is expected to save about 12% for this set of letters.

Huffman coding for all ASCII symbols should do better than this. The letters of Figure 5.18 are atypical in that there are too many common letters compared to the number of rare letters. Huffman coding for all 26 letters would yield an expected cost of 4.29 bits per letter. The equivalent fixed-length code would require about five bits. This is somewhat unfair to fixed-length coding since there is actually room for 32 codes in five bits, but only 26 letters. More generally, Huffman coding of a typical text file will save around 40% over ASCII coding if we charge ASCII coding at eight bits per character. Huffman coding for a binary file (such as a compiled executable) would have a very different set of distribution frequencies, and so would have a different space savings. Most commercial compression programs use two or three encoding schemes to adjust to different types of files.

In the preceding example, "DEED" was coded in 8 bits, a saving of 33% over the twelve bits required from a fixed-length coding. However, "FUZZ" requires 20 bits, more space than required by the corresponding fixed-length coding. The problem is that "FUZZ" is composed of letters that are not expected to occur often. If the message does not match the expected frequencies of the letters, than the length of the encoding will not be as expected either.

5.5   Binary Search Trees

Project 4.4 asks you to implement a simple city database using a list. Each record in the database contains the name of a city and its xy-coordinates. If the records are not stored in any particular order, then inserting a new record into the list can be performed quickly by putting it at the end. However, searching an unsorted list for a particular record by city name requires $\Theta(n)$ time in the average case. For a large database, this is probably much too slow. Alternatively, the records can be stored in the list in alphabetical order by city name. If the list is implemented using a linked list, then no speedup will result from storing the records in order. If the list is implemented using an array, then the binary search of Section 3.5 can be used to find a record in only $\Theta(\log n)$ time. However, insertion will now require $\Theta(n)$ time since, after the proper location for the new record in the sorted list has been found, many records must be shifted to make room for the new record. Is there some way to organize a collection of records so that both inserting records and searching for records can be done quickly?

This section presents the Binary Search Tree (BST), which allows an improved solution to this problem.

Before discussing the BST, let us first consider the issue of exactly what we are searching for. In the example above, a city record contains at least three pieces of information: its x coordinate, its y coordinate, and its name. In the example, we were interested in searching for a city by its name. Thus, the name field served as a **search key** for the record. Throughout the rest of the book, we will be discussing various data structures used to search for a particular record, or various sorting algorithms used to organized a collection of records. In each case, we assume that the data record is derived from an interface named **Elem**, as follows.

```
interface Elem {                  // Interface for generic element type
  public abstract int key(); // Key used for search and ordering
} // interface Elem
```

Interface **Elem** simply ensures that the records have a function named **key** that returns an **int** value to be used for comparison between elements during searching or sorting. This is something of an oversimplification, since there are situations where the desired key field should not be an **int** (such as the case of organizing city records by name). However, all of the principles for searching and sorting will remain the same, so it would be a simple matter to modify the implementations presented in this book to handle such cases.

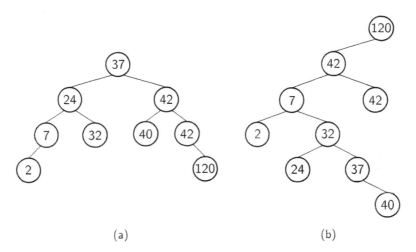

(a)   (b)

Figure 5.19 Two Binary Search Trees for a collection of values. The tree in (a) results if values are inserted in the order $(37, 24, 42, 7, 2, 40, 42, 32, 120)$. The tree in (b) results if the same values are inserted in the order $(120, 42, 42, 7, 2, 32, 37, 24, 40)$.

A BST is a binary tree that conforms to the following condition.

Definition 5.4 Binary Search Tree Property. All nodes stored in the left subtree of a node whose key value is K have key values less than K. All nodes stored in the right subtree of a node whose key value is K have key values greater than or equal to K.

Figure 5.19 shows two BSTs for a collection of values. One consequence of the Binary Search Tree Property is that if the BST nodes are printed using an inorder traversal, the resulting enumeration will be in sorted order from lowest to highest.

Figure 5.20 shows part of the implementation for Binary Search Trees. All of the public functions are shown. These include a constructor for the BST; a function `clear` to reinitialize the tree, functions to insert and remove records; a function to find a record with a given key value; and a function to print the records in ascending order of key value.

To find a record with key value K in a BST, begin at the root. If the root stores K, then the search is over. If not, then we must search deeper in the tree. What makes the BST search efficient is that we need search only one of the node's two subtrees. If K is less than the root node's value, we search only the left subtree. If K is greater than the root node's value, we

```
class BST { // Binary Search Tree implementation
  private BinNode root;                    // The root of the tree

  public BST() { root = null; }            // Initialize root to null
  public void clear() { root = null; } // Throw the nodes away
  public void insert(Elem val) { root = inserthelp(root, val); }
  public void remove(int key) { root = removehelp(root, key); }
  public Elem find(int key) { return findhelp(root, key); }
  public boolean isEmpty() { return root == null; }

  public void print() { // Print out the BST
    if (root == null)
      System.out.println("The BST is empty.");
    else {
      printhelp(root, 0);
      System.out.println();
    }
  }
} // class BST
```

Figure 5.20 Part of the Java implementation for the Binary Search Tree.

search only the right subtree. This process continues until K is found, or we reach a leaf node. If we reach a leaf node without encountering K, then K is not in the BST.

Consider searching for the value 32 in the tree of Figure 5.19(a). Since 32 is less than the root value of 37, the search proceeds to the left subtree. Since 32 is greater than 24, we search in 24's right subtree. At this point the node containing 32 is found. If the search value were 35, the same path would be followed to the node containing 32. Since this node contains no children, we know that 35 does not appear anywhere in the BST.

Notice that in Figure 5.20, **find** simply calls a private member function named **findhelp**. Function **find** takes the search key as an explicit parameter, and its BST as an implicit parameter. However, the find operation is most easily implemented as a recursive function whose parameters are the root of a BST subtree and the search key. Member **findhelp** is of the desired form for this recursive subroutine and is implemented as follows.

```
private Elem findhelp(BinNode rt, int key) {
  if (rt == null) return null;
  Elem it = (Elem)rt.element();
  if (it.key() > key)  return findhelp(rt.left(), key);
  else if (it.key() == key)  return it;
  else  return findhelp(rt.right(), key);
}
```

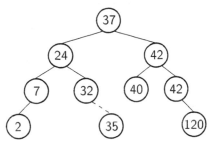

Figure 5.21 BST insert of a node with value 35. The node with value 32 becomes the parent of the new node containing 35.

Once the desired record is found, it is passed up the chain of recursive calls to `findhelp`.

Inserting a value K requires that we first find where K would have been if it were in the tree. This takes us to either a leaf node, or to an internal node with no child in the appropriate direction.[3] Call this node R'. We then add a new node containing K as a child of R'. Figure 5.21 illustrates this operation. The value 35 is added as the right child of the node with value 32. Here is the implementation for `inserthelp`.

```
private BinNode inserthelp(BinNode rt, Elem val) {
  if (rt == null) return new BinNode(val);
  Elem it = (Elem)rt.element();
  if (it.key() > val.key())
    rt.setLeft(inserthelp(rt.left(), val));
  else
    rt.setRight(inserthelp(rt.right(), val));
  return rt;
}
```

You should pay careful attention to the implementation for `inserthelp`. Note that `inserthelp` returns a `BinNode` reference. Logically, what is being returned is a subtree identical to the old subtree except that it has been modified to contain the new node being inserted. Each node along a path from the root to parent of the new node added to the tree will have its appropriate child pointer assigned to. Except for the last node in the path, none of these nodes will actually change their child's pointer value. In that

---

[3]This assumes that no node in the tree has value equal to the one being inserted. If we do find a node containing the value to be inserted, we have two options. If the application does not allow nodes with equal values, then this insertion should be treated as an error. If duplicate values are allowed, our convention is to insert the duplicate in the right subtree, as is done by member `inserthelp`.

sense, many of the assignments are unnecessary. However, the cost of these additional assignments is small compared to the simplicity of this approach.

The shape of a BST depends on the order in which elements are inserted. A new element is added to the BST as a new leaf node, potentially increasing the depth of the tree. Figure 5.19 illustrates two BSTs for a collection of values. It is possible for the BST containing n nodes to be a chain of nodes with height $n + 1$. This would happen if, for example, all elements were inserted in sorted order. In general, it is preferable for a BST to be as shallow as possible.

Removing a node from a BST is a bit trickier than inserting a node, but not too difficult to grasp if all of the possible cases are considered individually. Before tackling the general node removal process, let us first discuss how to get or remove the node with the smallest value in a subtree. These routines will be used later by the general node removal function. To remove the minimum value in a subtree, first find the minimum value by continuously moving down the `left` link until there is no further `left` link to follow. This will bring us to the node with minimum value; call it S. To remove S, simply have the parent of S change its pointer to point to the right child of S. We know that S has no left child (since if S did have a left child, S would not be the node with minimum value). Thus, changing the pointer as described will maintain a BST, with S removed. The code for the get and remove functions, named `getmin` and `deletemin`, respectively, is as follows:

```
private Elem getmin(BinNode rt) {
  if (rt.left() == null)
    return (Elem)rt.element();
  else return getmin(rt.left());
}

private BinNode deletemin(BinNode rt) {
  if (rt.left() == null)
    return rt.right();
  else {
    rt.setLeft(deletemin(rt.left()));
    return rt;
  }
}
```

Figure 5.22 illustrates the `deletemin` process. Beginning at the root node with value 10, `deletemin` follows the left link until there is no further left link, in this case reaching the node with value 5. It then returns a pointer to the right subtree. Of course, the prior (recursive) call to `deletemin` then assigns this right subtree as the left child of the node that used to point to

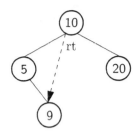

Figure 5.22 An example of deleting the node with minimum value. In this tree, the node with minimum value, 5, is the left child of the root. Thus, the root's `left` pointer is changed to point to 5's right child.

the minimum value, thus chopping the minimum value out of the tree. This is indicated in Figure 5.22 by a dashed line.

Removing an arbitrary node R from the BST requires that we first find R, and then remove it from the tree. So, the first part of the remove operation is a search to find R. Once R is found, there are several possibilities. If R has no children, then R's parent has its pointer set to `null`. If R has one child, then R's parent has its pointer set to R's child (similar to `deletemin`). The problem comes if R has two children. One simple approach, though expensive, is to set R's parent to point to one of R's subtrees, and then reinsert the remaining subtree's nodes one at a time. A better alternative is to find a value in one of the subtrees that can replace the value in R. Thus, the question becomes: Which value can substitute for the one being removed? It cannot be any arbitrary value, since we must preserve the BST property without making major changes to the structure of the tree. Which value is most like the one being removed? The answer is the least value greater than (or equal to) the one being removed, or else the greatest value less than the one being removed. If either of these values replace the one being removed, then the BST property is maintained. For example, assume that we wish to remove the value 37 from the BST of Figure 5.19(a). Instead of removing the root node, we remove the node with the least value in the right subtree (using the `getmin` and `deletemin` operations). This value can then replace the value in the root. In this example we first remove the node with value 40, since it contains the least value in the right subtree. We then substitute 40 as the new value of the root node. Figure 5.23 illustrates this process.

When no duplicate node values appear in the tree, it makes no difference whether the replacement is the greatest value from the left subtree or the least value from the right subtree. If duplicates are stored, then we must

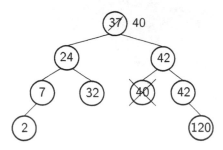

Figure 5.23 An example of removing the value 37 from the BST. The node containing this value has two children. We replace value 37 with the least value from the node's right subtree, in this case 40.

select the replacement from the *right* subtree. To see why, call the greatest value in the left subtree G. If other nodes in the left subtree also have value G, selecting G as the replacement value for the root of the subtree will result in a tree with equal values to the left of the node now containing G. Precisely this situation occurs if we replace value 120 with the greatest value in the left subtree of Figure 5.19(b). Selecting the least value from the right subtree does not have a similar problem, since it does not violate the Binary Search Tree Property if equal values appear in the right subtree.

From the above, we see that if we want to remove the value from a node with two children, then we simply call `getmin` and `deletemin` on the node's right subtree, and substitute the value returned by `getmin` for the value being removed. Below is the code for `removehelp`.

```
private BinNode removehelp(BinNode rt, int key) {
  if (rt == null) return null;
  Elem it = (Elem)rt.element();
  if (key < it.key())
    rt.setLeft(removehelp(rt.left(), key));
  else if (key > it.key())
    rt.setRight(removehelp(rt.right(), key));
  else { // Found it
    if (rt.left() == null)
      rt = rt.right();
    else if (rt.right() == null)
      rt = rt.left();
    else { // Two children
      Elem temp = getmin(rt.right());
      rt.setElement(temp);
      rt.setRight(deletemin(rt.right()));
    }
  }
  return rt;
}
```

The cost for `findhelp` and `inserthelp` is the depth of the node found or inserted. The cost for `removehelp` is the depth of the node being removed, or in the case when this node has two children, the depth of the node with smallest value in its right subtree. Thus, in the worst case, the cost of any one of these operations is the depth of the deepest node in the tree. This is why it is desirable to keep BSTs **balanced**, that is, with least possible height. If a binary tree is balanced, then the height for a tree of n nodes is approximately $\log n$. However, if the tree is completely unbalanced, for example in the shape of a linked list, then the height for a tree of n nodes can be as great as n. Thus, a balanced BST will in the average case have operations costing $\Theta(\log n)$, while a badly unbalanced BST can have operations in the worst case costing $\Theta(n)$. Consider the situation where we construct a BST of n nodes by inserting the nodes one at a time. If we are fortunate to have them arrive in an order that results in a balanced tree (a "random" order is likely to be good enough for this purpose), then each insertion will cost on average $\Theta(\log n)$, for a total cost of $\Theta(n \log n)$. However, if the nodes are inserted in order of increasing value, then the resulting tree will be a chain of height n. The cost of insertion in this case will be $\sum_{i=1}^{n} i$, which is $\Theta(n^2)$.

Traversing a BST costs $\Theta(n)$ regardless of the shape of the tree. Each node is visited exactly once, and each pointer of the tree is followed exactly once. As an example, below is function `printhelp`, which performs an inorder traversal to print out the contents of the tree from the least key value to greatest.

```
private void printhelp(BinNode rt, int level) {
  if (rt == null) return;
  printhelp(rt.left(), level+1);
  for (int i=0; i<level; i++)      // Indent based on level
    System.out.print("  ");
  System.out.println((Elem)rt.element()); // Print node value
  printhelp(rt.right(), level+1);
}
```

While the BST is simple to implement and efficient when the tree is balanced, the possibility of its being unbalanced is a serious liability. There are techniques for organizing a BST to guarantee good performance. One example is the Splay Tree of Section 13.2. Other search trees are guaranteed to remain balanced, such as the 2-3 tree of Section 11.4.

5.6   Heaps and Priority Queues

There are many situations, both in real life and in computing applications, where we wish to choose the next "most important" from a collection of people, tasks, or objects. For example, doctors in a hospital emergency room often choose to see next the "most critical" patient rather than the one who arrived first. When scheduling programs for execution in a multi-tasking operating system, at any given moment there may be several programs (usually called **jobs**) ready to run. The one that is selected should be the one with the highest **priority**. Priority is indicated by a particular value associated with the job. When a new job is to be executed, the one with highest priority should be selected from the queue.

When a collection of objects is organized by importance or priority, we call this a **priority queue**. A normal queue data structure will not implement a priority queue efficiently since search for the element with highest priority will take $\Theta(n)$ time. A list, whether sorted or not, will also require $\Theta(n)$ time for either insertion or removal. A BST that organizes records by priority could be used, with all operations requiring $\Theta(n \log n)$ time in the average case. However, there is always the possibility that the BST will become unbalanced, leading to bad performance. Instead, we would like to find a data structure that is guaranteed to have good performance for this special application.

This section presents the **heap** data structure. A heap is defined by two properties. First, it is a complete binary tree, so heaps are nearly always implemented using the array representation for complete binary trees presented in Section 5.3.3. Second, the values stored in a heap are **partially ordered**. This means that there is a relationship between the value stored at any node and the values of its children. There are two variants of the heap, depending on the definition of this relationship.

The **max-heap** has the property that every node stores a value that is *greater* than or equal to the value of either of its children. Since the root has a value greater than or equal to its children, which in turn have values greater than or equal to their children, the root stores the maximum of all values in the tree.

The other heap variant is called a **min-heap**. The min-heap stores at every node a value that is *less* than or equal to that of its children. Since the root has a value less than or equal to its children, which in turn have values less than or equal to their children, the root stores the minimum of all values in the tree.

Note that there is no necessary relationship between a node and its sibling in either the min-heap or the max-heap. For example, it is possible that the values for all nodes in the left subtree of the root are greater than for every node of the right subtree.

Both heap variants have their uses. For example, the Heapsort of Section 8.6 uses the max-heap, while the Replacement Selection algorithm of Section 9.7 uses a min-heap. The examples in the rest of this section will use a max-heap.

Students often confuse the logical representation of a heap with its physical implementation by means of the array-based complete binary tree. The two are not synonymous, since the logical view of the heap is actually a tree structure while the typical physical implementation uses an array.

Figure 5.24 presents an implementation for max-heaps. As with the BST, the heap stores elements of type `Elem`, which store an integer key value used to order the heap.

Class `MaxHeap` makes two concessions to the array-based implementation. First, heap nodes are indicated by their logical position within the heap rather than by a pointer to the node. In practice, the logical heap position corresponds to the identically numbered physical array position. Second, the constructor takes as input a pointer to the array to be used. This approach provides the greatest flexibility for using the heap since all data values can be loaded into the array directly. The advantage of this is described below. The constructor also takes an integer parameter indicating the initial size of the heap (based on the number of elements initially loaded into the array) and a second integer parameter indicating the maximum size allowed for the heap. Member function `heapsize` returns the current size of the heap. The call `H.isLeaf(pos)` will return `true` if position `pos` is a leaf in heap `H`. Members `leftchild`, `rightchild`, and `parent` return the position (actually, the array index) for the left child, right child, and parent of the position passed, respectively.

One way to build a heap is to insert the elements one at a time. Member function `insert` will insert a new element V into the heap. You might expect that the heap insertion process is similar to the insert function for a BST, starting at the root and working down through the heap. However, this approach is not likely to work since the heap must maintain the shape of a complete binary tree. Equivalently, if the heap takes up the first n positions of its array prior to the call to `insert`, it must take up the first $n+1$ positions after. To accomplish this, `insert` first places V at position n of the array.

```
public class MaxHeap {           // Max-heap implementation
private Elem[] Heap;             // Pointer to the heap array
private int size;                // Maximum size of the heap
private int n;                   // Number of elements now in heap

public MaxHeap(Elem[] h, int num, int max)   // Constructor
{ Heap = h;  n = num;  size = max;  buildheap(); }

public int heapsize() // Return current size of the heap
{ return n; }

public boolean isLeaf(int pos)  // True if pos is a leaf position
{ return (pos >= n/2) && (pos < n); }

// Return position for left child of pos
public int leftchild(int pos) {
  Assert.notFalse(pos < n/2, "Position has no left child");
  return 2*pos + 1;
}

// Return position for right child of pos
public int rightchild(int pos) {
  Assert.notFalse(pos < (n-1)/2, "Position has no right child");
  return 2*pos + 2;
}

public int parent(int pos) { // Return position for parent
  Assert.notFalse(pos > 0, "Position has no parent");
  return (pos-1)/2;
}

public void buildheap()          // Heapify contents of Heap
  { for (int i=n/2-1; i>=0; i--) siftdown(i); }

private void siftdown(int pos) { // Put element in its correct place
  Assert.notFalse((pos >= 0) && (pos < n), "Illegal heap position");
  while (!isLeaf(pos)) {
    int j = leftchild(pos);
    if ((j<(n-1)) && (Heap[j].key() < Heap[j+1].key()))
      j++; // j is now index of child with greater value
    if (Heap[pos].key() >= Heap[j].key()) return; // Done
    DSutil.swap(Heap, pos, j);
    pos = j;  // Move down
  }
}
}
```

Figure 5.24 A Java implementation for the max-heap.

```
public void insert(Elem val) { // Insert value into heap
  Assert.notFalse(n < size, "Heap is full");
  int curr = n++;
  Heap[curr] = val;                    // Start at end of heap
  // Now sift up until curr's parent's key > curr's key
  while ((curr!=0) && (Heap[curr].key()>Heap[parent(curr)].key())) {
    DSutil.swap(Heap, curr, parent(curr));
    curr = parent(curr);
  }
}

public Elem removemax() {            // Remove maximum value
  Assert.notFalse(n > 0, "Removing from empty heap");
  DSutil.swap(Heap, 0, --n); // Swap maximum with last value
  if (n != 0)        // Not on last element
    siftdown(0);    // Put new heap root val in correct place
  return Heap[n];
}

// Remove element at specified position
public Elem remove(int pos) {
  Assert.notFalse((pos >= 0) && (pos < n), "Illegal heap position");
  DSutil.swap(Heap, pos, --n); // Swap with last value
  while (Heap[pos].key() > Heap[parent(pos)].key()) // push up
    DSutil.swap(Heap, pos, parent(pos));
  if (n != 0) siftdown(pos);   // Push down
  return Heap[n];
}
} // class MaxHeap
```

Figure 5.24 (continued)

Of course, V is unlikely to be in the correct position. To move V to the
right place, it is compared to its parent's value. If the value of V is less than
or equal to the value of its parent, then it is in the correct place and the
insert routine is finished. If the value of V is greater than that of its parent,
then the two elements swap positions. From here, the process of comparing
V to its parent continues until V reaches its correct place.

Each call to **insert** takes $\Theta(\log n)$ time in the worst case, since the value
being inserted can move at most the distance from the bottom of the tree
to the top of the tree. Thus, the time to insert n values into the heap will
be $\Theta(n \log n)$.

We can build the heap more efficiently if all n values are available at
the beginning of the building process. Instead of inserting the values into
the heap one by one, we can take advantage of having them all together
to speed up the process. Consider Figure 5.25(a), which shows one way

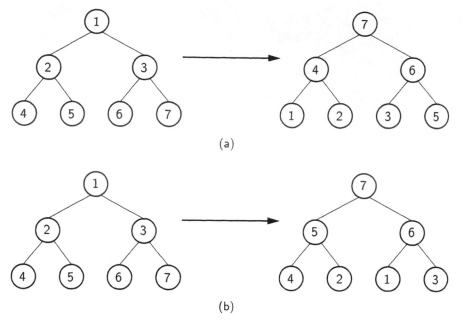

Figure 5.25 Two series of exchanges to build a heap. (a) This heap is built by a series of nine exchanges in the order (4-2), (4-1), (2-1), (5-2), (5-4), (6-3), (6-5), (7-5), (7-6). (b) This heap is built by a series of four exchanges in the order (5-2), (7-3), (7-1), (6-1).

to create a heap by a process of exchanging values. Note that this figure shows the input in its logical form as a complete binary tree, but you should realize that these values are physically stored in an array. All exchanges are between a node and one of its children. The heap is formed as a result of this exchange process. The array for the right-hand tree of Figure 5.25(a) would appear as follows.

7	4	6	1	2	3	5

Figure 5.25(b) shows an alternative series of exchanges that also forms a heap, but much more efficiently. From this example, it is clear that the heap for any given set of numbers is not unique, and we see that some rearrangements of the input values require fewer exchanges than others to build the heap. So, how do we pick the best rearrangement? One good algorithm stems from induction. Suppose that the left and right subtrees of the root are already heaps, and R is the name of the element at the root. This situation is illustrated by Figure 5.26. In this case there are two possibilities. (1) R has a value greater than or equal to its two children. In

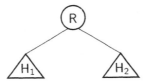

Figure 5.26 Final stage in the heap-building algorithm. Both subtrees of node R are heaps. All that remains is to push R down to its proper level in the heap.

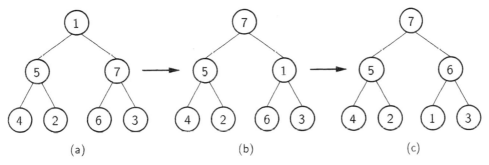

Figure 5.27 The siftdown operation. The subtrees of the root are assumed to be heaps. (a) The partially completed heap. (b) Values 1 and 7 are swapped. (c) Values 1 and 6 are swapped to form the final heap.

this case, construction is complete. (2) R has a value less than one or both of its children. In this case, R should be exchanged with the child that has greater value. The result will be a heap, except that R might still be less than one or both of its (new) children. In this case, we simply continue the process of "pushing down" R until it reaches a level where it is greater than its children, or is a leaf node. This process is implemented by the private member function **siftdown** of the heap class. The siftdown operation is illustrated by Figure 5.27.

This approach assumes that the subtrees are already heaps, suggesting that a complete algorithm may be obtained by visiting the nodes in some order such that the children of a node are visited *before* the node itself. One simple way to do this is simply to work from the high index of the array to the low index. Actually, the build process need not visit the leaf nodes (they can never move down since they are already at the bottom), so the building algorithm can start in the middle of the array with the first internal node. The exchanges shown in Figure 5.25(b) result from this process. Member function **buildheap** implements the building algorithm.

What is the cost of `buildheap`? One way to view the cost is to count the distance that each element must go to reach its final level. We will focus only on the distance that an element must go downward in the heap. Some elements move upwards in the heap, but for every up there must be a corresponding downward step by another element. We can ignore these upward movements, since no element will move up and later be moved down again. This is because once a node has been processed, all nodes below it must have lesser value so it can never be moved downward again.

Viewed in this way, we see that up to half of the nodes in a heap of height d are at depth $d - 1$, and so their elements cannot move downward at all. One quarter of the nodes are at depth $d - 2$, and so their elements can move down at most one level. At each step up the tree we get half the number of nodes as were at the previous level, and an additional height of one. The maximum sum of total distances that elements can go is therefore

$$\sum_{i=1}^{\log n} (i - 1)\frac{n}{2^i} = \Theta(n).$$

Thus, this algorithm takes $\Theta(n)$ time.

Removing the maximum (root) value from a heap containing n elements requires that we maintain the complete binary tree shape, and that the remaining $n - 1$ node values conform to the heap property. We can maintain the proper shape by moving the element in the last position in the heap (the current last element in the array) to the root position. We now consider the heap to be one element smaller. Unfortunately, the new root value is probably *not* the maximum value in the new heap. This problem is easily solved by using `siftdown` to reorder the heap. Since the heap is $\log n$ levels deep, the cost of deleting the maximum element is $\Theta(\log n)$ in the average and worst cases.

The heap is a natural implementation for the priority queues discussed at the beginning of this section. Jobs can be added to the heap (using their priority value as the ordering key) when needed. Function `removemax` can be called whenever a new job is to be executed.

Some applications of priority queues require the ability to change the priority of an object already stored in the queue. This may require that the object's position in the heap representation be updated. Unfortunately, a max-heap is not efficient when searching for an arbitrary value; it is only good for finding the maximum value. However, if we already know the index for an object within the heap, it is a simple matter to update its priority (including changing its position to maintain the heap property) or remove it. The **remove** member function takes as input the position of the node to be removed from the heap. A typical implementation for priority queues requiring updating of priorities will need to use an auxiliary data structure allowing efficient search for objects (such as a BST). Records in the auxiliary data structure will store the object's heap index, so that the object may be deleted from the heap and reinserted with its new priority (see Project 5.5). Section 7.5.1 presents one application of a priority queue with priority updating.

5.7   Further Reading

For an example of a tree implementation where the internal node pointer directly stores the value of the leaf node, see Shaffer and Brown [SB93].

The proof of Section 5.4.1 that the Huffman coding tree has minimum external path weight is from Knuth [Knu73]. For more information on data compression techniques, see *Data Compression: Methods and Theory* by James A. Storer [Sto88] and *Codes and Cryptography* by Dominic Welsh [Wel88]. Tables 5.11 and 5.12 are derived from Welsh [Wel88].

See Bentley's Programming Pearl "Thanks, Heaps" [Ben85, Ben88] for a good discussion on the heap data structure and its uses.

Many techniques exist for maintaining reasonably balanced BSTs in the face of unfriendly insert and delete operations. One example is the AVL tree of Adelson-Velskii and Landis, which is discussed by Knuth [Knu81]. The AVL tree is actually a BST whose insert and delete routines reorganize the tree structure so as to guarantee that the subtrees rooted by the children of any node will differ in height by at most one. Another example is the Splay Tree [ST85] discussed in Section 13.2.

5.8   Exercises

5.1 Section 5.1.1 claims that a full binary tree has the highest fraction of non-empty leaves. Prove that this is true.

5.2 Define the **degree** of a node as the number of its non-empty children. As an extension of the Full Binary Tree Theorem, prove by induction that the number of degree 2 nodes in any binary tree is one less than the number of leaves.

5.3 **(a)** Modify the preorder traversal of Section 5.2 to perform an inorder traversal of a binary tree.

(b) Modify the preorder traversal of Section 5.2 to perform a post-order traversal of a binary tree.

5.4 Find the overhead fraction for each of the full binary tree implementations with space requirements as follows:

(a) All nodes store data, two child pointers, and a parent pointer. The data field requires four bytes and each pointer requires four bytes.

(b) Both leaf nodes and internal nodes store data and two child pointers. The data field requires sixteen bytes and each pointer requires four bytes.

(c) Both leaf nodes and internal nodes store data, all nodes store a parent pointer, and internal nodes store two child pointers. The data field requires eight bytes and each pointer requires four bytes.

(d) Only leaf nodes store data; internal nodes store two child pointers. The data field requires four bytes and each pointer requires two bytes.

5.5 Write a recursive function named **search** that takes as input a binary tree (NOT a BST!) and a value K, and returns **true** if value K appears in the tree and **false** otherwise. Your function should have the following prototype:

```
boolean search(BinNode rt, int K).
```

5.6 Write an algorithm that takes as input a pointer to the root of a binary tree, and prints the node values of the tree in **level** order. Level order first prints the root, then all nodes of level 1, then all nodes of level 2, and so on. *Hint*: Preorder traversals make use of a stack through recursive calls. Consider making use of another data structure to help implement the level order traversal.

5.7 Define the **internal path length** for a tree as the sum of the depths of all internal nodes, while the **external path length** is the sum of the depths of all leaf nodes in the tree. Prove by induction that if tree **T** is a full binary tree with n internal nodes, I is **T**'s internal path length, and E is **T**'s external path length, then $E = I + 2n$ for $n \geq 0$.

5.8 Build the Huffman coding tree and determine the codes for the following set of letters and weights:

A	B	C	D	E	F	G	H	I	J	K	L
2	3	5	7	11	13	17	19	23	31	37	41

What is the expected length in bits of a message containing n characters for this frequency distribution?

5.9 What will the Huffman coding tree look like for a set of sixteen characters all with equal weight? What is the average code length for a letter in this case? How does this differ from the smallest possible fixed length code for sixteen characters?

5.10 A set of characters with varying weights is assigned Huffman codes. If one of the characters is assigned code 001, then:

(a) What other codes *cannot* have been assigned?

(b) What other codes *must* have been assigned?

5.11 Assume that a sample alphabet has the following weights:

Q	Z	F	M	T	S	O	E
2	3	10	10	10	15	20	30

(a) For this alphabet, what is the worst case number of bits required by the Huffman code for a string of n letters? What string(s) have the worst case performance?

(b) For this alphabet, what is the best case number of bits required by the Huffman code for a string of n letters? What string(s) have the best case performance?

(c) What is the average number of bits required by a character using the Huffman code for this alphabet?

5.12 What are the minimum and maximum number of elements in a heap of height h?

5.13 Where in a min-heap might the largest element reside?

5.14 The Huffman coding tree function `buildTree` of Figure 5.15 manipulates a sorted list. This could result in a $\Theta(n^2)$ algorithm, since placing an intermediate Huffman tree on the list could take $\Theta(n)$ time. Revise this algorithm to use a priority queue based on a min-heap instead of a list.

5.15 Why is the BST Property defined so that nodes with values equal to the value of the root appear only in the right subtree, rather than allow equal valued nodes to appear in either subtree?

5.16 Draw the BST that results from adding the value 5 to the BST of Figure 5.19(a).

5.17 Draw the BST that results from deleting the value 7 from the BST of Figure 5.19(b).

5.18 Write a recursive function named `count` that, given a BST and a value K, returns the number of nodes having values less than or equal to K. Function `count` should visit as few nodes in the BST as possible. Your function should have the following prototype:

```
int count(BinNode root, int K).
```

5.19 Write a recursive function named `printRange` that, given a BST, a low value and a high value, prints in sorted order all records that fall between the two values. Function `printRange` should visit as few nodes in the BST as possible. Function `printRange` should have the following prototype:

```
void printRange(BinNode root, int low, int high).
```

5.20 Show the max-heap that results from running `buildheap` on the following values stored in an array:

$$10 \quad 5 \quad 12 \quad 3 \quad 2 \quad 1 \quad 8 \quad 7 \quad 9 \quad 4$$

5.21 **(a)** Show the heap that results from deleting the maximum value from the max-heap of Figure 5.25b.
     (b) Show the heap that results from deleting the element with value 5 from the max-heap of Figure 5.25b.

5.22 Revise the heap definition of Figure 5.24 to implement a min-heap. The member function `removemax` should be replaced by a new function called `removemin`.

5.9 Projects

5.1 Complete the implementation of the Huffman coding tree, building on the code presented in Section 5.4. Include a function to compute the codes for each letter, and functions to encode and decode messages. This project can be further extended to support file compression. To do so requires adding two steps: (1) Read through the input file to generate actual frequencies for all letters in the file; and (2) store a representation for the Huffman tree at the beginning of the encoded output file to be used by the decoding function. If you have trouble with devising such a representation, see Section 6.5.

5.2 Complete the implementation from Section 5.4 for building a Huffman coding tree. Modify function `buildTree` of Figure 5.15, replacing the sorted list with a min-heap to store the partial Huffman trees.

5.3 One way to deal with the "problem" of `null` pointers in binary trees is to use that space for some other purpose. One example is the **threaded** binary tree. The threaded binary tree stores with each node two additional bit fields that indicate if the `left` and `right` members are regular pointers to child nodes or threads. If `left` is not a pointer to a child (i.e., if it would be `null` in a regular binary tree), then it instead stores a pointer to the **inorder predecessor** of that node. The inorder predecessor is the node that would be printed *before* the current node in an inorder traversal. If `right` is not a pointer to a child, then it instead stores a pointer to the node's **inorder successor**. The inorder successor is the node that would be printed *after* the current node in an inorder traversal. The main advantage of threaded binary trees is that operations such as inorder traversal can be implemented without using recursion or a stack.

Reimplement the BST as a threaded binary tree, and include a non recursive version of the preorder traversal

5.4 Implement a city database using a BST to store the database records. Each database record contains the name of the city (a string of arbitrary length) and the coordinates of the city expressed as integer x and y coordinates. The BST should be organized by city name. Your database should allow records to be inserted, deleted by name or coordinate, and searched by name or coordinate. Another operation that should be supported is to print all records within a given distance of a specified point. Collect running-time statistics for each operation. Which operations can be implemented reasonably efficiently (i.e., in $\Theta(\log n)$ time in the average case) using a BST? Can the database system be made more efficient by using one or more additional BSTs to organize the records by location?

5.5 Implement a priority queue based on the max-heap class implementation of Figure 5.24. The following commands should be supported for manipulating the priority queue:

```
void enqueue(int ObjectID, int priority);
int dequeue();
void changeweight(int ObjectID, int newPriority);
```

Function **enqueue** inserts a new object into the priority queue with ID number **ObjectID** and priority **priority**. Function **dequeue** removes the object with highest priority from the priority queue and returns its object ID. Function **changeweight** changes the priority of the object with ID number **ObjectID** to be **newPriority**. The type for **Elem** should be a class or structure that stores the object ID and the priority for that object. You will need a mechanism for finding the position of the desired object within the heap. Use an array, storing the object with **ObjectID** i in position i. (Be sure in your testing to keep the **ObjectID**s within the array bounds.) You must also modify the heap implementation to store the object's position in the array so that updates to objects in the heap can be recorded in the auxiliary structure.

6

General Trees

This chapter extends the discussion of Chapter 5 to general trees, whose nodes may have any number of children. This property makes general trees substantially harder to implement than binary trees.

Section 6.1 presents general tree terminology. Section 6.2 presents a simple representation for solving the important problem of processing equivalence classes. Several pointer-based implementations for general trees are covered in Section 6.3. Section 6.4 generalizes the properties of binary trees to trees whose nodes have K children. Sequential implementations are covered in Section 6.5.

6.1 General Tree Definitions and Terminology

A **tree T** is a finite set of one or more nodes such that there is one designated node R, called the root of **T**. The remaining nodes in $(\mathbf{T} - \{R\})$ are partitioned into $n \geq 0$ disjoint subsets $\mathbf{T}_1$, $\mathbf{T}_2$, ..., $\mathbf{T}_n$, each of which is a tree, and whose roots R_1, R_2, ..., R_n, respectively, are children of R. The subsets $\mathbf{T}_i$ $(1 \leq i \leq n)$ are said to be **subtrees** of **T**. These subtrees are ordered in that $\mathbf{T}_i$ is said to come before $\mathbf{T}_j$ if $i < j$. By convention, the subtrees are arranged from left to right with subtree $\mathbf{T}_1$ called the leftmost child of R. A node's **out degree** is the number of children for that node. A **forest** is a collection of one or more trees.

Figure 6.1 presents tree notation generalized from the notation for binary trees presented in Chapter 5. Some additional terms are specific to general trees.

Each node in a tree has precisely one parent, except for the root, which has no parent. From this observation, it immediately follows that a tree with n nodes must have $n - 1$ edges, since each node aside from the root has one edge connecting that node to its parent.

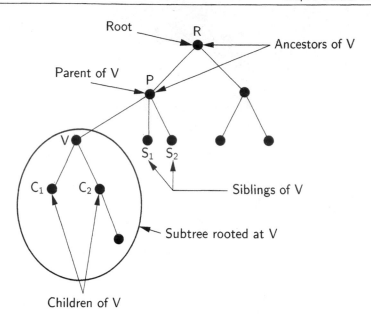

Figure 6.1 Notation for general trees. Node P is the parent of nodes V, S_1, and S_2. Thus, V, S_1, and S_2 are children of P. Nodes R and P are ancestors of V. Nodes V, S_1, and S_2 are called **siblings**. The oval surrounds the subtree having V as its root.

6.1.1   An ADT for General Tree Nodes

Before discussing general tree implementations, we should first make precise what operations such implementations must support. Any implementation must be able to initialize a tree. Given a tree, we may wish access to the root of that tree. Typically we wish to process the children of a node, in some order. We may want the value for a node, the leftmost child of a node, the node's next (right) sibling, or the node's parent. We also would like a way to remove nodes from a tree.

From this list, we see that there are things that we wish to do to nodes (reach the parent, sibling, or child), and things that we wish to do to trees (initialize, return the root). Thus, as with the binary tree, our general tree implementations include both a tree class and a node class. Figure 6.2 shows sample Java interfaces for these classes.

6.1.2   General Tree Traversals

Three tree traversals were presented for binary trees: preorder, postorder, and inorder. For general trees, preorder and postorder traversals are defined

```
interface GTNode {                    // General tree node ADT
  public Object value();              // Return the value
  public boolean isLeaf();            // TRUE if this node is a leaf
  public GTNode parent();             // Return the parent
  public GTNode leftmost_child();     // Return the leftmost child
  public GTNode right_sibling();      // Return the right sibling
  public void setValue(Object value); // Set the value
  public void setParent(GTNode par);  // Set the parent
  public void insert_first(GTNode n); // Add a new leftmost child
  public void insert_next(GTNode n);  // Insert a new right sibling
  public void remove_first();         // Remove the leftmost child
  public void remove_next();          // Remove the right sibling
} // interface GTNode

interface GenTree {           // General tree ADT
  public void clear();        // Clear the tree
  public GTNode root();       // Return the root
  // Make the tree have a new root with children first and sib
  public void newroot(Object value, GTNode first, GTNode sib);
  public void newleftchild(Object value); // Add left child
} // interface GenTree
```

Figure 6.2 The general tree node and general tree interfaces.

with meanings similar to their binary tree counterparts. Preorder traversal of a general tree first visits the root of the tree, then performs a preorder traversal of each subtree from left to right. A postorder traversal of a general tree performs a postorder traversal of the root's subtrees from left to right, then visits the root. Inorder traversal does not have a natural definition for the general tree, since there is no particular number of children for an internal node. An arbitrary definition – such as visit the leftmost subtree in inorder, then the root, then visit the remaining subtrees in inorder – can be invented. However, inorder traversals are generally not used with general trees.

A preorder traversal of the tree in Figure 6.3 visits the nodes in order

RACDEBF.

A postorder traversal of this tree would visit the nodes in order

CDEAFBR.

To perform a preorder traversal, it is necessary to visit each of the children for a given node (say R) from left to right. This is accomplished by starting at R's leftmost child (call it T). From T, we can move to T's right sibling, and then to that node's right sibling, and so on.

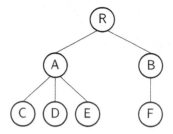

Figure 6.3 An example of a general tree.

Using the GTNode interface of Figure 6.2, here is a Java implementation to print the nodes of a general tree in preorder.

```
static void preorder(GTNode rt) { // Preorder traversal
  if (rt.isLeaf()) System.out.print("Leaf: ");
  else System.out.print("Internal: ");
  System.out.println(rt.value());  // Print or take other action
  GTNode temp = rt.leftmost_child();
  while (temp != null) {
    preorder(temp);
    temp = temp.right_sibling();
  }
}
```

6.2   The Parent Pointer Implementation

Perhaps the simplest general tree implementation is to store for each node only a pointer to that node's parent. We will call this the **Parent Pointer** implementation. Clearly this implementation is not general purpose, since it is inadequate for such important operations as finding the leftmost child or the right sibling for a node. Thus, it may seem to be a poor idea to implement a general tree in this way. However, the parent pointer implementation stores precisely the information required to answer the following, useful question: "Given two nodes, are they in the same tree?" To answer the question, we need only follow the series of parent pointers from each node to its respective root. If both nodes reach the same root, then they must be in the same tree. The process of finding the ultimate root for a given node is called FIND. If the roots are different, then the two nodes are not in the same tree.

One typical application for this procedure is to determine if two objects are in the same set, and if not, then to merge the sets together. Since the sets are then united, this operation is usually called UNION and the whole process goes by the name "UNION/FIND algorithm."

The UNION/FIND implementation represents each set by a general tree. Two objects are in the same set if they are in the same tree. Every node of the tree (except for the root) has precisely one parent. Thus, each node requires the same space. The only information that must be stored is the node's parent pointer. The tree itself is typically stored as an array of general tree nodes. Those nodes that are the root of their trees store a `null` value. Figure 6.4 shows the parent pointer implementation for the general tree and its nodes. These classes are greatly simplified from those of Figure 6.2 since we need only a limited subset of the operations. Class `GenTree` is given two new functions, `differ` and `UNION`. Function `differ` checks if two objects are in different sets, and function `UNION` merges two sets together. A private function `FIND` is used to find the ultimate root for an object.

An application using the UNION/FIND functions should store a set of n objects, where each object is assigned a unique index in the range 0 to $n - 1$. Class `GenTree` creates and initializes the UNION/FIND array, and functions `differ` and `UNION` take array indices as inputs.

Figure 6.5 illustrates the parent pointer implementation. Note that the nodes can appear in any order within the array, and the array can store any number of separate trees. For example, Figure 6.5 stores two trees in the same array. Thus, a single array can store a collection of items distributed among an arbitrary (and changing) number of disjoint subsets.

Consider the problem of assigning the members of a set to disjoint subsets called **equivalence classes**. The input is a series of equivalence pairs. An equivalence pair might say that object C is equivalent to object A. If so, C and A are placed in the same subset. If a later equivalence relates A and B, then by implication C is also equivalent to B. Thus, an equivalence pair may merge together two subsets, each containing several objects.

Equivalence classes can be managed efficiently with the UNION/FIND algorithm. Initially, each object is at the root of its own tree. An equivalence pair is processed by checking to see if both objects of the pair are in the same tree using function `differ`. If they are, then no change need be made since the objects are already in the same equivalence class. Otherwise, the two equivalence classes should be merged by the `UNION` function.

As an example of the equivalence class problem, consider the set of letters

$$(A, \ B, \ C, \ D, \ E, \ F, \ G, \ H, \ I, \ J).$$

Initially, we assume that they are each in a distinct equivalence class. This is represented by storing each letter as the root of its own tree. Figure 6.6(a) shows the initial configuration using the parent pointer array representation.

```
class GTNode {    // General tree node for UNION/FIND
  private GTNode par;                    // Parent pointer
  public GTNode() { par = null; }        // Constuctor
  public GTNode parent() { return par; } // Return node's parent
  public GTNode setParent(GTNode newpar) // Set the parent pointer
  { return par = newpar; }
} // class GTNode

class GenTree {    // General Tree class for UNION/FIND
  private GTNode[] array;                 // Node array

  public GenTree(int size) {              // Constructor
    array = new GTNode[size];             // Create node array
    for (int i=0; i<size; i++)
      array[i] = new GTNode();
  }

  public boolean differ(int a, int b) { // Nodes in different trees?
    GTNode root1 = FIND(array[a]);       // Find root of node a
    GTNode root2 = FIND(array[b]);       // Find root of node b
    return root1 != root2;               // Compare roots
  }

  public void UNION(int a, int b) {       // Merge two subtrees
    GTNode root1 = FIND(array[a]);        // Find root of node a
    GTNode root2 = FIND(array[b]);        // Find root of node b
    if (root1 != root2) root2.setParent(root1); // Merge subtrees
  }

  private GTNode FIND(GTNode curr) {      // Find root
    while (curr.parent() != null) curr = curr.parent();
    return curr;                          // At root
  }
} // class GenTree
```

Figure 6.4 General tree implementation for the UNION/FIND algorithm.

Now, consider what happens when equivalence relationship (A, B) is processed. The root of the tree containing A is A, and the root of the tree containing B is B. To make them equivalent, one of these two nodes is set to be the parent of the other. In this case it is irrelevant which points to which; arbitrarily select the first in alphabetical order to be the root. This is represented in the parent pointer array by setting the parent field of B (the node in array position 1) to store a pointer to A. Equivalence pairs (C, H), (G, F), and (D, E) are processed in similar fashion. Equivalence pair (I, F) is also similar. Objects I and F are both their own roots, so I is set to point to F. Note that this also makes G equivalent to I. The result of processing these five equivalences is shown in Figure 6.6(b).

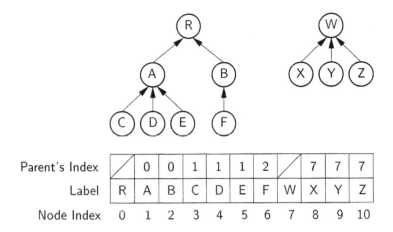

Parent's Index		0	0	1	1	1	2		7	7	7
Label	R	A	B	C	D	E	F	W	X	Y	Z
Node Index	0	1	2	3	4	5	6	7	8	9	10

Figure 6.5 The parent pointer array implementation. Each node stores its value and a pointer to its parent. For clarity, the parent pointers are shown in the array as the index of the parent's position in the array. The root of any tree stores `null`, represented graphically by a slash in the "Parent's Index" box. This figure shows two trees stored in the same parent pointer array, one rooted at R, and the other rooted at W.

The parent pointer representation places no limit on the number of nodes that can share a parent. To make equivalence processing as efficient as possible, the distance from each node to the root of its respective tree should be as small as possible. Thus, we would like to keep the height of the trees small when merging two equivalence classes together. Ideally, each tree would have all nodes pointing directly to the root. Achieving this goal may require too much additional processing to be worth the effort.

A low-cost approach to reducing the height is to be smart about how two trees are joined together. One simple technique, called the **weighted union rule**, joins the tree with fewer nodes to the tree with more nodes by making the smaller tree's root point to the root of the bigger tree. This will limit the total depth of the tree to $O(\log n)$, since the depth of all nodes in the smaller tree will now increase by one, but the total number of nodes in the combined tree is at least twice the number in the smaller subtree. Thus, the depth of any node can be increased at most $\log n$ times.

When processing equivalence pair (I, F) in Figure 6.6(b), F is the root of a tree with two nodes while I is the root of a tree with only one node. Thus, I is set to point to F rather than the other way around. Figure 6.6(c) shows the result of processing two more equivalence pairs: (H, A) and (E, G). For the first pair, the root for H is C while the root for A is itself. Both trees

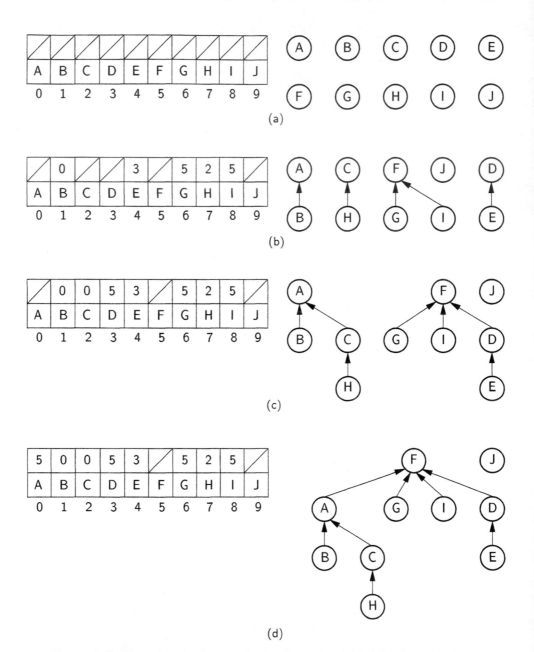

Figure 6.6 An example of equivalence processing. (a) Initial configuration for ten items in ten independent equivalence classes. (b) The result of processing five equivalence pairs: (A, B), (C, H), (G, F), (D, E), and (I, F). (c) The result of processing two more equivalence pairs: (H, A) and (E, G). (d) The result of processing the last equivalence pair (H, E).

```
GTNode FIND(GTNode curr) {
  if (curr.parent() == null) return curr;  // At root
    return curr.setParent(FIND(curr.parent()));
}
```

Figure 6.7 Java code for performing FIND with path compression.

contain two nodes, so it is an arbitrary decision as to which object is set to be the root for the combined tree. In the case of equivalence pair (E, G), the root of E is D while the root of G is F. Since F is the root of the larger tree, object D is set to point to F.

Not all equivalences will combine two trees. If the equivalence pair (F, G) is processed when the representation is in the state shown in Figure 6.6(c), no change will be made since F is already the root for G.

The weighted union rule helps to minimize the depth of the tree, but we can do better than this. **Path compression** is a method that tends to create extremely shallow trees. Path compression takes place while finding the root for a given node X. Call this root R. Path compression resets the parent of every node on the path from X to R to point directly to R. This can be implemented by first finding R. A second pass is then made along the path from X to R, assigning the parent field of each node encountered to R. Alternatively, a recursive algorithm can be implemented as shown in Figure 6.7. This version of FIND not only returns the root of the current node, but also makes all ancestors of the current node point to the root.

Path compression keeps the cost of each FIND operation very close to constant. To be more precise about what is meant by "very close to constant," the cost of path compression for n FIND operations on n nodes (when combined with the weighted union rule for joining sets) is $\Theta(n \log^* n)$. The notation "$\log^* n$" means the number of times that the log of n must be taken before $n \leq 1$. For example, $\log^* 65536$ is 4 since $\log 65536 = 16$, $\log 16 = 4$, $\log 4 = 2$, and finally $\log 2 = 1$. Thus, $\log^* n$ grows *very* slowly, so the cost of a series of n FIND operations is very close to $\Theta(n)$.

Note that this discussion does not mean that the tree resulting from processing n equivalence pairs necessarily has depth $\Theta(\log^* n)$. One can devise a series of equivalence operations that yields $\Theta(\log n)$ depth for the resulting tree. However, many of the equivalences in such a series will look only at the roots of the trees being merged, requiring little processing time. The *total* amount of processing time required will be $\Theta(n \log^* n)$, yielding nearly constant time for each equivalence operation. This is an example of the technique of amortized analysis, discussed in Section 14.3.

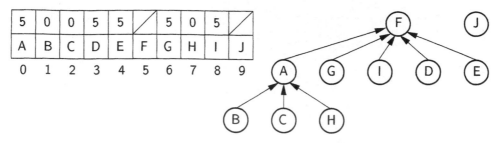

Figure 6.8 An example of path compression, showing the result of processing equivalence pair (H, E) on the representation of Figure 6.6(c).

Figure 6.6(d) shows the result of processing equivalence pair (H, E) on the the representation shown in Figure 6.6(c) using the standard weighted union rule without path compression. Figure 6.8 illustrates the path compression process for the same equivalence pair. After locating the root for node H, we can perform path compression to make H point directly to root object A. Likewise, E is set to point directly to its root, F. Finally, object A is set to point to root object F.

6.3 General Tree Implementations

We now tackle the problem of producing an implementation for general trees that allows efficient processing of all member functions of the ADT shown in Figure 6.2. This section presents several approaches to implementing general trees. Each implementation yields advantages and disadvantages in the amount of space required to store a node and the relative ease with which key operations may be performed.

General tree implementations should place no restriction on how many children a node may have. In some applications, once a node is created the number of children never changes. In such cases, a fixed amount of space can be allocated for the node when it is created, based on the number of children for the node. Matters become more complicated if children can be added to or deleted from a node, requiring that the node's space allocation be adjusted accordingly.

6.3.1 List of Children

Our first attempt to create a general tree implementation is called the "list of children" implementation for general trees. Quite simply, this implemen-

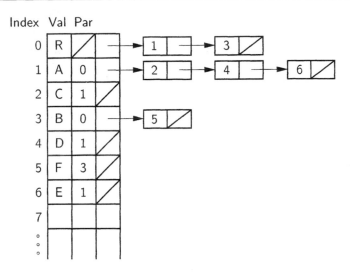

Figure 6.9 The "list of children" implementation for the general tree of Figure 6.3. The column of numbers to the left of the node array labels the array indices. The column labeled "Val" stores node values. The column labeled "Par" stores pointers to the parents. For clarity, these pointers are shown as array indices. The last column stores pointers to the linked list of children for each internal node. Each element on the linked list stores a pointer to one of the node's children (shown as the array index of the target node).

tation stores with each internal node a linked list of its children, in order from left to right. This concept is illustrated by Figure 6.9.

The "list of children" implementation stores tree nodes in an array. Each node contains a value, a pointer to its parent, and a pointer to a linked list of the node's children, stored from left to right. Each list element contains a pointer to one child. Thus, the leftmost child of a node can be found directly in the first linked list element. However, to find the right sibling for a node is more difficult. Consider the case of a node M and its parent P. To find M's right sibling, we must move down the child list of P until the linked list element storing the pointer to M has been found. The *next* linked list element stores a pointer to M's right sibling. Thus, in the worst case, to find M's right sibling requires that all children of M's parent be searched.

Combining trees using this representation is difficult if each tree is stored in a separate node array. If the nodes of both trees are stored in a single node array, then adding tree **T** as a subtree of node R is done by simply adding the root of **T** to R's list of children.

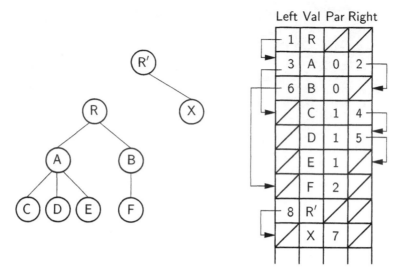

Figure 6.10 The "left child/right sibling" implementation.

6.3.2 The Left Child/Right Sibling Implementation

The "list of children" implementation makes it difficult to access a node's right sibling. Figure 6.10 shows an improved implementation. Here, each node stores its value and pointers to its parent, leftmost child, and right sibling. Thus, each of the basic ADT operations can be implemented by reading a value directly from the node. If two trees are stored within the same node array, then adding one as the subtree of the other simply requires setting three pointers. Combining trees in this way is illustrated by Figure 6.11. This implementation is more space efficient than the "list of children" implementation, and each node requires a fixed amount of space in the node array.

6.3.3 Dynamic Node Implementations

The general tree implementations of the previous two sections use an array to store the tree nodes. We next attempt to extend the concept of linked implementation to general trees. The linked implementation for binary trees stores each node as a separate dynamic object containing its value and pointers to its two children. Unfortunately, nodes of a general tree can have any number of children, and this number may change during the life of the node. A general tree node implementation must support these properties. One solution is simply to limit the number of children permitted for any node, and

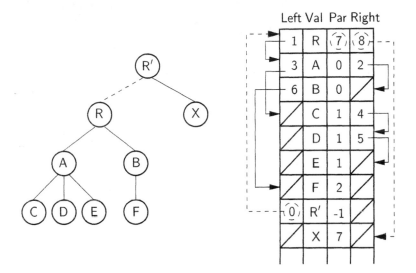

Figure 6.11 Combining two trees that use the "left child/right sibling" implementation. The subtree rooted at R in Figure 6.10 now becomes the first child of R'. Three pointers are adjusted in the node array: The left child field of R' now points to node R, while the right sibling field for R points to node X. The parent field of node R points to node R'.

allocate pointers for exactly that number of children. There are two major objections to this. First, it places an undesirable limit on the number of children, which makes certain trees unrepresentable by this implementation. Second, this is likely to be extremely wasteful of space since most nodes will have far fewer children and thus leave some pointer positions empty.

The alternative is to allocate variable space for each node. There are two basic approaches. One is to allocate as part of the node an array of child pointers. In essence, each node stores an array-based list of child pointers. Figure 6.12 illustrates the concept. This approach assumes that the number of children is known when the node is created, which is true for some applications but not for others. It also works best if the number of children does not change. If the number of children does change (especially if it increases) then some special recovery mechanism must be developed that allows for a change in the size of the child pointer array. One possibility is to allocate a new node of the correct size from free store, and return the old copy of the node to free store for later reuse. This works especially well in a garbage-collected language such as Java. For example, assume that a node M initially has two children, and that space for two child pointers is allocated when M is created. If a third child is added to M, space for a new

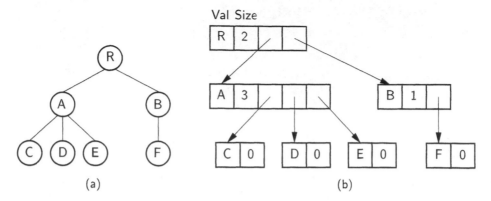

Figure 6.12 A dynamic general tree representation with fixed size arrays for the child pointers. (a) The general tree. (b) The tree representation. For each node, the first field stores the node value while the second field stores the size of the child pointer array.

node with three child pointers can be allocated, the contents of M copied over to the new space, and the old space dereferenced and left as garbage. As an alternative to relying on the system's garbage collector, a memory manager for variable size storage units can be implemented, as described in Section 12.4. Note in Figure 6.12 that the current number of children for each node is stored explicitly in a **size** field. The child pointers are stored in an array with **size** elements.

Another approach that is more flexible, but which requires more space, is to store a linked list of child pointers with each node as illustrated by Figure 6.13. This implementation is essentially the same as the "list of children" implementation of Section 6.3.1, but with dynamically allocated nodes rather than nodes stored in an array.

6.3.4 Dynamic "Left Child/Right Sibling" Implementation

The "left child/right sibling" implementation of Section 6.3.2 stores a fixed number of pointers with each node. This can be readily adapted to a dynamic implementation. In essence, we substitute a binary tree for a general tree (or a forest of general trees). Each node of the "left child/right sibling" implementation points to two "children" in a new binary tree structure. The left child of this new structure is the node's first child in the general tree. The right child is the node's right sibling. Converting from a forest of general trees to a single binary tree is illustrated by Figure 6.14. Here we simply include links from each node to its right sibling, and remove links to all children except the leftmost child.

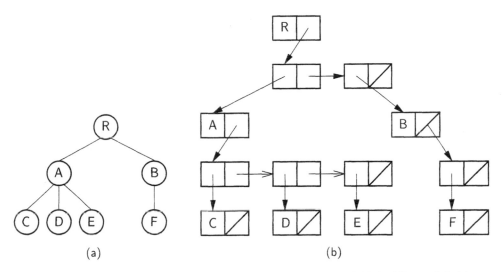

Figure 6.13 A dynamic general tree representation with linked lists of child pointers. (a) The general tree. (b) The tree representation.

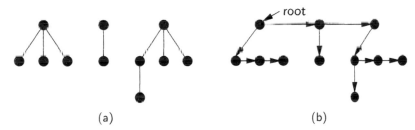

Figure 6.14 Converting from a forest of general trees to a single binary tree. Each node stores pointers to its left child and right sibling. The tree roots are assumed to be siblings for the purpose of converting.

Since each node of the general tree now contains a fixed number of pointers, and since each function of the general tree ADT can now be implemented efficiently, the dynamic "left child/right sibling" implementation is preferred to the other general tree implementations described in Sections 6.3.1 to 6.3.3.

6.4 *K*-ary Trees

K-ary trees are trees whose nodes have *K* children. Thus, a binary tree is a 2-ary tree. The PR quadtree discussed in Section 13.3 is an example of a 4-ary tree. Unlike general trees, *K*-ary tree nodes have a fixed number of children and so are relatively easy to implement. In general, *K*-ary trees

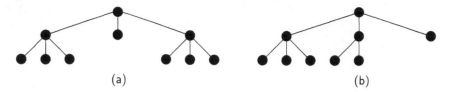

Figure 6.15 Full and complete 3-ary trees. (a) This tree is full (but not complete). (b) This tree is complete (but not full).

bear many similarities to binary trees, and similar implementations can be used for K-ary tree nodes. Note that as K becomes large, the potential number of **null** pointers grows, and the difference between the required size for internal nodes and leaf nodes increases. Thus, as K becomes larger, the advantage of choosing different implementations for the internal and leaf nodes increases.

Full and **complete** K-ary trees are analogous to full and complete binary trees, respectively. Figure 6.15 shows full and complete K-ary trees for $K = 3$.

Many of the properties of binary trees extend to K-ary trees. Equivalent theorems to those in Section 5.1.1 regarding the number of NULL pointers in a K-ary tree and the relationship between the number of leaves and the number of internal nodes in a K-ary tree can be derived. We can also store a complete K-ary tree in an array as shown in Section 5.3.3.

6.5   Sequential Tree Implementations

Next we consider a fundamentally different approach to implementing trees. The goal is to store a series of node values with the minimum information needed to reconstruct the tree structure. This approach, known as a **sequential** tree implementation, has the advantage of saving space because no pointers are stored. It has the disadvantage that accessing any node in the tree requires sequentially processing all nodes that appear before it in the node list. In other words, node access must start at the beginning of the node list, processing nodes in whatever order they are stored until the desired node is reached. Thus, one primary virtue of the other implementations discussed in this section is lost: efficient access (typically $\Theta(\log n)$ time) to arbitrary nodes in the tree. Sequential tree implementations are ideal for archiving trees on disk for later use since they save space, and the tree structure can easily be reconstructed as needed for later processing.

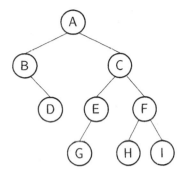

Figure 6.16 Sample binary tree for sequential tree implementation examples.

A sequential tree implementation stores the node values as they would be enumerated by a preorder traversal, along with sufficient information to describe the tree's shape. If the tree has restricted form, for example if it is a full binary tree, then less information about structure need be stored. A general tree, since it has the most flexible shape, requires the most additional shape information. There are many possible sequential tree implementation schemes. We will begin with methods appropriate to binary trees, then generalize to an implementation appropriate to a general tree structure.

Since every node of a binary tree is either a leaf or has two (possibly empty) children, we can take advantage of this fact to implicitly represent the structure of the tree. The most straightforward sequential tree implementation lists every node value as it would be encountered during a preorder traversal. Unfortunately, this is not enough information to know when a leaf node has been reached. However, we can treat all non-empty nodes as internal nodes with two (possibly empty) children. Only **null** values will be interpreted as leaf nodes. Such a node list provides enough information to recover the tree structure. For the binary tree of Figure 6.16, the list would be as follows (assuming that '/' stands for **null**):

$$AB/D//CEG///FH//I// \tag{6.1}$$

To reconstruct the tree structure from this node list, we begin by setting node A to be the root. A's left child will be node B. Node B's left child is a **null** pointer, so node D must be B's right child. Node D has two **null** children, so node C must be the right child of node A.

To illustrate the difficulty involved in using the sequential tree representation for processing, consider searching for the right child of the root node.

We must first move sequentially through the node list of the left subtree. Only at this point do we reach the value of the root's right child. Clearly the sequential representation is space efficient, but not time efficient.

Assume that each node value takes a constant amount of space (e.g., if the node value is a positive integer and `null` is indicated by the value zero). From the Full Binary Tree Theorem of Section 5.1.1, we know that the size of the node list will be about twice the number of nodes (i.e., the overhead fraction is $1/2$). The extra space is required by the `null` pointers. We should be able to store the node list more compactly. However, any sequential implementation must recognize when a leaf node has been reached (a leaf node indicates the end of a subtree). One way to do this is to explicitly list with each node whether it is an internal node or a leaf. If a node X is an internal node, then we know that its two children (which may be subtrees) immediately follow X in the node list. If X is a leaf node, then the next node in the list is the right child of some ancestor of X, not the right child of X. In particular, the next node will be the child of X's most recent ancestor that has not yet seen its right child. However, this assumes that each internal node does in fact have two children, in other words, that the tree is full. Empty children must be indicated in the node list explicitly. Assume that internal nodes are marked with a prime (') and that leaf nodes show no mark. Empty children of internal nodes are indicated by '/', but the (empty) children of leaf nodes are not represented at all. We can represent the tree of Figure 6.16 as follows:

$$A'B'/DC'E'G/F'HI \qquad\qquad (6.2)$$

This approach requires that an additional bit field be stored with each node. Storing n bits can be a considerable savings over storing n `null` values. Note that a full binary tree stores no `null` values with this implementation, and so requires less overhead.

Storing general trees by means of a sequential implementation requires that more explicit structural information be included with the node list. Not only must the general tree implementation indicate whether a node is leaf or internal, it must also indicate how many children the node has. Alternatively, the implementation can indicate when a node's child list has come to an end. The next example dispenses with marks for internal or leaf nodes. Instead it includes a special mark (the ")" symbol) to indicate the end of a child list. All leaf nodes are followed by a ")" symbol since they have no children. A leaf node that is also the last child for its parent would indicate this by two successive ")" symbols. For the tree of Figure 6.3, we get the list

$$RAC)D)E))BF)))\tag{6.3}$$

Note that F is followed by three ")" marks, since it is a leaf, the last node of B's rightmost subtree, and the last node of R's rightmost subtree.

6.6   Further Reading

The expression $\log^* n$ cited in Section 6.2 is closely related to the inverse of Ackermann's function. For more information about Ackermann's function and the cost of path compression, see Robert E. Tarjan's paper "On the efficiency of a good but not linear set merging algorithm" [Tar75]. The article "Data Structures and Algorithms for Disjoint Set Union Problems" by Galil and Italiano [GI91] covers many aspects of the equivalence class problem.

Applications of Spatial Data Structures by Hanan Samet [Sam90a] treats various implementations of tree structures in detail within the context of K-ary trees. Samet covers sequential implementations as well as the linked and array implementations such as described in this chapter and Chapter 5. While these books are ostensibly concerned with spatial data structures, many of the concepts treated are relevant to anyone who must implement tree structures.

6.7   Exercises

6.1 Write an algorithm to determine if two general trees are identical. Analyze your algorithm's running time.

6.2 Write an algorithm to determine if two general trees are identical when the ordering of the subtrees for a node is ignored. Analyze your algorithm's running time.

6.3 Write a postorder traversal function similar to the preorder traversal function named `print` given in Section 6.1.2.

6.4 Write a function that takes as input a general tree and returns the number of nodes in that tree. Write your function to use the `GTNode` interface of Figure 6.2.

6.5 Describe how to implement the weighted union rule efficiently. In particular, describe what information must be stored with each node and how this information is updated when two trees are merged.

6.6 Using the weighted union rule and path compression, show the array for the parent pointer implementation that results from the following series of equivalences on the set of integers from 0 through 15. Initially, each element in the set should be in a separate equivalence class. When two trees are of the same size, make the root with greater value be the child of the root with lesser value.

(0, 2) (1, 2) (3, 4) (3, 1) (3, 5) (9, 11) (12, 14) (3, 9) (4, 14) (6, 7) (8, 10) (8, 7) (7, 0) (10, 15) (10, 13)

6.7 Devise a series of equivalence statements for a collection of sixteen items that yields a tree of height 5 when both the weighted union rule and path compression are used. What is the total number of parent pointers followed to perform this series?

6.8 Analyze the fraction of overhead required by the "list of children" implementation, the "left child/right sibling" implementation, and the two linked implementations of Section 6.3.3. How do these implementations compare in space efficiency?

6.9 Using the general tree ADT of Figure 6.2, write a function that takes as input the root of a general tree and returns a binary tree generated by the conversion process illustrated by Figure 6.14.

6.10 Derive the formulae for computing the relatives of a non-empty complete K-ary tree node stored in the complete tree representation of Section 5.3.3.

6.11 Find the overhead fraction for a full K-ary tree implementation with space requirements as follows.

(a) All nodes store data, K child pointers, and a parent pointer. The data field requires four bytes and each pointer requires four bytes.

(b) Both leaf nodes and internal nodes store data and K child pointers. The data field requires sixteen bytes and each pointer requires four bytes.

(c) Both leaf nodes and internal nodes store data, all nodes store a parent pointer, and internal nodes store K child pointers. The data field requires eight bytes and each pointer requires four bytes.

(d) Only leaf nodes store data, only internal nodes store K child pointers. The data field requires four bytes and each pointer requires two bytes.

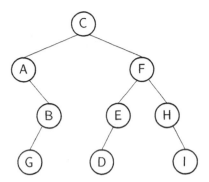

Figure 6.17 A sample tree for Exercise 6.13.

6.12 Use mathematical induction to prove that the number of leaves in a non-empty full K-ary tree is $(K-1)n+1$, where n is the number of internal nodes.

6.13 (a) Write out the sequential representation for Figure 6.17 using the coding illustrated by Equation 6.1.

(b) Write out the sequential representation for Figure 6.17 using the coding illustrated by Equation 6.2.

6.14 Draw the general tree represented by the following sequential representation for general trees illustrated by Equation 6.3.

$$XPC)Q)RV)M))))$$

6.15 (a) Write a function to decode the sequential representation for binary trees illustrated by Equation 6.1. The input should be the node list and the output should be a pointer to the root of the resulting binary tree.

(b) Write a function to decode the sequential representation for full binary trees illustrated by Equation 6.2. The input should be the node list and the output should be a pointer to the root of the resulting binary tree.

(c) Write a function to decode the sequential representation for general trees illustrated by Equation 6.3. The input should be the node list and the output should be a pointer to the root of the resulting general tree.

6.16 Devise a sequential representation for Huffman coding trees suitable for use as part of a file compression utility (see Project 5.1).

6.8   Projects

6.1 Write classes that implement the general tree interfaces of Figure 6.2 using the dynamic "left child/right sibling" representation described in Section 6.3.4.

6.2 Write classes that implement the general tree interfaces of Figure 6.2 using the linked general tree representation with child pointer arrays of Figure 6.12. Your implementation should support only fixed-size nodes that do not change their number of children once they are created. Then, reimplement these classes with the linked list of children representation of Figure 6.13. How do the two implementations compare in space and time efficiency and ease of implementation?

6.3 Write classes that implement the general tree interfaces of Figure 6.2 using the linked general tree representation with child pointer arrays of Figure 6.12. Your implementation must be able to support changes in the number of children for a node. When created, a node should be allocated only enough space to store its initial set of children. Whenever a new child is added to a node such that the array overflows, then allocate a new array from free store that can store twice as many children.

6.4 Implement a BST file archiver. Your program should take a BST created in main memory using the implementation of Figure 5.20 and write it out to disk using one of the sequential representations of Section 6.5. It should also be able to read in disk files using your sequential representation and create the equivalent main memory representation.

6.5 Use the UNION/FIND algorithm to implement a solution to the following problem. Given a set of points represented by their xy-coordinates, assign the points to clusters. Any two points are defined to be in the same cluster if they are within a specified distance d of each other. For the purpose of this problem, clustering is an equivalence relationship. In other words, points A, B, and C are defined to be in the same cluster if the distance between A and B is less than d and the distance between A and C is also less than d, even if the distance between B and C is greater than d. To solve the problem, compute the distance between each pair of points, using the equivalence processing algorithm to merge clusters whenever two points are within the specified distance. What is the asymptotic complexity of this algorithm? Where is the bottleneck in processing?

7

Graphs

This chapter introduces the graph data structure. A graph is defined by two sets. The first is a set of nodes, which are more commonly called **vertices** in graph terminology. The second is a set of connections linking pairs of vertices, called **edges**. In general, graphs allow an edge to connect any pair of vertices. Trees and lists can be viewed as restricted forms of graphs, so graphs can be viewed as the most general of all data structures.

Graphs are widely used to model both real-world systems and abstract problems. Graphs are regularly used in hundreds of applications. Here is a brief sampling of the types of problems that graphs are often applied to:

1. Modeling connectivity in computer and communications networks.

2. Representing a map as a set of locations with distances between locations; used to compute shortest routes between locations.

3. Modeling flow capacities in transportation networks.

4. Finding a path from a starting condition to a goal condition; for example, in artificial intelligence problem solving.

5. Modeling computer algorithms, showing transitions from one program state to another.

6. Finding an acceptable order for finishing subtasks in a complex activity, such as constructing large buildings.

7. Modeling relationships in families, business, or military organizations, and scientific taxonomies.

This chapter provides a sampling of graph algorithms used in such applications. Section 7.1 begins with some basic graph terminology and then defines two fundamental representations for graphs, the adjacency matrix and adjacency list. Section 7.2 presents a graph ADT and simple implementations based on the adjacency matrix and adjacency list. Section 7.3 presents the two most commonly used graph traversal algorithms, called depth-first and breadth-first search, with application to topological sorting. Section 7.4 presents algorithms for solving some problems related to finding shortest routes in a graph. Finally, Section 7.5 presents algorithms for finding the minimum-cost spanning tree, useful for determining lowest-cost connectivity in a network. Besides being useful and interesting in their own right, these algorithms illustrate the use of many of the data structures presented in earlier chapters.

7.1 Terminology and Representations

A graph $\mathbf{G} = (\mathbf{V}, \mathbf{E})$ consists of a set of vertices $\mathbf{V}$ and a set of edges $\mathbf{E}$, such that each edge in $\mathbf{E}$ is a connection between a pair of vertices in $\mathbf{V}$. The number of vertices is written $|\mathbf{V}|$, and the number of edges is written $|\mathbf{E}|$. $|\mathbf{E}|$ can range from zero to a maximum of $\Theta(|\mathbf{V}|^2)$. A graph with relatively few edges is called **sparse**, while a graph with many edges is called **dense**. A graph containing all possible edges is said to be **complete**.

A graph whose edges are directed from one vertex to another (as in Figure 7.1(b)) is called a **directed graph** or **digraph**. A graph whose edges are not directed is called an **undirected graph** (as in Figure 7.1(a)). A graph with labels associated with its vertices (as in Figure 7.1(c)) is called a **labeled graph**. Two vertices are **adjacent** if they are joined by an edge. Such vertices are also called **neighbors**. An edge connecting vertices u and v is written (u, v). Such an edge is said to be **incident** on vertices u and v. Associated with each edge may be a cost or **weight**. Graphs whose edges have weights (as in Figure 7.1(c)) are said to be **weighted**.

A sequence of vertices $v_1, v_2, ..., v_n$ forms a **path** of length $n - 1$ if there exist edges from v_i to v_{i+1} for $1 \leq i < n$. A path is **simple** if all vertices on the path are distinct. The **length** of a path is the number of edges it contains. A **cycle** is a path of length 3 or more that connects some vertex v_1 to itself. A cycle is **simple** if the path is simple, except for the first and last vertices being the same. Figure 7.1 illustrates the graph terminology defined here.

A **subgraph S** is formed from graph $\mathbf{G}$ by selecting a subset $\mathbf{V}_s$ of $\mathbf{G}$'s vertices and some edges of $\mathbf{G}$, both of whose vertices are in $\mathbf{V}_s$.

An undirected graph is **connected** if there is at least one path from any vertex to any other. The maximally connected subgraphs of an undirected

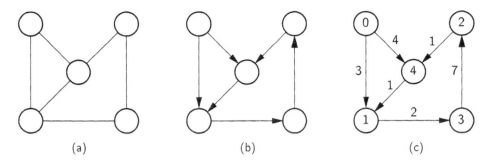

Figure 7.1 Examples of graphs and terminology. (a) A graph. (b) A directed graph (digraph). (c) A labeled (directed) graph with weights associated with the edges. In this example, there is a simple path from vertex 0 to vertex 3 containing vertices 0, 1, and 3. Vertices 0, 1, 3, 2, 4, and 1 also form a path, but not a simple path since vertex 1 appears twice. Vertices 1, 3, 2, 4, and 1 form a simple cycle.

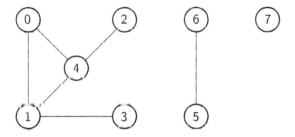

Figure 7.2 An undirected graph with three connected components. Vertices 0, 1, 2, 3, and 4 form one connected component. Vertices 5 and 6 form a second connected component. Vertex 7 by itself forms a third connected component.

graph are called **connected components**. For example, Figure 7.2 shows an undirected graph with three connected components.

A graph without cycles is called **acyclic**. Thus, a directed graph without cycles is called a **directed acyclic graph** or DAG.

A **free tree** is a connected, undirected graph with no simple cycles. Equivalently, a free tree is connected and has $|V| - 1$ edges.

There are two commonly used methods for representing graphs. The **adjacency matrix** is illustrated by Figure 7.3(b). The adjacency matrix for a graph is a $|V| \times |V|$ array. Assume that $|V| = n$ and that the vertices are labeled from v_0 through v_{n-1}. Row i of the adjacency matrix contains entries for vertex v_i. Column j in row i is marked if there is an edge from v_i to v_j, and is not marked otherwise. Thus, the adjacency matrix requires one

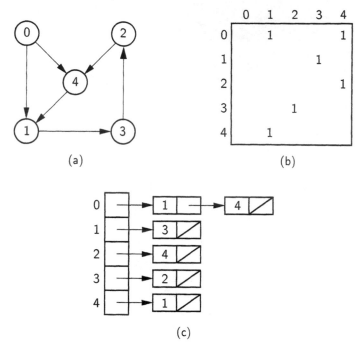

Figure 7.3 Two graph representations. (a) A directed graph. (b) The adjacency matrix for the graph of (a). (c) The adjacency list for the graph of (a).

bit at each position. Alternatively, if we wish to associate a number with each edge, such as the weight or distance between two vertices, then each matrix position must be large enough to store that number. In either case, the space requirements for the adjacency matrix are $\Theta(|\mathbf{V}|^2)$.

The second common representation for graphs is the **adjacency list**, illustrated by Figure 7.3(c). The adjacency list is an array of linked lists. The array is $|\mathbf{V}|$ items long, with position i storing a pointer to the linked list of edges for vertex v_i. This linked list stores the vertices that are adjacent to vertex v_i. The adjacency list is therefore a generalization of the "list of children" representation for trees described in Section 6.3.1.

The storage requirements for the adjacency list depend on both the number of edges and the number of vertices in the graph. There must be an array entry for each vertex (even if the vertex is not adjacent to any other vertex, and thus has no elements on its linked list), and each edge must appear on one of the lists. Thus, the cost is $\Theta(|\mathbf{V}| + |\mathbf{E}|)$.

Both the adjacency matrix and the adjacency list can be used to store directed or undirected graphs. Each edge of an undirected graph connecting

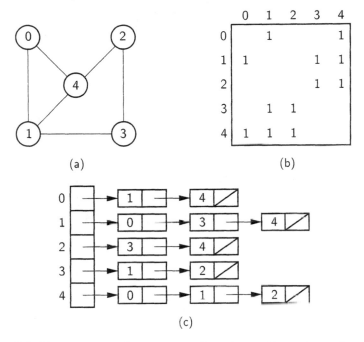

Figure 7.4 Using the graph representations for undirected graphs. (a) An undirected graph. (b) The adjacency matrix for the graph of (a). (c) The adjacency list for the graph of (a).

vertices u and v is represented by two directed edges: one from u to v and one from v to u. Figure 7.4 illustrates the use of the adjacency matrix and the adjacency list for undirected graphs.

Which graph representation is more space efficient depends on the number of edges in the graph. The adjacency list stores information only for those edges that actually appear in the graph, while the adjacency matrix requires space for each potential edge, whether it exists or not. However, the adjacency matrix requires no overhead for pointers, which can be a substantial cost, especially if the only information stored for an edge is one bit to indicate its existence. As the graph becomes denser, the adjacency matrix becomes relatively more space efficient. Sparse graphs are likely to have their adjacency list representation be more space efficient.

The adjacency matrix often leads to a higher asymptotic cost for an algorithm than would be required if the adjacency list were used. The reason is that it is common for a graph algorithm to visit each neighbor of each vertex. Using the adjacency list, only the actual edges connecting a vertex to its neighbors are examined. However, the adjacency matrix must look at

```
interface Graph {                        // Graph class ADT
  public int n();                        // Number of vertices
  public int e();                        // Number of edges
  public Edge first(int v);              // Get first edge for vertex
  public Edge next(Edge w);              // Get next edge for a vertex
  public boolean isEdge(Edge w);         // True if this is an edge
  public boolean isEdge(int i, int j);   // True if this is an edge
  public int v1(Edge w);                 // Where edge came from
  public int v2(Edge w);                 // Where edge goes to
  public void setEdge(int i, int j, int weight); // Set edge weight
  public void setEdge(Edge w, int weight);       // Set edge weight
  public void delEdge(Edge w);           // Delete edge w
  public void delEdge(int i, int j);     // Delete edge (i, j)
  public int weight(int i, int j);       // Return weight of edge
  public int weight(Edge w);             // Return weight of edge
  public void setMark(int v, int val);   // Set Mark for v
  public int getMark(int v);             // Get Mark for v
} // interface Graph
```

Figure 7.5 A graph ADT.

each of its $|\mathbf{V}|$ potential edges, yielding a total cost of $\Theta(|\mathbf{V}^2|)$ time when the algorithm might otherwise require only $\Theta(|\mathbf{V}| + |\mathbf{E}|)$ time. This is a considerable disadvantage when the graph is sparse.

7.2   Graph Implementations

We next turn to the problem of implementing a graph class. Figure 7.5 shows the Graph interface, with a listing of the key functions. We will assume throughout this chapter that an application using a graph of n vertices refers to those vertices by index values in the range 0 to $n - 1$.

Besides the constructor and destructor, class Graph has methods to return the number of vertices and edges (functions n and e, respectively). Since a common activity in graph algorithms is to visit edges extending from a given vertex, three methods are provided that work in a manner similar to list access functions. Function first returns the first edge for a given vertex. Function next returns the next edge for a vertex. Function isEdge is used to determine if a given edge exists in the graph. This can be used to determine when processing of a vertex's edge list is complete, since next will return null when it has reached the last edge. Given an edge, functions v1 and v2 return the vertex the edge comes from and the vertex the edge goes to, respectively. Two versions of the weight function are provided. The first returns the weight of a given edge. The second returns the weight of an edge specified by its vertices. If no such edge exists, the weight is defined to be INFINITY. Functions setEdge and delEdge set the weight of an edge and remove an edge from the graph, respectively. Two versions of each are provided, one to specify the edge by an Edge object, and one to specify an edge by its vertices. We will assume that the weight of an edge may not be set to zero. Functions getMark and setMark get and set a requested value in the Mark array (described below).

As indicated by the parameter types for the ADT functions, vertices are described by an index value. In other words, there is a Vertex 0, Vertex 1, and so on. We can assume that a graph application stores any additional information of interest about a given vertex elsewhere, such as a name or application-dependent value.

Edges are treated as special objects by the ADT. An Edge object is expected to have certain properties of its own, which will be used by the graph implementations. In particular, given an Edge, we will want access to the two vertices that it connects. Here is an interface for the Edge:

```
interface Edge {   // Interface for graph edges
  public int v1(); // Return the vertex it comes from
  public int v2(); // Return the vertex it goes to
} // interface Edge
```

Given our definition for graph and edge ADTs, it is reasonably straightforward to implement them using either the adjacency list or adjacency matrix. These implementations do not consider the problem of how the graph is actually created. The user of an implementation is expected to add functionality for this purpose, perhaps reading the graph description from a file. The graph can be built up by using the setEdge functions provided by the ADT.

Figure 7.6 shows an implementation for the adjacency matrix graph representation. Array Mark is used by the graph algorithms presented later in this chapter to track whether a given vertex has been visited. Function getMark and setMark access and change its contents, respectively. The edge matrix is implemented as an integer array of size $n \times n$ for a graph of n vertices. Position (i, j) in the matrix stores the weight for edge (i, j) if it exists. A weight of zero for edge (i, j) is used to indicate that no edge connects vertices i and j. Class Edgem is used to implement the Edge interface. It stores the vertices that the edge connects.

Given a vertex v, function first locates the position in matrix of the first edge (if any) of v by beginning with edge $(v, 0)$ and scanning through row v until an edge is found. If no edge is incident on v, then first returns

```
// Edge class for Adjacency Matrix graph representation
class Edgem implements Edge {
  private int vert1, vert2; // The vertex indices

  public Edgem(int vt1, int vt2) { vert1 = vt1; vert2 = vt2; }
  public int v1() { return vert1; }
  public int v2() { return vert2; }
} // class Edgem

class Graphm implements Graph { // Graph: Adjacency matrix
  private int[][] matrix;             // The edge matrix
  private int numEdge;                // Number of edges
  public int[] Mark;                  // The mark array

  public Graphm(int n) {              // Constructor
    Mark = new int[n];
    matrix = new int[n][n];
    numEdge = 0;
  }

  public int n() { return Mark.length; } // Number of vertices

  public int e() { return numEdge; }     // Number of edges

  public Edge first(int v) { // Get the first edge for a vertex
    for (int i=0; i<Mark.length; i++)
      if (matrix[v][i] != 0)
        return new Edgem(v, i);
    return null;  // No edge for this vertex
  }

  public Edge next(Edge w) { // Get next edge for a vertex
    if (w == null) return null;
    for (int i=w.v2()+1; i<Mark.length; i++)
      if (matrix[w.v1()][i] != 0)
        return new Edgem(w.v1(), i);
    return null;  // No next edge;
  }

  public boolean isEdge(Edge w) { // True if this is an edge
    if (w == null) return false;
    else return matrix[w.v1()][w.v2()] != 0;
  }

  public boolean isEdge(int i, int j) // True if this is an edge
    { return matrix[i][j] != 0; }
```

Figure 7.6 Adjacency matrix implementations for edges and graphs.

```
public int v1(Edge w) { return w.v1(); } // Where edge comes from

public int v2(Edge w) { return w.v2(); } // Where edge goes to

public void setEdge(int i, int j, int wt) { // Set edge weight
  Assert.notFalse(wt!=0, "Cannot set weight to 0");
  if (matrix[i][j] == 0) numEdge++;
  matrix[i][j] = wt;
}

public void setEdge(Edge w, int weight) // Set edge weight
  { if (w != null) setEdge(w.v1(), w.v2(), weight); }

public void delEdge(Edge w) {        // Delete edge w
  if (w != null)
    if (matrix[w.v1()][w.v2()] != 0) {
      matrix[w.v1()][w.v2()] = 0;
      numEdge--;
    }
}

public void delEdge(int i, int j) { // Delete edge (i, j)
  if (matrix[i][j] != 0) {
    matrix[i][j] = 0;
    numEdge--;
  }
}

public int weight(int i, int j) {  // Return weight of edge
  if (matrix[i][j] == 0) return Integer.MAX_VALUE;
  else return matrix[i][j];
}

public int weight(Edge w) {         // Return weight of edge
  Assert.notNull(w, "Can't take weight of null edge");
  if (matrix[w.v1()][w.v2()] == 0) return Integer.MAX_VALUE;
  else return matrix[w.v1()][w.v2()];
}

public void setMark(int v, int val) { Mark[v] = val; } // Set Mark

public int getMark(int v) { return Mark[v]; }          // Get Mark
} // class Graphm
```

Figure 7.6 (continued)

null. Function **next** locates the edge following edge (i, j) (if any) by continuing down the row of vertex i starting at position $j + 1$, looking for an edge. Function **isEdge** indicates whether a given edge exists in the graph. Function **getEdge** and **delEdge** allow the user to set the weight of an edge or delete an edge, respectively. Function **weight** returns the weight associated with a specified edge.

Figure 7.7 shows implementations for the **Edgel** and **Graphl** classes using the adjacency list. The **Graphl** class makes use of an extension on the standard **List** class from Chapter 4. This extension provides functions that allow access to the "current" link, either to get it or set it. This is helpful so that an **Edgel** object can gain direct access to the relevant edge in the adjacency list. Otherwise, access via an **Edge** object would require traversing a vertex's adjacency list from the beginning to find the adjacency list node corresponding to a specific edge. Here is the implementation of the **GraphList** extension to the linked list class **LList** of Figure 4.5.

```
// Linked list for graphs: Provides access to curr
class GraphList extends LList {
  public Link currLink() { return curr; }
  public void setCurr(Link who) { curr = who; }
} // class GraphList
```

Class **Edgel** stores the indices of the two vertices it connects, as well as a pointer directly to the corresponding **Link** node in the adjacency list. Implementation for **Graphl** member functions is straightforward once we have implemented function **isEdge**. **isEdge** must determine if a given edge exists in the graph. The edge can be described either by an **Edge** object, or by its vertices. Doing so has the side effect of setting the "current" pointer of the appropriate vertex's adjacency list. Thus, a function such as **setEdge** need merely verify that an edge exists, and then either change the value of the current edge in the appropriate vertex list, or insert a new edge at that point. The remaining functions work in a similar manner. The version of function **isEdge** that takes two vertices **v1** and **v2** as input is straightforward: Work down the adjacency list of **v1** until **v2** is found. The version of **isEdge** that takes an **Edge** as input will verify that the adjacency list node stored with the **Edge** object matches the vertices that it stores.

7.3 Graph Traversals

Often it is useful to visit the vertices of a graph in some specific order based on the graph's topology. This is known as a **graph traversal**, and is similar

```
// Edge class for Adjacency List graph representation
class Edgel implements Edge {
  private int vert1, vert2;   // Indices of v1, v2
  private Link itself; // Pointer to node in the adjacency list

  public Edgel(int vt1, int vt2, Link it) // Constructor
    { vert1 = vt1;  vert2 = vt2;  itself = it; }

  public int v1() { return vert1; }
  public int v2() { return vert2; }
  Link theLink() { return itself; } // Access into adjacency list
} // class Edgel


class Graphl implements Graph {          // Graph: Adjacency list
  private GraphList[] vertex;             // The vertex list
  private int numEdge;                    // Number of edges
  public int[] Mark;                      // The mark array

  public Graphl(int n) {                  // Constructor
    Mark = new int[n],
    vertex = new GraphList[n];
    for (int i=0; i<n; i++)
      vertex[i] = new GraphList();
    numEdge = 0;
  }

  public int n() { return Mark.length; } // Number of vertices

  public int e() { return numEdge; }     // Number of edges

  public Edge first(int v) { // Get the first edge for a vertex
    vertex[v].setFirst();
    if (vertex[v].currValue() == null) return null;
    return new Edgel(v, ((int[])vertex[v].currValue())[0],
                    vertex[v].currLink());
  }

  public boolean isEdge(Edge e) { // True if this is an edge
    if (e == null) return false;
    vertex[e.v1()].setCurr(((Edgel)e).theLink());
    if (!vertex[e.v1()].isInList()) return false;
    return ((int[])vertex[e.v1()].currValue())[0] == e.v2();
  }

  public int v1(Edge e) { return e.v1(); } // Where edge comes from

  public int v2(Edge e) { return e.v2(); } // Where edge goes to
```

Figure 7.7 Adjacency list implementations for edges and graphs.

```
   public boolean isEdge(int i, int j) { // True if this is an edge
     GraphList temp = vertex[i];
     for (temp.setFirst(); ((temp.currValue() != null) &&
            (((int[])temp.currValue())[0] < j)); temp.next());
     return (temp.currValue() != null) &&
            (((int[])temp.currValue())[0] == j);
   }

   public Edge next(Edge e) { // Get next edge for a vertex
     vertex[e.v1()].setCurr(((Edgel)e).theLink());
     vertex[e.v1()].next();
     if (vertex[e.v1()].currValue() == null) return null;
     return new Edgel(e.v1(), ((int[])vertex[e.v1()].currValue())[0],
                      vertex[e.v1()].currLink());
   }

   public void setEdge(int i, int j, int weight) { // Set edge weight
     Assert.notFalse(weight!=0, "Cannot set weight to 0");
     int[] currEdge = { j, weight };
     if (isEdge(i, j))              // Edge already exists in graph
       vertex[i].setValue(currEdge);
     else {                         // Add new edge to graph
       vertex[i].insert(currEdge);
       numEdge++;
     }
   }

   public void setEdge(Edge w, int weight) // Set edge weight
     { if (w != null) setEdge(w.v1(), w.v2(), weight); }

   public void delEdge(int i, int j)  // Delete edge
     { if (isEdge(i, j)) { vertex[i].remove(); numEdge--; } }

   public void delEdge(Edge w)        // Delete edge
     { if (w != null) delEdge(w.v1(), w.v2()); }

   public int weight(int i, int j) {  // Return weight of edge
     if (isEdge(i, j)) return ((int[])vertex[i].currValue())[1];
     else return Integer.MAX_VALUE;
   }

   public int weight(Edge e) {     // Return weight of edge
     if (isEdge(e)) return ((int[])vertex[e.v1()].currValue())[1];
     else return Integer.MAX_VALUE;
   }

   public void setMark(int v, int val) { Mark[v] = val; } // Set Mark

   public int getMark(int v) { return Mark[v]; }          // Get Mark
} // class Graphl
```

Figure 7.7 (continued)

in concept to a tree traversal. Recall that tree traversals visit every node exactly once, in some specified order such as preorder or postorder. In a similar manner, standard graph traversal orders exist, each appropriate for solving certain problems. In particular, many problems in artificial intelligence programming are modeled using graphs. The problem domain may consist of a large collection of states, with connections between various pairs of states. Solving the problem may require getting from a specified start state to a specified goal state by moving between states only through the connections. Typically, the start and goal states are not directly connected.

Graph traversal algorithms typically begin with a start vertex, and attempt to visit the remaining vertices from there. Graph traversals must deal with a number of troublesome cases. First, it may not be possible to reach all vertices from the start vertex. This occurs when the graph is not connected. Second, the graph may contain cycles, and we must make sure that cycles do not cause the algorithm to go into an infinite loop.

Graph traversal algorithms generally get around both of these problems by maintaining a **mark bit** for each vertex on the graph. At the beginning of the algorithm, the mark bit for all vertices is cleared. The mark bit for a vertex is set when the vertex is visited during the traversal. If a marked vertex is encountered during traversal, it is not visited a second time. This keeps the program from going into an infinite loop due when it encounters a cycle.

Once the traversal algorithm completes, we can check to see if all vertices have been processed by checking the mark bit array. If not all vertices are marked, we can continue the traversal from another unmarked vertex. Note that this process works regardless of whether the graph is directed or undirected. To ensure visiting all vertices, `graphTraverse` could be called as follows on a graph `G`:

```
void graphTraverse(Graph G) {
  for (v=0; v<G.n(); v++)
    G.setMark(v, UNVISITED);  // Initialize mark bits
  for (v=0; v<G.n(); v++)
    if (G.getMark(v) == UNVISITED)
      doTraverse(G, v);
}
```

Function "doTraverse" would correspond to one of the graph traversals described in the following subsections.

7.3.1 Depth-First Search

The first method of organized graph traversal is called **depth-first search** (DFS). Whenever a vertex v is visited during the search, recursively visit all of its unvisited neighbors. Alternatively, add all edges leading out of v to a stack. The next vertex to be visited is determined by popping the stack and following that edge. The effect is to follow one branch through the graph to its conclusion, then back up and follow another branch, and so on. The process of performing DFS creates a **depth-first search tree**. This tree is composed of the edges that were followed to any new (unvisited) vertex during the traversal, and leaves out the edges that lead to already visited vertices. DFS can be applied to directed or undirected graphs. Here is an implementation for the DFS algorithm:

```
static void DFS(Graph G, int v) { // Depth first search
  PreVisit(G, v);                 // Take appropriate action
  G.setMark(v, VISITED);
  for (Edge w = G.first(v); G.isEdge(w); w = G.next(w))
    if (G.getMark(G.v2(w)) == UNVISITED)
      DFS(G, G.v2(w));
  PostVisit(G, v);                // Take appropriate action
}
```

This implementation has calls to functions `PreVisit` and `PostVisit`. These functions specify what activity should take place during the search. Just as a preorder tree traversal requires action before the subtrees are visited, some graph traversals require that a vertex be processed before ones further along in the DFS. Alternatively, some applications require activity *after* the remaining vertices are processed; hence the call to function `PostVisit`.

Figure 7.8 shows a graph and the corresponding depth-first search tree. Figure 7.9 illustrates the DFS process for the graph of Figure 7.8(a).

DFS processes each edge once in a directed graph. In an undirected graph, DFS processes each edge from both directions. Each vertex must be visited, so the total cost is $\Theta(|\mathbf{V}| + |\mathbf{E}|)$.

7.3.2 Breadth-First Search

Our second graph traversal algorithm is known as a **breadth-first search** (BFS). BFS examines all vertices connected to the start vertex before visiting vertices further away. BFS is implemented similarly to DFS, except that a queue replaces the recursion stack. Note that if the graph is a tree and the

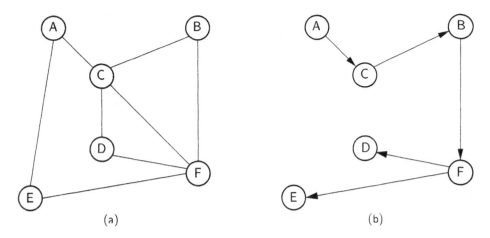

Figure 7.8 (a) A graph. (b) The depth-first search tree for the graph when starting at vertex A.

start vertex is at the root, BFS is equivalent to visiting vertices level by level from top to bottom. Here is an implementation for the BFS algorithm:

```
static void BFS(Graph G, int start) { // Breadth first search
  Queue Q = new AQueue(G.n());           // Use a Queue
  Q.enqueue(new Integer(start));
  G.setMark(start, VISITED);
  while (!Q.isEmpty()) {                  // Process each vertex on Q
    int v = ((Integer)Q.dequeue()).intValue();
    PreVisit(G, v);               // Take appropriate action
    for (Edge w = G.first(v); G.isEdge(w); w = G.next(w))
      if (G.getMark(G.v2(w)) == UNVISITED) { // Put neighbors on Q
        G.setMark(G.v2(w), VISITED);
        Q.enqueue(new Integer(G.v2(w)));
      }
    PostVisit(G, v);              // Take appropriate action
  }
}
```

Figure 7.10 shows a graph and the corresponding breadth-first search tree. Figure 7.11 illustrates the BFS process for the graph of Figure 7.10(a).

7.3.3 Topological Sort

Assume that we need to schedule a series of tasks such as classes or jobs, where we cannot start one task until after its prerequisites are completed. We wish to organize the tasks into a linear order that allows us to complete them one at a time without violating any prerequisites. We can model the problem using a DAG. The graph is directed because one task is a prerequisite of

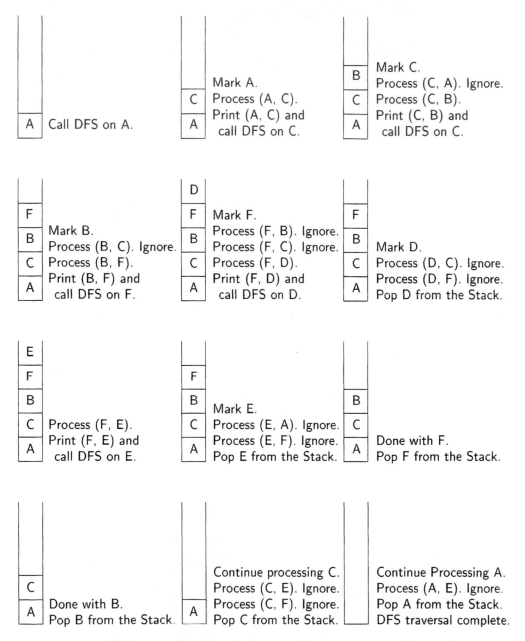

Figure 7.9 A detailed illustration of the DFS process for the graph of Figure 7.8(a) starting at vertex *A*. The steps leading to each change in the recursion stack are described.

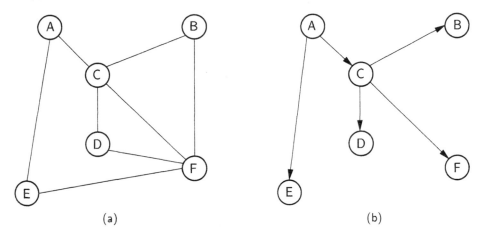

(a)   (b)

Figure 7.10 (a) A graph. (b) The breadth-first search tree for the graph
when starting at vertex A.

another – the vertices have a directed relationship. It is acyclic because
a cycle would indicate a conflicting series of prerequisites that could not
be completed without violating at least one prerequisite. The process of
laying out the vertices of a DAG in a linear order to meet the prerequisite
rules is called a **topological sort**. Figure 7.12 illustrates the problem. An
acceptable topological sort for this example is $J1$, $J2$, $J3$, $J4$, $J5$, $J6$, $J7$.

A topological sort may be found by performing a DFS on the graph.
When a vertex is visited, no action is taken (i.e., function `PreVisit` does
nothing). When the recursion pops back to that vertex, function `PostVisit`
prints the vertex. This yields a topological sort in reverse order. It does not
matter where the sort starts, so long as all vertices are visited in the end.
Here is an implementation for the algorithm:

```
static void topsort(Graph G) { // Topological sort: recursive
  for (int i=0; i<G.n(); i++)  // Initialize Mark array
    G.setMark(i, UNVISITED);
  for (int i=0; i<G.n(); i++)  // Process all vertices
    if (G.getMark(i) == UNVISITED)
      tophelp(G, i);           // Call recursive helper function
}

static void tophelp(Graph G, int v) { // Topsort helper function
  G.setMark(v, VISITED);
  for (Edge w = G.first(v); G.isEdge(w); w = G.next(w))
    if (G.getMark(G.v2(w)) == UNVISITED)
      tophelp(G, G.v2(w));
  printout(v);                         // PostVisit for Vertex v
}
```

A			

Initial call to BFS on A.
Mark A and put on the queue.

C	E		

Dequeue A.
Process (A, C).
Mark and enqueue C. Print (A, C).
Process (A, E).
Mark and enqueue E. Print(A, E).

E	B	D	F

Dequeue C.
Process (C, A). Ignore.
Process (C, B).
Mark and enqueue B. Print (C, B).
Process (C, D).
Mark and enqueue D. Print (C, D).
Process (C, F).
Mark and enqueue F. Print (C, F).

B	D	F	

Dequeue E.
Process (E, A). Ignore.
Process (E, F). Ignore.

D	F		

Dequeue B.
Process (B, C). Ignore.
Process (B, F). Ignore.

F			

Dequeue D.
Process (D, C). Ignore.
Process (D, F). Ignore.

Dequeue F.
Process (F, B). Ignore.
Process (F, C). Ignore.
Process (F, D). Ignore.
BFS is complete.

Figure 7.11 A detailed illustration of the BFS process for the graph of Figure 7.10(a) starting at vertex A. The steps leading to each change in the queue are described.

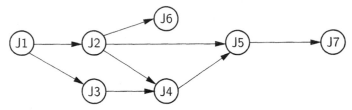

Figure 7.12 An example graph for topological sort. Seven tasks have dependencies as shown by the directed graph.

Using this algorithm starting at *J1* and visiting adjacent neighbors in lexicographic order, vertices of the graph in Figure 7.12 are printed out in the order *J7, J5, J4, J6, J2, J3, J1*. When reversed, this yields the legal topological sort *J1, J3, J2, J6, J4, J5, J7*.

We can also implement topological sort using a queue instead of recursion. To do so, we first visit all of the edges, counting the number of edges that lead to each vertex (i.e., count the number of prerequisites for each vertex). All vertices with no prerequisites are placed on the queue. We then begin processing the queue. Each vertex taken off of the queue is printed, and all neighbors have their counts decremented by one. Any neighbor whose count is now zero is placed on the queue. If the queue becomes empty without printing all of the vertices, then the graph contains a cycle (i.e., there is no possible ordering for the tasks that does not violate some prerequisite). The printed order for the vertices of the graph in Figure 7.12 using the queue version of topological sort is *J1, J2, J3, J6, J4, J5, J7*. Figure 7.13 shows an implementation for the queue-based topological sort algorithm.

7.4   Shortest-Paths Problems

On a road map, a road connecting two towns is typically labeled with its distance. We can model a road network as a directed graph whose edges are labeled with real numbers. The numbers represent the distance (or other cost metric, such as travel time) between two vertices. These labels may be called **weights**, **costs**, or **distances**, depending on the application. Given such a graph, a typical problem is to find the total length of the shortest path between two specified vertices. This is a nontrivial problem, since the shortest path may not be along the edge (if any) connecting two vertices, but rather may be along a path involving one or more intermediate vertices. For example, in Figure 7.14, the cost of the path from *A* to *B* to *D* is 15. The cost of the edge directly from *A* to *D* is 20. The cost of the path from

```
static void topsort(Graph G) { // Topological sort: Queue
  Queue Q = new AQueue(G.n());
  int[] Count = new int[G.n()];
  int v;
  for (v=0; v<G.n(); v++) Count[v] = 0; // Initialize
  for (v=0; v<G.n(); v++)         // Process every edge
    for (Edge w = G.first(v); G.isEdge(w); w = G.next(w))
      Count[G.v2(w)]++;           // Add to v2's prereq count
  for (v=0; v<G.n(); v++)         // Initialize Queue
    if (Count[v] == 0)           // Vertex has no prerequisites
      Q.enqueue(new Integer(v));
  while (!Q.isEmpty()) {          // Process the vertices
    v = ((Integer)Q.dequeue()).intValue();
    printout(v);                  // PreVisit for Vertex V
    for (Edge w = G.first(v); G.isEdge(w); w = G.next(w)) {
      Count[G.v2(w)]--;           // One less prerequisite
      if (Count[G.v2(w)] == 0) // This vertex is now free
        Q.enqueue(new Integer(G.v2(w)));
    }
  }
}
```

Figure 7.13 A queue-based topological sort algorithm.

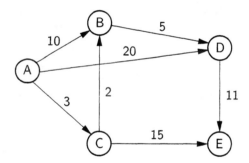

Figure 7.14 Example graph for shortest-path definitions.

A to C to B to D is 10. Thus, the shortest path from A to D is 10 (not along the edge connecting A to D). We use the notation $d(A, D) = 10$ to indicate that the shortest distance from A to D is 10. In Figure 7.14, there is no path from E to B, so we set $d(E, B) = \infty$. We define $w(A, D) = 20$ to be the weight of edge (A, D), that is, the weight of the direct connection from A to D. Since there is no edge from E to B, $w(E, B) = \infty$. Note that $w(D, A) = \infty$ since the graph of Figure 7.14 is directed. We assume that all weights are positive.

7.4.1   Single-Source Shortest Paths

The first shortest-paths problem we will study is called the **single-source shortest paths** problem. Given a vertex s in a graph **G**, find a shortest path from s to every other vertex in **G**. We might want only the shortest path between vertices s and t. Unfortunately, there is no better algorithm (in the worst case) for finding the shortest path to a single vertex than to find shortest paths to all vertices.

The algorithm described here will only compute the distance to every such vertex, rather than recording the actual path. Recording the path requires some modifications to the algorithm that are left as an exercise.

One instance of the single-source shortest-paths problem occurs in computer networking. The problem is to find the cheapest way for one computer to broadcast a message to all other computers on the network. The network is modeled by a graph with edge weights indicating time or cost to send a message to a neighboring computer.

For unweighted graphs (or where all edges have the same cost), the single-source shortest paths can be found using a simple breadth-first search. When weights are added, this method will not work.

One approach to solving this problem when the edges have differing weights might be to process the vertices in a fixed order. Label the vertices v_0 to v_{n-1}, with $s = v_0$. When processing vertex v_1, we take the edge connecting v_0 and v_1. When processing v_2, we consider the shortest distance from v_0 and compare that to the shortest distance from v_0 to v_1 to v_2. When processing vertex v_i, we consider the shortest paths for vertices v_0 through v_{i-1} that has already been processed. Unfortunately, the true shortest path to v_i might go through vertex v_j for $j > i$. Such a path will not be considered by this algorithm. However, the problem would not occur if we process the vertices in order of distance from s. Assume that we have processed in order of distance the first $i - 1$ vertices that are closest to s; call this set of vertices **S**. We are now about to process the ith closest vertex; call it x. A shortest path from s to x must have its next-to-last vertex in **S**. Thus,

$$\mathrm{d}(s, x) = \min_{u \in \mathbf{S}}(\mathrm{d}(s, u) + \mathrm{w}(u, x)).$$

In other words, the shortest path from s to x is the minimum over all paths that go from s to u, then have an edge from u to x, where u is a vertex in **S**.

This solution is usually referred to as Dijkstra's algorithm. It works by maintaining a distance estimate $\mathrm{D}(x)$ for all vertices in **V**. Vertices are processed in order of distance from s. Whenever a vertex v is processed, $\mathrm{D}(x)$ is

```
// Compute shortest path distances from s, store them in D
static void Dijkstra(Graph G, int s, int[] D) {
  for (int i=0; i<G.n(); i++)        // Initialize
    D[i] = Integer.MAX_VALUE;
  D[s] = 0;
  for (int i=0; i<G.n(); i++) {      // Process the vertices
    int v = minVertex(G, D);         // Find the next-closest vertex
    G.setMark(v, VISITED);
    if (D[v] == Integer.MAX_VALUE) return; // Unreachable vertices
    for (Edge w = G.first(v); G.isEdge(w); w = G.next(w))
      if (D[G.v2(w)] > (D[v] + G.weight(w)))
        D[G.v2(w)] = D[v] + G.weight(w);
  }
}
```

Figure 7.15 An implementation for Dijkstra's algorithm.

updated for every neighbor x of v. Figure 7.15 shows an implementation for Dijkstra's algorithm. At the end, array D will contain the shortest distance values.

There are two reasonable solutions to the key issue of finding the unvisited vertex with minimum D value during each pass through the main **for** loop. The first method is simply to scan through the list of $|\mathbf{V}|$ vertices searching for the minimum value, as follows.

```
static int minVertex(Graph G, int[] D) {
  int v = 0;  // Initialize v to any unvisited vertex;
  for (int i=0; i<G.n(); i++)
    if (G.getMark(i) == UNVISITED) { v = i; break; }
  for (int i=0; i<G.n(); i++)  // Now find smallest value
    if ((G.getMark(i) == UNVISITED) && (D[i] < D[v]))
      v = i;
  return v;
}
```

Since this scan is done $|\mathbf{V}|$ times, and since each edge requires a constant time update to D, the total cost for this approach is $\Theta(|\mathbf{V}|^2 + |\mathbf{E}|) = \Theta(|\mathbf{V}|^2)$, since $|\mathbf{E}|$ is in $O(|\mathbf{V}|^2)$.

The second method is to store unprocessed vertices in a min-heap ordered by D values. The next-closest vertex can be found in the heap in $\Theta(\log |\mathbf{V}|)$ time. Every time we modify $D(x)$, we could reorder x in the heap by deleting and reinserting it. This is an example of a priority queue with priority update, as described in Section 5.6. To implement true priority updating, we would need to store with each vertex its array index within the heap. A simpler approach is to add the new (smaller) distance value for a given vertex as a new record in the heap. The smallest value for a given vertex currently in the heap will be found first, and greater distance values found later will be ignored since the vertex will be marked as `VISITED`. The only disadvantage to repeatedly inserting distance values is that it will raise the number of elements in the heap from $\Theta(|\mathbf{V}|)$ to $\Theta(|\mathbf{E}|)$ in the worst case. The time complexity is $\Theta((|\mathbf{V}| + |\mathbf{E}|) \log |\mathbf{E}|)$, since for each edge we must reorder the heap.

We need to store on the heap some object that implements the `Elem` interface (i.e., that has a `key` function). In this case, the object stores a vertex and its (current) distance from the start vertex. The `key` function returns the distance to the start vertex. We can use the following class, named `DijkElem`, for the purpose.

```
class DijkElem implements Elem {
   private int vertex;
   private int distance;

   public DijkElem(int v, int d) { vertex = v; distance = d; }
   public DijkElem() {vertex = 0; distance = 0; }

   public int key() { return distance; }
   public int vertex() { return vertex; }
} // class DikjElem
```

Figure 7.16 shows an implementation for Dijkstra's algorithm using the priority queue.

Using `MinVertex` to scan the vertex list for the minimum value is more efficient when the graph is dense, that is, when $|\mathbf{E}|$ approaches $|\mathbf{V}|^2$. Using a priority queue is more efficient when the graph is sparse since its cost is $\Theta((|\mathbf{V}| + |\mathbf{E}|) \log |\mathbf{E}|)$. However, when the graph is dense this cost can be as great as $\Theta(|\mathbf{V}|^2 \log |\mathbf{E}|)$.

Figure 7.17 illustrates Dijkstra's algorithm. The start vertex is A. All vertices except A have an initial value of ∞. After processing vertex A, its neighbors have their D estimates updated to be the direct distance from A. After processing C (the closest vertex to A), vertices B and E are updated to reflect the shortest path through C. The remaining vertices are processed in order B, D, and E.

7.4.2 All-Pairs Shortest Paths

We next consider the problem of finding the shortest distance between all pairs of vertices in the graph, called the **all-pairs shortest-paths** problem. To be precise, for every $u, v \in \mathbf{V}$, calculate d(u, v).

```
// Dijkstra's shortest-paths algorithm: priority queue version
static void Dijkstra(Graph G, int s, int[] D) {
  int v;                                    // The current vertex
  DijkElem[] E = new DijkElem[G.e()]; // Heap with lots of space
  E[0] = new DijkElem(s, 0);              // Initialize heap array
  MinHeap H = new MinHeap(E, 1, G.e()); // Create the heap
  for (int i=0; i<G.n(); i++)           // Initialize distance array
    D[i] = Integer.MAX_VALUE;
  D[s] = 0;
  for (int i=0; i<G.n(); i++) {          // For each vertex
    do { v = ((DijkElem)H.removemin()).vertex(); } // Get position
      while (G.getMark(v) == VISITED);
    G.setMark(v, VISITED);
    if (D[v] == Integer.MAX_VALUE) return; // Unreachable vertices
    for (Edge w = G.first(v); G.isEdge(w); w = G.next(w))
      if (D[G.v2(w)] > (D[v] + G.weight(w))) {      // Update D
        D[G.v2(w)] = D[v] + G.weight(w);
        H.insert(new DijkElem(G.v2(w), D[G.v2(w)]));
      }
  }
}
```

Figure 7.16 An implementation for Dijkstra's algorithm using a priority queue.

	A	B	C	D	E
Initial	0	∞	∞	∞	∞
Process A	0	10	3	20	∞
Process C	0	5	3	20	18
Process B	0	5	3	10	18
Process D	0	5	3	10	18
Process E	0	5	3	10	18

Figure 7.17 A listing for the progress of Dijkstra's algorithm operating on the graph of Figure 7.14. The start vertex is A.

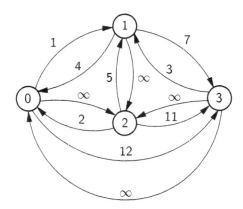

Figure 7.18 An example of k-paths in Floyd's algorithm. Path 1, 3 is a
0-path by definition. Path 3, 0, 2 is not a 0-path, but it is a 1-path (as well
as a 2-path, a 3-path, and a 4-path) since the largest intermediate vertex
is 0. Path 1, 3, 2 is a 4-path, but not a 3-path since the intermediate vertex
is 3. All paths in this graph are 4-paths.

One solution is to run Dijkstra's algorithm $|\mathbf{V}|$ times, each time com-
puting the shortest path from a different start vertex. If $\mathbf{G}$ is sparse ($|\mathbf{E}| =
O(|\mathbf{V}|)$) then this is a good solution, since the total cost will be $\Theta(|\mathbf{V}|^2 +
|\mathbf{V}||\mathbf{E}| \log |\mathbf{V}|) = \Theta(|\mathbf{V}|^2 \log |\mathbf{V}|)$ for the version of Dijkstra's algorithm based
on priority queues. For a dense graph, the priority queue version of Dijkstra's
algorithm yields a cost of $\Theta(|\mathbf{V}|^3 \log |\mathbf{V}|)$, but the version using `MinVertex`
yields a cost of $\Theta(|\mathbf{V}|^3)$.

Another solution that limits processing time to $\Theta(|\mathbf{V}|^3)$ regardless of the
number of edges is known as Floyd's algorithm. Define a **k-path** from vertex
v to vertex u to be any path whose intermediate vertices (aside from v and
u) all have indices less than k. A 0-path is defined to be a direct edge from
v to u. Figure 7.18 illustrates the concept of k-paths.

Define $\mathrm{D}_k(v, u)$ to be the length of the shortest k-path from vertex v to
vertex u. Assume that we already know the shortest k-path from v to u.
The shortest $(k + 1)$-path either goes through vertex k or it does not. If it
does go through k, then the best path is the best k-path from v to k followed
by the best k-path from k to u. Otherwise, we should keep the best k-path
seen before. Floyd's algorithm simply checks all of the possibilities in a triple
loop. Here is the implementation for Floyd's algorithm. At the end of the
algorithm, array D stores the all-pairs shortest distances.

```
// Compute all-pairs shortest paths
static void Floyd(Graph G, int[][] D) {
  for (int i=0; i<G.n(); i++) // Initialize D with initial weights
    for (int j=0; j<G.n(); j++)
      D[i][j] = G.weight(i, j);
  for (int k=0; k<G.n(); k++) // Compute all k paths
    for (int i=0; i<G.n(); i++)
      for (int j=0; j<G.n(); j++)
        if ((D[i][k] != Integer.MAX_VALUE) &&
            (D[k][j] != Integer.MAX_VALUE) &&
            (D[i][j] > (D[i][k] + D[k][j])))
          D[i][j] = D[i][k] + D[k][j];
}
```

Clearly this algorithm requires $\Theta(|\mathbf{V}|^3)$ running time, and it is the best choice for dense graphs because it is (relatively) fast and easy to implement.

7.5   Minimum-Cost Spanning Trees

This section presents two algorithms for determining the **minimum-cost spanning tree** (MST) of a graph. The MST problem takes as input a connected, undirected graph $\mathbf{G}$, where each edge has a distance or weight measure attached. The MST is the graph containing the vertices of $\mathbf{G}$ along with the subset of $\mathbf{G}$'s edges that (1) has minimum total cost as measured by summing the values for all of the edges in the subset, and (2) keeps the vertices connected. Examples of applications where a solution to this problem is useful include soldering the shortest set of wires needed to connect a set of terminals on a circuit board, and connecting a set of cities by telephone in such a way as to require the least amount of wire.

The MST contains no cycles. If a proposed set of edges did have a cycle, a cheaper MST could be had by removing any one of the edges in the cycle. Thus, the MST is a free tree with $|\mathbf{V}| - 1$ edges. The name minimum-cost spanning tree comes from the fact that the required set of edges forms a tree, it spans the vertices (i.e., it connects them together), and it has minimum cost. Figure 7.19 shows the MST for an example graph.

7.5.1   Prim's Algorithm

The first of our two algorithms for finding MSTs is commonly referred to as Prim's algorithm. Prim's algorithm is very simple. Start with any vertex N in the graph, setting the MST to be N initially. Pick the least-cost edge connected to N. This edge connects N to another vertex; call this M. Add

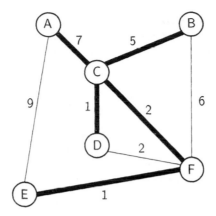

Figure 7.19 A graph and its MST. All lines are edges in the original graph; heavy lines indicate the subset of edges making up the MST. Note that edge (C, F) could be replaced with edge (D, F) to form a different MST.

vertex M and edge (N, M) to the MST. Next, pick the least-cost edge coming from either N or M to any other vertex in the graph. Add this edge and the new vertex it reaches to the MST. This process continues, at each step expanding the MST by selecting the least-cost edge from a vertex currently in the MST to a vertex not currently in the MST.

Prim's algorithm is quite similar to Dijkstra's algorithm for finding the single-source shortest paths. The primary difference is that we are seeking not the next closest vertex to the start vertex, but rather the next closest vertex to any vertex currently in the MST. Figure 7.20 shows an implementation for Prim's algorithm that searches the distance matrix for the next closest vertex. Array `V[i]` stores the previously visited vertex that is closest to vertex i, so that we know which edge goes into the MST when vertex i is processed.

Alternatively, we can implement Prim's algorithm using a priority queue to find the next closest vertex, as shown in Figure 7.21. As with the priority queue version of Dijkstra's algorithm, the heap's `Elem` type stores a `DijkElem` object, and the **key** function returns the D value for a vertex, where D is the distance to the closest vertex in the MST.

Prim's algorithm is an example of a **greedy** algorithm. At each step in the **for** loop, we select the least-cost edge that connects a marked vertex to an unmarked vertex. There is no concern for whether the MST really should include this next least-cost edge or not. This leads to an important question: Does Prim's algorithm work correctly? Clearly it generates a

```java
// Compute a minimal-cost spanning tree
static void Prim(Graph G, int s, int[] D) {
  int[] V = new int[G.n()];       // V[i] stores closest vertex to i
  for (int i=0; i<G.n(); i++)     // Initialize
    D[i] = Integer.MAX_VALUE;
  D[s] = 0;
  for (int i=0; i<G.n(); i++) { // Process the vertices
    int v = minVertex(G, D);
    G.setMark(v, VISITED);
    if (v != s) AddEdgetoMST(V[v], v);
    if (D[v] == Integer.MAX_VALUE) return; // Unreachable vertices
    for (Edge w = G.first(v); G.isEdge(w); w = G.next(w))
      if (D[G.v2(w)] > G.weight(w)) {
        D[G.v2(w)] = G.weight(w);
        V[G.v2(w)] = v;
      }
  }
}
```

Figure 7.20 An implementation for Prim's algorithm.

```java
// Prims's MST algorithm: priority queue version
static void Prim(Graph G, int s, int[] D) {
  int v;                                  // The current vertex
  int[] V = new int[G.n()]; // V[i] stores closest vertex to i
  DijkElem[] E = new DijkElem[G.e()];   // Heap with lots of space
  E[0] = new DijkElem(s, 0);            // Initialize heap array
  MinHeap H = new MinHeap(E, 1, G.e()); // Create the heap
  for (int i=0; i<G.n(); i++)           // Initialize distance array
    D[i] = Integer.MAX_VALUE;
  D[s] = 0;
  for (int i=0; i<G.n(); i++) {         // Now, get distances
    do { v = ((DijkElem)H.removemin()).vertex(); } // Get position
      while (G.getMark(v) == VISITED);
    G.setMark(v, VISITED);
    if (v != s) AddEdgetoMST(V[v], v); // Add this edge to MST
    if (D[v] == Integer.MAX_VALUE) return; // Unreachable vertices
    for (Edge w = G.first(v); G.isEdge(w); w = G.next(w))
      if (D[G.v2(w)] > G.weight(w)) {  // Update D
        D[G.v2(w)] = G.weight(w);
        V[G.v2(w)] = v;                 // Update who it came from
        H.insert(new DijkElem(G.v2(w), D[G.v2(w)]));
      }
  }
}
```

Figure 7.21 An implementation of Prim's algorithm using a priority queue.

spanning tree (since each pass through the `for` loop adds an unmarked vertex to the spanning tree until all vertices have been added), but does this tree have minimum cost?

Theorem 7.1 *Prim's algorithm produces a minimum-cost spanning tree.*

Proof: The theorem is proved by contradiction. Let $G = (V, E)$ be a graph for which the algorithm does *not* generate an MST. Define an ordering on the vertices according to the order in which they were added by Prim's algorithm to the MST: $v_0, v_1, ..., v_{n-1}$. Let edge e_i connect (v_x, v_i) for some $x < i$ and $i \geq 1$. Let e_j be the lowest numbered (first) edge added by Prim's algorithm such that the set of edges selected so far *cannot* be extended to form an MST for G. In other words, e_j is the first edge where Prim's algorithm "went wrong." Let T be the "true" MST. Call v_p the vertex connected by edge e_j, that is, $e_j = (v_p, v_j)$.

Since T is a tree, there exists some path in T connecting v_p and v_j. There must be some edge e' in this path connecting vertices v_u and v_w, with $u < j$ and $w \geq j$. Since e_j is not part of T, adding edge e_j to T forms a cycle. Edge e' must be of lower cost than edge e_j, since Prim's algorithm did not generate an MST. This situation is illustrated in Figure 7.22. However, Prim's algorithm would have selected the least-cost edge available. It would have selected e', not e_j! Thus, it is a contradiction that Prim's algorithm would have selected the wrong edge, and thus, Prim's algorithm must be correct.   □

Here is an example of how Prim's algorithm operates. For the graph of Figure 7.19, assume that we begin by marking vertex A. From A, the least-cost edge leads to vertex C. Vertex C and edge (A, C) are added to the MST. The least-cost edge from the MST at this point is (C, D). The next step marks vertex F. Since edges (C, F) and (D, F) happen to have equal cost, it is an arbitrary decision as to which gets selected. The next step marks vertex E and adds edge (F, E) to the MST. Following in this manner, vertex B (through edge (C, B)) is marked. At this point, the algorithm terminates.

7.5.2   Kruskal's Algorithm

Our next MST algorithm is commonly referred to as Kruskal's algorithm. Kruskal's algorithm is also a simple, greedy algorithm. We first partition the set of vertices into $|V|$ equivalence classes, each consisting of one vertex. We then process the edges in order of weight. An edge is added to the

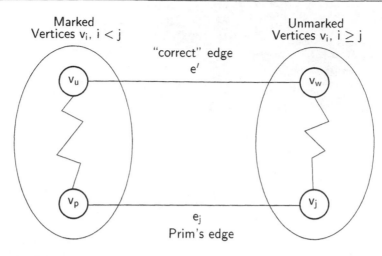

Figure 7.22 Illustration of Prim's MST algorithm proof. The left oval contains that portion of the graph where Prim's MST and "true" MST **T** agree. The right oval contains the rest of the graph. The two portions of the graph are connected by (at least) edges e_j (selected by Prim's algorithm to be in the MST) and e' (the "correct" edge to be placed in the MST). Note that the path from v_w to v_{j+1} cannot include any marked vertex v_i, $i \le j$, because to do so would form a cycle.

MST, and the two equivalence classes combined, if the edge connects two vertices in different equivalence classes. This process is repeated until only one equivalence class remains.

The edges can be processed in order of weight by using a min-heap. This is generally faster than sorting the edges first, since in practice we need only visit a small fraction of the edges before completing the MST. This is an example of finding only a few smallest elements in a list, as discussed in Section 8.6.

The only tricky part to this algorithm is determining if two vertices belong to the same equivalence class. Fortunately, the ideal algorithm is available for the purpose – the UNION/FIND algorithm based on the parent pointer representation for trees described in Section 6.2. Figure 7.23 illustrates the first three steps of Kruskal's MST algorithm. Figure 7.24 shows an implementation for the algorithm, along with the `KruskalElem` class that is used for storing the edges on the minheap.

Kruskal's algorithm is dominated by the time required to process the edges. The `differ` and `UNION` functions are nearly constant in time if path compression is used. Thus, the total cost of the algorithm is $\Theta(|\mathbf{E}| \log |\mathbf{E}|)$ in the worst case, and often close to $\Theta(|\mathbf{V}| \log |\mathbf{E}|)$ in the average case.

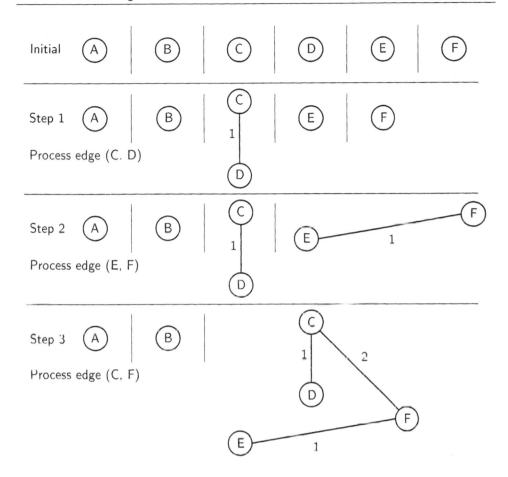

Figure 7.23 Illustration of the first three steps of Kruskal's MST algorithm as applied to the graph of Figure 7.19.

7.6 Further Reading

Many interesting properties of graphs can be investigated by playing with the programs in the Stanford Graphbase. This is a collection of benchmark databases and graph processing programs. The Stanford Graphbase is documented in [Knu94].

7.7 Exercises

7.1 Prove by induction that a graph with n vertices has at most $n(n-1)/2$ edges.

```
class KruskalElem implements Elem {
  private Edge edge;
  private Graph G;

  public KruskalElem(Graph inG, Edge w) { G = inG; edge = w; }
  public int key() { return G.weight(edge); }
  public Edge edge() { return edge; }
} // class KruskalElem

static void Kruskal(Graph G) {    // Kruskal's MST algorithm
  GenTree A = new GenTree(G.n()); // Equivalence class array
  KruskalElem[] E = new KruskalElem[G.e()]; // Minheap array
  int edgecnt = 0; // Count of edges

  for (int i=0; i<G.n(); i++)     // Put the edges on the array
    for (Edge w = G.first(i); G.isEdge(w); w = G.next(w))
      E[edgecnt++] = new KruskalElem(G, w);
  MinHeap H = new MinHeap(E, edgecnt, edgecnt); // Heapify the edges
  int numMST = G.n();             // Initially n equiv classes
  for (int i=0; numMST>1; i++) { // Combine equiv classes
    KruskalElem temp = (KruskalElem)H.removemin(); // Next cheapest
    Edge w = temp.edge();
    int v = G.v1(w);  int u = G.v2(w);
    if (A.differ(v, u)) {         // If in different equiv classes
      A.UNION(v, u);              // Combine equiv classes
      AddEdgetoMST(G.v1(w), G.v2(w));  // Add this edge to MST
      numMST--;                   // One less MST
    }
  }
}
```

Figure 7.24 An implementation for Kruskal's algorithm.

7.2 Prove the following implications regarding free trees.

    (a) IF an undirected graph is connected and has no simple cycles THEN the graph has $|V| - 1$ edges.

    (b) IF an undirected graph has $|V| - 1$ edges and no cycles, THEN the graph is connected.

7.3 **(a)** Draw the adjacency matrix representation for the graph of Figure 7.25.

    (b) Draw the adjacency list representation for the same graph.

    (c) If a pointer requires four bytes, a vertex label requires two bytes, and an edge weight requires two bytes, which representation requires more space for this graph?

7.4 Show the DFS tree for the graph of Figure 7.25, starting at Vertex 1.

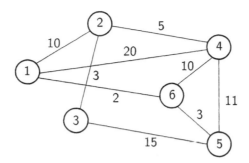

Figure 7.25 Example graph for Chapter 7 exercises.

7.5 Show the BFS tree for the graph of Figure 7.25, starting at Vertex 1.

7.6 The BFS topological sort algorithm can report the existence of a cycle if one is encountered. Modify this algorithm to print the vertices appearing in cycles (if any).

7.7 Show the shortest paths generated by running Dijkstra's shortest-paths algorithm on the graph of Figure 7.25, beginning at Vertex 4. Show the D values as each vertex is processed, as in Figure 7.17.

7.8 Modify the algorithm for single-source shortest paths to actually store and return the shortest paths rather than just compute the distances.

7.9 The root of a DAG is a vertex R such that every vertex of the DAG can be reached by a directed path from R. Write an algorithm that takes a directed graph as input and determines the root (if there is one) for the graph. The running time for your algorithm should be $\Theta(|\mathbf{V} + \mathbf{E}|)$.

7.10 Write an algorithm to find the longest path in a DAG, where the length of the path is measured by the number of edges that it contains. What is the asymptotic complexity of your algorithm?

7.11 Write an algorithm to determine whether a directed graph of $|\mathbf{V}|$ vertices contains a cycle. Your algorithm should run in $\Theta(|\mathbf{V}|+|\mathbf{E}|)$ time.

7.12 Write an algorithm to determine whether an undirected graph of $|\mathbf{V}|$ vertices contains a cycle. Your algorithm should run in $\Theta(|\mathbf{V}|)$ time.

7.13 The **single-destination shortest paths** problem for a directed graph is to find the shortest path *from* every vertex to given vertex v. Write an algorithm to solve the single-destination shortest paths problem.

7.14 Show the result of running Floyd's all-pairs shortest-paths algorithm on the graph of Figure 7.25.

7.15 The implementation for Floyd's algorithm given in Section 7.4.2 is inefficient for adjacency lists because the edges are visited in a bad order when initializing array D. What is the cost of of this initialization step for the adjacency list? How can this initialization step be revised so that it costs $\Theta(|\mathbf{V}|^2)$ in the worst case?

7.16 State the greatest possible lower bound that you can for the all-pairs shortest-paths problem, and justify your answer.

7.17 List the order in which the edges of the graph in Figure 7.25 are visited when running Prim's MST algorithm starting at vertex 3. Show the final MST.

7.18 List the order in which the edges of the graph in Figure 7.25 are visited when running Kruskal's MST algorithm. Each time an edge is added to the MST, show the result on the equivalence array, (e.g., show the array as in Figure 6.6).

7.19 Write an algorithm to find a **maximal** cost spanning tree, that is, the spanning tree with highest possible cost.

7.20 When can Prim's and Kruskal's algorithms yield different MSTs?

7.21 Prove that, if the costs for the edges of Graph **G** are distinct, then only one MST exists for **G**.

7.22 Does either Prim's or Kruskal's algorithm work if there are negative edge weights?

7.23 Consider the collection of edges selected by Dijkstra's algorithm as the shortest paths to the graph's vertices from the start vertex. Do these edges form a spanning tree (not necessarily of minimum cost)? Do these edges form an MST? Explain why or why not.

7.24 Write an algorithm to label the connected components of an undirected graph. In other words, all vertices of the first component are given the first component's label, all vertices of the second component are given the second component's label, and so on.

7.8 Projects

7.1 Design a format for storing graphs in files. Then implement two functions: one to read a graph from a file and the other to write a graph to a file. Test your functions by implementing a complete MST program that reads an undirected graph in from a file, constructs the MST, and then writes to a second file the directed graph representing the MST.

Part III

Sorting and Searching

8

Internal Sorting

Sorting is one of the most frequently performed computing tasks, so naturally it has been intensively studied and many algorithms have been devised. After years of analysis, there are still unsolved problems related to sorting and new algorithms are still being developed and refined for special purpose applications. This chapter, while introducing this central problem in computer science, also touches on many important issues in algorithm analysis. Sorting algorithms serve to illustrate a wide variety of analysis techniques. Sorting also motivates an introduction to file processing in Chapter 9. Many programs must sort collections of records too large to fit in main memory, and disk-based sorting requires special techniques. These are covered in Chapter 9, after the principles of disk-based processing have been introduced.

This chapter covers several standard algorithms appropriate for sorting a collection of records that fit in the computer's main memory. It begins with a discussion of three simple, but relatively slow algorithms requiring $\Theta(n^2)$ time in the average and worst cases. Several algorithms with considerably better performance are then presented, some with $\Theta(n \log n)$ worst-case running time. The final sorting method presented requires only $\Theta(n)$ worst-case time under special conditions. The chapter concludes with a proof that sorting in general requires $\Omega(n \log n)$ time in the worst case.

8.1 Sorting Terminology and Notation

Except where noted otherwise, input to the sorting algorithms presented in this chapter is a collection of records stored in an array. Each record contains a field called the **sort key**, or more simply the **key**. The key may be of any type so long as there is a linear ordering relationship between keys (see Section 2.1). The key field can be a character, string, integer, real, or any other (possibly more complicated) type for which a suitable comparison function can be defined. We assume that for any record type, there is a function named **key** that returns the key for that record. Further, we assume that comparison operators have been defined for the key type. Thus, a typical sorting algorithm shown in this chapter might have a comparison between records R and S in the form

```
if (R.key() <= S.key()) ...
```

We also assume that for every record type there is a **DSutil.swap** function defined. Function **DSutil.swap** takes as arguments an array and the indices within the array for two records, and swaps these records within the array.

Definition 8.1 The Sorting Problem. Given a set of records r_1, r_2, ..., r_n with key values k_1, k_2, ..., k_n, respectively, arrange the records into any order s such that records r_{s_1}, r_{s_2}, ..., r_{s_n} have keys obeying the property $k_{s_1} \le k_{s_2} \le ... \le k_{s_n}$. In other words, the sorting problem is to arrange a set of records so that the values of their key fields are in nondecreasing order.

As defined, the Sorting Problem allows input with two or more records that have the same key value. Certain applications require that input not contain duplicate key values. The sorting algorithms presented in this chapter and in Chapter 9 can handle duplicate key values unless noted otherwise.

When duplicate key values are allowed, there may be an implicit ordering to the duplicates, typically based on their order of occurrence within the input. It may be desirable to maintain this initial ordering among duplicates. A sorting algorithm is said to be **stable** if it does not change the relative ordering of records with identical key values. Many, but not all, of the sorting algorithms presented in this chapter are stable.

When comparing two sorting algorithms, the most straightforward approach is simply to program both and measure their running time. Examples of such timings are presented in Figures 8.14 and 8.15. However, such a comparison can be misleading since the running time for many sorting algorithms depends on specifics of the input values. In particular, the number of records, the size of the keys and the records, the allowable range of the key values, and the amount by which the input records are "out of order" can all greatly affect the relative running times for sorting algorithms.

When analyzing sorting algorithms, it is traditional to measure the number of comparisons made between keys. This measure is usually closely related to the running time for the algorithm, and has the advantage of being machine and data-type independent. However, in some cases records may be so large that their physical movement may take a significant fraction of the total running time. If so, it may be appropriate to measure the number of swap operations performed by the algorithm. In most applications we can assume that all records and keys are of fixed length, and that a single comparison or a single swap operation requires a constant amount of time regardless of which keys are involved. Some special situations "change the rules" for comparing sorting algorithms. For example, an application with records or keys having widely varying length (such as sorting a sequence of variable length strings) will benefit from a special purpose sorting technique. Some applications require that a small number of records be sorted, but that the sort be performed frequently. An example would be an application that repeatedly sorts groups of five numbers. In such cases, the constants in the runtime equations that are usually ignored in an asymptotic analysis now become crucial. Finally, some situations require that a sorting algorithm use as little memory as possible.

8.2   Three $\Theta(n^2)$ Sorting Algorithms

This section presents three simple sorting algorithms. While easy to understand and implement, we will soon see that they are unacceptably slow when there are many records to be sorted. Nonetheless, there are situations where one of these simple algorithms is the best tool for the job.

8.2.1   Insertion Sort

Our first sorting algorithm is called **Insertion Sort**. Insertion Sort sequentially processes a list of records. Each record is inserted in turn at the correct position within a sorted list composed of those records already processed. The following is a Java implementation for Insertion Sort. The input is an array of records to be sorted.

```
static void inssort(Elem[] array) {  // Insertion Sort
  for (int i=1; i<array.length; i++) // Insert i'th record
    for (int j=i; (j>0) && (array[j].key()<array[j-1].key()); j--)
      DSutil.swap(array, j, j-1);
}
```

i=1	2	3	4	5	6	7
42	20	17	13	13	13	13
20	42	20	17	17	14	14
17	17	42	20	20	17	15
13	13	13	42	28	20	17
28	28	28	28	42	28	20
14	14	14	14	14	42	23
23	23	23	23	23	23	28
15	15	15	15	15	15	42

Figure 8.1 An illustration of Insertion Sort. Each column shows the array after the iteration with the indicated value of i in the outer for loop. Values above the line in each column have been sorted. Each arrow indicates the upward motion of a record through the array.

Consider the case where inssort is processing the ith record, with key value X. The record is moved upward in the array as long as X is less than the key value immediately above it. As soon as a key value less than or equal to X is encountered, inssort is done with that record because all records above it in the array must have smaller keys. Figure 8.1 illustrates how Insertion Sort works.

The body of inssort is made up of two nested for loops. The outer for loop is executed $n - 1$ times. The inner for loop is harder to analyze since the number of times it executes depends on how many keys in positions 1 to $i - 1$ have a value less than that of the key in position i. In the worst case, each record must make its way to the top of the array. This would occur if the keys are initially arranged from highest to lowest, in the reverse of sorted order. In this case, the number of comparisons will be one the first time through the for loop, two the second time, and so on. Thus, the total number of comparisons will be

$$\sum_{i=2}^{n} i = \Theta(n^2).$$

In contrast, consider the best-case cost. This occurs when the keys begin in sorted order from lowest to highest. In this case, every pass through the inner for loop will fail immediately, and no values will be moved. The total number of comparisons will be $n - 1$, which is the number of times the outer for loop executes. Thus, the cost for Insertion Sort in the best case is $\Theta(n)$.

While the best case is significantly faster than the worst case, the worst case is usually a more reliable indication of "typical" running time behavior. However, there are situations where we can expect the input to be in sorted or nearly sorted order. One example is when an already sorted list is slightly disordered; resorting it using Insertion Sort may be a good idea if we know that the disordering is slight. Examples of algorithms that take advantage of Insertion Sort's best-case running time are the Shellsort algorithm of Section 8.3 and the Quicksort algorithm of Section 8.4.

What is the average-case cost of Insertion Sort? When record i is processed, the number of times through the inner **for** loop depends on how far "out of order" the record is. In particular, the **for** loop is executed once for each key greater than the key of record i that appears in array positions 0 through $i-1$. For example, in the leftmost column of Figure 8.1 the value 15 is preceded by five values greater than 15. Each such occurrence is called an **inversion**. The number of inversions (i.e., the number of values greater than a given value that occur prior to it in the array) will determine the number of comparisons and swaps that must take place. We need to determine what the average number of inversions will be for the record in position i. We expect on average that half of the keys in the first $i-1$ array positions will have a value greater than that of the key at position i. Thus, the average case should be about half the cost of the worst case, which is still $\Theta(n^2)$. So, the average case is no better than the worst case in asymptotic complexity.

Counting comparisons or swaps yields similar results since each time through the inner **for** loop yields both a comparison and a swap, except the last (i.e., the comparison that fails the inner **for** loop's test), which has no swap. Thus, the number of swaps for the entire sort operation is $n-1$ less than the number of comparisons. This is 0 in the best case, and $\Theta(n^2)$ in the average and worst cases.

8.2.2   Bubble Sort

Our next sort is called **Bubble Sort**. Bubble Sort is often taught to novice programmers in introductory computer science courses. This is unfortunate, since Bubble Sort has no redeeming features whatsoever. It is a relatively slow sort, and unlike Insertion Sort, it has a poor best-case running time. However, Bubble Sort serves as the basis for a better sort, presented next.

Bubble Sort consists of a simple double **for** loop. The first iteration of the inner **for** loop moves through the record array from bottom to top, comparing adjacent keys. If the lower-indexed key's value is greater than its higher-indexed neighbor, then the two values are swapped. Once the smallest value is encountered, this process will cause it to "bubble" up to the top of

	i=0	1	2	3	4	5	6
42	13	13	13	13	13	13	13
20	42	14	14	14	14	14	14
17	20	42	15	15	15	15	15
13	17	20	42	17	17	17	17
28	14	17	20	42	20	20	20
14	28	15	17	20	42	23	23
23	15	28	23	23	23	42	28
15	23	23	28	28	28	28	42

Figure 8.2 An illustration of Bubble Sort. Each column shows the array after the iteration with the indicated value of i in the outer for loop. Values above the line in each column have been sorted. Arrows indicate the swaps that take place during a given iteration.

the array. The second pass through the array repeats this process. However, since we know that the smallest value reached the top of the array on the first pass, there is no need to compare the top two elements on the second pass. Likewise, each succeeding pass through the array compares adjacent elements, looking at one less value than the preceding pass. Figure 8.2 illustrates Bubble Sort. A Java implementation is as follows.

```java
static void bubsort(Elem[] array) {    // Bubble Sort
  for (int i=0; i<array.length-1; i++) // Bubble up i'th record
    for (int j=array.length-1; j>i; j--)
      if (array[j].key() < array[j-1].key())
        DSutil.swap(array, j, j-1);
}
```

Determining Bubble Sort's number of comparisons is easy. Regardless of the arrangement of the values in the array, the number of comparisons made by the inner for loop is always i, leading to a total cost of

$$\sum_{i=1}^{n} i = \Theta(n^2).$$

Bubble Sort's running time is roughly the same in the best, average, and worst cases.

The number of swaps required depends on how often a value is less than the one immediately preceding it in the array. We can expect this to occur for about half the comparisons in the average case, leading to $\Theta(n^2)$ for the expected number of swaps. The actual number of swaps performed by Bubble Sort will be identical to that performed by Insertion Sort.

i=0	1	2	3	4	5	6
42	13	13	13	13	13	13	13
20	20	14	14	14	14	14	14
17	17	17	15	15	15	15	15
13	42	42	42	17	17	17	17
28	28	28	28	28	20	20	20
14	14	20	20	20	28	23	23
23	23	23	23	23	23	28	28
15	15	15	17	42	42	42	42

Figure 8.3 An example of Selection Sort. Each column shows the array after the iteration with the indicated value of i in the outer for loop. Numbers above the line in each column have been sorted and are in their final positions.

8.2.3   Selection Sort

Our last $\Theta(n^2)$ sort is called **Selection Sort**. The ith pass of Selection Sort "selects" the ith smallest key in the array, placing that record into position i. In other words, Selection Sort first finds the smallest key in an unsorted list, then the second smallest, and so on. Its unique feature is that there are few record swaps. To find the next smallest key value requires searching through the entire unsorted portion of the array, but only one swap is required to put the record in place. Thus, the total number of swaps required will be $n - 1$ (we get the last record in place "for free").

Figure 8.3 illustrates Selection Sort. Here is a Java implementation.

```
static void selsort(Elem[] array) {      // Selection Sort
  for (int i=0; i<array.length-1; i++) { // Select i'th record
    int lowindex = i;              // Remember its index
    for (int j=array.length-1; j>i; j--) // Find the least value
      if (array[j].key() < array[lowindex].key())
        lowindex = j;                // Put it in place
    DSutil.swap(array, i, lowindex);
  }
}
```

Selection Sort is essentially a Bubble Sort, except that rather than repeatedly swapping adjacent values to get the next smallest record into place, we instead remember the position of the element to be selected and do one swap at the end. Thus, the number of comparisons is still $\Theta(n^2)$, but the number of swaps is much less than required by bubble sort. Selection Sort is particularly advantageous when the cost to do a swap is high, for example, when the elements are long strings or other large records. Selection

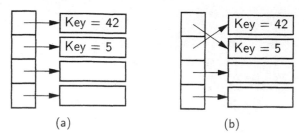

(a)   (b)

Figure 8.4 An example of swapping pointers to records. (a) A series of four records. The record with key value 42 comes before the record with key value 5. (b) The four records after the top two pointers have been swapped. Now the record with key value 5 comes before the record with key value 42.

Sort is more efficient than Bubble Sort (by a constant factor) in most other situations as well.

There is another approach to keeping the cost of swapping records low that can be used by any sorting algorithm even when the records are large. This is to have each element of the array store a pointer to a record rather than store the record itself. In this implementation, a swap operation need only exchange the pointer values; the records themselves do not move. This technique is illustrated by Figure 8.4. Additional space is needed to store the pointers, but the return is a faster swap operation. Note that the sorting implementations presented in this chapter take as input an array of type **Elem**. Since Java arrays store references to objects rather than storing the objects themselves, Java naturally encourages a pointer-swapping implementation.

8.2.4 The Cost of Exchange Sorting

Figure 8.5 summarizes the cost of Insertion, Bubble, and Selection Sort[1] in terms of their required number of comparisons and swaps in the best, average, and worst cases. The running time for each of these sorts is $\Theta(n^2)$ in the average and worst cases.

The remaining sorting algorithms presented in this chapter are significantly better than these three under typical conditions. But before continuing on, it is instructive to investigate what makes these three sorts so

---

[1]There is a slight anomaly with Selection Sort in that the best-case number of swaps is worse than that for Insertion Sort or Bubble Sort. This is because the implementation given here does not avoid a swap in the case where record i is already in position i. The reason is that it usually takes more time to repeatedly check for this situation than would be saved by avoiding such swaps.

	Insertion	**Bubble**	**Selection**
Comparisons:			
Best Case	$\Theta(n)$	$\Theta(n^2)$	$\Theta(n^2)$
Average Case	$\Theta(n^2)$	$\Theta(n^2)$	$\Theta(n^2)$
Worst Case	$\Theta(n^2)$	$\Theta(n^2)$	$\Theta(n^2)$
Swaps:			
Best Case	0	0	$\Theta(n)$
Average Case	$\Theta(n^2)$	$\Theta(n^2)$	$\Theta(n)$
Worst Case	$\Theta(n^2)$	$\Theta(n^2)$	$\Theta(n)$

Figure 8.5 A comparison of the asymptotic complexities for three simple sorting algorithms.

slow. The crucial bottleneck is that only *adjacent* records are compared. Thus, comparisons and moves (in all but Selection Sort) are by single steps. Swapping adjacent records is called an **exchange**. Thus, these sorts are sometimes referred to as **exchange sorts**.

The cost of any exchange sort can be at best the total number of steps that the records in the array must move to reach their "correct" location. To determine the cost of the best possible exchange sort in the average case, we need to sum the difference for each record between its initial position and its final position in the sorted array (i.e., the number of inversions for each record).

What is the minimum cost (in the average case) for an exchange sort? Consider a list $\mathbf{L}$ containing n values. $\mathbf{L}$ has $n(n-1)/2$ distinct pairs of values, each of which could potentially be an inversion. Each such pair must either be an inversion in $\mathbf{L}$, or in $\mathbf{L}_R$, the reverse of $\mathbf{L}$. Thus, the total number of inversions in $\mathbf{L}$ and $\mathbf{L}_R$ together is exactly $n(n-1)/2$ for an average of $n(n-1)/4$ per list. We can therefore say that any sorting algorithm which limits comparisons to adjacent items will cost $\Omega(n^2)$ in the average case.

8.3 Shellsort

The next sort we consider is called **Shellsort** after its inventor, D.L. Shell. It is also sometimes called the **diminishing increment** sort. Unlike the exchange sorts, Shellsort makes comparisons and swaps between nonadjacent elements. Shellsort also exploits the best-case performance of Insertion Sort. Shellsort attempts to make the list "mostly sorted" so that a final Insertion Sort can finish the job. When properly implemented, Shellsort will give substantially better performance than $\Theta(n^2)$ in the worst case.

Shellsort uses a process that forms the basis for many of the sorts presented in the following sections: Break the list into sublists, sort them, then recombine the sublists. Shellsort breaks the array of elements into "virtual" sublists. Each sublist is sorted using an Insertion Sort. Another group of sublists is then chosen and sorted, and so on.

During each iteration, Shellsort breaks the list into disjoint sublists so that each element in a sublist is a fixed number of positions apart. For example, let us assume for convenience that n, the number of values to be sorted, is a power of two. One possible implementation of Shellsort will begin by breaking the list into $n/2$ sublists of 2 elements each, where the array index of the 2 elements in each sublist differs by $n/2$. If there are 16 elements in the array indexed from 0 to 15, there would initially be 8 sublists of 2 elements each. The first sublist would be the elements in positions 0 and 8, the second in positions 1 and 9, and so on. Each list of two elements is sorted using Insertion Sort.

The second pass of Shellsort looks at fewer, bigger lists. For our example the second pass would have $n/4$ lists of size 4, with the elements in the list being $n/4$ positions apart. Thus, the second pass would have as its first sublist the 4 elements in positions 0, 4, 8, and 12; the second sublist would have elements in positions 1, 5, 9, and 13; and so on. Each sublist of four elements would also be sorted using an Insertion Sort.

The third pass would be made on two lists, one consisting of the odd positions and the other consisting of the even positions. The culminating pass in this example would be a "normal" Insertion Sort of all elements. Figure 8.6 illustrates the process for an array of 16 values where the sizes of the increments (the distances between elements on the successive passes) are 8, 4, 2, and 1. Below is a Java implementation:

```java
static void shellsort(Elem[] array) {    // Shellsort
  for (int i=array.length/2; i>2; i/=2) // For each increment
    for (int j=0; j<i; j++)             // Sort each sublist
      inssort2(array, j, i);
  inssort2(array, 0, 1);     // Could call regular inssort here
}

// Modified version of Insertion Sort for varying increments
static void inssort2(Elem[] A, int start, int incr) {
  for (int i=start+incr; i<A.length; i+=incr)
    for (int j=i; (j>=incr)&&(A[j].key()<A[j-incr].key()); j-=incr)
      DSutil.swap(A, j, j-incr);
}
```

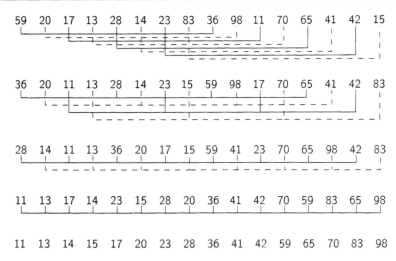

Figure 8.6 An example of Shellsort. Sixteen items are sorted in four passes. The first pass sorts 8 sublists of size 2 and increment 8. The second pass sorts 4 sublists of size 4 and increment 4. The third pass sorts 2 sublists of size 8 and increment 2. The fourth pass sorts 1 list of size 16 and increment 1 (a regular Insertion Sort).

Shellsort will work correctly regardless of the size of the increments, *provided that the final pass has increment 1* (i.e., provided the final pass is a regular Insertion Sort). The expectation is that each of the sublist sorts will make the list "more sorted" than it was before. It is not necessarily the case that this will be true, but it is almost always true in practice. When the final Insertion Sort is conducted, the list should be "almost sorted," yielding a relatively cheap final Insertion Sort pass.

Some choices for increments will make Shellsort run more efficiently than others. In particular, the choice of increments described above (2^k, 2^{k-1}, ..., 2, 1) turns out to be relatively inefficient. A better choice is the following series based on division by three: (..., 121, 40, 13, 4, 1).

The analysis of Shellsort is difficult, so we must accept without proof that the average case performance of Shellsort (for "divisions by three" increments) is $O(n^{1.5})$. Other choices for the increment series can reduce this upper bound somewhat. Thus, Shellsort is substantially better than Insertion Sort, or any of the $\Theta(n^2)$ sorts presented in Section 8.2. In fact, Shellsort is competitive with the asymptotically better sorts to be presented whenever n is of medium size. Shellsort illustrates how we can sometimes exploit the special properties of an algorithm (in this case Insertion Sort) even if in general that algorithm is unacceptably slow.

8.4   Quicksort

Quicksort is aptly named since, when properly implemented, it is the fastest known general purpose in-memory sorting algorithm in the average case. Quicksort is widely used, and is typically the algorithm implemented in a library sort routine such as the UNIX `qsort` function. Interestingly, Quicksort is hampered by exceedingly poor worst-case performance, thus making it inappropriate for certain applications.

Before we get to Quicksort, consider for a moment the practicality of using a Binary Search Tree for sorting. You could insert all of the values to be sorted into the BST one by one, then traverse the completed tree using an inorder traversal. The output would form a sorted list. This approach has a number of drawbacks, not least of which is the extra space required by BST nodes and the amount of time required to insert nodes into the tree. However, this method introduces some interesting ideas. First, the root of the BST (i.e., the first node inserted) splits the array into two subarrays: The left subtree contains those values in the array less than the root value while the right subtree contains those values in the array greater than or equal to the root value. Thus, the BST implicitly implements a "divide and conquer" approach to sorting the left and right subtrees. Quicksort implements this concept in a much more efficient way.

Quicksort first selects a value called the **pivot**. Assume that the input array contains k values less than the pivot. The records are then rearranged in such a way that the k values less than the pivot are placed in the first, or leftmost k positions in the array, and the values greater than or equal to the pivot are placed in the last, or rightmost, $n - k$ positions. This is called a **partition** of the array. The values placed in a given partition need not (and typically will not) be sorted with respect to each other. All that is required is that all values end up in the correct partition. The pivot value itself is placed in position k. Quicksort then proceeds to sort the resulting subarrays now on either side of the pivot, one of size k and the other of size $n - k - 1$. How are these values sorted? Since Quicksort is such a good algorithm, using Quicksort on the subarrays would be appropriate. The Java code for Quicksort is as follows. Parameters i and j define the left and right indices, respectively, for the subarray being sorted. The initial call to Quicksort would be `qsort(array, 0, n-1)`.

```
static void qsort(Elem[] array, int i, int j) { // Quicksort
  int pivotindex = findpivot(array, i, j);       // Pick a pivot
  DSutil.swap(array, pivotindex, j);    // Stick pivot at end
  // k will be the first position in the right subarray
  int k = partition(array, i-1, j, array[j].key());
  DSutil.swap(array, k, j);             // Put pivot in place
  if ((k-i) > 1) qsort(array, i, k-1); // Sort left partition
  if ((j-k) > 1) qsort(array, k+1, j); // Sort right partition
}
```

Note that the pivot value is initially placed at the end of the array (position j). Function **partition** will return k, the first position in the right partition. Thus, **partition** must not affect the value of array position j. After partitioning, the pivot value is placed in position k, which is its correct position in the final, sorted array. By doing so, we guarantee that at least one value (the pivot) will not be processed in the recursive calls to **qsort**. Even if a bad pivot is selected, yielding a completely empty partition to one side of the pivot, the larger partition will contain at most $n - 1$ elements.

Selecting a pivot can be done in many ways. The simplest is to use the first key. However, if the input is sorted or reverse sorted, this will produce a poor partitioning with all values to one side of the pivot. It is better to pick a value at random, thereby reducing the chance of a bad input order affecting the sort. Unfortunately, using a random number generator is relatively expensive, and we can do nearly as well by selecting the middle value in the array. Here is a simple **findpivot** function:

```
static int findpivot(Elem[] array, int i, int j)
  { return (i+j)/2; }
```

We now turn to function **partition**. If we knew in advance how many keys are less than the pivot, **partition** could simply copy elements with key values less than the pivot to the low end of the array, and elements with larger keys to the high end. Since we do not know in advance how many keys are less than the pivot, we use a clever algorithm that moves indices inwards from the ends of the subarray, swapping values as necessary until the two indices meet. Here is a Java implementation for the partition algorithm:

```
static int partition(Elem[] array, int l, int r, int pivot) {
  do {                      // Move the bounds inward until they meet
    while (array[++l].key() < pivot); // Move left bound right
    while ((r!=0) && (array[--r].key()>pivot)); // Move right bound
    DSutil.swap(array, l, r);       // Swap out-of-place values
  } while (l < r);                  // Stop when they cross
  DSutil.swap(array, l, r);         // Reverse last, wasted swap
  return l;            // Return first position in right partition
}
```

Figure 8.7 illustrates `partition`. Initially, variables `l` and `r` are immediately outside the actual array bounds. Each pass through the outer `do` loop moves the counters `l` and `r` inwards, until eventually they cross. Note that at each iteration of the inner `while` loops, the bounds are moved prior to checking against the pivot value. This ensures that progress is made by each `while` loop, even when the two values swapped on the last iteration of the `do` loop were equal to the pivot. Also note the check that `r` remains positive in the second `while` loop. This ensures that `r` does not run off the low end of the array in the case where the pivot value for the leftmost partition is the least value in that partition. Function `partition` returns the first index of the right partition so that the subarray bound for the recursive calls to `qsort` can be determined. Figure 8.8 illustrates the complete Quicksort algorithm.

To analyze Quicksort, we first analyze the `findpivot` and `partition` functions operating on a subarray of length k. Clearly, `findpivot` takes constant time. Function `partition` contains a `do` loop with two nested `while` loops. The total cost of the partition operation is constrained by how far `l` and `r` can move inwards. In particular, these two bounds variables together can move a total of s steps for a subarray of length s. However, this does not directly tell us how much work is done by the nested `while` loops. The `do` loop as a whole is guaranteed to move both `l` and `r` inward at least one position on each first pass. Each `while` loop moves its variable at least once (except in the special case where `r` is at the left edge of the array, but this can happen only once). Thus, we see that the `do` loop can be executed at most s times, the total amount of work done moving `l` and `r` is s, and each `while` loop can fail its test at most s times. The total work for the entire `partition` function is therefore $\Theta(s)$.

Knowing the cost of `findpivot` and `partition`, we can determine the cost of Quicksort. We begin with a worst-case analysis. The worst case will occur when the pivot does a poor job of breaking the array, that is, when there are no elements in one partition, and $n - 1$ elements in the other. In this case, the divide and conquer strategy has done a poor job of dividing, so the conquer phase will work on a subproblem only one less than the size of the original problem. If this happens at each partition step, then the total cost of the algorithm will be

$$\sum_{k=1}^{n} k = \Theta(n^2).$$

Initial		72	6	57	88	85	42	83	73	48	60
		l									r
Pass 1		72	6	57	88	85	42	83	73	48	60
		l								r	
Swap 1		48	6	57	88	85	42	83	73	72	60
		l								r	
Pass 2		48	6	57	88	85	42	83	73	72	60
					l		r				
Swap 2		48	6	57	42	85	88	83	73	72	60
					l		r				
Pass 3		48	6	57	42	85	88	83	73	72	60
					r	l					
Swap 3		48	6	57	85	42	88	83	73	72	60
					r	l					
Reverse Swap		48	6	57	42 |	85	88	83	73	72	60
					r	l					

Figure 8.7 The Quicksort partition step. The first row shows the initial positions for a collection of ten key values. The pivot value is 60, which has been swapped to the end of the array. The do loop makes three iterations, each time moving counters l and r inwards until they cross in the third pass. A final swap reverses the unwanted swap of the last pass. In the end, the left partition contains four values and the right partition contains six values. Function qsort will place the pivot value into position 4.

In the worst case Quicksort is $\Theta(n^2)$. This is terrible, no better than Bubble Sort.[2] When will this worst case occur? Only when each pivot yields a bad partitioning of the array. If the pivot values are selected at random, then this is extremely unlikely to happen. When selecting the middle position of the current subarray, it is still unlikely to happen. It does not take many good partitionings for Quicksort to work fairly well.

Quicksort's best case occurs when findpivot always breaks the array into two equal halves. Quicksort repeatedly splits the array into smaller partitions, as shown in Figure 8.8. In the best case, the result will be $\log n$ levels of partitions, with the top level having one array of size n, the second

---

[2]The worst insult that I can think of for a sorting algorithm.

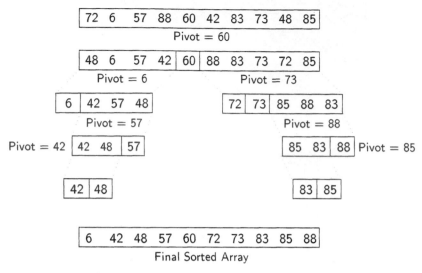

Figure 8.8 An illustration of Quicksort.

level two arrays of size $n/2$, the next with four arrays of size $n/4$, and so on. Thus, at each level, all partition steps for that level do a total of n work, for an overall cost of $n \log n$ work when Quicksort finds perfect pivots.

Quicksort's average-case behavior falls somewhere between the extremes of worst and best case. Average-case analysis considers the cost for all possible arrangements of input, summing the costs and dividing by the number of cases. We make one reasonable simplifying assumption: At each partition step, the pivot is equally likely to end in any position in the (sorted) array. In other words, the pivot is equally likely to break an array into partitions of sizes 0 and $n - 1$, or 1 and $n - 2$, and so on.

Given this assumption, the average-case cost is computed from the following equation:

$$\mathbf{T}(n) = cn + \frac{1}{n}\sum_{k=0}^{n-1}[\mathbf{T}(k) + \mathbf{T}(n - 1 - k)], \quad \mathbf{T}(0) = \mathbf{T}(1) = c.$$

This equation is in the form of a **recurrence relation** where $\mathbf{T}(k)$ refers to the cost of running Quicksort on an array of size k. Recurrence relations are discussed in Chapter 14, and this one is solved in Section 14.2.4. This equation says that there is one chance in n that the pivot breaks the array into subarrays of size 0 and $n - 1$, one chance in n that the pivot breaks the array into subarrays of size 1 and $n - 2$, and so on. The expression "$\mathbf{T}(k) + \mathbf{T}(n - 1 - k)$" is the cost for the two recursive calls to Quicksort on two arrays of size k and $n - 1 - k$. The initial cn term is the cost of doing the `findpivot` and `partition` steps. The closed form solution to this recurrence relation is $\Theta(n \log n)$. Thus, Quicksort has average-case cost $\Theta(n \log n)$.

The running time for Quicksort can be improved (by a constant factor), and much study has gone into optimizing this algorithm. The most obvious place for improvement is the `findpivot` function. Quicksort's worst case arises when the pivot does a poor job of splitting the array into equal size subarrays. If we are willing to do more work searching for a better pivot, the effects of a bad pivot can be decreased or even eliminated. One good choice is to use the "median of three" algorithm, which uses as a pivot the middle of three randomly selected values. Using a random number generator to choose the positions is relatively expensive, so a common compromise is to look at the first, middle, and last positions of the current subarray.

A significant improvement can be gained by recognizing that Quicksort is slow when n is small. This might not seem to be relevant if most of the time we sort large arrays, nor should it matter how long Quicksort takes in the rare instance when a small array is sorted since it will be fast anyway. But you should notice that Quicksort itself repeatedly sorts small arrays! This happens as a natural by-product of the divide and conquer approach.

A simple solution might then be to replace Quicksort with a faster sort for small numbers, say Insertion Sort or Selection Sort. However, there is an even better – and still simpler – optimization. When Quicksort partitions are below a certain size, do nothing! The values within that partition will be out of order. However, we do know that all values in the array to the left of the partition are smaller than all values in the partition. All values in the array to the right of the partition are greater than all values in the partition. Thus, even if Quicksort only gets the values to "nearly" the right locations, the array will be close to sorted. This is an ideal situation in which to take advantage of the best-case performance of Insertion Sort. The final step is a single call to Insertion Sort to process the entire array, putting the elements into final sorted order. Empirical testing shows that the subarrays should be left unordered when they get down to nine or fewer elements.

The last speedup to be considered reduces the cost of making recursive calls. Quicksort is inherently recursive, since each Quicksort operation must sort two sublists. Thus, there is no simple way to turn Quicksort into an iterative algorithm. However, Quicksort can be implemented using a stack to imitate recursion, as the amount of information that must be stored is small. We need not store copies of a subarray, only the subarray bounds. Furthermore, the stack depth can be kept small if care is taken on the order in which Quicksort's recursive calls are executed. We can also place the code for `findpivot` and `partition` inline to eliminate the remaining function calls. Note however that by not processing sublists of size nine or less as suggested above, about 80 to 90% of the function calls will already have been eliminated. Thus, eliminating the remaining function calls will yield only a modest speedup. Figure 8.9 shows a version of the Quicksort algorithm using a stack and no function calls to `findpivot` or `partition`.

8.5 Mergesort

Mergesort is conceptually one of the simplest sorting algorithms, and has good runtime behavior both in the asymptotic sense and in empirical running time. Unfortunately, it is also relatively difficult to implement in practice. Like Quicksort, Mergesort is based on the principle of divide and conquer. Mergesort splits a list into two equal sublists, sorts each sublist, and then recombines them into one sorted list. The process of combining two sorted sublists is called **merging**. The running time of Mergesort does not depend on the arrangement of the input values, thus it does not have poor worst-case performance in the sense of Quicksort. However, Mergesort is usually less efficient than a properly implemented Quicksort (by a constant factor) in the average case. Figure 8.10 illustrates Mergesort. A pseudocode sketch of Mergesort is as follows:

```
List mergesort(List inlist) {
   if (inlist.length() <= 1) return inlist;;
   List l1 = half of the items from inlist;
   List l2 = other half of the items from inlist;
   return merge(mergesort(l1), mergesort(l2));
}
```

Before discussing how to implement Mergesort, we will first examine the `merge` function. Merging two sorted sublists is quite simple. Function `merge` examines the first element of each sublist, and picks the smaller value as the smallest element overall. This smaller value is removed from its sublist, and placed into the output list. Merging continues in this way, comparing the front elements of the sublists and continually appending the smaller to the output list until no more input elements remain.

Implementing Mergesort presents a number of technical difficulties. The first decision is how to represent the lists. Mergesort lends itself well to sorting a singly linked list since merging does not require random access to the list elements. Thus, Mergesort is the method of choice when the

```
// Non-recursive Quicksort
static void qsort(Elem[] array, int oi, int oj) {
  int[] Stack = new int[MAXSTACKSIZE]; // Stack for array bounds
  int listsize = oj-oi+1;
  int top = -1;
  int pivot;
  int pivotindex, l, r;

  Stack[++top] = oi;  // Initialize stack
  Stack[++top] = oj;

  while (top > 0) {    // While there are unprocessed subarrays
    // Pop Stack
    int j = Stack[top--];
    int i = Stack[top--];

    // Findpivot
    pivotindex = (i+j)/2;
    pivot = array[pivotindex].key();
    DSutil.swap(array, pivotindex, j); // Stick pivot at end

    // Partition
    l = i-1;
    r = j;
    do {
      while (array[++l].key() < pivot);
      while ((r!=0) && (array[--r].key() > pivot));
      DSutil.swap(array, l, r);
    } while (l < r);
    DSutil.swap(array, l, r);  // Undo final swap
    DSutil.swap(array, l, j);  // Put pivot value in place

    // Put new subarrays onto Stack if they are small
    if ((l-i) > THRESHOLD) {   // Left partition
      Stack[++top] = i;
      Stack[++top] = l-1;
    }
    if ((j-l) > THRESHOLD) {   // Right partition
      Stack[++top] = l+1;
      Stack[++top] = j;
    }
  }
  inssort(array);              // Final Insertion Sort
}
```

Figure 8.9 An optimized version of Quicksort. Recursion has been replaced by a stack, findpivot and partition have been placed in-line, and subarrays smaller than THRESHOLD are not processed. At the end, a single call to Insertion Sort sorts the small partitions.

```
36  20  17  13  28  14  23  15

20  36 │ 13  17 │ 14  28 │ 15  23

13  17  20  36 │ 14  15  23  28

13  14  15  17  20  23  28  36
```

Figure 8.10 An illustration of Mergesort. The first row shows eight numbers to be sorted. Mergesort will recursively subdivide the list into sublists of one element each, then recombine the sublists. The second row shows the four sublists of size 2 created by the first merging pass. The third row shows the two sublists of size 4 created by the next merging pass on the sublists of row 2. The last row shows the final sorted list created by merging the two sublists of row 3.

input is in the form of a linked list. Implementing **merge** for linked lists is straightforward, since we need only remove items from the front of the input lists and append items to the output list. Breaking the input list into two equal halves presents some difficulty. Ideally we would just break the lists into front and back halves. However, even if we know the length of the list in advance, it would still be necessary to traverse halfway down the linked list to reach the beginning of the second half. A simpler method, which does not rely on knowing the length of the list in advance, assigns elements of the input list alternating between the two sublists. The first element is assigned to the first sublist, the second element to the second sublist, the third to first sublist, the fourth to the second sublist, and so on. This requires one complete pass through the input list to build the sublists.

When the input to Mergesort is an array, splitting input into two subarrays is easy if we know the array bounds. Merging is also easy if we merge the subarrays into a second array. Note that this approach requires twice the amount of space as any of the sorting methods presented so far, which is a serious disadvantage for Mergesort. It is possible to merge the subarrays without using a second array, but this is extremely difficult to do efficiently, and is not really practical. Merging the two subarrays into a second array, while simple to implement, presents another difficulty. The merge process ends with the sorted list in the auxiliary array. Consider how the recursive nature of Mergesort breaks the original array into subarrays, as shown in Figure 8.10. Mergesort is recursively called until subarrays of size 1 have been created, requiring $\log n$ levels of recursion. These subarrays are merged into subarrays of size 2, which are in turn merged into subarrays of size 4, and so on. We need to avoid having each merge operation require a new array. With some difficulty, an algorithm can be devised that alternates between two arrays. A much simpler approach is to copy the sorted sublists to the auxiliary array first, and then merge them back to the original array. Here is a complete implementation for mergesort that follows this approach.

```
static void mergesort(Elem[] array, Elem[] temp, int l, int r) {
  int mid = (l+r)/2;                  // Select midpoint
  if (l == r) return;                 // List has one element
  mergesort(array, temp, l, mid);     // Mergesort first half
  mergesort(array, temp, mid+1, r);   // Mergesort second half
  for (int i=l; i<=r; i++)            // Copy subarray to temp
    temp[i] = array[i];
  // Do the merge operation back to array
  int i1 = l; int i2 = mid + 1;
  for (int curr=l; curr<=r; curr++) {
    if (i1 == mid+1)                  // Left sublist exhausted
      array[curr] = temp[i2++];
    else if (i2 > r)                  // Right sublist exhausted
      array[curr] = temp[i1++];
    else if (temp[i1].key() < temp[i2].key()) // Get smaller value
      array[curr] = temp[i1++];
    else array[curr] = temp[i2++];
  }
}
```

An optimized Mergesort implementation from R. Sedgewick is shown next. It is particularly clever, since it reverses the order of the second subarray during the initial copy. Now the current positions of the two subarrays work inwards from the ends, allowing the end of each subarray to act as a sentinel for the other. Unlike the previous implementation, no test is needed to check for when one of the two subarrays becomes empty. This version also uses Insertion Sort to sort small subarrays.

```
static void mergesort(Elem[] array, Elem[] temp, int l, int r) {
  int i, j, k, mid = (l+r)/2;   // Select the midpoint
  if (l == r) return;           // List has one element
  if ((mid-l) >= THRESHOLD) mergesort(array, temp, l, mid);
  else inssort(array, l, mid-l+1);
  if ((r-mid) > THRESHOLD) mergesort(array, temp, mid+1, r);
  else inssort(array, mid+1, r-mid);
  // Do the merge operation. First, copy 2 halves to temp.
  for (i=l; i<=mid; i++) temp[i] = array[i];
  for (j=1; j<=r-mid; j++) temp[r-j+1] = array[j+mid];
  // Merge sublists back to array
  int a = temp[l].key(); int b = temp[r].key();
  for (i=l,j=r,k=l; k<=r; k++)
    if (a < b) { array[k] = temp[i++]; a = temp[i].key(); }
    else { array[k] = temp[j--]; b = temp[j].key(); }
}
```

```
// Insertion Sort for subarrays: sort len elements from index start
static void inssort(Elem[] array, int start, int len) {
  for (int i=start+1; i<start+len; i++)        // Insert i'th record
    for (int j=i; (j>start) &&
                  (array[j].key()<array[j-1].key()); j--)
      DSutil.swap(array, j, j-1);
}
```

Analysis of Mergesort is straightforward, despite the fact that it is a recursive algorithm. The merging part takes time $\Theta(i)$ where i is the total
length of the two subarrays being merged. The array to be sorted is repeatedly split in half until subarrays of size 1 are reached, at which time they
are merged to be of size 2, these merged to subarrays of size 4, and so on as
shown in Figure 8.10. Thus, the depth of the recursion is $\log n$ for n elements
(assume for simplicity that n is a power of two). The first level of recursion
can be thought of as working on one array of size n, the next level working
on two arrays of size $n/2$, the next on four arrays of size $n/4$, and so on.
The bottom of the recursion has n arrays of size 1. Thus, n arrays of size 1
are merged (requiring n total steps), $n/2$ arrays of size 2 (again requiring
n total steps), $n/4$ arrays of size 4, and so on. At each of the $\log n$ levels
of recursion, $\Theta(n)$ work is done, for a total cost of $\Theta(n \log n)$. This cost is
unaffected by the relative order of the values being sorted, thus this analysis
holds for the best, average, and worst cases.

8.6 Heapsort

Our discussion of Quicksort began by considering the practicality of using a
Binary Search Tree for sorting. The BST requires more space than the other
sorting methods, and will be slower than Quicksort or Mergesort due to the
relative expense of inserting values into the tree. There is also the possibility
that the BST might be unbalanced, leading to a $\Theta(n^2)$ worst-case running
time. Subtree balance in the BST is closely related to Quicksort's partition
step. Quicksort's pivot serves roughly the same purpose as the BST root
value in that the left partition (subtree) stores values less than the pivot
(root) value, while the right partition (subtree) stores values greater than or
equal to the pivot (root).

A good sorting algorithm can be devised based on a tree structure more
suited to the purpose. In particular, we would like the tree to be balanced,
space efficient, and fast. The algorithm should take advantage of the fact
that sorting is a special-purpose application in that all of the values to be

stored are available at the start. This means that we do not necessarily need to insert one value at a time into the tree structure.

Heapsort is based on the heap data structure presented in Section 5.6. Heapsort has all of the advantages just listed. The complete binary tree is balanced, its array representation is space efficient, and we can load all values into the tree at once, taking advantage of the efficient `buildheap` function. The asymptotic performance of Heapsort is $\Theta(n \log n)$ in the best, average, and worst cases. It is not as fast as Quicksort in the average case (by a constant factor), but Heapsort has special properties that will make it particularly useful when sorting data sets too large to fit in main memory, as discussed in Chapter 9.

A sorting algorithm based on max-heaps is quite straightforward. First we use the heap building algorithm of Section 5.6 to convert the array into max-heap order. Then we repeatedly remove the maximum value from the heap, restoring the heap property each time that we do so, until the heap is empty. Note that each time we remove the maximum element from the heap, it is placed at the end of the array. Assume the n elements are stored in array positions 0 through $n - 1$. After removing the maximum value from the heap and readjusting, the maximum value will now be placed in position $n - 1$ of the array. The heap is now considered to be of size $n - 1$. Removing the new maximum (root) value places the second largest value in position $n - 2$ of the array. At the end of the process, the array will be properly sorted from least to greatest. This is why Heapsort uses a max-heap rather than a min-heap as might have been expected. Figure 8.11 illustrates Heapsort. The complete Java implementation is as follows.

```
static void heapsort(Elem[] array) {  // Heapsort
  MaxHeap H = new MaxHeap(array, array.length, array.length);
  for (int i=0; i<array.length; i++)  // Now sort
    H.removemax();    // Removemax places max value at end of heap
}
```

Since building the heap takes $\Theta(n)$ time, and since n deletions of the maximum element each take $\Theta(\log n)$ time, we see that the entire heapsort operation takes $\Theta(n \log n)$ time in the worst, average, and best cases. While typically slower than Quicksort by a constant factor, Heapsort has one special advantage over the other sorts studied so far. Building the heap is relatively cheap, requiring $\Theta(n)$ time. Removing the maximum element from the heap requires $\Theta(\log n)$ time. Thus, if we wish to find the k largest elements in an array, we can do so in time $\Theta(n + k \log n)$. If k is small, this is a substantial

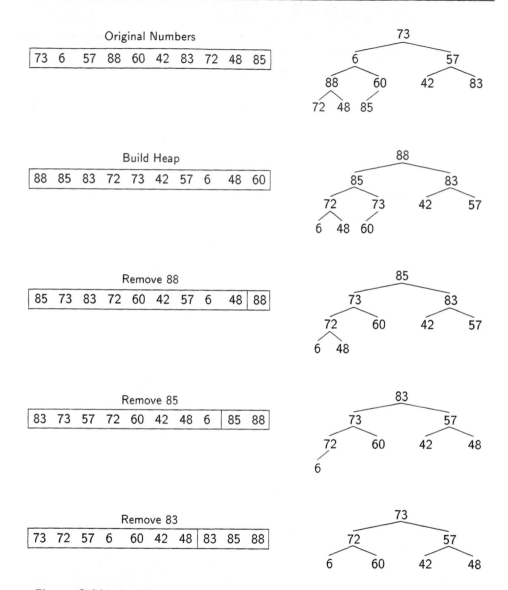

Figure 8.11 An illustration of Heapsort. The top row shows the values in their original order. The second row shows the values after building the heap. The third row shows the result of the first deletemax operation on key value 88. Note that 88 is now at the end of the array. The fourth row shows the result of the second deletemax operation on key value 85. The fifth row shows the result of the third deletemax operation on key value 83. At this point, the last three positions of the array hold the three greatest values in sorted order. Heapsort continues in this manner until the entire array is sorted.

improvement over the time required to find the k largest elements using one of the other sorting methods described earlier. One situation where we are able to take advantage of this concept is in the implementation of Kruskal's minimal cost spanning tree (MST) algorithm of Section 7.5.2. That algorithm requires that edges be visited in ascending order (so, use a min-heap), but this process stops as soon as the MST is complete. Thus, only a relatively small fraction of the edges need be sorted.

8.7   Binsort and Radix Sort

Section 3.8 presented the following code fragment to sort a permutation of the numbers 0 through $n - 1$:

```
for (i=0; i<n; i++)
  B[A[i].key()] = A[i];
```

Here the key value is used to determine the position for a record in the final sorted array. This is the most basic example of a **Binsort**, where key values are used to assign records to **bins**. This algorithm is extremely efficient, taking $\Theta(n)$ time regardless of the initial ordering of the keys. This is far better than the performance of any sorting algorithm that we have seen so far. The only problem is that this algorithm has limited use since it works only for a permutation of the numbers from 0 to $n - 1$.

There are a number of ways that we can extend this simple Binsort algorithm to be more useful. The simplest extension is to allow for duplicate values among the keys. This can be done by turning array slots into arbitrary length bins by making each element in array B the head of a linked list. In this way, all records with key value i can be placed in bin B[i]. A second extension allows for a key range greater than n. For example, a set of n records might have keys in the range 1 to $2n$. The only requirement is that each possible key value have a corresponding bin in B. The extended Binsort algorithm is as follows:

```
void binsort(ELEM *A, int n) {
  list B[MaxKeyValue];
  for (i=0; i<n; i++) B[A[i].key()].append(A[i]);
  for (i=0; i<MaxKeyValue; i++)
    for (B[i].first(); B[i].isInList(); B[i].next())
      output(B[i].currValue());
}
```

This version of Binsort can sort any collection of records whose key values fall in the range from 0 to `MaxKeyValue` $- 1$. The amount of work required is simply that needed to place each record into the appropriate bin, and then take all of the records out of the bins. Thus, we need to process each record twice, for $\Theta(n)$ work.

Unfortunately, there is a small but crucial detail missing in this analysis. Binsort must also look at each of the bins to see if it contains a record. The algorithm must process `MaxKeyValue` bins, regardless of how many actually hold records. If `MaxKeyValue` is small compared to n, then this is not a great expense. Suppose that `MaxKeyValue` $= n^2$. In this case, the total amount of work done will be $\Theta(n + n^2) = \Theta(n^2)$. This results in a poor sorting algorithm, and the algorithm becomes even worse as the disparity between n and `MaxKeyValue` increases. In addition, a large key range requires an unacceptably large array B. Thus, even the extended Binsort is useful only for a limited key range.

A simple generalization to Binsort yields a **bucket sort**. Each bin is associated with not just one key, but rather a range of key values. A bucket sort assigns records to bins and then relies on some other sorting technique to sort the records within each bin. The hope is that the relatively inexpensive bucketing process will put only a small number of records in each bin, and that a "cleanup sort" within the bins will then be relatively cheap.

There is a way to keep the number of bins and the related processing small while allowing the cleanup sort to be based on Binsort. Consider a sequence of records with keys in the range 0 to 99. If we have ten bins available, we can first assign records to bins by taking their key value modulo 10. Thus, every key will be assigned to the bin matching its rightmost decimal digit. We can then take these records from the bins *in order*, and reassign them to the bins on the basis of their leftmost (10's place) digit (define values in the range 0 to 9 to have a leftmost digit of 0). In other words, assign the ith record from array A to a bin using the formula `A[i].key()/10`. If we now gather the values from the bins in order, the result is a sorted list. Figure 8.12 illustrates this process.

In this example, we have $r = 10$ bins and $n = 12$ keys in the range 0 to $r^2 - 1$. The total computation is $\Theta(n)$ since we look at each record and each bin a constant number of times. This is a great improvement over the simple Binsort where the number of bins must be as large as the key range. Note that the example uses $r = 10$ so as to make the bin computations easy to visualize: Records were placed into bins based on the value of first the

Initial List:　　27　91　1　97　17　23　84　28　72　5　67　25

First pass
(on right digit)

Second pass
(on left digit)

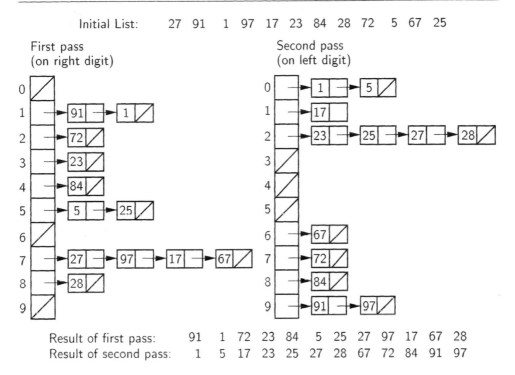

Result of first pass:　　91　1　72　23　84　5　25　27　97　17　67　28
Result of second pass:　　1　5　17　23　25　27　28　67　72　84　91　97

Figure 8.12 An example of Radix Sort for twelve two-digit numbers in base ten. Two passes are required to sort the list.

rightmost and then the leftmost decimal digits. Any number of bins would have worked. This is an example of a **Radix Sort**, so called because the bin computations are based on the **radix** or the **base** of the key values. This sorting algorithm can be extended to any number of keys in any key range. We simply assign records to bins based on the keys' digit values working from the rightmost digit to the leftmost. If there are k digits, then this requires that we assign keys to bins k times.

As with Mergesort, an efficient implementation of Radix Sort is somewhat difficult to achieve. In particular, we would prefer to sort an array of values and avoid processing linked lists. If we know how many values will be in each bin, then an auxiliary array of size n can be used to hold the bins. For example, if during the first pass the 0 bin will receive three records and the 1 bin will receive five records, then we could simply reserve the first three array positions for the 0 bin and the next five array positions for the 1 bin. Exactly this approach is taken by the following Java implementation. At the end of each pass, the records are copied back to the original array.

```
static void radix(Elem[] A, Elem[] B, int k, int r, int[] count) {
  // Count[i] stores number of records in bin[i]
  int i, j, rtok;

  for (i=0, rtok=1; i<k; i++, rtok*=r) { // For k digits
    for (j=0; j<r; j++) count[j] = 0;     // Initialize count

    // Count the number of records for each bin on this pass
    for (j=0; j<A.length; j++) count[(A[j].key()/rtok)%r]++;

    // Index B: count[j] will be index for last slot of bin j.
    for (j=1; j<r; j++) count[j] = count[j-1] + count[j];

    // Put records into bins working from bottom of each bin.
    // Since bins fill from bottom, j counts downwards
    for (j=A.length-1; j>=0; j--)
      B[--count[(A[j].key()/rtok)%r]] = A[j];

    for (j=0; j<A.length; j++) A[j] = B[j]; // Copy B back to A
  }
}
```

The first inner **for** loop initializes array **count**. The second loop counts the number of records to be assigned to each bin. The third loop sets the values in **count** to their proper indices within array **B**. Note that the index stored in **count[j]** is the *last* index for bin j; bins are filled from the bottom. The fourth loop assigns the records to the bins (within array **B**). The final loop simply copies the records back to array **A** to be ready for the next pass. Variable **rtok** stores r^k for use in bin computation. Figure 8.13 shows how this algorithm processes the input shown in Figure 8.12.

This algorithm requires k passes over the list of n numbers in base r, with $\Theta(n + r)$ work done at each pass. Thus the total work is $\Theta(nk + rk)$. What is this in terms of n? Since r is the size of the base, it may be rather small. One could use base 2 or 10. Base 26 would be appropriate for sorting character strings. For now, we will treat r as a constant value and ignore it for the purpose of determining asymptotic complexity. Variable k is related to the key range: It is the maximum number of digits that a key may have in base r. In some applications we can determine k to be of limited size, and so may wish to consider it a constant. In this case, Radix Sort is $\Theta(n)$ in the best, average, and worst cases, making it the sort with best asymptotic complexity that we have studied.

Is it a reasonable assumption to treat k as a constant? Or is there some relationship between k and n? If the key range is limited and duplicate key values are common, there may be no relationship between k and n. However,

| 1 | 97 | 17 | 23 | 84 | 28 | 72 | 5 | 67 | 25 |

2	3	4	5	6	7	8	9
1	1	1	2	0	4	1	0

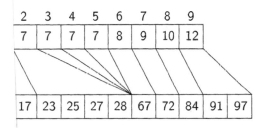

2	3	4	5	6	7	8	9
3	4	5	7	7	11	12	12

| 72 | 23 | 84 | 5 | 25 | 27 | 97 | 17 | 67 | 28 |

2	3	4	5	6	7	8	9
4	0	0	0	1	1	1	2

2	3	4	5	6	7	8	9
7	7	7	7	8	9	10	12

| 17 | 23 | 25 | 27 | 28 | 67 | 72 | 84 | 91 | 97 |

function **radix** applied to the input of l values within the input array. Row 2 after counting the number of records lex values stored in array **count**. For no input values are in bin 0. **Count[1]** s 0 and 1 will hold the values for bin 1. ...y B position 2 will hold the (single) value for bin 2. **Count[7]** is 11, indicating that array B positions 7 through 10 will hold the four values for bin 7. Row 4 shows the results of the first pass of the radix sort. Rows 5 through 7 show the equivalent steps for the second pass.

consider the situation in which no keys are duplicated. If there are n unique keys, then it requires n distinct code values to represent them. To represent n distinct code values requires a minimum of $\log_2 n$ binary bits. In terms of radix r, we require $\log_r n$ base r digits. Thus, in general, it requires *at least* $\Omega(\log n)$ digits (within a constant factor) to store the n distinct numbers. In other words, k is in $\Omega(\log n)$. This yields an asymptotic complexity of $\Omega(n \log n)$ for Radix Sort to process n distinct key values.

It is possible that the key range is much larger; $\log_r n$ bits is merely the best case possible for n distinct values. Thus, the $\log_r n$ estimate for k could be overly optimistic. The moral of this analysis is that, for the general case of n distinct key values, radix sort is at best a $\Omega(n \log n)$ sorting algorithm.

Radix sort can be much improved by making base r be as large as possible. Consider the case of an integer key value. Set $r = 2^i$ for some i. In other words, the value of r is related to the number of bits of the key processed on each pass. Each time the number of bits is doubled, the number of passes is cut in half. When processing an integer key value, setting $r = 256$ allows the key to be processed one byte at a time. Processing a 32-bit key requires only four passes. It is not unreasonable on most computers to use $r = 2^{16} = 64K$, resulting in only two passes. Of course, this requires a `count` array of size 64K. Performance will be good only if the number of records is close to 64K or greater. In other words, the number of records must be large compared to the key size for radix sort to be efficient. In many sorting applications, radix sort can be tuned in this way to give good performance.

Radix Sort depends on the ability to make a fixed number of multiway choices based on a digit value, as well as random access to the bins. Thus, Radix Sort may be difficult to implement for certain key types. For example, if the keys are real numbers or arbitrary length strings, then some care will be necessary in implementation. In particular, Radix Sort will need to be careful about deciding when the "last digit" has been found to distinguish among real numbers, or the last character in variable length strings. Applying the concept of Radix Sort to the trie data structure (Section 13.1) is most appropriate for these situations.

At this point, the perceptive reader might begin to question our earlier assumption that key comparison takes constant time. If the keys are "normal integer" values stored in, say, an integer variable, what is the size of this variable compared to n? In fact, it is almost certain that 32 (the number of bits in a Java `int`) is greater than $\log n$ for any practical computation. In this sense, comparison of two long integers requires $\Omega(\log n)$ work.

Computers normally do arithmetic in units of a particular size, such as a 32-bit word. Regardless of the size of the variables, comparisons use this native word size and require a constant amount of time. In practice, comparisons of two 32-bit values take constant time, even though 32 is much greater than $\log n$. To some extent the truth of the proposition that there are constant time operations (such as integer comparison) is in the eye of the beholder. At the gate level of computer architecture, individual bits are compared. However, constant time comparison for integers is true in practice on most computers, and we rely on such assumptions as the basis for our analyses. In contrast, Radix Sort must do several arithmetic calculations on key values (each requiring constant time), where the number of such calculations is proportional to the key length. Thus, radix sort truly does $\Omega(n \log n)$ work to process n distinct key values.

8.8   An Empirical Comparison of Sorting Algorithms

Which sorting algorithm is fastest? Asymptotic complexity analysis lets us distinguish between $\Theta(n^2)$ and $\Theta(n \log n)$ algorithms, but it does not help distinguish between algorithms with the same asymptotic complexity. Nor does asymptotic analysis say anything about which algorithm is best for sorting small lists. For answers to these questions, we must turn to empirical testing.

Figures 8.14 and 8.15 show timing results for actual implementations of the sorting algorithms presented in this chapter. The algorithms compared include Insertion Sort, Bubble Sort, Selection Sort, Shell Sort, Quicksort, Mergesort, Heapsort and Radix Sort. For Quicksort, two versions are compared: the basic implementation from Section 8.4 and an optimized, nonrecursive version that does not partition sublists below length ten. Mergesort shows both the basic implementation from Section 8.5 and the optimized version with calls to Insertion Sort for lists of length below ten.

The input to each algorithm is a random array of integers. This affects the timing for some of the sorting algorithms. For example, Selection Sort is not being used to best advantage since the record size is small, so it does not get the best possible showing. The Radix Sort implementation certainly takes advantage of this short key range and does not look at more digits than necessary. In particular, Radix Sort assumes that the values are less than 2^{16}. To support full 32-bit integers, the running times would double. Figure 8.14 shows the running time for arrays of sizes 10, 100, 1000, and 10,000 on an IBM-compatible PC running the Windows95™ operating

Algorithm	10	100	1000	10,000	Up	Down
Insert. Sort	.10	9.5	957.9	98,086	22	192,656
Bubble Sort	.13	14.3	1470.3	157,230	101,926	193,337
Select. Sort	.11	9.9	1018.9	104,897	102,398	102,711
Shellsort	.09	2.5	45.6	829	247	484
Quicksort	.15	1.8	23.6	291	176	193
Quicksort/O	.10	1.6	20.9	274	127	170
Mergesort	.12	2.4	36.8	505	395	390
Mergesort/O	.08	1.8	28.0	390	302	450
Heapsort	–	50.0	60.0	880	980	940
Radix Sort/1	.87	8.6	89.5	939	923	923
Radix Sort/2	.44	4.3	44.5	478	461	462
Radix Sort/4	.23	2.3	22.5	236	231	236
Radix Sort/8	.19	1.2	11.5	115	120	121

Figure 8.14 Empirical comparison of sorting algorithms on a PC running Windows95 and Visual **J++**. All times are in milliseconds. For each algorithm, times are shown for sorting arrays of 10, 100, 1000, and 10,000 records. Also shown are times for sorting 10,000 records in ascending key order (column "up") and sorting 10,000 records in descending key order ("down"). Quicksort and Mergesort are each shown with regular and optimized versions. Radix Sort is shown for 1, 2, 4 and 8 bit-per-pass versions.

Algorithm	10	100	1000	10,000	Up	Down
Insert. Sort	.66	65.9	6423	661,711	129	1,176,829
Bubble Sort	.90	85.5	8447	1,068,268	673,057	1,411,337
Select. Sort	.73	67.4	6678	668,056	686,090	682,790
Shellsort	.62	18.5	321	5,593	1,717	3,259
Quicksort	.92	12.7	169	1,836	1,187	1,384
Quicksort/O	.65	10.7	141	1,781	907	1,165
Mergesort	.76	16.8	234	3,231	2,493	2,446
Mergesort/O	.53	11.8	189	2,649	1,955	2,985
Heapsort	–	41.0	565	7,973	9,151	8,013
Radix Sort/1	7.40	67.4	679	6,895	6,852	6,898
Radix Sort/2	3.90	33.6	331	3,628	3,340	3,266
Radix Sort/4	2.10	18.7	160	1,678	1,693	1,648
Radix Sort/8	4.10	11.5	97	808	815	805

Figure 8.15 Empirical comparison of sorting algorithms on a Sun SPARC-station for the sorts shown in Figure 8.14. All times are in milliseconds.

system with the Visual **J++**™ compiler. Figure 8.15 shows the running time for equivalent sizes on a Sun SPARCstation™ running UNIX. The final two columns of each figure show the performance for the algorithms when run on inputs of size 10,000 where the numbers are in ascending (sorted) and descending (reverse sorted) order, respectively. These columns demonstrate best-case performance for some algorithms and worst-case performance for others. These columns also show that for some algorithms, the order of input has little effect.

These figures show a number of interesting results. As expected, Quicksort is consistently a good performer. Surprisingly, the optimized version is only slightly better than the original version. Such optimizations are highly language dependent; under **C** or **C++** equivalent optimizations would typically save roughly one quarter of the total time. The optimized Mergesort is a clear improvement over the regular version. Heapsort is a relatively poor performer on both machines, but the penalty is much worse on the UNIX machine. For small lists, Insertion Sort performs as well as Quicksort and Mergesort.

Radix Sort using 8 bits per pass is by far the best performer for large lists. Note however that this applies to 16-bit key values. If 32-bit key values are used, Radix Sort will take twice as long while times for the other sorts will not change significantly.

8.9   Lower Bounds for Sorting

This book contains many analyses for algorithms. These analyses generally define the upper and lower bounds for algorithms in their worst and average cases. For most of the algorithms presented so far, analysis is easy. This section considers a more difficult task – an analysis for the cost of a *problem* as opposed to an *algorithm*. The upper bound for a problem can be defined as the asymptotic cost of the fastest known algorithm. The lower bound defines the best possible efficiency for *any* algorithm that solves the problem, including algorithms not yet invented. Once the upper and lower bounds for the problem meet, we know that no future algorithm can possibly be (asymptotically) more efficient.

A simple estimate for a problem's lower bound can be obtained by measuring the size of the input that must be read and the output that must be written. Certainly no algorithm can be more efficient than the problem's minimum I/O time. From this we see that the problem of sorting cannot be solved by *any* algorithm in less than $\Omega(n)$ time since it takes at least n steps to read and write the n values to be sorted. Based on our current knowledge of sorting algorithms and the size of the input, we know that the *problem* of sorting is bounded by $\Omega(n)$ and $O(n \log n)$.

Computer scientists have spent much time devising efficient general purpose sorting algorithms, but no one has ever found one that is faster than $O(n \log n)$ in the worst or average cases. Should we keep searching for a faster sorting algorithm? Or can we prove that there is no faster sorting algorithm by finding a tighter lower bound?

This section presents one of the most important and most useful proofs in computer science: that no sorting algorithm based on key comparisons can possibly be faster than $\Omega(n \log n)$ in the worst case. This proof is important for three reasons. First, knowing that widely used sorting algorithms are asymptotically optimal is reassuring. In particular, it means that you need not bang your head against the wall searching for an $O(n)$ sorting algorithm (or at least not one in any way based on key comparisons). Second, this proof is one of the few nontrivial lower-bounds proofs that we have for any problem; that is, this proof provides one of the few instances where our lower bound is tighter than simply measuring the size of the input and output. As such, it provides a useful model for proving lower bounds on other problems. Finally, knowing a lower bound for sorting gives us a lower bound in turn for other problems whose solution could be used as the basis for a sorting algorithm. The process of deriving asymptotic bounds for one problem from the asymptotic bounds of another is called a **reduction**, a concept further explored in Chapter 15.

Except for the Radix Sort and Binsort, all of the sorting algorithms presented in this chapter make decisions based on the direct comparison of two key values. For example, Insertion Sort sequentially compares the value to be inserted into the sorted list until a comparison against the next value in the list fails. In contrast, Radix Sort has no direct comparison of key values. All decisions are based on the value of specific digits in the key value. So it is possible to take approaches to sorting that do not involve key comparisons. Of course, Radix Sort in the end does not provide a more efficient sorting algorithm than comparison-based sorting. Thus, empirical evidence suggests that comparison-based sorting is a good approach.[3]

---

[3]The truth is stronger than this statement implies. In reality, Radix Sort relies on comparisons as well, and so can be modeled by the technique used in this section. The result is an $\Omega(n \log n)$ bound in the general case even for algorithms that look like Radix Sort.

The proof that any comparison sort requires $\Omega(n \log n)$ comparisons in the worst case is structured as follows. First, you will see how comparison decisions can be modeled as the branches in a binary tree. This means that any sorting algorithm based on comparisons can be viewed as a binary tree whose internal nodes correspond to comparisons. Next, the minimum number of leaves in the resulting tree is shown to be the factorial of n. Finally, the minimum depth of a tree with $n!$ leaves is shown to be in $\Omega(n \log n)$.

Before presenting the proof of an $\Omega(n \log n)$ lower bound for sorting, we first must define the concept of a **decision tree**. A decision tree is a binary tree that can model the processing for any algorithm that makes decisions. Each (binary) decision is represented by a branch in the tree. For the purpose of modeling sorting algorithms, we count all comparisons of key values as decisions. If two keys are compared and the first is less than the second, then this is modeled as a left branch in the decision tree. In the case where the first-value is greater than the second, the algorithm takes the right branch.

Figure 8.16 shows the decision tree that models Insertion Sort on three input values. The first input value is labeled X, the second Y, and the third Z. They are are initially stored in positions 0, 1, and 2, respectively, of input array A. Consider the possible outputs. Initially, we know nothing about the final positions of the three values in the sorted output array. The correct output could be any permutation of the input values. For three values, there are $n! = 6$ permutations. Thus, the root node of the decision tree lists all six permutations that might be the eventual result of the algorithm.

When $n = 3$, the first comparison made by Insertion Sort is between the second item in the input array (Y) and the first item in the array (X). There are two possibilities: Either the value of Y is less than that of X, or the value of Y is *not* less than that of X. This decision is modeled by the first branch in the tree. If Y is less than X, then the left branch should be taken and Y must appear before X in the final output. Only three of the original six permutations have this property, so the left child of the root lists the three permutations where Y appears before X: YXZ, YZX, and ZYX. Likewise, if Y were not less than X, then the right branch would be taken, and only the three permutations in which Y appears after X are possible outcomes: XYZ, XZY, and ZXY. These are listed in the right child of the root.

Let us assume for the moment that Y is less than X and so the left branch is taken. In this case, Insertion Sort swaps the two values. At this point the array stores YXZ. Thus, in Figure 8.16 the left child of the root shows YXZ above the line. Next, the third value in the array is compared against the

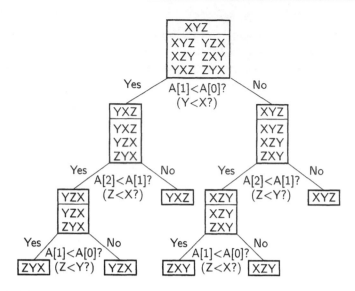

Figure 8.16 Decision tree for Insertion Sort when processing three values labeled X, Y, and Z, initially stored at positions 0, 1, and 2, respectively, in input array A.

second (i.e., Z is compared with X). Again, there are two possibilities. If Z is less than X, then these items should be swapped (the left branch). If Z is not less than X, then Insertion Sort is complete (the right branch). Note that the right branch reaches a leaf node, and that this leaf node contains only permutation YXZ. This means that only permutation YXZ can be the outcome based on the results of the decisions taken to reach this node. In other words, Insertion Sort has "found" the single permutation of the original input that yields a sorted list. Likewise, if the second decision resulted in taking the left branch, a third comparison, regardless of the outcome, yields nodes in the decision tree with only single permutations. Again, Insertion Sort has "found" the correct permutation that yields a sorted list.

Any sorting algorithm based on comparisons can be modeled by a decision tree in this way, regardless of the size of the input. Thus, all sorting algorithms can be viewed as algorithms to "find" the correct permutation of the input that yields a sorted list. Each algorithm based on comparisons can be viewed as proceeding by making branches in the tree based on the results of key comparisons, and each algorithm can terminate once a node with a single permutation has been reached.

How is the worst-case cost of an algorithm expressed by the decision tree? The decision tree shows the decisions made by an algorithm for all possible inputs of a given size. Each path through the tree from the root to a leaf is one possible series of decisions taken by the algorithm. The depth of the deepest node represents the longest series of decisions required by the algorithm to reach an answer.

There are many comparison-based sorting algorithms, and each will be modeled by a different decision tree. Some decision trees may be well-balanced, others may be unbalanced. Some trees will have more nodes than others (those with more nodes may be making "unnecessary" comparisons). In fact, a poor sorting algorithm may have an arbitrarily large number of nodes in its decision tree, with leaves of arbitrary depth. There is no limit to how slow the "worst" possible sorting algorithm could be. However, we are interested here in knowing what the *best* sorting algorithm could have as its minimum cost in the worst case. In other words, we would like to know what is the *smallest* depth possible for the *deepest* node in the tree for any sorting algorithm.

The smallest depth of the deepest node will depend on the number of nodes in the tree. Clearly we would like to "push up" the nodes in the tree, but there is limited room at the top. A tree of height 1 can only store one node (the root); the tree of height 2 can store three nodes; the tree of height 3 can store seven nodes, and so on.

> **Facts to Remember**. A binary tree of height n can store at most $2^n - 1$ nodes. Equivalently, a tree with n nodes requires at least $\lceil \log(n + 1) \rceil$ levels.

What is the minimum number of nodes that must be in the decision tree for any comparison-based sorting algorithm for n values? Since sorting algorithms are in the business of determining which unique permutation of the input corresponds to the sorted list, all sorting algorithms must contain at least one leaf node for each possible permutation. There are $n!$ permutations for a set of n numbers (see Section 2.2).

Since there are at least $n!$ nodes in the tree, we know that the tree must have $\Omega(\log n!)$ levels. From Stirling's approximation (Section 2.2), we know $\log n!$ is in $\Omega(n \log n)$. The decision tree for any comparison-based sorting algorithm must have nodes $\Omega(n \log n)$ levels deep. Thus, in the worst case, any such sorting algorithm must require $\Omega(n \log n)$ comparisons.

Any sorting algorithm requiring $\Omega(n \log n)$ comparisons in the worst case requires $\Omega(n \log n)$ running time in the worst case. Since any sorting algorithm requires $\Omega(n \log n)$ running time, the problem of sorting also requires $\Omega(n \log n)$ time. We already know of sorting algorithms with $O(n \log n)$ running time, so we can conclude that the problem of sorting requires $\Theta(n \log n)$ time. As a corollary, we know that no comparison-based sorting algorithm can improve on existing $\Theta(n \log n)$ time sorting algorithms by more than a constant factor.

8.10   Further Reading

The definitive reference on sorting is Donald E. Knuth's *Sorting and Searching* [Knu81]. A wealth of details is covered there, including optimal sorts for small size n and special purpose sorting networks. It is a thorough (although somewhat dated) treatment on sorting. For a more recent analysis of Quicksort and a thorough survey on its optimizations, see Robert Sedgewick's *Quicksort* [Sed80]. Sedgewick's *Algorithms* [Sed88] discusses most of the sorting algorithms described here, and pays special attention to efficient implementation.

While $\Omega(n \log n)$ is the theoretical lower bound in the worst case for sorting, many times the input is sufficiently well-ordered that certain algorithms can take advantage of this fact to speed the sorting process. A simple example is Insertion Sort's best-case running time. Sorting algorithms whose running time is based on the amount of disorder of the input are called **adaptive**. For more information on adaptive sorting algorithms, see "A Survey of Adaptive Sorting Algorithms" by Estivill-Castro and Wood [ECW92].

8.11   Exercises

8.1 Using induction, prove that Insertion Sort will always produce a sorted array.

8.2 Write an Insertion Sort algorithm for integer key values. However, here's the catch: The input is a stack (*not* an array), and the only variables that your algorithm may use are a fixed number of integers and a fixed number of stacks. The algorithm should return a stack containing the records in sorted order (with the least value being at the top of the stack). Your algorithm should be $\Theta(n^2)$ in the worst case.

8.3 The Bubble Sort implementation has the following inner **for** loop:

```
for (int j=n-1; j>i; j--)
```

Consider the effect of replacing this with the following statement:

```
for (int j=n-1; j>0; j--)
```

Would the new implementation work correctly? Would the change affect the asymptotic complexity of the algorithm? How would the change affect the running time of the algorithm?

8.4 When implementing Insertion Sort, a binary search could be used to locate the position within the first $i - 1$ elements of the array into which element i should be inserted. Why would using such a binary search not speed up the asymptotic running time for Insertion Sort?

8.5 Figure 8.5 shows the best-case number of swaps for Selection Sort as $\Theta(n)$. This is because the algorithm does not check to see if the ith record is already in the ith position; that is, it may perform unnecessary swaps.

(a) Modify the algorithm so that it does not make unnecessary swaps.

(b) What is your prediction regarding whether this modification actually improves the running time?

(c) Write two programs to compare the actual running times of the original Selection Sort and the modified algorithm. Which one is actually faster?

8.6 Recall that a sorting algorithm is said to be stable if the original ordering for duplicate keys is preserved. Which of the sorting algorithms presented in this chapter are stable, and which are not? For each one, describe either why it is or is not stable. If a minor change to the implementation would make it stable, describe the change.

8.7 Figure 8.9 presents an optimized version of Quicksort that uses a stack instead of recursion. How deep can the stack get in the worst case? How can the order of calls be managed to minimize the stack size, and how deep can the stack become if this is done? Show the appropriate modification to Figure 8.9.

8.8 Assume L is an array, `L.length` returns the number of records in the array, and `qsort(L, 0, i)` sorts the records of L from 0 to i (leaving the records sorted in L) using the Quicksort algorithm. What is the average-case time complexity for each of the following code fragments?

(a)
```
for (i=0; i<L.length; i++)
    qsort(L, 0, i);
```

(b) `for (i=0; i<L.length; i++)`
    `qsort(L, 0, L.length-1);`

8.9 Modify Quicksort to sort a sequence of variable length strings stored one after the other in a character array, with a second array (storing pointers to strings) used to index the strings. Your function should modify the index array so that the first pointer points to the beginning of the lowest-valued string, and so on.

8.10 Graph $f_1(n) = n \log n$, $f_2(n) = n^{1.5}$, and $f_3(n) = n^2$ in the range $1 \leq n \leq 1000$ to visually compare their growth rates. Typically, the constant factor in the running-time expression for an implementation of Insertion Sort will be less than the constant factors for Shellsort or Quicksort. How many times greater can the constant factor be for Shellsort to be faster than Insertion Sort when $n = 1000$? How many times greater can the constant factor be for Quicksort to be faster than Insertion Sort when $n = 1000$?

8.11 Imagine that there exists an algorithm SPLITk that can split a list **L** of n elements into k sublists, each containing one or more elements, such that sublist i contains only elements whose values are less than all elements in sublist j for $i < j <= k$. If $n < k$, then $k - n$ sublists are empty, and the rest are of length 1. Assume that SPLITk has time complexity O(length of **L**). Furthermore, assume that the k lists can be concatenated together again in constant time. Consider the following algorithm:

```
List SORTk(List L) {
  List sub[k];  // To hold the sublists
  if (L.length() > 1) {
    SPLITk(L, sub);  // SPLITk places the sublists into sub
    for (i=0; i<k; i++)
      sub[i] = SORTk(sub[i]);  // Sort each sublist
    L = concatenation of k sublists in sub;
    return L;
  }
}
```

(a) What is the worst-case asymptotic running time for SORTk? Why?

(b) What is the average-case asymptotic running time of SORTk? Why?

8.12 Here is a variation on sorting. The problem is to sort a collection of n nuts and n bolts by size. It is assumed that for each bolt in the collection, there is a corresponding nut of the same size, but initially we do not know which nut goes with which bolt. The differences in size between two nuts or two bolts can be too small to see by eye, so you cannot rely on comparing the sizes of two nuts or two bolts directly. Instead, you can only compare the sizes of a nut and a bolt by attempting to screw one into the other (assume this comparison to be a constant time operation). This operation tells you that either the nut is bigger than the bolt, the bolt is bigger than the nut, or they are the same size. What is the minimum number of comparisons needed to sort the nuts and bolts in the worst case?

8.13 (a) Devise an algorithm to sort three numbers. Try to make it as efficient as possible. How many comparisons and swaps are required in the best, worst, and average cases?

    (b) Devise an algorithm to sort five numbers. Try to make it as efficient as possible. How many comparisons and swaps are required in the best, worst, and average cases?

    (c) Devise an algorithm to sort eight numbers. Try to make it as efficient as possible. How many comparisons and swaps are required in the best, worst, and average cases?

8.14 Devise an algorithm to sort a set of numbers in the range 0 to 30,000. There are no duplicates. Keep memory requirements to a minimum.

8.15 Which of the following operations are best implemented by first sorting the list of numbers? For each operation, briefly describe an algorithm to implement it, and state the algorithm's asymptotic complexity.

    (a) Find the minimum value.

    (b) Find the maximum value.

    (c) Compute the arithmetic mean.

    (d) Find the median (i.e., the middle value).

    (e) Find the mode (i.e., the value that appears the most times).

8.16 Consider a recursive Mergesort implementation that calls Insertion Sort on sublists smaller than some threshold. If there are n calls to Mergesort, how many calls will there be to Insertion Sort? Why?

8.17 Implement Mergesort for the case where the input is a linked list.

8.18 Use an argument similar to that given in Section 8.9 to prove that $\log n$ is a worst-case lower bound for the problem of searching for a given value in a sorted array containing n elements.

8.19 Give a permutation for the values 0 through 7 that will cause Quicksort (as implemented in Section 8.4) to have its worst case behavior.

8.12 Projects

8.1 Starting with the Java code for Quicksort given in this chapter, write a series of Quicksort implementations to test the following optimizations on a wide range of input data sizes. Try these optimizations in various combinations to try and develop the fastest possible Quicksort implementation that you can.

   (a) Look at more values when selecting a pivot.

   (b) Do not make a recursive call to `qsort` when the list size falls below a given threshold, and use Insertion Sort to complete the sorting process. Test various values for the threshold size.

   (c) Eliminate recursion by using a stack and inline functions.

8.2 Write your own collection of sorting programs to implement the algorithms described in this chapter, and compare their running times. Be sure to implement optimized versions, trying to make each program as fast as possible. Do you get the same relative timings as shown in Figure 8.14 or 8.15? If not, why do you think this happened? How do your results compare to those of your classmates? What does this say about the difficulty of doing empirical timing studies?

8.3 Perform a study of Shell Sort, using different increments. Compare the version shown in Section 8.3, where each increment is half the previous one, with others. In particular, try implementing "division by 3" where the increments on a list of length n will be $n/3$, $n/9$, etc. Do other increment schemes work as well?

9

File Processing and External Sorting

This chapter describes the fundamental differences between primary memory and secondary storage (such as disk and tape drives) as they affect algorithm and data structure designers. These differences have primarily to do with speed of access, quantity, and persistence of data stored in the medium. Most file processing techniques derive from one fundamental fact: Access to disk and tape drives is tremendously slower than access to primary memory. How this tremendous difference in speed affects disk-based applications motivates a study of disk-based sorting as distinct from in-memory sorting.

We begin with a description of the significant differences between primary memory and secondary storage. Section 9.2 discusses the physical aspects of disk and tape drives. Section 9.3 presents basic methods for managing buffer pools. Buffer pools will be used several times in the following chapters. Section 9.4 discusses the random access model of access to data stored on disk. Sections 9.5 to 9.8 discuss the basic principles of sorting collections of records too large to fit in main memory.

9.1 Primary Versus Secondary Storage

Computer storage devices are typically classified into **primary** or **main** memory and **secondary** or **peripheral** storage. Primary memory usually refers to **Random Access Memory** (RAM), while secondary storage refers to devices such as hard disk drives, floppy disk drives and tape drives. Primary memory also includes cache and video memories, but we will ignore them since their existence does not affect the principal differences between primary and secondary memory.

Medium	Price	Price per Megabyte
32MB RAM	$225	$7.00/MB
1.4MB floppy disk	$.50	$0.36/MB
2.1GB disk drive	$210	$0.10/MB
1GB JAZ cassette	$100	$0.10/MB
2GB cartridge tape	$20	$0.01/MB

Figure 9.1 Price comparison table for writable electronic data storage media in common use. Prices are representative of mid 1997.

Along with a faster CPU, every new model of computer seems to come with more main memory. As memory size continues to increase, is it possible that relatively slow disk storage will be unnecessary? Probably not, since the desire to store and process larger files grows at least as fast as main memory size. While prices for both main memory and peripheral storage devices are dropping rapidly, a look at the price chart of Figure 9.1 shows that disk drive storage per megabyte is about two orders of magnitude less than RAM. Floppy disks used to be considerably cheaper per megabyte than hard disk drives, but now their price per megabyte is actually greater. Filling in the gap between hard drives and floppy disks are removable drives, whose price per storage unit is comparable to that of a fixed disk drive. Magnetic tape is perhaps an order of magnitude cheaper than disk. Optical storage such as CD-ROMs provide even greater storage at further reductions in price.[1]

Secondary storage devices have at least two other advantages over RAM memory. Perhaps most importantly, disk and tape files are **persistent**, meaning that they are not erased from disk and tape when the power is turned off. In contrast, RAM used for main memory is usually **volatile** – all information is lost with the power. A second advantage is that floppy disks, removable drives, CD-ROMs, and magnetic tape can easily be transferred between computers. This provides a convenient way to take information from one computer to another.

In exchange for reduced storage costs, persistence, and portability, secondary storage devices must pay a penalty in terms of increased access time. While not all accesses to disk take the same amount of time (more on this later), the typical time required to access a byte of storage from a disk drive in 1997 is around 10 ms (i.e., 10 *thousandths* of a second). This may not seem slow, but compared to the time required to access a byte from main

---

[1]As of this writing, CD-ROMs are generally read-only (hence the name) and are sold by information content, not storage capacity. Thus, they are not included in Figure 9.1.

memory, this is fantastically slow. Access time from standard personal computer RAM in 1997 is about 60 or 70 nanoseconds (i.e., 60 or 70 *billionths* of a second). Thus, the time to access a byte of data from a disk drive is about a quarter million times longer than that required to access a byte from main memory. While disk drive and RAM access times are both decreasing, they have done so at roughly the same rate. Ten years ago, the relative speeds were about the same as they are today, in that the difference in access time between RAM and a disk drive has remained in the range between a factor of 100,000 and 1,000,000.

To gain some intuition for the significance of this speed difference, consider the time that it might take for you to look up the entry for disk drives in the index of this book, and then turn to the appropriate page. Call this your "primary memory" access time. If it takes you about 20 seconds to perform this access, then an access taking a quarter million times longer would require about two months.

Due to the relatively slow access time for data on disk, great care is required to create efficient applications that process disk-based information. The million-to-one ratio of disk access time versus main memory access time makes the following rule of paramount importance when designing disk-based applications:

Minimize the number of disk accesses!

There are generally two approaches to minimizing disk accesses. The first is to arrange information so that if you do access data from secondary memory, you will get what you need in as few accesses as possible, and preferably on the first access. **File structure** is the term used for a data structure that organizes data stored in secondary memory. File structures should be organized so as to minimize disk accesses. The other way to minimize disk accesses is to arrange information so that each disk access retrieves additional data that can be used to minimize the need for future accesses, that is, to guess accurately what information will be needed later and retrieve it from disk now, if this can be done cheaply. As you shall see, there is little or no difference in the time required to read several hundred contiguous bytes from disk or tape as compared to reading one byte, so this technique is indeed practical.

One way to minimize disk accesses is to compress the information stored on disk. Section 3.8 discusses the space/time tradeoff in which space requirements can be reduced if you are willing to sacrifice time. However, the disk-based space/time tradeoff principle stated that the smaller you can make your disk storage requirements, the faster your program will run. This is because the time to read information from disk is enormous compared to computation time, so almost any amount of additional computation to unpack the data is going to be less than the disk read time saved by reducing the storage requirements. This is precisely what happens when files are compressed. CPU time is required to uncompress information, but this time is likely to be much less than the time saved by reducing the number of bytes read. Current file compression programs are not designed to allow random access to parts of a compressed file, so the disk-based space/time tradeoff principle cannot easily be taken advantage of in normal processing using commercial disk compression utilities. However, in the future disk drive controllers may automatically compress and decompress files stored on disk, thus taking advantage of the disk-based space/time tradeoff principle to save both space and time. Many cartridge tape drives today automatically compress and decompress information during I/O.

9.2   Disk and Tape Drives

A Java programmer views a random access file stored on disk as a contiguous series of bytes, with those bytes possibly combining to form data records. This is called the **logical** file. The **physical** file actually stored on disk is usually not a contiguous series of bytes. It could well be in pieces spread all over the disk. The **file manager**, a part of the operating system, is responsible for taking requests for data from a logical file and mapping those requests to the physical location of the data on disk. Likewise, when writing to a particular logical byte position with respect to the beginning of the file, this position must be converted by the file manager into the corresponding physical location on the disk. To gain some appreciation for the the approximate time costs for these operations, you need to understand the physical structure and basic workings of a disk drive.

Disk drives are often referred to as **direct access** storage devices. This means that it takes roughly equal time to access any record in the file. This is in contrast to **sequential access** storage devices such as tape drives, which require the tape reader to process data from the beginning of the tape until the desired position has been reached. As you will see, the disk drive is only approximately direct access: At any given time, some records are more quickly accessible than others.

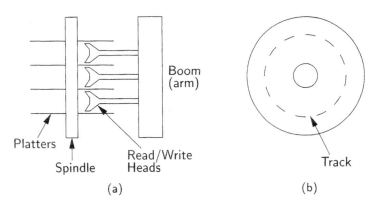

Figure 9.2 (a) A typical disk drive arranged as a stack of platters. (b) One track on a disk drive platter.

A hard disk drive is composed of one or more round **platters**, stacked one on top of another and attached to a central **spindle**. Platters spin continuously at a constant rate, like a record on a phonograph. Each usable surface of each platter is assigned a **read/write head** or **I/O head** through which data are read or written, somewhat like the arrangement of a phonograph player's arm "reading" sound from a phonograph record. Unlike a phonograph needle, the disk read/write head does not actually touch the surface of a hard disk. Instead, it remains slightly above the surface, and any contact during normal operation would damage the disk. This distance is very small, much smaller than the height of a dust particle. It can be likened to a 5000 kilometer airplane trip across the United States, with the plane flying at a height of one meter! In contrast, the read/write head on a floppy disk drive is in contact with the surface of the disk, which in part accounts for its relatively slow access time.

A hard disk drive typically has several platters and several read/write heads, as shown in Figure 9.2(a). Each head is attached to an **arm**, which connects to the **boom**. The boom moves all of the heads in or out together. When the heads are in some position over the platters, there are data on each platter directly accessible to each head. The data on a single platter that are accessible to any one position of the head for that platter are collectively called a **track**, that is, all data on a platter that are a fixed distance from the spindle, as shown in Figure 9.2(b). The collection of all tracks that are a fixed distance from the spindle is called a **cylinder**. Thus, a cylinder is all of the data that can be read when the arms are in a particular position.

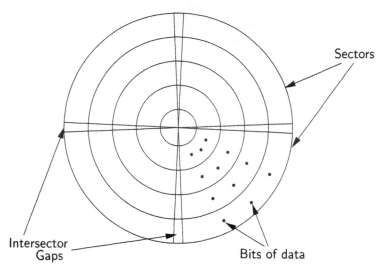

Figure 9.3 The organization of a disk platter. Dots indicate density of information.

Each track is subdivided into **sectors**. Between each sector there are **intersector gaps** in which no data are stored. These gaps allow the read head to recognize the end of a sector. Note that each sector contains the same amount of data. Since the outer tracks have greater length, they contain less bits per inch than do the inner tracks. Thus, about half of the potential storage space is wasted, since only the innermost tracks are stored at the highest possible data density. This arrangement is illustrated by Figure 9.3.

In contrast to the physical layout of a hard disk, a CD-ROM (and some floppy disk configurations) consists of a single spiral track. Bits of information along the track are equally spaced, so the information density is the same at both the outer and inner portions of the track. To keep the information flow at a constant rate along the spiral, the drive must slow down the rate of disk spin as the I/O head moves toward the center of the disk. This makes for a more complicated and slower mechanism.

Three separate steps take place when reading a particular byte or series of bytes of data from a hard disk. First, the I/O head moves so it is positioned over the track containing the data. This movement is called a **seek**. Second, the sector containing the data rotates to come under the head. When in use the disk is always spinning, typically at the rate of 3600 or 7200 rotations per minute. The time spent waiting for the desired sector to come under the I/O head is called **rotational delay** or **rotational latency**. Third is the actual transfer (i.e., reading or writing) of data. It takes relatively little time to read information once it is positioned under the I/O head, simply the amount of time required for it to move under the head. In fact, disk drives are designed not to read one byte of data, but rather to read an entire sector of data at each request. Thus, a sector is the minimum amount of data that can be read or written at one time.

After reading a sector of data, the computer must take time to process it. While processing takes place, the disk continues to rotate. When reading several contiguous sectors of data at one time, this rotation creates a problem since the drive will read the first sector, process data, and find that the second sector has moved out from under the I/O head in the meantime. The disk must then rotate to bring the second sector under the I/O head.

Since each disk has fixed rotation rate and fixed processing time for one sector of data, system designers can know how far the disk will rotate between the time when a sector is read and when the I/O head is ready for the next sector. Instead of having the second logical sector physically adjacent to the first, it is better for the second logical sector to be at the position that will be under the I/O head when the I/O head is ready for it. Arranging data in this way is called **interleaving**, and the physical distance between logically adjacent sectors is called the **interleaving factor**. Figure 9.4(b) shows the sectors within one track arranged with an interleaving factor of three. Sector 2 is separated from sector 1 by sectors 4 and 7. Reading an entire track will require three rotations of the disk from the time when sector 1 first moves under the I/O head. During the first rotation, sectors 1, 2, and 3 can be read. During the second rotation, sectors 4, 5, and 6 can be read. Sectors 7 and 8 can be read during the third rotation.

Contrast reading the interleaved sectors of Figure 9.4(b) with the simple contiguous arrangement of Figure 9.4(a). After reading the first sector, and following some delay to process the information just read, the disk must rotate until sector 2 is once again under the I/O head, nearly a full rotation. Without interleaving, eight rotations of the disk are needed to read the entire track of Figure 9.4(a).

In general, it is desirable to keep all sectors for a file together. This stems from two assumptions:

1. Seek time is slow (it is typically the most expensive part of an I/O operation), and

2. If one sector of the file is read, the next sector will probably soon be read.

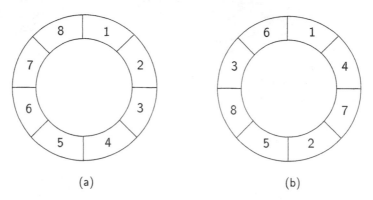

Figure 9.4 The organization of a disk drive track. (a) No interleaving of sectors. (b) Sectors arranged with an interleaving factor of three.

Assumption (2) is called **locality of reference**, and is a concept that comes up repeatedly in computer science.

Sectors are often grouped to form a **cluster**. The sectors making up a cluster may be interleaved. A cluster is the smallest unit of allocation for a file, so all files are a multiple of the cluster size. The cluster size is determined by the operating system. The file manager keeps track of which clusters make up each file. In MS-DOS systems, there is a designated portion of the disk called the **File Allocation Table**, which stores information about which sectors belong to which file. In contrast, UNIX does not use clusters. The smallest unit of file allocation and the smallest unit that can be read/written is a sector, which in UNIX terminology is called a **block**. UNIX maintains information about file organization in certain blocks called **i-nodes**.

A group of physically contiguous clusters from the same file is called an **extent**. Ideally, all clusters making up a file will be contiguous on the disk (i.e., the file will consist of one extent), so as to minimize seek time required to access different portions of the file. If the disk is nearly full when a file is created, there may not be a extent available that is large enough to hold the new file. Furthermore, if a file grows, there may not be free space physically adjacent. Thus, a file may consist of several extents widely spaced on the disk. The fuller the disk, and the more that files on the disk change, the worse this file fragmentation (and the resulting seek time) becomes. File fragmentation leads to a noticeable degradation in performance as additional seeks are required to access data.

Another type of problem arises when the file's logical record size does not match the sector size. If the sector size is not a multiple of the record size (or vice versa), records will not fit evenly within a sector. For example, a sector

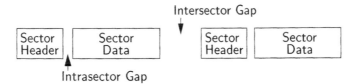

Figure 9.5 An illustration of sector gaps within a track. Each sector begins with a sector header containing the sector address and an error detection code for the contents of that sector. The sector header is followed by a small intrasector gap, followed in turn by the sector data. Each sector is separated from the next sector by a larger intersector gap.

might be 2048 bytes long, and a logical record 100 bytes. This leaves room to store 20 records with 48 bytes left over. Either the extra space is wasted, or else records are allowed to cross sector boundaries. If a record crosses a sector boundary, two disk accesses may be required to read it. If the space is left empty instead, such wasted space is called **internal fragmentation**.

A second example of internal fragmentation occurs at cluster boundaries. Files whose size is not an even multiple of the cluster size must waste some space at the end of the last cluster. The worst case will occur when file size modulo cluster size is one (for example, a file of 2049 bytes and a cluster of 2048 bytes). Thus, cluster size is a tradeoff between large files processed sequentially (where a large cluster size is desirable to minimize seeks) and small files (where small clusters are desirable to minimize wasted storage).

Every disk drive organization requires that some disk space be used to organize the sectors, clusters, and so forth. The layout of sectors within a track is illustrated by Figure 9.5. Typical information that must be stored on the disk itself includes the File Allocation Table, **sector headers** that contain address marks and information about the condition (whether usable or not) for each sector, and gaps between sectors. The sector header also contains error detection codes to help verify that the data have not been corrupted. This is why most disk drives have a "nominal" size that is greater than the actual amount of useful data that can be stored on the drive. A typical example might be a disk drive with a nominal size of 1044MB that actually provides 1000MB of disk space after formatting. The difference is the amount of space required to organize the information on the disk. Additional space will be lost due to fragmentation.

9.2.1 Disk Access Costs

The primary cost when accessing a sector on disk is normally the seek time. This assumes of course that a seek is necessary. When reading a file in sequential order (if the sectors comprising the file are physically contiguous), little seeking is necessary. However, when accessing a random disk sector, the average distance between the current track and the desired track is one third the number of tracks on the disk. This expected cost is derived by averaging the distances for all of the possible cases for seeking between two random tracks. The cost of a seek can be further broken into **startup time** to get the arm moving, and the time required to traverse one track. Thus, the cost to seek a distance of n tracks can be expressed by the equation $f(n) = t * n + s$ where t is the time to traverse one track and s is the startup time. A typical example is the 675MB Maxtor disk drive. The manufacturer's specifications indicate that $t = 0.08$ ms and $s = 3$ ms on a platter with 612 tracks. Thus, the average seek time for this disk drive can be computed as $0.08 * 612/3 + 3 \approx 19.3$ ms.

For many years, typical rotation speed for disk drives was 3600 rpm, or one rotation every 16.7 ms. Newer disk drives have a rotation speed of 7200 rpm. When reading a sector at random, you can expect that the disk will need to rotate halfway around to bring the desired sector under the I/O head, or 8.3 ms for a 3600 rpm disk drive.

Once under the I/O head, a sector of data can be transferred as fast as that sector rotates under the head. If an entire track is to be read, then it will require one rotation (16.7 ms) to move the full track under the head. If only part of the track is to be read, then proportionately less time will be required. For example, if there are 32 sectors on the track and one sector is to be read, this will require about 0.5 ms.

> **Example 9.1** Assume that a disk drive has a total (nominal) capacity of 675MB spread among 15 platters, yielding 45MB/platter. Each platter contains 612 tracks and each track contains 150 sectors of 512 bytes/sector. I/O head startup time is 3 ms and the time for the head to traverse one track during a seek is 0.08 ms. Assume the operating system maintains a cluster size of 8 sectors per cluster (4KB), yielding 18 clusters per track (the remaining space is lost). Based on this information we can estimate the cost for disk access.
>
> Assume that the interleaving factor is three. How many revolutions of the disk will be required to read one track once the first

sector of the track is under the I/O head? The answer is three, since one third of the sectors will be read during each rotation. How much time is required to read the track? Since it requires three rotations at 16.7 ms per rotation, the entire time is 50.1 ms.

How long will it take to read a file of 128KB divided into 256 sector-sized (512 byte) records? This file will be stored in 32 clusters, since each cluster holds exactly 8 sectors. The answer to the question depends in large measure on how the file is stored on the disk, that is, whether it is all together or broken into multiple extents. We will calculate both cases to see how much difference this makes. If the file is stored so as to fill all 144 usable sectors of one track and 112 sectors of an adjacent track, then the cost will be the time to seek to the first track (assuming this requires a random seek of one third the width of the disk), then a wait for the initial rotational delay, then the time to read (requiring three rotations due to interleaving), then the time to seek to the adjacent track, a second rotational delay, and finally the time to read the remaining sectors (which we will simplify by assuming it requires three complete rotations, which is nearly correct). Thus, the total expected time is

Total Time = (Initial Seek) + (Rotational Delay + Transfer Time)+
(Second Seek) + (Rotational Delay + Transfer Time) =
(612/3*0.08+3)+((.5+3)16.7)+(0.08+3)+((.5+3)16.7) = 139.3 ms.

If the file's clusters are spread randomly across the disk, then the time required is the time to read 32 clusters at random, which means a random seek followed by the rotational delay, followed by the time for the disk to rotate through 24/150 of a rotation (since we want to read 8 sectors with an interleaving factor of three). This yields

$$32 * (612/3 * 0.08 + 3 + 16.7/2 + 24/150 * 16.7)$$
$$= 32 * 30.3 = 969.6 \text{ ms,}$$

or nearly a second. This example illustrates why it is important to keep disk files from becoming fragmented, and why so-called "disk defragmenters" can speed up file processing time. File fragmentation happens most commonly when the disk is nearly full and the file manager must search for free space whenever a file is created or changed.

Example 9.2 To read a single sector of information requires a seek, followed by rotational delay as the desired sector comes under the I/O head, and finally the time for the sector to pass under the head. Using the specifications from Example 9.1, this is

$$612/3 * 0.08 + 3 + 16.7/2 + 1/150 * 16.7 = 27.8 \text{ ms}.$$

This value is sometimes referred to as the **average access time** for the disk drive. Actually, this is something of an over-simplification. When most disk drive manufacturers today calculate average access time, they also take into consideration the probability that the desired information will already reside in the **disk cache**, which stores sectors recently read. For example, the manufacturer of this disk drive claims an average access time of roughly one half our computed value. Section 9.3 discusses the concept of caching.

9.2.2 Magnetic Tape

Magnetic tape is typically much cheaper than hard disk space. Typical 9-track tapes costing $20 are designed to store data at 6250 bytes per inch (bpi), and are 2400 feet long. Thus, a 9-track tape is theoretically able to hold about 170MB, at a cost of less than 12 cents per megabyte. Unfortunately, a good 9-track tape drive costs more than a workstation these days, perhaps $10,000 to $20,000. Thus, 9-track tape is not commonly used for workstations, but is still widely used at larger computing facilities. Cartridge tape is similar to 9-track tape and is commonly used with workstations and personal computers. A 1GB cartridge tape costs about $20, or 1¢ per megabyte.

Magnetic tape drives are different from disk drives in that tape can only be accessed sequentially. In other words, you can't get to the middle of the tape without winding or rewinding the tape from the current location through to the desired location. This makes tapes unacceptably slow for random access. A second physical characteristic that affects tape drive performance is that it takes some time for the tape drive to stop the tape. Thus, a large **interblock gap** must separate data so that the I/O head can recognize that a gap has occurred, and stop the drive. This interblock gap is typically the size of many records. Thus, putting a gap between each record would waste a lot of space. To avoid this waste, records are grouped into **blocks**; the number of records in a block is called the **blocking factor**. The tape can only stop a high-speed wind or rewind at the block gaps. To find a particular record or file requires that the tape (relatively) quickly reach the desired block. The I/O head must then slowly read that block, allowing the CPU to receive the desired record. Thus, large block size saves space, but at the price of increased time needed to process an individual record within the block. If blocks are always processed sequentially as a unit, then this is not an issue.

The second performance measure for tape drives is how fast they can transfer data. A typical 9-track tape drive can process data at the rate of 200 inches per second (ips). The nominal (or peak) transfer rate for a 6250 bpi tape on a 200 ips tape drive is then

$$6250 \text{ bpi} \times 200 \text{ ips} = 1.25 \text{MB/s}.$$

However, the interblock gap reduces the actual data density on the tape, and thus the fastest possible transfer rate. Time to find the desired record and processing time further reduce peak transmission rates.

Since tape is so cheap, but also so slow and appropriate only for sequential access, it is usually not used to store data intended for rapid access. Rather, tapes are normally used for backup and archiving. Since tapes are no longer commonly used for on-line processing, they are not discussed further in this book.

9.3   Buffers and Buffer Pools

Consider once more the time required to read data from a disk drive. Given the specifications of the disk drive from Example 9.1, we find that it takes about $612/3 * 0.08 + 3 + 3.5 * 16.7 = 77.8$ ms to read one track of data on average. It takes about $612/3*0.08+3+16.7/2+16.7/150 = 27.8$ ms to read a single sector of data. This is a good savings (slightly over one third the time), but less than 1% of the data on the track is read. If we want to read only a single byte of data, it would require about $612/3*0.08+3+16.7/2 = 27.7$ ms to do so. This is an insignificant savings in time compared to that required to read one sector of information. For this reason, nearly all disk drives automatically read or write an entire sector's worth of information whenever the disk is accessed, even when only one byte of information is requested.

Once a sector is read, its information is stored in main memory. This is known as **buffering** or **caching** the information. If the next disk request is to that same sector, then it is not necessary to read from disk again; the information is already stored in main memory. Buffering is an example of one method for minimizing disk accesses stated at the beginning of the chapter: Bring off additional information from disk to satisfy future requests. If information from files were accessed at random, then the chance that two consecutive disk requests are to the same sector would be low. However, in practice most disk requests are close to the location (in the logical file at least) of the previous request. This means that the probability of the next request "hitting the cache" is much higher than chance would indicate.

This principle explains one reason why new disk drives are faster than in the past. Not only is the hardware faster, but information is now stored using better algorithms and larger caches that minimize the number of times information needs to be fetched from disk. This same concept is also used to store parts of programs in faster memory within the CPU, the so-called CPU cache that is prevalent in modern microprocessors.

Sector-level buffering is now automatic in nearly all operating systems and is often built directly into the disk drive controller hardware. Most operating systems maintain at least two buffers, one for input and one for output. Consider what would happen if there were only one buffer during a byte-by-byte copy operation. The sector containing the first byte would be read into the I/O buffer. The output operation would need to destroy the contents of the single I/O buffer to write this byte. Then the buffer would need to be filled again from disk for the second byte, only to be destroyed during output. The simple solution to this problem is to keep one buffer for input, and a second for output.

Most disk drive controllers operate independently from the CPU once an I/O request is received. This is useful since the CPU can typically execute millions of instructions during the time required for a single I/O operation. A technique that takes maximum advantage of this microparallelism is **double buffering**. Imagine that a file is being processed sequentially. While the first block is being read, the CPU cannot process that information and so must wait or find something else to do in the meantime. Once the first block is read, the CPU can start processing while the disk drive (in parallel) begins reading the second block. If the time required for the CPU to process a sector is approximately the same as the time required by the disk controller to read a sector, it may be possible to keep the CPU continuously fed with data from the file. The same concept can also be applied to output, writing one sector to disk while the CPU is writing to a second output buffer in memory. Thus, in computers that support double buffering, it pays to have at least two input buffers and two output buffers available.

Caching information in memory is such a good idea that it is usually extended to multiple buffers. The operating system or an application program may store many buffers of information. The information stored in a buffer is often called a **page**, and the collection of buffers is called a **buffer pool**. The goal of the buffer pool is to increase the amount of information stored in memory in hopes of increasing the likelihood that new information requests can be satisfied from the buffer pool rather than requiring new information to be read from disk.

So long as there is an unused buffer available in the buffer pool, new information can be read in from disk on demand. When an application continues to read new information from disk, eventually all of the buffers in the buffer pool will become full. Once this happens, some decision must be made about what information in the buffer pool will be sacrificed to make room for newly requested information.

When replacing information contained in the buffer pool, the goal is to select a buffer that has "unnecessary" information, that is, that information least likely to be requested again. There are several approaches to making this decision. One is "first-in, first-out" (FIFO). This scheme simply orders the buffers in a queue. The buffer at the front of the queue is used next to store new information, and then placed at the end of the queue. In this way, the buffer to be replaced is the one that has held its information the longest, in hopes that this information is no longer needed. This is a reasonable assumption when processing moves along the file at some steady pace in roughly sequential order. However, many programs work with certain key pieces of information over and over again, and the importance of information has little to do with how long ago the information was first accessed, but everything to do with how *recently* the information was last accessed.

Another approach is called "least frequently used" (LFU). LFU tracks the number of accesses to each buffer in the buffer pool. When a buffer must be reused, the buffer that has been accessed the fewest number of times is considered to contain the "least important" information, and so it is used next. LFU, while it seems intuitively reasonable, has many drawbacks. First, it is necessary to store and update access counts for each buffer. Second, what was referenced many times in the past may now be irrelevant. Thus, some time mechanism where counts "expire" is often desirable. This also avoids the problem of buffers that slowly build up big counts because they get used just often enough to avoid being replaced (unless counts are maintained for all sectors ever read, not just the sectors currently in the buffer pool).

The third approach is called "least recently used" (LRU). LRU simply keeps the buffers in a linked list. Whenever information in a buffer is accessed, this buffer is brought to the front of the list. When new information must be read, the buffer at the back of the list (the one least recently used) is taken and its "old" information is discarded. This is an easily implemented approximation to LFU, and is the method of choice for managing buffer pools unless special knowledge about information access patterns for an application suggests a special-purpose buffer management scheme.

9.4   The Programmer's View of Files

As stated earlier, the Java programmer's logical view of a random access file is a single stream of bytes. Interaction with a file can be viewed as a communications channel for issuing one of three instructions: read bytes from the current position in the file, write bytes to the current position in the file, and move the current position within the file. You do not normally see how the bytes are stored in sectors, clusters, and so forth. Sector-level buffering is done automatically by the operating system.

When processing records in a disk file, the order of access can have a great affect on I/O time. A **random access** procedure processes records in an order independent of their logical order within the file. **Sequential access** processes records in order of their logical appearance within the file. Sequential processing requires less seek time if the physical layout of the disk file matches its logical layout, as would be expected if the file was created on a disk with a high percentage of free space.

Many operating systems support **virtual memory**. Virtual memory is a technique that allows the programmer to pretend that there is more main memory than actually exists. This is done by means of a buffer pool reading blocks from disk. The disk stores the complete contents of the virtual memory; blocks are read into main memory as demanded by memory accesses. Naturally, programs using virtual memory techniques are slower than programs whose data are stored in physical memory. The advantage is reduced programmer effort since a good virtual memory system provides the appearance of larger main memory without modifying the program. Figure 9.6 illustrates the concept of virtual memory.

Following are the primary Java functions for accessing information from random access disk files when using class `RandomAccessFile`.

Physical Memory
(on disk)

Virtual Memory
(in main memory)

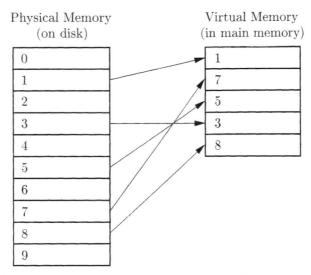

Figure 9.6 An illustration of virtual memory. The complete collection of information resides on disk (physical memory). Those sectors recently accessed are held in main memory (virtual memory). In this example, copies of sectors 1, 7, 5, 3, and 8 from physical memory are currently stored in the virtual memory. If a memory access to sector 9 is received, one of the sectors currently in main memory must be replaced.

- `RandomAccessFile(String name, String mode)`: Class constructor, opens a disk file for processing.

- `read(byte[] b)`: Read some bytes from the current position in the file. The current position moves forward as the bytes are read.

- `write(byte[] b)`: Write some bytes at the current position in the file (overwriting the bytes already at that position). The current position moves forward as the bytes are written.

- `seek(long pos)`: Move the current position in the file. This allows bytes at other places within the file to be read or written.

- `close()`: Close a file at the end of processing.

9.5 External Sorting

We now consider the problem of sorting collections of records too large to fit in main memory. Since the records must reside in peripheral or external memory, such sorting methods are called **external sorts** in contrast to the internal sorts discussed in Chapter 8.

Sorting large collections of records is central to many applications, such as processing payrolls and other large business databases. As a consequence, many external sorting algorithms have been devised. Years ago, sorting algorithm designers sought to optimize the use of specific hardware configurations, such as multiple tape or disk drives. Most computing today is done on personal computers and low-end workstations with relatively powerful CPUs, but only one or at most two disk drives. The techniques presented here are geared toward optimized processing on a single disk drive. This approach allows us to cover the most important issues in external sorting while skipping many less important machine-dependent details. Readers who have a need to implement efficient external sorting algorithms that take advantage of more sophisticated hardware configurations should consult the references in Section 9.9.

When a collection of records is too large to fit in main memory, the only practical way to sort is to read some records from disk, do some rearranging, then write them back to disk. This process is repeated until the file is sorted, with each record read perhaps many times. Armed with the basic knowledge about disk drives presented in Section 9.2, it should come as no surprise that the primary goal of an external sorting algorithm is to minimize the amount of information that must be read from or written to disk. A certain amount of additional CPU processing can profitably be traded for reduced disk access.

Before discussing external sorting techniques, consider again the basic model for accessing information from disk. The file to be sorted is viewed by the programmer as a sequential series of fixed-size **blocks**. Assume (for simplicity) that each block contains the same number of fixed-size data records. Depending on the application, a record may be only a few bytes – composed of little or nothing more than the key – or may be hundreds of bytes with a relatively small key field. Records are assumed not to cross block boundaries. These assumptions can be relaxed for special-purpose sorting applications, but ignoring these complications makes the principles clearer.

As explained in Section 9.2, a sector is the basic unit of I/O. In other words, all disk reads and writes are for a single, complete sector. Sector sizes are typically a power of two, in the range 512 to 8K bytes, depending on the computing system and the size and speed of the disk drive. The block size used for external sorting algorithms should be equal to or a multiple of the sector size.

Under this model, a sorting algorithm reads a block of data into a buffer in main memory, performs some processing on it, and at some future time writes it back to disk. From Section 9.1 we see that reading or writing a block from disk takes on the order of one million times longer than a memory access. Based on this fact, we can reasonably expect that the records contained in a single block can be sorted by an internal sorting algorithm such as Quicksort in less time than is required to read or write the block.

Under good conditions, reading from a file in sequential order is more efficient than reading blocks in random order. Given the significant impact of seek time on disk access, it may seem obvious that sequential processing is faster. However, it is important to understand precisely under what circumstances sequential file processing is actually faster than random access, since it affects our approach to designing an external sorting algorithm.

Efficient sequential access relies on seek time being kept to a minimum. The first requirement is that the blocks making up a file are in fact stored on disk in sequential order and close together, preferably filling a small number of contiguous tracks. At the very least, the number of extents making up the file should be small. Users typically do not have much control over the layout of their file on disk, but writing a file all at once in sequential order to a disk drive with a high percentage of free space increases the likelihood of such an arrangement.

The second requirement is that the disk drive's I/O head remain positioned over the file throughout sequential processing. This will not happen if there is competition of any kind for the I/O head. For example, on a multi-user timeshared computer the sorting process may compete for the I/O head with the process of another user. Even when the sorting process has sole control of the I/O head, it is still likely that sequential processing will not be efficient. Imagine the situation where all processing is done on a single disk drive, with the typical arrangement of a single bank of read/write heads that move together over a stack of platters. If the sorting process involves reading from an input file, alternated with writing to an output file, then the I/O head will continuously seek between the input file and the output file. Similarly, if two input files are being processed simultaneously (such as during a merge process), then the I/O head will continuously seek between these two files.

The moral is that, with a single disk drive, there often is no such thing as efficient, sequential processing of a data file. Thus, a sorting algorithm may be more efficient if it performs a smaller number of nonsequential disk operations rather than a larger number of logically sequential disk operations that require a large number of seeks in practice.

As mentioned previously, the record size may be quite large compared to the size of the key. For example, payroll entries for a large business may each store hundreds of bytes of information including the name, ID, address, and job title for each employee. The sort key may be the ID number, requiring only a few bytes. The simplest sorting algorithm may be to process such records as a whole, reading the entire record whenever it is processed. However, this will greatly increase the amount of I/O required, since only a relatively few records will fit into a single disk block. Another alternative is to do a **key sort**. Under this method, the keys are all read and stored together in an **index file**, where each key is stored along with a pointer indicating the position of the corresponding record in the original data file. The key and pointer combination should be substantially smaller than the size of the original record; thus, the index file will be much smaller than the complete data file. The index file will then be sorted, requiring much less I/O since the index records are smaller than the complete records.

Once the index file is sorted, it is possible to reorder the records in the original file. This is typically not done for two reasons. First, reading the records in sorted order from the record file requires a random access for each record. This can take a substantial amount of time, and is only of value if the complete collection of records needs to be viewed or processed in sorted order (as opposed to a search for selected records). Second, database systems typically allow searches to be done on multiple keys. In other words, today's processing may be done in order of ID numbers. Tomorrow, the boss may want information sorted by salary. Thus, there may be no single "sorted" order for the full record. Instead, multiple index files are often maintained, one for each sort key. These ideas are explored further in Chapter 11.

9.6   Simple Approaches to External Sorting

If your operating system supports virtual memory, the simplest "external" sort is to read the entire file into virtual memory and run an internal sorting method such as Quicksort. This approach allows the virtual memory manager to use its normal buffer pool mechanism to control disk accesses. Unfortunately, this may not always be a viable option. One potential drawback is that the size of virtual memory is usually limited to something much smaller than the disk space available. Thus, your input file may not fit into virtual memory. Limited virtual memory can be overcome by adapting an internal sorting method to make use of your own buffer pool combined with one of the buffer management techniques discussed in Section 9.3.

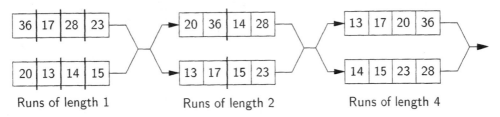

Runs of length 1   Runs of length 2   Runs of length 4

Figure 9.7 Illustration of a simple external Mergesort algorithm. Input records are divided equally among two input files. The first runs from each input file are merged and placed in the first output file. The second runs from each input file are merged and placed in the second output file. Merging alternates between the two output files until the input files are empty. The role of input and output files are then reversed, allowing the runlength to be doubled with each pass.

A more general problem with adapting an internal sorting algorithm to external sorting is that it is not likely to be as efficient as designing a new algorithm with the specific goal of minimizing disk fetches. Consider the simple adaptation of Quicksort to external sorting. Quicksort begins by processing the entire array of records, with the first partition step moving indices inward from the two ends. This can be implemented efficiently using a buffer pool. However, the next step is to process each of the subarrays, followed by processing of sub-subarrays, and so on. As the subarrays get smaller, processing quickly approaches random access to the disk drive. Even if the I/O can be made efficient, Quicksort still must process each record $\log n$ times on average. You will soon see that it is possible to do much better than this.

A better approach to external sorting can be derived from the Mergesort algorithm. The simplest form of Mergesort performs a series of sequential passes over the records, merging larger and larger sublists on each pass. Thus, the first pass merges sublists of size 1 into sublists of size 2; the second pass merges the sublists of size 2 into sublists of size 4; and so on. Such sorted sublists are called **runs**. Each sublist-merging pass copies the contents of the file to another file. Here is a sketch of the algorithm, illustrated by Figure 9.7:

1. Split the original file into two equal-sized **run files**.

2. Read one block from each run file into input buffers.

3. Take the first record from each input buffer, and write them to an output run buffer in sorted order.

4. Take the next record from each input buffer, and write them to a second output run buffer in sorted order.

5. Repeat until finished, alternating output between the two output run buffers. When an input block is exhausted, read the next block from the appropriate input file. When an output run buffer is full, write it to the appropriate output file.

6. Repeat steps 2 through 5, using the original output files as input files. On the second pass, the first two records of each input run file are already in sorted order. Thus, these two runs may be merged and output as a single run of four elements.

7. Each pass through the run files provides larger and larger runs until only one run remains.

This algorithm can easily take advantage of the double buffering techniques described in Section 9.3. Note that the various passes read the input run files sequentially and write the output run files sequentially. For sequential processing and double buffering to be effective, however, it is necessary that there be a separate I/O head available for each file. This typically means that each of the input and output files must be on separate disk drives, requiring a total of four disk drives for maximum efficiency.

The simple Mergesort requires that $\log n$ passes be made to sort a file of n records. Thus, each record must be read from disk and written to disk $\log n$ times. The number of passes can be significantly reduced by observing that it is not necessary to use Mergesort on small runs. A simple modification is to read in a block of data, sort it in memory, and then output it as a single sorted run. For example, assume that we have 4KB blocks, and 8-byte records each containing four bytes of data and a 4-byte key. Thus, each block contains 512 records. Standard Mergesort would require nine passes to generate runs of 512 records, whereas processing each block as a unit can be done in one pass with an internal sort. These runs can then be merged by Mergesort. Standard Mergesort requires eighteen passes to process 256K records. Using an internal sort to create initial runs of 512 records reduces this to one initial pass to create the runs and nine merge passes to put them all together, approximately half as many passes.

We can extend this concept even further. Available main memory is usually much more than one block in size. If we process larger initial runs, then the number of passes required by Mergesort is further reduced. For example, most modern computers can make anywhere from half a megabyte to a few tens of megabytes of RAM available for processing. If all of this memory (excepting a small amount for buffers and local variables) is devoted to building initial runs as large as possible, then quite large files can be processed in relatively few passes. The next section presents a technique for producing large runs, typically twice as large as could fit directly into main memory.

Another way to reduce the number of passes required is to increase the number of runs that are merged together during each pass. While the standard Mergesort algorithm merges two runs at a time, there is no reason why merging needs to be limited in this way. Section 9.8 discusses the technique of multiway merging.

Over the years, many variants on external sorting have been presented. However, most follow the same principles. In general, all good external sorting algorithms are based on the following two steps:

1. Break the file into large initial runs.

2. Merge the runs together to form a single sorted file.

9.7 Replacement Selection

This section treats the problem of creating initial runs as large as possible from a disk file, assuming a fixed amount of RAM is available for processing. As mentioned previously, a simple approach is to allocate as much RAM as possible to a large array, fill this array from disk, and sort the array using Quicksort. Thus, if the size of memory available for the array is M records, then the input file can be broken into initial runs of length M. A better approach is to use an algorithm called **Replacement Selection** that, on average, creates runs that are $2M$ records in length. Replacement Selection is actually a slight variation on the Heapsort algorithm. The fact that Heapsort is slower than Quicksort is irrelevant in this context since I/O time will dominate the total running time of any reasonable external sorting algorithm.

Replacement Selection views RAM as consisting of an array of size M in addition to an input buffer and an output buffer. (Additional I/O buffers may be desirable if the operating system supports double buffering, since Replacement Selection does sequential processing on both its input and its output.) Imagine that the input and output files are streams of records. Replacement Selection takes the next record in sequential order from the input stream when needed, and outputs runs one record at a time to the

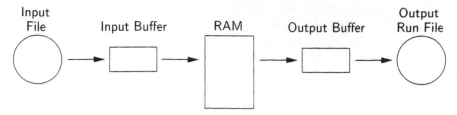

Figure 9.8 Overview of Replacement Selection. Input records are processed sequentially. Initially RAM is filled with M records. As records are processed, they are written to an output buffer. When this buffer becomes full it is written to disk. Meanwhile, as Replacement Selection needs records, it reads them from the input buffer. Whenever this buffer becomes empty, the next block of records is read from disk.

output stream. Buffering is used so that disk I/O is performed one block at a time. A block of records is initially read and held in the input buffer. Replacement Selection removes records from the input buffer one at a time until the buffer is empty. At this point the next block of records is read in. Output to a buffer is similar: Once the buffer fills up it is written to disk as a unit. This process is illustrated by Figure 9.8.

Replacement Selection works as follows. Assume that the main processing is done in an array of size M records.

1. Fill the array from disk. Set LAST $= M - 1$.
2. Build a min-heap. (Recall that a min-heap is defined such that the record at each node has a key value *less* than the key values of its children.)
3. Repeat until the array is empty:
   (a) Send the record with the minimum key value (the root) to the output buffer.
   (b) Let R be the next record in the input buffer. If R's key value is greater than the key value just output ...
      i. Then place R at the root.
      ii. Else replace the root with the record in array position LAST, and place R at position LAST. Set LAST $=$ LAST $- 1$.
   (c) Sift down the root to reorder the heap.

When the test at step 3(b) is successful, a new record is added to the heap, eventually to be output as part of the run. So long as records coming from the input file have key values greater than the last key value output to the run, they can be safely added to the heap. Records with smaller key values cannot be output as part of this run since they would not be in sorted order. Such values must be stored somewhere for future processing as part of another run. However, since the heap will shrink by one element in this case, there is now a free space where the last element of the heap used to be! Thus, Replacement Selection will slowly shrink the heap, and at the same time use the discarded heap space to store records for the next run. Once the first run is complete (i.e., the heap becomes empty), the array will be filled with records ready to be processed for the second run. Figure 9.9 illustrates part of a run being created by Replacement Selection.

It should be clear that the minimum length of a run will be M records if the size of the heap is M, since at least those records originally in the heap will be part of the run. Under good conditions (e.g., if the input is sorted), then an arbitrarily long run is possible – in fact, the entire file could be processed as one run. If conditions are bad (e.g., if the input is reverse sorted), then runs of only size M result.

What is the expected length of a run generated by Replacement Selection? It can be deduced from an analogy called the **snowplow argument**.

Imagine that a snowplow is going around a circular track during a heavy, but steady, snowstorm. After the plow has been around at least once, we can imagine the situation regarding snow on the track. Immediately behind the plow, the track is empty since it was just plowed. The greatest level of snow on the track is immediately in front of the plow, since this is the place least recently plowed. At any instant in time, there is a certain amount of snow S on the track. Snow is constantly falling throughout the track at a steady rate, with some snow falling "in front" of the plow and some "behind" the plow. (On a circular track, everything is actually "in front" of the plow, but Figure 9.10 illustrates the idea.) During the next revolution of the plow, all snow S on the track is removed, plus half of what falls. Since everything is assumed to be in steady state, after one revolution S snow is still on the track, so $2S$ snow must fall during a revolution, and $2S$ snow is removed during a revolution (leaving S snow behind).

At the beginning of Replacement Selection, nearly all values coming from the input file are greater (i.e., "before the plow") than the latest key value output for this run, since initial key values of the run should be small. As the run progresses, the latest key value output becomes greater and so new key values coming from the input file are more likely to be too small (i.e., "after the plow"); such records go to the bottom of the array. The total

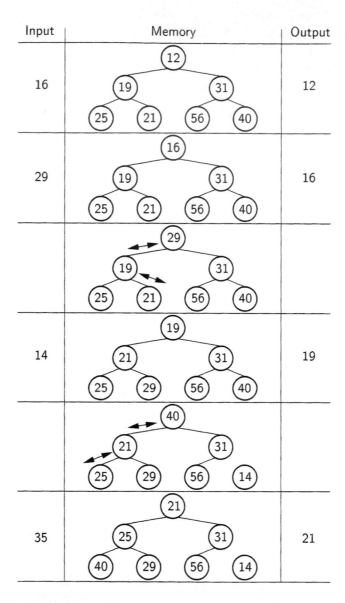

Figure 9.9 Replacement Selection example. After building the heap, root value 12 is output and incoming value 16 replaces it. Value 16 is output next, replaced with incoming value 29. The heap is reordered, with 19 rising to the root. Value 19 is output next. Incoming value 14 is too small for this run, and is placed at end of the array, moving value 40 to the root. Reordering the heap results in 21 rising to the root, which is output next.

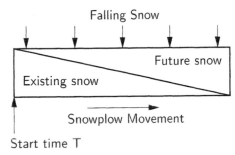

Figure 9.10 Illustration of the snowplow analogy showing the action during one revolution of the snowplow. A circular track is laid out straight for purposes of illustration, and is shown in cross-section. At any time T, the most snow is directly in front of the snowplow. As the plow moves around the track, the same amount of snow is always in front of the plow. As the plow moves forward, less of this is snow that was in the track at time T; more is snow that has fallen since.

length of the run is expected to be twice the size of the array. Of course, this assumes that incoming key values are evenly distributed within the key range (in terms of the snowplow analogy, we assume that snow falls evenly throughout the track). Sorted and reverse sorted inputs do not meet this expectation, and so change the length of the run.

9.8   Multiway Merging

The second stage of a typical external sorting algorithm merges the runs created by the first stage. If a simple two-way merge is used, then R runs will require $\log R$ passes through the file. While R should be much less than the total number of records (since the initial runs should each contain many records), we would like to reduce still further the number of passes required to merge the runs together. Note that two-way merging does not make good use of available memory. Since merging is a sequential process on the two runs, only one block of records per run need be in memory at a time. Thus, most of the space just used by the heap for Replacement Selection (typically many blocks in length) is not being used by the merge process.

We can make better use of this space and at the same time greatly reduce the number of passes needed to merge the runs if we merge several runs at a time. Multiway merging is similar to two-way merging. If we have B runs to merge, with a block from each run available in memory, then the B-way merge algorithm simply looks at B values (the front-most value for each input run) and selects the smallest one to output. This value is removed

Input Runs

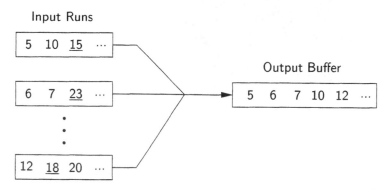

Figure 9.11 Illustration of multiway merge. The first value in each input run is examined and the smallest sent to the output. This value is removed from the input and the process repeated. In this example, values 5, 6, and 12 are compared first. Value 5 is removed from the first run and sent to the output. Values 10, 6, and 12 will be compared next. After the first five values have been output, the "current" value of each block is the one underlined.

from its run, and the process is repeated. When the current block for any run is exhausted, the next block from that run is read from disk. Figure 9.11 illustrates a multiway merge.

Conceptually, multiway merge assumes that each run is stored in a separate file. However, this is not necessary in practice. We only need to know the position of each run within a single file, and use **fseek** to move to the appropriate block whenever we need new data from a particular run. Naturally, this approach destroys the ability to do sequential processing on the input file. However, if all runs were stored on a single disk drive, then processing would not be sequential anyway since the I/O head would be alternating between the runs. Thus, multiway merging replaces several (potentially) sequential passes with a single random access pass. If the processing would not be sequential anyway (such as when all processing is on a single disk drive), no time is lost by doing so.

Multiway merging can greatly reduce the number of passes required. If there is room in memory to store one block for each run, then all runs can be merged in a single pass. Thus, Replacement Selection can build initial runs in one pass, and multiway merging can merge all runs in one pass, yielding a total cost of two passes. However, for truly large files, there may be too many runs for each to get a block in memory. If there is room to allocate B blocks for a B-way merge, and the number of runs R is greater than B, then it will be necessary to do multiple merge passes. In other words, the

	Time (seconds)	
Algorithm	1MB	4MB
Simple Mergesort	123,310	543,870
128KB initial runs	25,650	151,320
128KB initial runs with K-way merge	14,340	67,670

Figure 9.12 A comparison of three external sorts on a collection of small records for files with 1MB and 4MB total sizes, using 128KB of working memory made up of 32 blocks of size 4KB. Times are in milliseconds. Comparisons were made under Microsoft Window95 running Visual **J++**.

first B runs are merged, then the next B, and so on. These super-runs are then merged by subsequent passes, B super-runs at a time.

How big a file can be merged in one pass? Assuming B blocks were allocated to the heap for Replacement Selection (resulting in runs of average length $2B$ blocks), followed by a B-way merge, we can process on average a file of size $2B^2$ blocks in a single multiway merge. $2B^{k+1}$ blocks on average can be processed in k B-way merges. To gain some appreciation for how quickly this grows, assume that we have available .5MB of working memory, and that a block is 4KB, yielding 128 blocks in working memory. The average run size is 1MB (twice the working memory size). In one pass, 128 runs can be merged. Thus, a file of size 128MB can, on average, be processed in two passes (one to build the runs, one to do the merge) with only .5MB of working memory. A larger block size would reduce the size of the file that can be processed in one merge pass for a fixed-size working memory; a smaller block size or larger working memory would increase the file size that can be processed in one merge pass. With .5MB of working memory and 4KB blocks, a file of size 16 gigabytes could be processed in two merge passes, which is big enough for most applications. Thus, this is a very effective algorithm for single disk drive external sorting.

Figure 9.12 shows a comparison of the running time to sort 1MB and 4MB files for the following implementations: (1) standard Mergesort with two input files and two output files, (2) two-way Mergesort with initial runs of 128KB, and (3) R-way Mergesort on the runs of 128KB. In each case, the file was composed of a series of four-byte key values, or 2^{18} and 2^{20} records, respectively.

We see from this experiment that building large initial runs reduces the running time to about one quarter that of standard Mergesort. Using a multiway merge further cuts the time in half.

In summary, a good external sorting algorithm will seek to do the following:

- Make the initial runs as long as possible.

- At all stages, overlap input, processing, and output as much as possible.

- Use as much working memory as possible. Applying more memory usually speeds processing. In fact, more memory will have a greater effect than a faster disk. A faster CPU is unlikely to yield much improvement in running time for external sorting.

- If possible, use additional disk drives for more overlapping of processing with I/O, and to allow for sequential file processing.

9.9   Further Reading

A good general text on file processing is Folk and Zoellig's *File Structures: A Conceptual Toolkit* [FZ92]. A somewhat more advanced discussion on key issues in file processing is Betty Salzberg's *File Structures: An Analytical Approach* [Sal88]. A great discussion on external sorting methods can be found in Salzberg's book. The presentation in this chapter is similar in spirit to Salzberg's.

For details on disk drive modeling and measurement, see the article by Ruemmler and Wilkes, "An Introduction to Disk Drive Modeling" [RW94]. See Andrew S. Tanenbaum's *Structured Computer Organization* [Tan90] for an introduction to computer hardware and organization.

Any good reference guide to the UNIX operating system will describe the internal organization of the UNIX file structure. One such guide is *UNIX for Programmers and Users* by Graham Glass [Gla93].

The snowplow argument comes from Donald E. Knuth's *Sorting and Searching* [Knu81], which also contains a wide variety of external sorting algorithms.

9.10   Exercises

9.1 Computer memory prices change rapidly. Find out what the current prices are for the media listed in Figure 9.1. Does your information change any of the basic conclusions regarding disk processing?

9.2 Assume a rather old disk drive is configured as follows. The total storage is approximately 40MB divided among 10 surfaces. Each surface has 128 tracks; there are 64 sectors/track, 512 bytes/sector, and 16 sectors/cluster. The interleaving factor is four. The disk turns at 3600 rpm. The average startup time for the read/write arm is 20 ms, and the average time to move the arm is 0.3 ms per track. Now assume that there is a 128KB file on the disk. On average, how long does it take to read all of the data in the file? Assume that the first track of the file is randomly placed on the disk, that the entire file lies on adjacent tracks, and that the file completely fills each track on which it is found. A seek must be performed each time the I/O head moves to a new track. Show your calculations.

9.3 Prove that two tracks selected at random from a disk are separated on average by one third the number of tracks on the disk.

9.4 Assume that a disk drive is configured as follows. The total storage is approximately 1033MB divided among 16 surfaces. Each surface has 2100 tracks, there are 63 sectors/track, 512 bytes/sector, and 8 sectors/cluster. The interleaving factor is three. The disk turns at 7200 rpm. The average startup time for the read/write arm is 3 ms, and the average time to move the arm is 0.08 ms per track. Now assume that there is a 128KB file on the disk. On average, how long does it take to read all of the data on the file? Assume that the first track of the file is randomly placed on the disk, that the entire file lies on adjacent tracks, and that the file completely fills each track on which it is found. A seek must be performed each time the I/O head moves to a new track. Show your calculations.

9.5 Given a 6250 bpi tape drive, a record size of 160 bytes, and an interblock gap of 0.3 inches, what blocking factor is required to have 90% of the tape contain data?

9.6 For a database application, assume it takes 100 ms to read a block from disk, 20 ms to search for a record in a block, and that there is room in memory for a buffer pool of 5 blocks. Requests come in for records, with the request specifying which block contains the record. If a block is accessed, there is a 10% probability for each of the next ten requests that the request will be to the same block. What will be the expected performance improvement for each of the following modifications to the system? For each modification, estimate the amount of speedup that will occur.

(a) Get a CPU that is twice as fast.

(b) Get a disk drive that is twice as fast.

(c) Get enough memory to double the buffer pool size.

9.7 A file contains one million records sorted by key value. Each query refers to the key of one record. Files are stored on disk in sectors each containing 100 records. The average time to read a sector selected at random is 50 ms. A sequential sector read takes 5 ms. The "batch" algorithm for processing queries is to first sort the queries by order of appearance in the file, and then read the entire file sequentially, processing all queries in sequential order as the file is read. This algorithm implies that the queries must all be available before processing begins. The "interactive" algorithm is to process each query in order of its arrival, searching for the requested sector each time (unless by chance two queries in a row are to the same sector). Carefully define under what conditions the batch method is more efficient than the interactive method.

9.8 Assume that a virtual memory is managed using a buffer pool. The buffer pool contains five buffers and each buffer stores one block of data. Memory accesses are by block ID. Assume the following series of memory accesses takes place:

$$5\ 2\ 5\ 12\ 3\ 6\ 5\ 9\ 3\ 2\ 4\ 1\ 5\ 9\ 8\ 15\ 3\ 7\ 2\ 5\ 9\ 10\ 4\ 6\ 8\ 5$$

For each of the following buffer pool replacement strategies, show the contents of the buffer pool at the end of the series. Assume that the buffer pool is initially empty.

(a) First-in, first out.

(b) Least frequently used (with counts kept only for blocks currently in memory).

(c) Least frequently used (with counts kept for all blocks).

(d) Least recently used.

9.9 Suppose that a record is 32 bytes, a block is 1024 bytes (so there are 32 records per block), and that working memory is 1MB (there is also additional space available for I/O buffers, program variables, etc.). What is the *expected* size for the largest file that can be merged using replacement selection followed by a *single* pass of multiway merge? Explain how you got your answer.

9.10 Assume that working memory size is 256KB broken into blocks of 8192 bytes (there is also additional space available for I/O buffers, program variables, etc.). What is the *expected size* for the largest file that can be merged using replacement selection followed by *two* passes of multiway merge? Explain how you got your answer.

9.11 Prove or disprove the following proposition: Given space in memory for a heap of M records, replacement selection will completely sort a file if no record in the file is preceded by M or more keys of greater value.

9.12 Imagine a database containing one million records, with each record being 100 bytes long. Provide an estimate of how long it would take to sort the database on a typical workstation.

9.13 Assume that a company has a computer configuration satisfactory for processing their monthly payroll. Further assume that the bottleneck in payroll processing is a sorting operation on all of the employee records, and that an external sorting algorithm is used. The company's payroll program is so good that it plans to hire out its services to do payroll processing for other companies. The president has an offer from a second company with 100 times as many employees. She realizes that her computer is not up to the job of sorting 100 times as many records in an acceptable amount of time. Describe what impact each of the following modifications to the computing system is likely to have in terms of reducing the time required to process the larger payroll database.

  (a) A factor of two speedup to the CPU.
  (b) A factor of two speedup to disk I/O time.
  (c) A factor of two speedup to main memory access time.
  (d) A factor of two increase to main memory size.

9.14 How can the external sorting algorithm described in this chapter be extended to handle variable length records?

9.11 Projects

9.1 Pictures are typically stored as an array, row by row, on disk. Consider the case where the picture has 16 colors. Thus, each pixel can be represented using 4 bits. If you allow 8 bits per pixel, no processing is required to unpack the pixels (since a pixel corresponds to a byte, the lowest level of addressing on most machines). If you pack two pixels per byte, space is saved but the pixels must be unpacked. Which takes more time to read from disk and access every pixel of the image: 8 bits per pixel or 4 bits per pixel packed? Program both and compare the times.

9.2 Implement a disk-based buffer pool library based on the LRU buffer pool replacement strategy. Disk blocks are numbered consecutively from the beginning of the file with the first block numbered as 0. Assume that blocks are 1024 bytes in size, with the first 4 bytes used to store the block ID corresponding to that buffer. The following four functions make up the ADT for the buffer pool library.

- `Object New_Block()`: Request that a new disk block be created. The buffer pool manager determines the next free block on disk and returns a reference to the buffer storing the new block. (Don't forget to put the block ID in the first 4 bytes of the new buffer).

- `Object Get_Block(int ID)`: Given a block ID, return a reference to the buffer containing that block. If the requested block is not currently in the buffer pool, it must be read from disk.

- `void Free_Block(int ID)`: Release a block of information. The buffer pool manager should consider this block as unused, and so can service the next `New_Block` request.

- `void Dirty_Block(int ID)`: The indicated block should be considered to have updated information. Blocks that are not "dirty" need not be written to disk when they are removed from the buffer pool. Blocks that are "dirty" must have their contents copied to disk when removed from the buffer pool.

9.3 Implement an external sort based on Replacement Selection and multiway merging as described in this chapter. Test your program both on files with small records and on files with large records. For what size record do you find that key sorting would be worthwhile?

10

Searching

Organizing and retrieving information is at the heart of most computer applications, and searching is surely the most frequently performed of all computing tasks. Search can be viewed abstractly as a process to determine if an element with a particular value is a member of a particular set. The more common view of searching is an attempt to find the record within a sequence of records that has a particular key value, or those records in a sequence whose key values meet some criteria such as falling within a range of values.

We can define searching formally as follows.

Definition 10.1 Suppose k_1, k_2, ... k_n are distinct keys, and that we have a collection T of n records of the form

$$(k_1, I_1), (k_2, I_2), ..., (k_n, I_n),$$

where I_j is information associated with key k_j for $1 \leq j \leq n$. Given a particular key value K, the **search problem** is to locate the record (k_j, I_j) in T such that $k_j = K$. **Searching** is a systematic method for locating the record (or records) with key value $k_j = K$.

A **successful** search is one in which a record with key $k_j = K$ is found. An **unsuccessful** search is one in which no record with $k_j = K$ is found (and no such record exists).

An **exact-match query** is a search for the record whose key value matches a specified key value. A **range query** is a search for all records whose key value falls within a specified range of key values.

We can categorize search algorithms into three general approaches:

1. Sequential and list methods.

2. Direct access by key value (hashing).

3. Tree indexing methods.

This and the following chapter treat these approaches in turn. The current chapter considers methods for searching data stored in lists and tables. A **table** is simply another term for an array. List in this context means any list implementation including a linked list or an array. Most of these methods are appropriate for sequences (i.e., duplicate key values are allowed), although special techniques applicable to sets are discussed in Section 10.3. The techniques from the first three sections of this chapter are most appropriate for searching a collection of records stored in RAM. Section 10.4 discusses hashing, a technique for organizing data in a table such that the location of each record within the table is a function of its key value.

Chapter 11 discusses tree-based methods for organizing information, including a commonly used data structure called the B-tree. Nearly all programs that must organize large collections of records stored on disk use some variant of either hashing or the B-tree. Hashing is practical for only certain access functions (such as exact-match queries) and is generally appropriate only when duplicate key values are not allowed. B-trees are the method of choice for disk-based applications whenever hashing is not appropriate.

10.1   Searching Sorted Arrays

The simplest form of search has already been presented in Example 3.1: the sequential search algorithm. Sequential search on an unsorted list requires $\Theta(n)$ time in the average and worst cases. For large collections of records that are searched repeatedly, sequential search is unacceptably slow. One way to reduce search time is to preprocess the records by sorting them.

The most commonly used search algorithm for sorted tables is the binary search described in Section 3.5. If we know nothing about the distribution of key values, then binary search is the best algorithm available for searching a sorted table. However, sometimes we do know something about the expected key distribution. Consider the typical behavior of a person looking up a name in a large dictionary. Most people certainly do not use sequential search! Typically, people use a modified form of binary search, at least until they get close to the word that they are looking for. The search generally does not start at the middle of the dictionary. A person looking for a word starting with 'S' generally assumes that entries beginning with 'S' start about three quarters of the way through the dictionary. Thus, they will first open the dictionary about three quarters of the way through, and then make a decision based on what they find as to where to look next. In other words, people typically use some knowledge about the expected distribution of key values to "compute" where to look next. This form of "computed" binary search is called a **dictionary search** or an **interpolation search**.

A dictionary search attempts to take advantage of knowledge about the expected distribution of key values for records stored in the table. The location of a particular key within the key range is translated into the expected position for the corresponding record in the table, and this position is checked first. As with binary search, the value of the key found eliminates all records either above or below that position. The actual value of the key found can then be used to compute a new position within the remaining range of the table. The next check is made based on the new computation. This proceeds until either the desired record is found, or the table is narrowed until no records are left.

Dictionary search should be more efficient than binary search when the expected distribution matches the true distribution of the key values. If the expected distribution is significantly different from the actual distribution, then dictionary search can be extremely inefficient. For example, imagine that you are searching a telephone directory for the name "Young." Normally you would look near the back of the book. If you found a name beginning with 'Z,' you might look just a little ways toward the front. If the next name you find also begins with 'Z', you would look a little farther toward the front. If this particular telephone directory were unusual in that half of the entries begin with 'Z,' then you would need to move toward the front many times, each time eliminating relatively few records from the search. In the extreme, the performance of dictionary search might not be much better than sequential search if the distribution of key values is badly calculated.

10.2 Self-Organizing Lists

While lists are most commonly ordered by key value, this is not the only viable option. Another approach to organizing lists for fast search is to order the records by expected frequency of access. Assume that we know, for each key k_i, the probability p_i that the record with key k_i will be requested. Assume also that the list is ordered so that the most frequently requested record is first, then the next most frequently requested record, and so on. Search in the list will be done sequentially, beginning with the first position. Over the course of many searches, the expected number of comparisons required for one search is:

$$\overline{C}_n = 1p_1 + 2p_2 + ... + np_n.$$

In other words, the cost to access the first record is one (since one key value is looked at), and the probability of this occurring is p_1. The cost to access the second record is two (since we must look at the first and the second records' key values), with probability p_2, and so on. For n records, assuming that all searches are for records that actually exist, the probabilities p_1 through p_n must sum to one.

Certain probability distributions give easily computed results.

Example 10.1 Calculate the expected cost to search a list when each record has equal chance of being accessed (the classic sequential search through an unsorted list). Setting $p_i = 1/n$ yields

$$\overline{C}_n = \sum_{i=1}^{n} i/n = (n + 1)/2.$$

This result matches our expectation that half the records will be accessed on average by normal sequential search. If the records truly have equal access probabilities, then ordering records by frequency yields no benefit.

An exponential probability distribution yields quite different results.

Example 10.2 Calculate the expected cost for searching a list ordered by frequency when the probabilities are defined as

$$p_i = \begin{cases} 1/2^i & \text{if } 1 \leq i \leq n - 1 \\ 1/2^{n-1} & \text{if } i = n. \end{cases}$$

Then,

$$\overline{C}_n \approx \sum_{i=1}^{n} (i/2^i) \approx 2.$$

For this example, the expected number of accesses is a constant. This is because the probability for accessing the first record is high, the second is much lower but still much higher than for record three, and so on. This shows that for some probability distributions, ordering the list by frequency can yield an efficient search technique.

In many search applications, real access patterns follow a rule of thumb called the **80/20 rule**. The 80/20 rule says that 80% of the record accesses are to 20% of the records. The values of 80 and 20 are only estimates; every application has its own values. However, behavior of this nature occurs surprisingly often in practice (which explains the success of caching techniques widely used by disk drive and CPU manufacturers for speeding access to data stored in slower memory; see the discussion on buffer pools in Section 9.3). When the 80/20 rule applies, we can expect reasonable search performance from a list ordered by frequency of access.

> **Example 10.3** Naturally occurring distributions often follow a pattern called a **Zipf distribution**. Examples include the observed frequency for the use of words in a natural language such as English, and the size of the population for cities (i.e., view the relative proportions for the populations as equivalent to the "frequency of use"). Zipf distributions are related to the Harmonic Series defined in Equation 2.10. Define the Zipf frequency for item i in the distribution for n records as $1/i\mathcal{H}_n$. The expected cost for the series whose members follow this Zipf distribution will be
>
> $$\overline{C}_n = \sum_{i=1}^{n} i/i\mathcal{H}_n = n/\mathcal{H}_n \approx n/\log_e n.$$

When a frequency distribution follows the 80/20 rule, the average search looks at about one tenth of the records in a table ordered by frequency.

In many applications, we have no means of knowing in advance which records will be accessed most often. To complicate matters further, certain records may be accessed frequently for a brief period of time, and then rarely thereafter. Thus, the probability of access for records may change over time. **Self-organizing lists** seek to solve both of these problems.

Self-organizing lists modify the order of records within the list based on the actual pattern of record access. Self-organizing lists use a heuristic for deciding how to to reorder the list.[1] These heuristics are similar to the rules for managing buffer pools (see Section 9.3). In fact, a buffer pool is a form

---

[1] A heuristic is a "rule of thumb," that is, a simple rule that works well in practice.

of self-organizing list. Ordering the buffer pool by expected frequency of access is a good strategy, since typically we must search the contents of the buffers to determine if the desired information is already in main memory. When ordered by frequency of access, the buffer at the end of the list will be the one most appropriate for reuse when a new page of information must be read. Below are three traditional heuristics for managing self-organizing lists:

1. The most obvious way to keep a list ordered by frequency would be to store a count of accesses to each record, and always maintain records in this order. This method will be referred to as **count**. Count is similar to the least frequently used buffer replacement strategy. Thus, whenever a record is accessed, it may move toward the front of the list if its number of accesses becomes greater than a record preceding it. Clearly, count will store the records in the order of frequency that has actually occurred so far. Besides requiring space for the access counts, count does not react well to changing frequency of access over time. Once a record has been accessed a large number of times under the frequency count system, it will remain near the front of the list regardless of further access history.

2. Bring a record to the front of the list when it is found, pushing the other records back one position. This is analogous to the least recently used buffer replacement strategy, and is called **move-to-front**. This heuristic is easy to implement if the records are stored using a linked list. When records are stored in an array, bringing a record forward from near the end of the array will result in a large number of records changing position. Move-to-front is an efficient heuristic in that it requires at most twice the accesses required by the **optimal static ordering** for n records when at least n searches are performed. In other words, if we had known the series of (at least n) searches in advance, and had stored the records in order of frequency so as to minimize the total cost for these accesses, this cost would be at least half the cost required by the move-to-front heuristic. (This will be proved using amortized analysis in Section 14.3.) Finally, move-to-front responds well to local changes in frequency of access, in that if a record is frequently accessed for a brief period of time it will be near the front of the list during that period of access.

3. Swap any record found with the record immediately preceding it in the list. This heuristic is called **transpose**. Transpose is good for

list implementations based on either linked lists or arrays. Frequently used records will, over time, move to the front of the list. Records that were once frequently accessed but are no longer used will slowly drift toward the back. Thus, it appears to have good properties with respect to changing frequency of access. Unfortunately, there are some pathological sequences of access that can make transpose perform poorly. Consider the case where the last record of the list (call it X) is accessed. This record is then swapped with the next-to-last record (call it Y), making Y the last record. If Y is now accessed, it swaps with X. A repeated series of accesses alternating between X and Y will continually search to the end of the list, since neither record will ever make progress toward the front. However, such pathological cases are unusual in practice.

Example 10.4 Assume that we have eight records, with key values 0 to 7, and that they are initially placed in ascending order of key. Now, consider the result of applying the following access pattern:

$$5\ 3\ 5\ 6\ 4\ 6\ 5\ 0\ 3\ 5\ 6\ 4.$$

If the list is organized by the count heuristic, the final list resulting from these accesses will be

$$5\ 6\ 3\ 4\ 0\ 1\ 2\ 7,$$

and the total cost for the twelve accesses will be 44 comparisons. (Assume that when a record's frequency count goes up, it moves forward in the list to become the last record with that value for its frequency count. After the first two accesses, 5 will be the first record and 3 will be the second.)

If the list is organized by the move-to-front heuristic, then the final list will be

$$4\ 6\ 5\ 3\ 0\ 1\ 2\ 7,$$

and the total number of comparisons required is 54.

Finally, if the list is organized by the transpose heuristic, then the final list will be

$$0\ 1\ 5\ 3\ 6\ 4\ 2\ 7,$$

and the total number of comparisons required is 62.

While self-organizing lists do not generally perform as well as search trees or a sorted list, both of which require $O(\log n)$ search time, there are many situations in which self-organizing lists prove a valuable tool. Obviously they have an advantage over sorted lists in that they need not be sorted. This means that the cost to insert a new record is low, which could more than make up for the higher search cost when insertions are frequent. Self-organizing lists are simpler to implement than search trees, and are likely to be more efficient for small lists. Nor do they require additional space. Finally, in the case where sequential search is "almost" fast enough, changing an unsorted list to a self-organizing list may greatly speed the application at a minor cost in additional code.

As an example of applying self-organizing lists, consider an algorithm for compressing and transmitting messages. The list is self-organized by the move-to-front rule. Transmission is in the form of words and numbers, by the following rules:

1. If the word has been seen before, transmit the current position of the word in the list. Move the word to the front of the list.

2. If the word is seen for the first time, transmit the word. Place the word at the front of the list.

Both the sender and the receiver keep track of the position of words in the list in the same way (using the move-to-front rule), so they agree on the meaning of the numbers that encode repeated occurrences of words. For example, consider the following example message to be transmitted (for simplicity, ignore case in letters).

The car on the left hit the car I left.

The first three words have not been seen before, so they must be sent as full words. The fourth word is the second appearance of "the," which at this point is the third word in the list. Thus, we only need to transmit the position value "3." The next two words have not yet been seen, so must be sent as full words. The seventh word is the third appearance of "the," which coincidentally is again in the third position. The eighth word is the second appearance of "car," which is now in the fifth position of the list. "I" is a new word, and the last word "left" is now in the fifth position. Thus the entire transmission would be:

The car on 3 left hit 3 5 I 5.

0	1	2	3	4	5	6	7	8	9	10	11	12	13	14	15
0	0	1	1	0	1	0	1	0	0	0	1	0	1	0	0

Figure 10.1 The bit table for the set of primes in the range 0 to 15. The bit at position i is set to 1 if and only if i is prime.

This approach to compression is similar in spirit to Ziv-Lempel coding, which is a class of coding algorithms commonly used in file compression utilities. Ziv-Lempel coding will replace repeated occurrences of strings with a pointer to the location in the file of the first occurrence of the string. The codes are stored in a self-organizing list in order to speed up the time required to search for a string that has previously been seen.

10.3 Searching in Sets

Determining whether a value is a member of a particular set is a special case of searching for keys in a sequence of records. Thus, any of the methods for searching discussed in this book can be used to check for set membership. However, we can also take advantage of the restricted circumstances imposed by this problem to speed up the search process.

One simple technique that can be used in the case of a limited key range is to store a bit array with a bit position allocated for each potential member. Those members actually in the set store a value of 1 in their corresponding bit; those members not in the set store a value of 0 in their corresponding bit. For example, consider the set of primes between 0 and 15. Figure 10.1 shows the corresponding bit table. To determine if a particular value is prime, we simply check the corresponding bit. This representation scheme is called a **bit vector**.

If the set fits within a single computer word, then set union, intersection, and difference can be performed by logical bitwise operations. The union of sets A and B is the bitwise OR function (whose symbol is | in Java). The intersection of sets A and B is the bitwise AND function (whose symbol is & in Java). For example, if we would like to compute the set of numbers between 0 and 15 that are both prime and odd numbers, we need only compute the expression

0011010100010100 & 0101010101010101.

The set difference $A - B$ can be implemented in Java using the expression A&~B (~ is the symbol for bitwise negation). For larger sets that do not fit into a single computer word, the equivalent operations can be performed in turn on the words making up the entire bit vector.

This method of computing sets from bit vectors is sometimes applied to document retrieval. Consider the problem of picking from a collection of documents those few which contain selected keywords. For each keyword, the document retrieval system stores a bit vector with one bit for each document. If the user wants to know which documents contain a certain three keywords, the corresponding three bit vectors are AND'ed together. Those bit positions resulting in a value of 1 correspond to the desired documents. Alternatively, a bit vector can be stored for each document to indicate those keywords appearing in the document. Such an organization is called a **signature file**. The signatures can be manipulated to find documents with desired combinations of keywords.

10.4   Hashing

This section presents a completely different approach to searching tables: by direct access based on key value. The process of accessing a record by mapping a key value to a position in the table is called **hashing**. Most hashing schemes place records in the table in whatever order satisfies the needs of the address calculation, thus the records are not ordered by value or frequency. The function that maps key values to positions is called a **hash function**, and is usually denoted by **h**. The array that holds the records is called the **hash table**, and will be denoted by **T**. A position in the hash table is also known as a **slot**. The number of slots in hash table **T** will be denoted by the variable M, with slots numbered from 0 to $M - 1$. The goal when hashing is to arrange things such that for any key value K and some hash function **h**, $0 \leq \mathbf{h}(K) < M$, and `T[i].key()` $= K$.

Hashing is generally appropriate only for sets; that is, hashing is generally not used for applications where multiple records with the same key value are permitted. Hashing is generally not suitable for range searches. In other words, we cannot easily find all records (if any) whose key values fall within a certain range. Nor can we easily find the record with the minimum or maximum key value, or visit the records in key order. Hashing is most appropriate for answering the question "What record, if any, has key value K?" For applications where access can be restricted to this query, hashing is usually the search method of choice since it is extremely efficient when implemented correctly. As you shall see in this section, however, there are many approaches to hashing and it is easy to devise an inappropriate implementation. Hashing is suitable for both in-memory and disk-based searching, and is one of the two widely used methods for organizing large databases stored on disk (the other is the B-tree, which is covered in Chapter 11).

As a simple, though unrealistic, introduction to the concept of hashing, consider the case where the key range is small compared to the number of records, for example, when there are n records with unique key values in the range 0 to $n - 1$. In this simple case, a record with key i can be stored in $\mathbf{T}[i]$, and the hash function is simply $\mathbf{h}(K) = K$ (in fact, we don't even need to store the key value as part of the record in this situation since it is the same as the index). To find the record with key value i, simply look in $\mathbf{T}[i]$.

Typically, there are many more values in the key range than there are slots in the hash table. For a more realistic example, suppose the key can take any value in the range 0 to 65,535 (i.e., the key is a two-byte unsigned integer), and we expect to store approximately 1000 records at any given time. It is probably impractical in this situation to use a hash table with 65,536 slots, leaving most of them empty. Instead, we must devise a hash function that allows us to store the records in a much smaller table. Since the possible key range is larger than the size of the table, at least some of the slots must be mapped to by multiple key values. Given a hash function $\mathbf{h}$ and two keys k_1 and k_2, if $\mathbf{h}(k_1) = \beta = \mathbf{h}(k_2)$ where β is a slot in the table, then we say that k_1 and k_2 have a **collision** at slot β under hash function $\mathbf{h}$.

Finding a record with key value K in a database organized by hashing follows a two-step procedure:

1. Compute the table location $\mathbf{h}(K)$.

2. Starting with slot $\mathbf{h}(K)$, locate the record containing key K using (if necessary) a **collision resolution policy**.

10.4.1 Hash Functions

Hashing generally takes records whose key values come from a large range, and stores those records in a table with a relatively small number of slots. Collisions occur when two records hash to the same slot in the table. If we are careful – or lucky – when selecting a hash function, then the actual number of collisions will be few. Unfortunately, even under the best of circumstances collisions are nearly unavoidable.[2] For example, consider a classroom full of

---

[2]The exception to this is **perfect hashing**. Perfect hashing is a system in which records are hashed such that there are no collisions. A hash function is selected for the

students. What is the probability that some pair of students shares the same birthday (i.e., the same day of the year, not necessarily the same year)? If there are 23 students, then the odds are about even that two will share a birthday. This is despite the fact that there are 365 days in which students may have birthdays (ignoring leap years), on most of which no student in the class has a birthday. With more students, the probability of a shared birthday increases. The mapping of students to days based on their birthday is similar to assigning records to slots in a table (of size 365) using the birthday as a hash function. Note that this says nothing about *which* students share a birthday, or on *which* days of the year shared birthdays fall.

To be practical, a database organized by hashing must store records in a high percentage of the hash table slots, typically keeping the table at least half full. Since collisions are extremely likely to occur under these conditions, does this mean that we need not worry about the ability of a hash function to avoid collisions? Absolutely not. Technically, any function that maps all possible key values to a slot in the hash table is a hash function. Even a function that maps all records to the same slot is a hash function, but it does nothing to help us find records during a search operation.

In general, we would like to pick a hash function that distributes the records with equal probability to all hash table slots. How well any particular hash function does this depends on the distribution of the keys within the allowable key range. In some cases, incoming data are well-distributed across their key range. For example, if the input is a set of random numbers selected uniformly from the key range, any hash function that assigns the key range so that each slot in the hash table receives an equal share of the range will likely also distribute the input records uniformly within the table. However, in many applications the incoming records are highly clustered or otherwise poorly distributed. When input records are not well-distributed throughout the key range it can be difficult to devise a hash function that does a good job of distributing the records throughout the table, especially if the input distribution is not known in advance.

---

specific set of records being hashed, which requires that the entire collection of records is available before selecting the hash function. Perfect hashing is efficient because it always finds the record that we are looking for exactly where the hash function computes it to be; only one access is required. Selecting a perfect hash function can be expensive, but may be worthwhile when extremely efficient search performance is required. An example is searching for data on a CD-ROM. Here the database will never change, the time for each access is expensive, and the database designer can build the hash table before issuing the CD-ROM.

There are many reasons why data values may be poorly distributed. Natural distributions are exponential. For example, the populations of the 100 largest cities in the US will be clustered toward the bottom of the range, with a few outliers at the top (this is an example of a Zipf distribution, see Section 10.2). Collected data are likely to be skewed in some way. For example, samples from the field may be rounded to, say, the nearest 5 (i.e., all numbers end in 5 or 0). If the input is a collection of common English words, the beginning letter will be poorly distributed. Note that in each of these examples, either high- or low-order bits of the key are poorly distributed.

When designing hash functions, we are generally faced with one of two situations:

1. We know nothing about the distribution of the incoming keys. In this case, we wish to select a hash function that generates a uniform random distribution of the values in the key range, while avoiding obvious opportunities for clustering such as hash functions that are sensitive to the high- or low-order bits of the key value.

2. We know something about the distribution of the incoming keys. In this case, we should use a distribution-dependent hash function that avoids assigning clusters of related key values to the same hash table slot. For example, if hashing English words, we should *not* hash on the value of the first character because this is likely to be unevenly distributed.

Below are several examples of hash functions that illustrate these points.

Example 10.5 Consider the following hash function used to hash integers to a table of sixteen slots:

```
static int h(int x) {
  return(x % 16);
}
```

The value returned by this hash function depends solely on the least significant four bits of the key. Since these bits are likely to be poorly distributed (e.g., a high percentage may be even numbers with the low order bit being zero), the result will also be poorly distributed. This example shows that the size of the table M (typically the value used as the modulus) is critical to a good hash function.

Example 10.6 One good hash function for numerical values is called the **mid-square** method. The mid-square method squares the key value, and then takes the middle r bits of the result for a table of size 2^r. This works well since most or all bits of the key value contribute to the result.

Example 10.7 Here is a hash function for strings of characters:

```
static int h(String x, int M) {
  int i, sum;
  for (sum=0, i=0; i<x.length(); i++)
    sum += (int)x.charAt(i);
  return(sum % M);
}
```

This function sums the ASCII values of the letters in the string. If M is small, it should do a good job of distributing strings evenly among the hash table slots, since it gives equal weight to all characters. This is an example of the **folding method**. Note that the order of the characters in the string has no effect on the result of this hash function. A similar method for integers would add the digits of the key value, assuming that there are enough digits to (1) keep any one or two digits with bad distribution from skewing the results of the process and (2) generate a sum much larger than M. As with many hash functions, the final step is to apply the modulus operator to the result, using table size M to generate a value within the table range. If the sum is not sufficiently large, then the modulus operator will yield a poor distribution. Since the ASCII value for "A" is 65, sum will always be in the range 650 to 900 for a string of ten upper case letters. For a hash table of size 100 or less, a good distribution results. For a hash table of size 1000, the distribution is terrible.

Example 10.8 Here is a much better hash function for strings:

```
static long ELFhash(String key, int M) {
  long h = 0;
  for (int i=0; i<key.length(); i++) {
    h = (h << 4) + (int) key.charAt(i);
    long g = h & 0xF0000000L;
    if (g != 0) h ^= g >>> 24;
    h &= ~g;
  }
  return h % M;
}
```

This function is called `ELFhash` because it is used in conjunction with the "Executable and Linking Format" (ELF) for executable and object files in UNIX System V Release 4. It is typical of the black art involved in real-life hash functions. `ELFhash` takes as input a string of arbitrary length. It works well with both short and long strings, and every letter of the string has equal effect. It mixes up the decimal values of the characters in a way that is likely to give an even distribution among positions in the hash table.

10.4.2   Open Hashing

While the goal of a hash function is to minimize collisions, collisions are normally unavoidable in practice. Thus, hashing implementations must include some form of collision resolution policy. Collision resolution techniques can be broken into two classes: **open hashing** (also called **separate chaining**) and **closed hashing** (also called **open addressing**).[3] The difference between the two has to do with whether collisions are stored outside the table (open hashing), or whether collisions result in storing one of the records at another slot in the table (closed hashing). Open hashing is treated in this section, and closed hashing in Section 10.4.3.

A simple form of open hashing defines each slot in the hash table to be the head of a linked list. All records that hash to a particular slot are placed on that slot's linked list. Figure 10.2 illustrates a hash table where each slot stores one record and a link pointer to the rest of the list.

Records within a slot's list can be ordered in several ways: by order of insertion, by key value order, or by frequency-of-access order. Ordering the list by key value provides an advantage in the case of an unsuccessful search, since we know to stop searching the list once we encounter a key that is greater than the one being searched for. If records on the list are unordered or ordered by frequency, then an unsuccessful search will need to visit every record on the list.

Given a table of size M storing N records, the hash function will (ideally) spread the records evenly among the M positions in the table, yielding on average N/M records for each list. Assuming that the table has more slots than there are records to be stored, we can hope that few slots will contain more than one record. In the case where a list is empty or has only one record, a search requires only one access to the list. Thus, the average cost

---

[3]Yes, it is confusing when "open hashing" means the opposite of "open addressing," but unfortunately, that is the way it is.

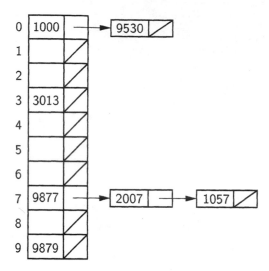

Figure 10.2 An illustration of open hashing for seven numbers stored in a ten-slot hash table using the hash function $\mathbf{h}(K) = K \bmod 10$. The numbers are inserted in the order 9877, 2007, 1000, 9530, 3013, 9879, and 1057. Two of the values hash to slot 0, one value hashes to slot 2, three of the values hash to slot 7, and one value hashes to slot 9.

for hashing should be $\Theta(1)$. However, if clustering causes many records to hash to a few of the slots, then the cost to access a record will be much higher as many elements on the linked list must be searched.

Open hashing is most appropriate when the hash table is kept in main memory, implemented with a standard in-memory linked list. Storing an open hash table on disk in an efficient way is difficult, since members of a given linked list may be stored on different disk blocks. This would result in multiple disk accesses when searching for a particular key value, which defeats the purpose of using hashing.

There are similarities to be observed between open hashing and Binsort. One way to view open hashing is that each record is placed in a bin. Multiple records may hash to the same bin, but this initial binning should greatly reduce the number of records accessed by a search operation. In a similar fashion, a simple Binsort reduces the number of records in each bin to a small number that can be sorted in some other way.

10.4.3 Closed Hashing

Closed hashing stores all records directly in the hash table. Each record i has a **home position** that is $\mathbf{h}(k_i)$, the slot computed by the hash function.

If a record R is to be inserted and another record already occupies R's home position, then R will be stored at some other slot in the table. It is the business of the collision resolution policy to determine which slot that will be. Naturally, the same policy must be followed during search as during insertion, so that any record not found in its home position can be recovered by repeating the collision resolution process.

Bucket Hashing

One approach to closed hashing is to group hash table slots into **buckets**. The hash table is viewed as an array of M slots divided into B buckets, with each bucket consisting of M/B slots. The hash function then assigns each record to the first slot within one of the buckets. If this slot is already occupied, then the record is moved downwards within the bucket until an open slot is found. If a bucket is entirely full, then the record is stored in an **overflow bucket** of infinite capacity at the end of the table. All buckets share the same overflow bucket. A good implementation will use a hash function that distributes the records evenly among the buckets so that as few records as possible go into the overflow bucket. Figure 10.3 illustrates bucket hashing.

When searching for a record, the first step is to hash the key to determine which bucket should contain the record. The records in this bucket are then searched. If the desired key value is not found and the bucket still has free slots, then the search is complete. If the bucket is full, then it is possible that the desired record is stored in the overflow bucket. In this case, the overflow bucket must be searched until the record is found or all records in the overflow bucket have been checked. If many records are in the overflow bucket, this will be an expensive process.

A simple variation on bucketing first hashes the key value to its home position as though bucketing were not being used. If the home position is full, then the record is pushed down toward the end of the bucket. If the bottom of the bucket is reached, then the collision resolution routine moves to the top of the bucket looking for an open slot. For example, assume that buckets contain eight records, with the first bucket consisting of slots 0 through 7. If a record is hashed to slot 5, the collision resolution process will attempt to insert the record into the table in the order 5, 6, 7, 0, 1, 2, 3, and finally 4. If all slots in this bucket are full, then the record is assigned to the overflow bucket. The advantage of this approach is that collisions are reduced, since any slot can be a home position rather than just the first slot in the bucket. This form of bucketing is well suited to hash tables stored

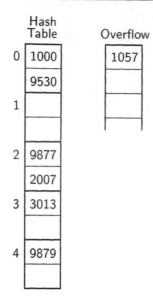

Figure 10.3 An illustration of bucket hashing for seven numbers stored in
a five-bucket hash table using the hash function $\mathbf{h}(K) = K \bmod 5$. Each
bucket contains two slots. The numbers are inserted in the order 9877, 2007,
1000, 9530, 3013, 9879, and 1057. Two of the values hash to bucket 0, three
values hash to bucket 2, one value hashes to bucket 3, and one value hashes
to bucket 4. Since bucket 2 cannot hold three values, the third one ends up
in the overflow bucket.

on disk. By making the bucket size equal to a disk block, we maximize the
likelihood that a record is stored in the same disk block as its home position.

Bucket methods are good for implementing hash tables stored on disk,
since the bucket size can be set to the size of a disk block. Whenever search
or insertion occurs, the entire bucket is read into memory. Processing an
insert or search operation requires only one disk access, unless the bucket is
full. If the bucket is full, the overflow bucket must be retrieved from disk as
well. Naturally, overflow should be kept small to minimize unnecessary disk
accesses.

Linear Probing

We now turn to the "classic" form of hashing: closed hashing with no bucketing, and a collision resolution policy that can potentially use any slot in
the hash table.

During insertion, the goal of collision resolution is to find a free slot in
the hash table when the home position for the record is already occupied.

We can view any collision resolution method as generating a sequence of hash table slots that can potentially hold the record. The first slot in the sequence will be the home position for the key. If the home position is occupied, then the collision resolution policy goes to the next slot in the sequence. If this is occupied as well, then another slot must be found, and so on. This sequence of slots is known as the **probe sequence** generated by the collision resolution policy. Insertion works as follows:

```
void hashInsert(Elem R) {            // Insert record R into T
  int home;                          // Home position for R
  int pos = home = h(R.key());       // Initial position
  for (int i=1; T[pos] != null; i++) {
    pos = (home + p(R.key(), i)) % M; // Next pobe slot
    Assert.notFalse(T[pos].key() != R.key(),
                "Duplicates not allowed");
  }
  T[pos] = R;                        // Insert R
}
```

In this implementation, $p(K, i)$ is the **probe function**, returning an offset from the home position for the ith slot on the probe sequence of key K.

Searching in a hash table follows the same probe sequence that was followed when inserting records. In this way, a record not in its home position may be recovered. A Java implementation for the search procedure is as follows:

```
Elem hashSearch(int K) { // Search for the record with key K
  int home;              // Home position for K
  int pos = home = h(K); // Initial position
  for (int i = 1; (T[pos] != null) && (T[pos].key() != K); i++)
    pos = (home + p(K, i)) % M;   // Next probe position
  if (T[pos] == null) return null; // K not in hash table
  else return T[pos];             // Found it
}
```

Both the insert and the search routines assume that at least one slot on the probe sequence of every key will be empty, otherwise they will continue in an infinite loop.

The discussion on bucket hashing presented a simple method of collision resolution. If the home position for the record is occupied, then move down the bucket until a free slot is found. This is an example of a technique for collision resolution known as **linear probing**. The probe function for simple linear probing is:

$$\mathbf{p}(K, i) = i.$$

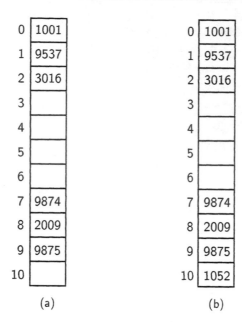

Figure 10.4 Example of problems with linear probing. (a) Six values are inserted in the order 9874, 2009, 1001, 9537, 3016, and 9875 using hash function $\mathbf{h}(K) = K$ mod 11. (b) The value 1052 is added to the hash table.

Once the bottom of the table is reached, the probe sequence wraps around to the beginning of the table. Linear probing has the virtue that all slots in the table will be candidates for inserting a new record before the probe sequence returns to the home position.

Linear probing has some definite drawbacks as a technique for collision resolution. The main problem is illustrated by Figure 10.4. Here, we see a hash table of eleven slots used to store four-digit numbers, with hash function $\mathbf{h}(K) = K$ mod 11. In Figure 10.4(a), six numbers have been placed in the table, leaving five slots remaining.

Ideally, each empty slot in the table will have equal probability of receiving the next record inserted. In this example, the hash function gives each slot (roughly) equal probability of being the home position for the next key. However, consider what happens to the next record if its key has home position at slot 0. Linear probing will send the record to slot 3. The same will happen to records whose home position is at slot 1 or 2. A record with home position at slot 3 will naturally remain in slot 3. Thus, the probability is 4/11 that the next record inserted will end up in slot 3. In a similar manner, records hashing to slots 7, 8, or 9 will end up in slot 10. However, only records hashing to slot 4 will be stored in slot 4, yielding one chance in eleven of this happening. Likewise, there is only one chance in eleven that the next record will be stored in slot 5, and one chance in eleven for slot 6. Thus, the resulting probabilities are not equal.

To make matters worse, if the next record ends up in slot 10 as illustrated by Figure 10.4(b), then the following record will end up in slot 3 with probability 8/11. This tendency of linear probing to cluster items together is known as **primary clustering**. Small clusters tend to merge into big clusters, making the problem worse. The objection to primary clustering is that it leads to long probe sequences.

Improved Collision Resolution Methods

How can we avoid primary clustering? One possibility is to use linear probing, but to skip slots by a constant c other than 1. In other words, the ith slot in the probe sequence will be $(\mathbf{h}(K) + ic) \bmod M$. In this way, records with adjacent home positions will not follow the same probe sequence.

The probe sequence should cycle through all slots in the hash table before returning to the home position. Not all probe functions have this property. For example, if $c = 2$ and the table contains an even number of slots, then any key whose home position is in an even slot will have a probe sequence that cycles through only the even slots. Likewise, the probe sequence for a key whose home position is in an odd slot will cycle through the odd slots. Thus, this combination of table size and linear probing constant effectively divides the key values into two sets stored in two disjoint sections of the hash table. Constant c must be relatively prime to M to have a probe sequence that visits all slots in the table. For a hash table of size $M = 10$, if c is any one of 1, 3, 7, or 9, then the probe sequence will visit all slots for any key. When $M = 11$, any value for c between 1 and 10 generates a probe sequence that visits all slots for every key.

Consider the situation where $c = 2$ and we wish to insert a record with key k_1 such that $\mathbf{h}(k_1) = 3$. The probe sequence for k_1 is 3, 5, 7, 9, and so on. If another key k_2 has home position at slot 5, then its probe sequence will be 5, 7, 9, and so on. The probe sequences of k_1 and k_2 are linked together in a manner that contributes to clustering. In other words, linear probing with a value of $c > 1$ does not solve the problem of primary clustering. We would like to find a probe function that does not link keys together in this way. We would prefer that the probe sequence for k_1 after the first step on the sequence should not be identical to the probe sequence of k_2. Instead, their probe sequences should diverge.

The ideal probe function would select the next position on the probe sequence at random from among the unvisited slots; that is, the probe sequence should be a random permutation of the hash table positions. Unfortunately, we cannot actually select the next position in the probe sequence at random, since then we would not be able to duplicate this same probe sequence when searching for the key. However, we can do something similar called **pseudo-random probing**. In pseudo-random probing, the ith slot in the probe sequence is $(\mathbf{h}(K) + r_i) \bmod M$ where r_i is the ith value in a random permutation of the numbers from 1 to $M - 1$. All insertions and searches use the same sequence of "random" numbers. The probe function would be

$$\mathbf{p}(K, i) = \texttt{Perm}[i - 1],$$

where `Perm` is an array of length $M - 1$ containing a random permutation of the values from 1 to $M - 1$.

> **Example 10.9** Consider a table of size $M = 101$, with $r_1 = 2$, $r_2 = 5$, and $r_3 = 32$. Assume that we have two keys k_1 and k_2 where $\mathbf{h}(k_1) = 30$ and $\mathbf{h}(k_2) = 28$. The probe sequence for k_1 is 30, then 32, then 35, then 62. The probe sequence for k_2 is 28, then 30, then 33, then 60. Thus, while k_2 will probe to k_1's home position as its second choice, the two keys' probe sequences diverge immediately thereafter.

Another technique that eliminates primary clustering is called **quadratic probing**. Here, the ith value in the probe sequence is $(\mathbf{h}(K) + i^2) \bmod M$. Thus, the probe function is

$$\mathbf{p}(K, i) = i^2.$$

Once again, two keys with different home positions will have diverging probe sequences. Quadratic probing has the disadvantage that not all slots in the hash table will necessarily be on the probe sequence.

> **Example 10.10** For a hash table of size $M = 101$, assume for keys k_1 and k_2 that $\mathbf{h}(k_1) = 30$ and $\mathbf{h}(k_2) = 29$. The probe sequence for k_1 is 30, then 31, then 34, then 39. The probe sequence for k_2 is 29, then 30, then 33, then 38. Thus, while k_2 will probe to k_1's home position as its second choice, the two keys' probe sequences diverge immediately thereafter.

Both pseudo-random probing and quadratic probing eliminate primary clustering, the problem of keys sharing substantial segments of a probe sequence. If two keys hash to the same home position, however, then they will follow the same probe sequence. This is because the probe sequences generated by pseudo-random and quadratic probing are entirely a function of the home position, not the original key value. (Note that function p does not use its input parameter K for either pseudo-random or quadratic probing.) If the hash function causes a cluster to a particular home position, then the cluster remains under pseudo-random and quadratic probing. This problem is called **secondary clustering**.

To avoid secondary clustering, we need to have the probe sequence be a function of the original key value, not the home position. A simple technique for doing this is to return to linear probing for the probe function, but to have the constant be based on a second hash function. Thus, the probe sequence would be of the form:

$$\mathbf{p}(K, i) = i * \mathbf{h}_2(K).$$

This method is called **double hashing**.

> **Example 10.11** Again, assume a hash table has size $M = 101$, and that there are three keys k_1, k_2, and k_3 with $\mathbf{h}(k_1) = 30$, $\mathbf{h}(k_2) = 28$, $\mathbf{h}(k_3) = 30$, $\mathbf{h}_2(k_1) = 2$, $\mathbf{h}_2(k_2) = 5$, and $\mathbf{h}_2(k_3) = 5$. Then, the probe sequence for k_1 will be 30, 32, 34, 36, and so on. The probe sequence for k_2 will be 28, 33, 38, 43, and so on. The probe sequence for k_3 will be 30, 35, 40, 45, and so on. Thus, none of the keys share substantial portions of the same probe sequence. Of course, if a fourth key k_4 has $\mathbf{h}(k_4) = 28$ and $\mathbf{h}_2(k_4) = 2$, then it will follow the same probe sequence as k_1. Pseudo-random or quadratic probing can be combined with double hashing to solve this problem.

A good implementation of double hashing should ensure that all of the probe sequence constants are relatively prime to the table size M. This can be achieved easily. One way is to select M to be a prime number, and have $\mathbf{h}_2$ return a value in the range $1 \leq \mathbf{h}_2(K) \leq M - 1$. Another way is to set $M = 2^m$ for some value m and let $\mathbf{h}_2$ return an odd value between 1 and 2^m.

Analysis of Closed Hashing

How efficient is hashing? We can measure hashing performance in terms of the number of record accesses required when performing an operation. The primary operations of concern are insertion, deletion, and search. It is useful to distinguish between successful and unsuccessful searches. Before a record can be deleted, it must be found. Thus, the number of accesses required to delete a record is equivalent to the number required to successfully search for it. To insert a record, an empty slot along the record's probe sequence must be found. This is equivalent to an unsuccessful search for the record (recall that a successful search for the record should generate an error since two records with the same key are not allowed).

When the hash table is empty, the first record inserted will always find its home position free. Thus, it will require only one record access to find a free slot. If all records are stored in their home positions, then successful searches will also require only one record access. As the table begins to fill up, the probability that a record can be inserted in its home position decreases. If a record hashes to an occupied slot, then the collision resolution policy must locate another slot in which to store it. Finding records not stored in their home position also requires additional record accesses as the record is searched for along its probe sequence. As the table fills up, more and more records are likely to be located ever further from their home positions.

From this discussion, we see that the expected cost of hashing is a function of how full the table is. Define the **load factor** for the table as $\alpha = N/M$, where N is the number of records currently in the table.

An estimate of the expected cost for an insertion (or an unsuccessful search) can be derived analytically as a function of α in the case where we assume that the probe sequence follows a random permutation of the slots in the hash table. The probability of finding the home position occupied is α. The probability of finding both the home position occupied and the next slot on the probe sequence occupied is $\frac{N(N-1)}{M(M-1)}$. The probability of i collisions is

$$\frac{N(N-1)\cdots(N-i+1)}{M(M-1)\cdots(M-i+1)}.$$

If N and M are large, then this is approximately $(N/M)^i$. The expected number of probes is one plus the sum over $i \geq 1$ of the probability of i collisions, which is approximately

$$1 + \sum_{i=1}^{\infty} (N/M)^i = 1/(1-\alpha).$$

The cost for a successful search (or a deletion) has the same cost as originally inserting that record. However, the expected value for the insertion cost depends on the value of α not at the time of deletion, but rather at the time of the original insertion. We can derive an estimate of this cost (essentially an average over all the insertion costs) by integrating from 0 to the current value of α, yielding a result of

$$\frac{1}{\alpha} \int_0^\alpha \frac{1}{1-x} dx = \frac{1}{\alpha} \log_e \frac{1}{1-\alpha}.$$

It is important to realize that these equations represent the expected cost for operations using the unrealistic assumption that the probe sequence is based on a random permutation of the slots in the hash table (thus avoiding all expense resulting from clustering). Thus, these costs are lower-bound estimates in the average case. Analysis shows that the average cost under linear probing is $\frac{1}{2}(1 + 1/(1-\alpha)^2)$ for insertions or unsuccessful searches and $\frac{1}{2}(1 + 1/(1-\alpha))$ for deletions or successful searches. Proofs of these results can be found in the references cited in Section 10.5.

Figure 10.5 shows the graphs of these four equations to help you visualize the expected performance of hashing based on the load factor. The two solid lines show the costs in the case of a "random" probe sequence for (1) insertion or unsuccessful search and (2) deletion or successful search. As expected, the cost for insertion or unsuccessful search grows faster, since these operations typically search further down the probe sequence. The two dashed lines show equivalent costs for linear probing. As expected, the cost of linear probing grows faster than the cost for "random" probing.

From Figure 10.5 we see that the cost for hashing is typically close to one record access, which is extraordinarily efficient, much better than binary search which requires $\log n$ record accesses. As α increases, so does the expected cost. For small values of α, the expected cost is low. It remains below two until the hash table is about half full. Based on this analysis, the rule of thumb is to design the system so that the hash table gets only about half full, since beyond that point performance will degrade rapidly. This requires that the implementor have some idea of how many records are likely to be in the table at maximum loading, and select the table size accordingly.

You may notice that this recommendation to limit α to 50% contradicts the disk-based space/time tradeoff principle, which strives to minimize disk space to increase information density. Hashing represents an unusual situation in that there is no benefit to be expected from locality of reference. In a sense, the hashing system implementor does everything possible to eliminate the effects of locality of reference! Given the disk block containing the last

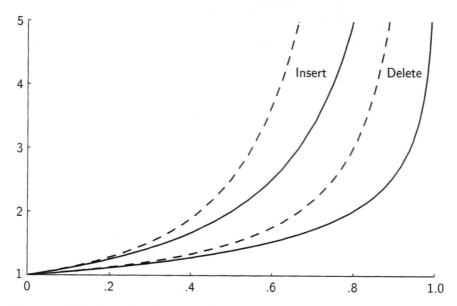

Figure 10.5 Growth of expected record accesses with α. The horizontal axis is the value for α, the vertical axis is the expected number of accesses to the hash table. Solid lines show the cost for "random" probing, while dashed lines show the cost for linear probing. The two leftmost lines show the cost for insertion and unsuccessful search; the rightmost two lines show the cost for deletion and successful search.

record accessed, the chance of the next record access coming to the same disk block is no better than random chance in a well-designed hash system. This is because a good hashing implementation breaks up relationships between search keys. Instead of improving performance by taking advantage of locality of reference, hashing trades increased hash table space for an improved chance that the record would be in its home position. Thus, the more space available for the hash table, the more efficient hashing should be.

Depending on the pattern of record accesses, it may be possible to reduce the expected cost of access even in the face of collisions. Recall the 80/20 rule: that 80% of the accesses will come to 20% of the data. In other words, some records are accessed more frequently. If two records hash to the same home position, which would be better placed in the home position, and which in a slot further down the probe sequence? The answer is that the record with higher frequency of access should be placed in the home position, since this will reduce the total number of record accesses. Ideally, records along a probe sequence will be ordered by their frequency of access.

One approach to approximating this goal is to modify the order of records along the probe sequence whenever a record is accessed. If a search is made to a record that is not in its home position, a self-organizing list heuristic can be used. For example, if the linear probing collision resolution policy is used, then whenever a record is located that is not in its home position, it can be swapped with the record preceding it in the probe sequence. That other record will now be further from its home position, but hopefully it will be accessed less frequently. Note that this approach will not work for the other collision resolution policies presented in this section, since swapping a pair of records to improve access to one may remove the other from its probe sequence.

Another approach is to keep access counts for records and periodically rehash the entire table. The records should be inserted into the hash table in frequency order, insuring that records that were frequently accessed during the last cycle have the best chance of being near their home positions.

Deletion

When deleting records from a hash table, there are two important considerations:

1. Deleting a record must not hinder later searches. In other words, the search process must still pass through the newly emptied slot. Thus, the delete process cannot simply mark the slot as empty, since this will isolate records further down the probe sequence. For example, in Figure 10.4(a), keys 1001 and 9537 both hash to slot 0. Key 9537 is placed in slot 1 by the collision resolution policy. If 1001 is deleted from the table, a search for 9537 must still probe to slot 1.

2. We do not want to make positions in the hash table unusable because of deletion. The freed slot should be available to a future insertion.

Both of these problems can be resolved by placing a special mark in place of the deleted record, called a **tombstone**. The tombstone indicates that a record once occupied the slot, but does so no longer. If a tombstone is encountered when searching through a probe sequence, the search procedure is to continue with the search. When a tombstone is encountered during insertion, that slot can be used to store the new record. However, to avoid inserting duplicate keys, it will still be necessary for the search procedure to follow the probe sequence until a truly empty position has been found.

The use of tombstones allows searches to work correctly, and allows reuse of deleted slots. However, after a series of intermixed insertion and deletion operations, some slots will contain tombstones. This will tend to lengthen the average distance from a record's home position to the record itself, beyond where it could be if the tombstones did not exist. A typical database application will first load a collection of records into the hash table and then progress to a phase of intermixed insertions and deletions. After the table is loaded with the initial collection of records, the first few deletions will lengthen the average probe sequence distance for records (it will add tombstones). Over time, the average distance will reach an equilibrium point since insertions will tend to decrease the average distance by filling in tombstone slots. For example, after initially loading records into the database, the average path distance might be 1.2 (i.e., an average of 0.2 accesses per search beyond the home position will be required). After a series of insertions and deletions, this average distance might increase to 1.6 due to tombstones. This seems like a small increase, but it is three times longer on average beyond the home position than before deletions.

Two possible solutions to this problem are:

1. Do a local reorganization upon deletion to try to shorten the average path length. For example, after deleting a key, continue to follow the probe sequence of that key and swap records further down the probe sequence into the slot of the recently deleted record (being careful not to remove a key from its probe sequence).

2. Periodically rehash the table. In other words, reinsert all records into a new hash table. Not only will this remove the tombstones, but it also provides an opportunity to place the most frequently accessed records into their home positions.

10.5 Further Reading

For a comparison of the efficiencies for various self-organizing techniques, see Bentley and McGeoch, "Amortized Analysis of Self-Organizing Sequential Search Heuristics" [BM85]. The text compression example of Section 10.2 comes from Bentley et al., "A Locally Adaptive Data Compression Scheme" [BSTW86]. For more on Ziv-Lempel coding, see *Data Compression: Methods and Theory* by James A. Storer [Sto88].

See *Introduction to Modern Information Retrieval* by Salton and McGill [SM83] for more information about document retrieval techniques.

See the paper "Practical Minimal Perfect Hash Functions for Large Databases" by Fox et al. [FHCD92], for an introduction and a good algorithm for perfect hashing.

For further details on the analysis for various collision resolution policies, see Knuth, Volume 3 [Knu81].

The model of hashing presented in this chapter has been of a fixed-size hash table. A problem not addressed is what to do when the hash table gets full and more records must be inserted. This is the domain of dynamic hashing methods. A good introduction to this topic is "Dynamic Hashing Schemes" by R.J. Enbody and H.C. Du [ED88].

10.6   Exercises

10.1 Modify the binary search routine of Section 3.5 to implement dictionary search. Assume that keys are in the range 1 to 10,000, and that key values are equally distributed within the range.

10.2 Modify Quicksort to find the Kth smallest value in an unsorted array of n numbers ($K <= n$). Your algorithm should require $\Theta(n)$ time in the average case.

10.3 Graph the equations $\mathbf{T}(n) = \log_2 n$ and $\mathbf{T}(n) = n/\log_e n$. Which gives the better performance, binary search on a sorted list, or sequential search on a list ordered by frequency where the frequence conforms to a Zipf distribution? Characterize the difference in running times.

10.4 Assume that the values 0 through 7 are stored in a self-organizing list, initially in ascending order. For each of the three self-organizing heuristics suggested in Section 10.2, show the resulting list and the total number of comparisons required resulting from the following series of accesses:

3 7 7 6 7 4 6 7 6 7 4 2 4 7 6.

10.5 For each of the three self-organizing list heuristics, describe a series of record accesses for which it would require the greatest number of comparisons of the three.

10.6 Write an algorithm to implement the frequency count self-organizing list heuristic, assuming that the list is implemented using an array. In particular, write a function **FreqCount** that takes as input a value to be searched for and which adjusts the list appropriately. If the value is not in the list, add it to the end of the list with a frequency count of one.

10.7 Write an algorithm to implement the move-to-front self-organizing list heuristic, assuming that the list is implemented using an array. In particular, write a function MoveToFront that takes as input a value to be searched for and which adjusts the list appropriately. If the value is not in the list, add it to the beginning of the list.

10.8 Write an algorithm to implement the transpose self-organizing list heuristic, assuming that the list is implemented using an array. In particular, write a function transpose that takes as input a value to be searched for and which adjusts the list appropriately. If the value is not in the list, add it to the end of the list.

10.9 Write functions for computing union, intersection, and set difference on arbitrarily long bit vectors used to represent set membership as described in Section 10.3. Assume that for each operation both vectors are of equal length.

10.10 Compute the probabilities for the following situations. These probabilities can be computed analytically, or you may write a computer program to generate the probabilities by simulation.

(a) Out of a group of 23 students, what is the probability that 2 students share the same birthday?

(b) Out of a group of 100 students, what is the probability that 3 students share the same birthday?

(c) How many students must be in the class for the probability to be at least 50% that there are 2 who share a birthday in the same month?

10.11 Assume that you are hashing key K to a hash table of n slots (indexed from 0 to $n - 1$). For each of the following functions $h(K)$, is the function acceptable as a hash function (i.e., would the hash program work correctly for both insertions and searches), and if so, is it a good hash function? Function Random(n) returns a random integer between 0 and $n - 1$, inclusive.

(a) $h(k) = k/n$ where k and n are integers.

(b) $h(k) = 1$.

(c) $h(k) = (k + \text{Random}(n)) \bmod n$.

(d) $h(k) = k \bmod n$ where n is a prime number.

10.12 Assume that you have a seven-slot hash table (with slots numbered 0 through 6). Show the final hash table that would result if you used the hash function $h(\mathbf{k}) = \mathbf{k}$ mod 7 and linear probing on this list of numbers: 3, 12, 9, 2. After inserting the key with value 2, list for each empty slot the probability that it will be the next one filled.

10.13 What is the result of running **ELFhash** on the following strings? Assume a hash table size of 101 slots.

   (a) HELLO WORLD
   (b) NOW HEAR THIS
   (c) HEAR THIS NOW

10.14 Using closed hashing, with double hashing to resolve collisions, insert the following keys into a hash table of thirteen slots (with slots numbered 0 through 12). The hash functions to be used are H1 and H2, defined below. You should show the hash table after all eight keys have been inserted. Be sure to indicate how you are using H1 and H2 to do the hashing. Function Rev(k) reverses the decimal digits of k, for example, Rev(37) = 73; Rev(7) = 7.

H1(k) = k mod 13.
H2(k) = (Rev($k + 1$) mod 11).

Keys: 2, 8, 31, 20, 19, 18, 53, 27.

10.15 Write an algorithm for a deletion function for hash tables that replaces the record with a special value indicating a tombstone. Modify the functions **hashInsert** and **hashSearch** to work correctly with tombstones.

10.16 Consider the following "random" permutation for the numbers 1 to 6:

$$2, 4, 6, 1, 3, 5.$$

Now, consider using this permutation for an implementation of pseudo-random probing on a hash table of size seven. Will this permutation solve the problem of primary clustering? What does this say about selecting a permutation for use when implementing pseudo-random probing?

10.7   Projects

10.1 Implement a database stored on disk using bucket hashing. Define records to be 128 bytes long with a 4-byte key and 120 bytes of data.

The remaining 4 bytes are available for you to store necessary information to support the hash table. A bucket in the hash table will be 1024 bytes long, so each bucket has space for 8 records. The hash table should consist of 27 buckets (total space for 216 records with slots indexed by positions 0 to 215) followed by the overflow bucket at record position 216 in the file. The hash function should be R.key() % 213. (Note that this means the last three slots in the table will not be home positions for any record.) The collision resolution function should be linear probing with wrap-around within the bucket. For example, if a record is hashed to slot 5, the collision resolution process will attempt to insert the record into the table in the order 5, 6, 7, 0, 1, 2, 3, and finally 4. If a bucket is full, the record should be placed in the overflow section at the end of the file.

Your system should support record insert, delete, and search. When you do your testing, consider that the system is designed to store about 100 or so records at a time.

10.2 Implement the text compression system described in Section 10.2.

10.3 Implement the three self-organizing list heuristics count, move-to-front, and transpose. Compare the cost for running the three heuristics on various input data. The cost metric should be the total number of comparisons required when searching the list. It is important to compare the heuristics using input data for which self-organizing lists are reasonable, that is, on frequency distributions that are uneven. One good approach is to read text files. The list should store individual words in the text file. Begin with an empty list, as was done for the text compression example of Section 10.2. Each time a word is encountered in the text file, search for it in the self-organizing list. If the word is found, reorder the list as appropriate. If the word is not in the list, add it to the end of the list and then reorder as appropriate.

10.4 Implement hashing with linear probing. Using empirical simulation, determine the cost of insert and delete as α grows (i.e., reconstruct the dashed lines of Figure 10.5).

11

Indexing

This chapter introduces file structures used to organize a large collection of records stored on disk. Such file structures support efficient insertion, deletion, and search operations. Hashing provides outstanding performance for the limited case in which all searches are of the form "find the record with key value K." Unfortunately, many applications require more general search capabilities. One example is a range query search for all records whose key lies within some range. Another query might require visiting all records in order of their key value. Hash tables are not organized to support either operation efficiently.

An **entry-sequenced file** contains records stored on disk in the order that they were entered into the system. Entry-sequenced files are the disk-based equivalent to an unsorted list, and so do not support efficient search. The natural solution is to sort the records by order of the search key. A typical database, such as a collection of employee or customer records maintained by a business, may contain multiple search keys. To answer a question about a particular customer may require a search on the name of the customer. Businesses often wish to sort and output the records by zip code order for a bulk mailing. Government paperwork may require the ability to process by order of Social Security number. Thus, there may not be a single "correct" order in which to store the records.

Section 9.5 discussed the concept of a key sort, in which an **index file** is created whose records consist of key values associated with pointers to a complete record in the main database file. The index file imposes an order on the records without physically rearranging them. One database may have several associated index files, each supporting efficient access through a different key field. Besides allowing access by multiple keys, index files help avoid the expense of reorganizing the original record file. The index allows direct access to specific records regardless of their order in the database.

Each record of a database normally has a unique identifier, called the **primary key**. For example, the primary key for a set of personnel records might be the Social Security number or ID number for the individual. Unfortunately, the ID number is generally an inconvenient value on which to perform a search since the searcher is unlikely to know it. Instead, the searcher might know the desired employee's name. Alternatively, the searcher might be interested in finding all employees whose salary is in a certain range. If these are typical search requests to the database then the name and salary fields deserve separate indexes. However, key values in the salary index are not likely to be unique. A key such as salary, where a particular key value may be duplicated in multiple records, is called a **secondary key**. Most searches are performed using a secondary key. The secondary key index will associate a secondary key value with the primary key of each record having that secondary key value. At this point, the full database might be searched directly for the record with that primary key, or there may be a primary key index with pointers to actual records on disk. In the latter case, only the primary key index provides the location of the actual record on disk.

Indexing is an important technique for organizing large databases, and many indexing methods have been developed. Direct access through hashing is discussed in Section 10.4. A simple list sorted by key value can also serve as an index to the record file. Techniques for searching sorted lists in memory are discussed in Section 10.1. Some additional issues relevant to indexing disk files by lists are discussed in the following section. Unfortunately, a sorted list does not perform well for insert and delete operations.

The third approach to indexing is the tree index. Trees are typically used to organize large databases that must support record insertion, deletion, and key range searches. Section 11.2 briefly describes ISAM, a tentative step towards solving the problem of storing a large database that must support insertion and deletion of records. Its failures help to illustrate the value of tree indexing techniques. Section 11.3 introduces the basic issues related to tree indexing. Section 11.4 introduces the 2-3 tree, a balanced tree structure that is a simple form of the B-tree covered in Section 11.5. B-trees are the most widely used indexing method for large disk-based databases, and many variations have been invented. Section 11.5 begins with a discussion of the variant normally referred to simply as a "B-tree." Section 11.5.1 presents the most widely implemented variant, the B^+-tree.

Linear Index

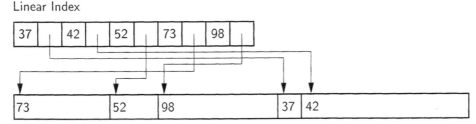

Database Records

Figure 11.1 Illustration of linear indexing for variable length records. Each record in the index file is of fixed length and contains a pointer to the beginning of the corresponding record in the database file.

11.1 Linear Indexing

A **linear index** is an index file organized as a sequence of key/pointer pairs where the keys are in sorted order and the pointers point to the position of the complete record on disk. Depending on its size, a linear index may be stored in main memory or on disk. A linear index provides a number of advantages. It provides convenient access to variable length database records, since each entry in the index file contains a fixed-length key field and a fixed-length pointer to the beginning of a (variable length) record as shown in Figure 11.1. A linear index also allows for efficient search and random access to database records, since it is amenable to binary search.

Linear indexing has significant limitations. If the database contains many records, the linear index may itself be too large to store in main memory. This makes binary search more expensive since many disk accesses may be required by the search process. One solution to this problem is to store a second level linear index in main memory that indicates the disk block in the index file storing a desired key. For example, the linear index on disk may reside in a series of 1024-byte blocks. If each key/pointer pair in the linear index requires 8 bytes, then 128 keys are stored per block. The second-level index in main memory consists of a table storing the value of the key in the first position of each block in the linear index file. If the linear index requires 100 disk blocks (100KB), the second-level index contains only 100 entries. To find the disk block containing a search key value, first search through the 100-entry table to find the greatest value less than or equal to the search key. This indicates the proper page in the index file, which is then read into memory. At this point, a binary search within this page will produce a pointer to the actual record in the database. This process is illustrated

1	2003	5894	10528

Second Level Index

1		2001	2003		5688	5894		9942	10528		10984

Linear Index: Disk Pages

Figure 11.2 A simple two-level linear index. The linear index is stored on disk. The smaller, second-level index is stored in main memory. Each element in the second-level index stores the first key value in the corresponding disk block of the index file.

Jones	AA10	AB12	AB39	FF37
Smith	AX33	AX35	ZX45	
Zukowski	ZQ99			

Figure 11.3 A two-dimensional linear index. Each row lists the primary keys associated with a particular secondary key value. In this example, the secondary key is a name. The primary key is a unique four character code.

by Figure 11.2. Typically the second-level index is stored in main memory. Thus, accessing a record by this method requires two disk reads: once from the index file and once from the database file for the actual record.

Every time a record is inserted to or deleted from the database, all associated secondary indices must be updated. Updates to a linear index are expensive, since the entire contents of the array might be shifted by one position. Another problem is that multiple records with the same secondary key each duplicate that key value within the index. When the secondary key field has a limited range (e.g., a field to indicate job category from among a small number of possible values), this duplication may waste considerable space.

One improvement on the simple sorted array is a two-dimensional array where each row corresponds to a secondary key value. A row contains the primary keys whose records have the indicated secondary key value. Figure 11.3 illustrates this approach. Now there is no duplication of secondary key values, possibly yielding a considerable space savings. The cost of insertion and deletion is reduced, since only one row of the table need be adjusted. Note that a new row is added to the array when a new secondary

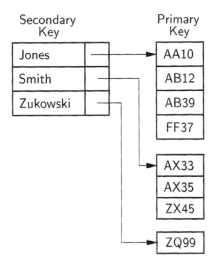

Figure 11.4 Illustration of an inverted list. Each secondary key value is stored in the secondary key index list. Each secondary key value on the list has a pointer to a list of the primary keys whose associated records have that secondary key value.

key value is added. This may lead to moving many records, but it should happen infrequently.

A drawback to this approach is that the array must be of fixed size, which imposes an upper limit on the number of primary keys that may be associated with a particular secondary key. Furthermore, those secondary keys with fewer records than the width of the array will waste the remainder of their row. A better approach is to have a one-dimensional array of secondary key values each associated with a linked list. This works well if the index is stored in main memory, but not so well when it is stored on disk since the linked list for a given key might be scattered across several disk blocks.

Consider a large database of employee records. If the primary key is the employee's ID number and the secondary key is the employee's name, then each record in the name index associates a name with one or more ID numbers. The ID number index in turn associates an ID number with a unique pointer to the full record on disk. The secondary key index in such an organization is also known as an **inverted list** or **inverted file**. It is inverted in that searches work backwards from the secondary key to the primary key to the actual data record. It is called a list because each secondary key value has (conceptually) a list of primary keys associated with it. Figure 11.4 illustrates this arrangement. Here, we have last names as the secondary key. The primary key is a four-character unique identifier.

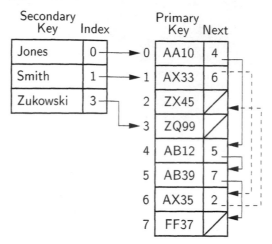

Figure 11.5 An inverted list implemented as an array of secondary keys and combined lists of primary keys. Each record in the secondary key array contains a pointer to a record in the primary key array. The `Next` field of the primary key array indicates the next record with that secondary key value.

Figure 11.5 shows a better approach to storing inverted lists. An array of secondary key values is shown as before. Associated with each secondary key is a pointer to an array of primary keys. The primary key array uses a linked list implementation. This approach combines the storage for all of the secondary key lists into a single array, probably saving space. Each record in this array consists of a primary key value and a pointer to the next element on the list. It is easy to insert and delete secondary keys from this array, making this a good implementation for disk-based inverted files.

11.2 ISAM

How do we handle large databases that require frequent update? The main problem with the linear index is that it is a single, large unit that does not lend itself to updates because a single update can require changing the position of every key in the index. Inverted lists reduce this problem, but they are only suitable for secondary key indices with relatively few secondary key values and a high degree of duplication. The linear index would perform well as a primary key index if it could somehow be broken into pieces such that individual updates affect only a part of the index. This concept will be pursued throughout the rest of this chapter, eventually culminating in the B^+-tree, the most widely used indexing method today. But first, we begin

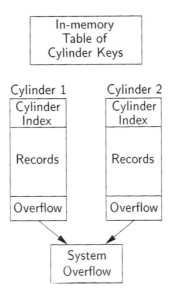

Figure 11.6 Illustration of the ISAM indexing system.

by studying ISAM, an early attempt to solve the problem of large databases requiring frequent update.

Before the invention of effective tree indexing schemes, a variety of disk-based indexing methods were in use. All were rather cumbersome, largely because no adequate method for handling updates was known. Typically, updates would cause the index to degrade in performance. ISAM is one example of such an index, and was widely used by IBM prior to adoption of the B-tree.

ISAM is based on a modified form of the linear index, as illustrated by Figure 11.6. Records are stored in sorted order by primary key. The disk file is organized by cylinders on disk. In memory is a table listing the lowest key value for each cylinder of the file. Each cylinder contains a table listing the lowest key value for each block in the cylinder. Each cylinder also contains an overflow area. When new records are inserted, they are placed in the correct cylinder's overflow area (in effect, a cylinder acts as a bucket). If a cylinder's overflow area fills completely, then a system-wide overflow area is used. Search proceeds by determining the proper cylinder from the system-wide table kept in main memory. The cylinder's block table is brought in from disk and consulted for the correct block. If the record is found in that block, then the search is complete. Otherwise, the cylinder's overflow area is searched.

After initial construction of the database, as long as no new records are inserted or deleted, access is efficient, requiring only two disk fetches. The first disk fetch recovers the block table for the desired cylinder. The second disk fetch recovers the block that, under good conditions, contains the record. After many inserts, the overflow list becomes too long, resulting in significant search time as the cylinder overflow area fills up. Under extreme conditions, many searches may eventually lead to the system overflow area. The "solution" to this problem is to periodically reorganize the entire database. This means rebalancing the records among the cylinders, sorting the records within each cylinder, and updating both the system index table and the within-cylinder block table. Such reorganization was typical of database systems during the 1960s, and would normally be done at night.

11.3 Tree Indexing

Linear indexing is efficient when the database is static, that is, when records are inserted and deleted rarely or never. ISAM is adequate for a limited number of updates, but not for frequent changes. Since it has essentially two levels of indexing, ISAM will also break down for a truly large database where the number of cylinders is too great for the top-level index to fit in main memory.

In their most general form, database applications have the following characteristics:

1. Large sets of records are frequently updated.

2. Search is by one or a combination of several keys.

3. Key range queries are used.

For such databases, a better organization must be found. One approach would be to use the binary search tree (BST) to store primary and secondary key indices. BSTs can store duplicate key values, they provide efficient insertion and deletion as well as efficient search, and they can perform efficient range queries. When there is enough main memory, the BST is a viable option for implementing both primary and secondary key indices.

Unfortunately, the BST can become unbalanced. Even under relatively good conditions, the depth of leaf nodes can easily vary by a factor of two. This may not be a significant concern when the tree is stored in main memory since the time required is still $\Theta(\log n)$ for search and update. When the tree is stored on disk, however, the depth of nodes in the tree becomes crucial.

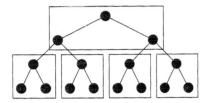

Figure 11.7 Breaking the BST into pages. The BST is divided among disk blocks, each with space for three nodes. The path from the root to any leaf is contained on two pages.

Every time a BST node B is visited, it is necessary to visit all nodes along the path from the root to B. Each node on this path must be retrieved from disk. Each disk access returns a block of information. If a node is on the same page as its parent, then the cost to find that node is trivial once its parent is in main memory. Thus, it is desirable to keep subtrees together on the same page. Unfortunately, each access to a BST node could require another block to be read from disk. Using a buffer pool to store multiple pages in memory can mitigate disk access problems if BST accesses display good locality of reference. But a buffer pool cannot eliminate the problem entirely. The problem becomes greater if the BST is unbalanced, since nodes deep in the tree have the potential of causing many disk blocks to be read. Thus, there are two significant issues that must be addressed to have efficient search from a disk-based BST. The first is how to keep the tree balanced. The second is how to arrange the nodes on pages so as to keep the number of pages encountered on any path from the root to the leaves at a minimum.

We could select a scheme for balancing the BST and allocating BST nodes to pages in a way that minimizes disk I/O, as illustrated by Figure 11.7. However, maintaining such a scheme in the face of insertions and deletions is difficult. In particular, the tree should remain balanced when an update takes place, but doing so may require much reorganization. Each update should affect only a few pages. As you can see from Figure 11.8, adopting a rule such as requiring the BST to be complete can cause a great deal of rearranging of data within the tree.

We can solve these problems by selecting another tree structure that automatically remains balanced after updates, and which is amenable to storing in pages. There are a number of widely used balanced tree data structures, and there are also techniques for keeping BSTs balanced. One example is the Splay tree discussed in Section 13.2. As an alternative, Section 11.4 presents the **2-3 tree**, which has the property that its leaves are

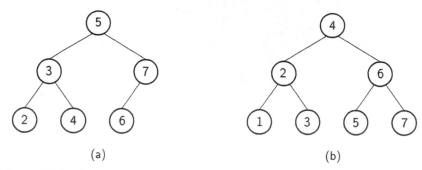

Figure 11.8 An attempt to rebalance a BST after insertion can be expensive. (a) A BST with six nodes in the shape of a complete binary tree. (b) A node with value 1 is inserted into the BST of (a). To maintain both the complete binary tree shape and the BST property, a major reorganization of the tree is required.

always at the same level. The main reason for discussing the 2-3 tree here in preference to the other balanced search trees is that it naturally leads to the B-tree of Section 11.5, which is by far the most widely used indexing method today.

11.4   2-3 Trees

This section describes a type of search tree called the 2-3 tree. The 2-3 tree is not a binary tree, but rather is a tree whose shape obeys the following definition.

Definition 11.1 A 2-3 tree has the following shape properties:

1. A node contains one or two keys.

2. Every internal node has either two children (if it contains one key) or three children (if it contains two keys). Hence the name.

3. All leaves are at the same level in the tree, so the tree is always height balanced.

In addition to these shape properties, the 2-3 tree has a search tree property analogous to that of a BST. For every node, the values of all descendants in the left subtree are less than the value of the first key, while values in the center subtree are greater than or equal to the value of the first key. If there is a right subtree (equivalently, if the node stores two keys), then the values of all descendants in the center subtree are less than the value of the second

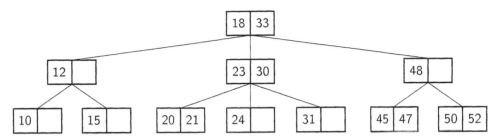

Figure 11.9 A 2-3 tree.

key, while values in the right subtree are greater than or equal to the value of the second key. To maintain these shape and search properties requires that special action be taken when nodes are inserted and deleted. The 2-3 tree has the advantage that it can be kept height balanced at relatively low cost.

Figure 11.9 illustrates the 2-3 tree. Nodes are indicated as rectangular boxes with two value fields. Internal nodes with only two children have an empty right value field. Leaf nodes may contain either one or two keys. Figure 11.10 shows the Java class declaration for the 2-3 tree node. Note that this sample declaration does not distinguish between leaf and internal nodes and so is space inefficient, since leaf nodes store three pointers each. The techniques of Section 5.3.1 can be applied here to implement separate internal and leaf node types.

From the defining rules for 2-3 trees we can derive relationships between the number of nodes in the tree and the depth of the tree. A 2-3 tree of height k has at least 2^{k-1} leaves, since if every internal node has two children it degenerates to the shape of a complete binary tree. A 2-3 tree of height k has at most 3^{k-1} leaves, since each internal node can have at most three children.

Searching for a value in a 2-3 tree is similar to searching in a BST. Search begins at the root. If the root does not contain the search key K, then the search progresses to the only subtree that can possibly contain K. The value(s) stored in the root node determine which is the correct subtree. For example, if searching for the value 30 in the tree of Figure 11.9, we begin with the root node. Since 30 is between 18 and 33, it can only be in the middle subtree. Searching the middle child of the root node yields the key. If searching for 15, then the first step is again to search the root node. Since 15 is less than 18, the first (left) branch is taken. At the next level, we take the second branch to the leaf node containing 15. If the search key were 16, then upon encountering the leaf containing 15 we would find that the search

```
class TTNode {               // 2-3 tree node implementation
  private Elem lkey;         // The node's left key
  private Elem rkey;         // The node's right key
  private int numKeys;       // Number of key values stored
  private TTNode left;       // Pointer to left child
  private TTNode center;     // Pointer to middle child
  private TTNode right;      // Pointer to right child

  public TTNode() { center = left = right = null; numKeys = 0; }
  public TTNode(Elem l, Elem r, TTNode p1, TTNode p2, TTNode p3) {
        lkey = l; rkey = r;
        if (r == null) numKeys = 1; else numKeys = 2;
        left = p1; center = p2; right = p3;
  }

  // Add key and subtree to internal node
  public void addKey(Elem val, TTNode child) {
    Assert.notFalse(numKeys==1, "Illegal addKey");
    numKeys = 2;
    if (val.key() < lkey.key()) {
      rkey = lkey; lkey = val;
      right = center; center = child;
    }
    else { rkey = val; right = child; }
  }

  public int numKeys() { return numKeys; }
  public TTNode lchild() { return left; }
  public TTNode rchild() { return right; }
  public TTNode cchild() { return center; }
  public TTNode setCenter(TTNode val) { return center = val; }
  public Elem lkey() { return lkey; }   // Left key value
  public Elem rkey() { return rkey; }   // Right key value
  public boolean isLeaf() { return left == null; }

  public void setLkey(Elem val) { // Change left key
    Assert.notFalse(val!=null, "Can't nullify left value");
    lkey = val;
  }

  public void setRkey(Elem val) { // Change right key
    Assert.notFalse(numKeys!=0,"Can't set right key of empty node");
    if ((val == null)&&(numKeys == 2)) // Clear subtree
      {right = null; numKeys = 1;}
    rkey = val; numKeys = 2;
  }
} // class TTNode
```

Figure 11.10 A Java implementation for the 2-3 tree node.

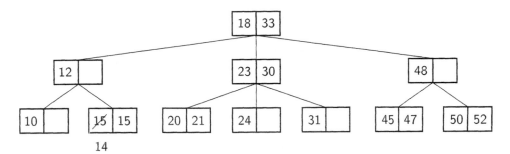

Figure 11.11 Simple insert into the 2-3 tree of Figure 11.9. The value 14 is inserted into the tree at the leaf node containing 15. Since there is room in the node for a second key, it is simply added to the left position with 15 moved to the right position.

key is not in the tree. Below is a Java implementation for 2-3 tree search, which is the functional equivalent to the `findhelp` function of the BST.

```
private Elem findhelp(TTNode root, int val) {
    if (root == null) return null;            // val not found
    if (val == root.lkey().key()) return root.lkey(); // val found
    if ((root.numKeys() == 2) && (val == root.rkey().key()))
        return root.rkey();
    if (val < root.lkey().key())              // Search left subtree
        return findhelp(root.lchild(), val);
    else if (root.numKeys() == 1)             // Search center subtree
        return findhelp(root.cchild(), val);
    else if (val < root.rkey().key())         // Search center subtree
        return findhelp(root.cchild(), val);
    else return findhelp(root.rchild(), val); // Search right
}
```

Insertion into a 2-3 tree is similar to insertion into a BST to the extent that the new record is placed in the appropriate leaf node. Unlike BST insertion, a new child is not created to hold the record being inserted. The first step is to find the leaf node that would contain the key if it were in the tree. If this leaf node contains only one value, then the new key can be added to that node with no further modification to the tree, as illustrated in Figure 11.11. In this example, the value 14 is inserted. Searching from the root, we come to the leaf node that stores 15. We add 14 as the left value (pushing the record with key 15 to the right position).

If the new key is to be inserted into a leaf node L that already contains two keys, then more space must be created. Consider the two key values of node L and the key to be inserted without further concern for which two were already in L and which is the one new key. The first step is to split L

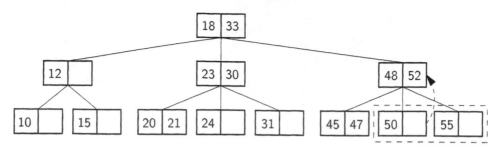

Figure 11.12 A simple node-splitting insert for a 2-3 tree. The value 55 is added to the 2-3 tree of Figure 11.9. This makes the node containing values 50 and 52 split, promoting value 52 to the parent node.

into two nodes. Thus, a new node – call it L' – must be created from free store. L receives the least of the three key values. L' receives the greatest of the three. The middle key value is passed back up to the parent node along with a pointer to L'. This is called a **promotion**. The promoted key is then inserted into the parent. If the parent currently contains only one key (and thus has only two children), then the promoted key and the pointer to L' are simply added to the parent node. If the parent is full, then the split-and-promote process is repeated. Figure 11.12 illustrates a simple promotion. Figure 11.13 illustrates what happens when promotions require the root to split, adding a new level to the tree. In either case, all leaf nodes continue to have equal depth. Figure 11.14 presents a Java implementation for the insertion process.

Note that **inserthelp** of Figure 11.14 takes two parameters. The first is a pointer to the root of the current subtree. The second is the value to be inserted. The return type is an array of **Objects**, used to return information in the case where a split takes place during insertion. If this occurs, the first object in the array is the element being promoted, while the second object is the newly-added subtree. These values constitute the information returned by the splitting process (which is implemented by the helper function **splitnode** in Figure 11.14).

When deleting a key from the 2-3 tree, there are three cases to consider. The simplest occurs when the key is removed from a leaf node containing two records. The key is simply removed, and no other nodes are affected. The second case occurs when the only key is removed from a leaf node. The third case occurs when a key is removed from an internal node. In both the second and the third cases, the deleted key is replaced with another that can take its place while maintaining the correct order, similar to removing a node from a

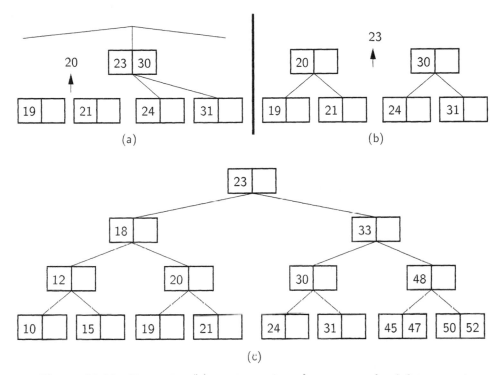

Figure 11.13 Example of inserting a key that causes the 2-3 tree root to split. (a) The value 19 is added to the 2-3 tree of Figure 11.9. This causes the node containing 20 and 21 to split, promoting 20. (b) This in turn causes the internal node containing 23 and 30 to split, promoting 23. (c) Finally, the root node splits, promoting 23 to become the left key in the new root. The result is that the tree becomes one level higher.

BST. If the tree is sparse enough, there is no such key available that will allow all nodes to still maintain at least one key. In this situation, sibling nodes may be merged together. The delete operation for the 2-3 tree is excessively complex, and will not be described further. Instead, a complete discussion of deletion will wait to the next section, where it can be generalized for a particular variant of the B-tree.

The 2-3 tree insert and delete routines do not add new nodes at the bottom of the tree. Instead they cause leaf nodes to split or merge, possibly causing a ripple effect moving up the tree to the root. If necessary the root may split, causing a new root node to be created and making the tree one level deeper. On deletion, the last two children of the root may merge, removing the root node and causing the tree to lose a level. In either case, all leaf nodes are at the same level. When all leaf nodes are at the same

```
private Object[] inserthelp(TTNode rt, Elem val) { // Do insert
  if (rt == null) { // Empty tree.
    rt = new TTNode(val, null, null, null, null);
    Object[] temp = {rt};  return temp;
  }
  if (rt.isLeaf())  // At leaf node -- insert here
    if (rt.numKeys() == 1) // Easy case
      { rt.addKey(val, null);  return null; }
    else return splitnode(rt, val, null);
  // Now at Internal node
  Object[] retval;                        // Hold result from insert
  if (val.key() < rt.lkey().key())
    retval = inserthelp(rt.lchild(), val);
  else if((rt.numKeys() == 1) || (val.key() < rt.rkey().key()))
    retval = inserthelp(rt.cchild(), val);
  else retval = inserthelp(rt.rchild(), val);
  if (retval == null) return null; // No split of child node
  // If here, child node split
  if (rt.numKeys() == 1) {                // Just add to rt
    rt.addKey((Elem)retval[0], (TTNode)retval[1]);
    return null;                         // No further splitting
  }
  // Split this node as well
  return splitnode(rt, (Elem)retval[0], (TTNode)retval[1]);
}

// Split a node into two; return info on promoted value
Object[] splitnode(TTNode rt, Elem val, TTNode child) {
  Object[] temp = new Object[2];    // Store info to be returned
  if (val.key() > rt.rkey().key()) { // Val is rightmost
    temp[0] = rt.rkey();              // Promote old right key
    TTNode hold = rt.rchild();
    rt.setRkey(null);                // Clear it
    temp[1] = new TTNode(val, null, hold, child, null);
  }
  else if (val.key() > rt.lkey().key()) { // Middle
    temp[0] = val;                   // Promote val
    temp[1] = new TTNode(rt.rkey(), null, child, rt.rchild(), null);
    rt.setRkey(null);                // Clear it
  }
  else {                             // Val is leftmost
    temp[0] = rt.lkey();             // Promote old left key
    temp[1] = new TTNode(rt.rkey(), null, rt.cchild(),
                         rt.rchild(), null);
    rt.setCenter(child);  rt.setLkey(val);
    rt.setRkey(null);                // Clear it
  }
  return temp;          // Return promoted element and its subtree
}
```

Figure 11.14 The 2-3 tree insert routine.

level, we say that a tree is **height balanced**. Since the 2-3 tree is height balanced, and every internal node has at least two children, we know that the maximum depth of the tree is $\log n$. Thus, all 2-3 tree insert, find, and delete operations require $\Theta(\log n)$ time.

11.5 B-Trees

This section presents the B-tree. B-trees are usually attributed to R. Bayer and E. McCreight who described the B-tree in a 1972 paper. By 1979, B-trees had replaced virtually all large file access methods other than hashing. B-trees, or some variant of B-trees, are *the* standard file organization for applications requiring insertion, deletion, and key range searches. B-trees address all of the major problems encountered when implementing disk-based search trees:

1. B-trees are always height balanced, with all leaf nodes at the same level.

2. Update and search operations affect only a few disk pages, so performance is good.

3. B-trees keep related records on the same disk block, which takes advantage of locality of reference.

4. B-trees guarantee that every node in the tree will be full at least to a certain minimum percentage. This improves space efficiency while reducing the typical number of disk fetches necessary during a search or update operation.

A B-tree of order m is a tree where each internal node contains up to m branches. Internal nodes have m children and store $m - 1$ key values.

Definition 11.2 A B-tree of order m has the following properties:

- The root is either a leaf or has at least two children.

- Each node, except for the root and the leaves, has between $\lceil m/2 \rceil$ and m children.

- All leaves are at the same level in the tree, so the tree is always height balanced.

You should note that the B-tree is just a generalization of the 2-3 tree. Put another way, a 2-3 tree is a B-tree of order three. Normally, the size

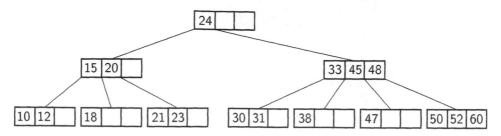

Figure 11.15 A B-tree of order four.

of a node in the B-tree is chosen to fill a disk block. A B-tree node implementation typically allows 100 or more children. Thus, a B-tree node is equivalent to a disk block, and a "pointer" value stored in the tree is actually the number of the block containing the child node (usually as an offset from the beginning of the corresponding disk file). In a typical application, B-tree block I/O will be managed using a buffer pool and a page-replacement scheme such as LRU (see Section 9.3).

Figure 11.15 shows a B-tree of order four. Each node contains up to three keys, and internal nodes have up to four children.

Search in a B-tree is a generalization of search in a 2-3 tree. It is an alternating two-step process, beginning with the root node of the B-tree.

1. Perform a binary search on the keys in the current node. If the search key is found, then return the record. If the current node is a leaf node and the key is not found, then report an unsuccessful search.

2. Otherwise, follow the proper branch and repeat the process.

For example, consider a search for the record with key 47 in the tree of Figure 11.15. The root node is examined and the second (right) branch taken. After examining the node at level 1, the third branch is taken to the next level to arrive at the leaf node containing key 47.

B-tree insertion is a generalization of 2-3 tree insertion. The first step is to find the leaf node that should contain the key to be inserted, space permitting. If there is room in this node, then insert the key. If there is not, then split the node into two and promote the middle key to the parent. If the parent becomes full, then it is split in turn, and the middle key promoted.

Note that this insertion process is guaranteed to keep all nodes at least half full. For example, when an internal node of a B-tree of order four becomes full, there will be five children. The node is split into two nodes containing two keys each, thus retaining the B-tree property.

11.5.1 B$^+$-Trees

The previous section mentioned that B-trees are universally used to implement large-scale disk-based systems. Actually, the B-tree as described in the previous section is almost never implemented, nor is the 2-3 tree as described in Section 11.4. What is most commonly implemented is a variant of the B-tree, called the B$^+$-tree. When greater efficiency is required, a slightly more complicated variant known as the B*-tree is used.

The most significant difference between the B$^+$-tree and the BST or the 2-3 tree of Section 11.4 is that the B$^+$-tree stores records only at the leaf nodes. Internal nodes store key values, but these are used solely as place-holders to guide the search. This means that internal nodes are significantly different in structure from leaf nodes. Internal nodes store keys to guide the search, associating each key with a pointer to a child node. Leaf nodes store actual records, or else keys and pointers to actual records in a separate disk file in the case where the B$^+$-tree serves purely as an index. Depending on the size of a record as compared to the size of a key, a leaf node in a B$^+$-tree of order m may store more or less than m records. The requirement is simply that the leaf nodes store enough records to remain at least half full. The leaf nodes of a B$^+$-tree are normally linked together to form a doubly-linked list. Thus, the entire collection of records can be traversed in sorted order by visiting all the leaf nodes on the linked list. Here is a Java-like pseudocode representation for the B$^+$-tree node class.

```
class Pair {        // Each BPNode stores an array of Pair
  Object pointer;   // BPNode leaves point to Elem,
                    // BPNode internal nodes point to BPNode
  int key;          // The key value for this pair
} // class Pair

class BPNode {                   // The BPNode class
  boolean isLeaf;                // True if this is a leaf
  Pair recarray[];               // Array of key/pointer pairs
  int numrec;                    // Number of pairs currently in node
  BPNode leftptr, rightptr;      // Each level forms a doubly-linked list
} // class BPNode
```

An important implementation detail to node is that while Figure 11.15 shows internal nodes containing three keys and four pointers, class **BPNode** stores key/pointer pairs. Figure 11.15 shows the B$^+$-tree as it is traditionally drawn. To simplify implementation in practice, nodes really do associate a key with each pointer. Each internal node should be assumed to hold in the leftmost position an additional key that is less than or equal to any possible

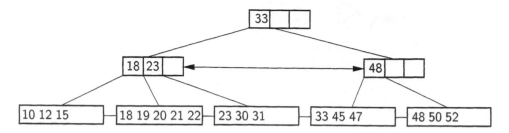

Figure 11.16 Example of a B$^+$-tree of order four. Internal nodes must store between two and four children. For this example, the record size is assumed to be such that leaf nodes can store between three and five records.

key value in the node's leftmost subtree. B$^+$-tree implementations typically store an additional dummy record with key value less than any legal key value.

B$^+$-trees are exceptionally good for range queries. Once the first record in the range has been found, the rest of the records in the range can be found by sequential processing of the remaining records in the node, and then continuing down the linked list of leaf nodes as far as necessary. Figure 11.16 illustrates the B$^+$-tree.

Search in a B$^+$-tree is nearly identical to search in a regular B-tree, except that the search must always continue to the proper leaf node. Even if the search-key value is found in an internal node, this is only a placeholder and does not provide access to the actual record. To find value 33 in the B$^+$-tree of Figure 11.16, search begins at the root. The value 33 stored in the root merely serves as a placeholder, indicating that keys with values greater than or equal to 33 are found in the second subtree. From the second child of the root, the first branch is taken to reach the leaf node containing the actual record (or a pointer to the actual record) with key value 33. Here is a pseudocode sketch of the B$^+$-tree search algorithm:

```
Elem findhelp(BPNode root, int K) {
  // function binaryle(A, n, K) returns the greatest value
  //   less than or equal to K in array A containing n records.
  int currec = binaryle(root.recarray, root.numrec, K);
  if (root.isLeaf())                        // If its a leaf node...
    if (root.recarray[currec].key() == K) //   Children are Elems
      return (Elem)root.recarray[currec].pointer;
    else return null;                       // K not in this node
  else return findhelp((BPNode)root.recarray[currec].pointer, K);
}
```

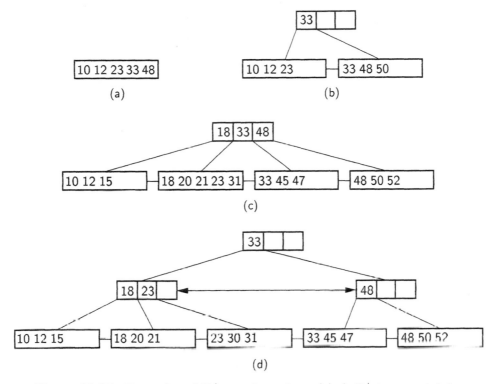

Figure 11.17 Examples of B+-tree insertion. (a) A B+-tree containing five records. (b) The result of inserting a record with key value 50 into the tree of (a). The leaf node splits, causing creation of the first internal node. (c) The B+-tree of (b) after further insertions. (d) The result of inserting a record with key value 30 into the tree of (c). The second leaf node splits, which causes the internal node to split in turn, creating a new root.

Inserting a record into the B+-tree is similar to B-tree insertion. First, the leaf that should contain the record is found. If that leaf is not full, then the new record is added, and no other B+-tree nodes are affected. If the leaf is already full, split it in two (dividing the records evenly among the two nodes) and promote a copy of the least-valued key in the newly-formed right node. As with the 2-3 tree, promotion may cause the parent to split in turn, perhaps eventually leading to splitting the root and causing the B+-tree to gain a new level. B+-tree insertion keeps all leaf nodes at equal depth. Figure 11.17 illustrates the insertion process through several examples. The following is a Java-like pseudocode sketch of the B+-tree insert algorithm.

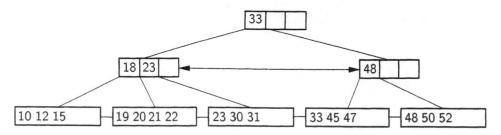

Figure 11.18 Simple deletion from a B⁺-tree. The record with key value 18 is removed from the tree of Figure 11.16. Note that since 18 is simply a placeholder used to direct search in the parent node, it need not be changed even if no record in the tree has key value 18.

```
// B+-tree pseudocode: insert
// putinarray(A, pos, pair) places pair in array A at position pos.
// Function splitnode(rt, pos, pair) places pair in rt at pos.
//    But, in the process, rt is split into two nodes, each node
//    taking half of the records, and the new node is returned.
Pair inserthelp(BPNode root, Elem rec) {
  Pair temp;        // Hold a key/pointer pair
  int currec = binaryle(root.recarray, root.numrec, rec.key());
  if (root.isLeaf()) { // Leaf node -- set up values to insert
    Assert.notFalse(root.recarray[currec].key() != rec.key(),
                    "Duplicates are not allowed");
    temp = new Pair(rec.key(), rec);
  }
  else { // internal node
    temp = inserthelp((BPnode)root.recarray[currec].pointer, rec);
    if (temp == null) return null; // Child did not split, so no
  }                                //    insert into current node

  // Now, do the insert to the current node.  Split if necessary
  if (!root.isFull()) putinarray(root.recarray, currec, temp);
  else {
    BPNode tp = splitnode(root, currec, temp);
    return new Pair(tp.recarray[0].key(), tp);
  }
  return null;
}
```

To delete a record from the B⁺-tree, first locate the leaf that contains the record to be deleted. If that leaf node is more than half full, then we need only remove the record, leaving the leaf node still at least half full. This is demonstrated by Figure 11.18.

If deleting a record reduces the number of records in the node below the minimum threshold (called an **underflow**), then we must do something to keep the node sufficiently full. The first choice is to look at the node's

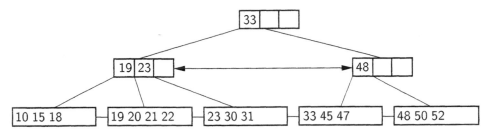

Figure 11.19 Deletion from the B⁺-tree of Figure 11.16 via borrowing from a sibling. The key with value 12 is deleted from the leftmost leaf, causing the record with key value 18 to shift to the leftmost leaf to take its place. Note that the parent must be updated to properly indicate the key range within the subtrees. In this example, the parent node has its leftmost key value changed to 19.

adjacent siblings to determine if they have a spare record that can be used to fill the gap. If so, then enough records are transferred from the sibling so that both nodes have the same number of records. This is done so as to delay as long as possible the next time when a delete causes this node to underflow again. This process may require that the parent node has its placeholder key value revised to reflect the true first key value in each node. Figure 11.19 illustrates the process.

If neither sibling can lend a node to the underfull node (call it N), then N must give its keys to a sibling and be removed from the tree. There is certainly room to do this, since the sibling is at most half full (remember that it had no records to contribute to the current node), and N is less than half full since it is underflowing. This merge process combines two subtrees of the parent, which may cause it to underflow in turn. If the last two children of the root merge together, then the tree loses a level. Figure 11.20 illustrates the node-merge deletion process.

Figure 11.21 shows a Java-like pseudocode sketch of the B⁺-tree delete algorithm.

The B⁺-tree requires that all nodes be at least one half full (except for the root). Thus, the storage utilization must be at least 50%. This is satisfactory for many implementations, but note that keeping nodes fuller will result both in less space required (since there is less empty space in the disk file) and in more efficient processing (fewer blocks on average will be read into memory since the amount of information in each block is greater). Since B-trees have become so popular, many have tried to improve their performance. One method for doing so is to use the B⁺-tree variant known

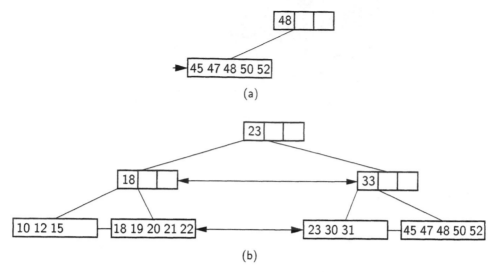

Figure 11.20 Deleting the record with key value 33 from the B$^+$-tree of Figure 11.16 via collapsing siblings. (a) The two leftmost leafnodes merge together to form a single leaf. Unfortunately, the parent node now has only one child. (b) Since the left subtree has a spare leaf node, that node is passed to the right subtree. The placeholder values of the root and the right internal node are updated to reflect the changes. Value 23 moves to the root, and old root value 33 moves to the rightmost internal node.

as the B*-tree. The B*-tree is identical to the B$^+$-tree, except for the rules used to split and merge nodes. Instead of splitting a node in half when it overflows, the B*-tree gives some records to its neighboring sibling. If the neighbor is also full, then the two nodes split into three. Similarly, when a node underflows, it is combined with its two siblings, and the total reduced to two nodes. Thus, the nodes are always at least two thirds full.[1]

11.5.2   B-Tree Analysis

The asymptotic cost of search, insertion, and deletion of records from B-trees, B$^+$-trees, and B*-trees is $\Theta(\log n)$ where n is the total number of records in the tree. However, the base of the log is the (average) branching factor

---

[1]This concept can be extended further if higher space utilization is required. However, the update routines become much more complicated. I once worked on a project where we implemented 3-for-4 node split and merge routines. This gave better performance than the 2-for-3 node split and merge routines of the B*-tree. However, the spitting and merging routines were so complicated that even their author could no longer understand them once they were completed!

```
// removehelp returns position of the child node adjusted, if any.
//   If the child node did not underflow or change its first record,
//   then return -1, to indicate the parent shouldn't be modified.
// Function removerec(A, n, c) removes the record at position c from
//   array A containing n records.
// Function merge_nodes(N1, N2) merges together the record arrays of
//   BPNodes N1 and N2.
// Function shuffle_nodes(N1, N2) copies records as necessary within
//   BPnodes N1 and N2, so that both have equal number of records.
int removehelp(BPNode root, int K, int thispos) {
  int currec = binaryle(root.recarray, root.numrec, K);
  if (root.isLeaf())
    if (root.recarray[currec].key() != K) return -1;// K not found
  else { // Delete from child
    currec = removehelp((BPNode)root.recarray[currec].pointer,
                        K, currec);
    if (currec == -1)   // Child did not underflow
      return -1;
    else if(root.recarray[currec].pointer.numrec != 0) {
      // Child was shuffled -- adust key value
      root.recarray[currec].key =
        ((BPNode)root.recarray[currec].pointer).recarray[0].key;
      return -1;        // Child did not underflow
    }
  }
  // Now, remove record at position currec
  removerec(root.recarray, root.numrec--, currec);
  if (root.numrec > THRESHOLD) // Enough records, just remove it
    return -1;
  else {                            // Underflow
    if (root.leftptr == null)   // No left neighbor
      if (root.numrec + root.rightptr.numrec <= MAXREC) {
        merge_nodes(root, root.rightptr);
        return thispos+1; // Right neighbor is now empty
      }
      else {
        shuffle_nodes(root, root.rightptr);
        return thispos+1; // Right neighbor has new first record
      }
    else if (root.numrec + root.leftptr.numrec <= MAXREC) {
      merge_nodes(root.leftptr, root);
      return thispos;     // This node is now empty
    }
    else {
      shuffle_nodes(root.leftptr, root);
      return thispos;     // This node has new first record
    }
  }
}
```

Figure 11.21 A Java-like pseudocode sketch of the B$^+$-tree delete algorithm.

of the tree. Typical database applications use extremely high branching factors, perhaps 100 or more. Thus, in practice the B-tree and its variants are extremely shallow.

As an illustration, consider a B^+-tree of order 100 and leaf nodes that contain up to 100 records. A one level B^+-tree can have at most 100 records. A two-level B^+-tree must have at least 100 records (2 leaves with 50 records each). It has at most 10,000 records (100 leaves with 100 records each). A three-level B^+-tree must have at least 5000 records (two second-level nodes with 50 children containing 50 records each) and at most one million records (100 second level nodes with 100 full children each). A four-level B^+-tree must have at least 250,000 records and at most 100 million records. Thus, it would require an *extremely* large database to generate a B^+-tree of more than four levels.

We can reduce the number of disk fetches required for the B-tree even more by using the following methods. First, the upper levels of the tree can be stored in main memory at all times. Since the tree branches so quickly, the top two levels require relatively little space. If the B-tree is only four levels deep, then at most two disk fetches (level two and the leaves at level three) are required to reach the pointer to any given record.

As mentioned earlier, a buffer pool should be used to manage nodes of the B-tree. Several nodes of the tree would typically be in main memory at one time. The most straightforward approach is to use a standard method such as LRU to do node replacement. However, sometimes it may be desirable to "lock" certain nodes such as the root into the buffer pool. In general, if the buffer pool is even of modest size (say at least twice the depth of the tree), no special techniques for node replacement will be required since the upper level nodes will naturally be accessed frequently.

11.6   Further Reading

For an expanded discussion of the issues touched on in this chapter, see a general file processing text such as *File Structures: A Conceptual Toolkit* by Folk and Zoellick [FZ92]. In particular, Folk and Zoellick provide a good discussion of the relationship between primary and secondary indices. The most thorough discussion on various implementations for the B-tree is the survey article by Comer [Com79]. Also see [Sal88] for further details on implementing B-trees. See Shaffer and Brown [SB93] for a discussion of buffer pool management strategies for B^+-tree-like data structures.

11.7 Exercises

11.1 Assume that a computer system has disk blocks of 1024 bytes, and that you are storing records with 4-byte keys and 4-byte data fields. Furthermore, 256KB of memory is available to store a linear index. The records are sorted and packed sequentially into the disk file. The first record of each block is used in the linear index.

(a) How many records can be in the file while still maintaining an index to the file in available memory?

(b) How many records can be stored when using a second-level index of 1024 bytes (i.e., 256 key values) as illustrated by Figure 11.2?

11.2 Assume that a computer system has disk blocks of 4096 bytes, and that you are storing records with 4-byte keys and 64-byte data fields. Records in the disk file are accessed through a linear index. The records are sorted and packed sequentially into the disk file. The first record of each block is used in the linear index.

(a) How large a disk file can the linear index maintain if the maximum space available for the index is 2MB?

(b) How many records can be stored in the disk file if a second-level linear index of 4096 bytes (i.e., 1024 key values) is used, as illustrated by Figure 11.2, and the first-level linear index is also stored on disk?

11.3 How must the function `binary` of Section 3.5 be modified so as to support variable length records with fixed-length keys indexed by a simple linear index as illustrated by Figure 11.1?

11.4 Assume that a database stores records consisting of a 2-byte integer key and a variable length data field consisting of a string. Show the linear index (as illustrated by Figure 11.1) for the following collection of records:

397	Hello world!
82	XYZ
1038	This string is rather long
1037	This is shorter
42	ABC
2222	Hello new world!

11.5 Each of the following series of records consists of a four-digit primary key (with no duplicates) and a four-character secondary key (with many duplicates).

> 3456 DEER
> 2398 DEER
> 2926 DUCK
> 9737 DEER
> 7739 GOAT
> 9279 DUCK
> 1111 FROG
> 8133 DEER
> 7183 DUCK
> 7186 FROG

(a) Show the inverted list (as illustrated by Figure 11.4) for this collection of records.

(b) Show the improved inverted list (as illustrated by Figure 11.5) for this collection of records.

11.6 Under what conditions will ISAM be more efficient than a B^+-tree implementation?

11.7 Prove that the number of leaf nodes in a 2-3 tree with k levels is between 2^{k-1} and 3^{k-1}.

11.8 Show the result if inserting the values 55 and 46 into the 2-3 tree of Figure 11.9.

11.9 You are given a series of records whose keys are letters. The records are inserted in the following order: C, S, D, T, A, M, P, I, B, W, N, G, U, R, K, E, H, O, L, J. Show the 2-3 tree that results from inserting these records.

11.10 You are given a series of records whose keys are letters. The records arrive in the following order: C, S, D, T, A, M, P, I, B, W, N, G, U, R, K, E, H, O, L, J. Show the 2-3 tree that results from inserting these records when the 2-3 tree is modified to be a 2-3^+ tree, that is, the internal nodes act only as placeholders. Assume that the leaf nodes are capable of holding up to two records.

11.11 Show the result of inserting the value 55 into the B-tree of Figure 11.15.

11.12 Show the result of inserting the values 1, 2, 3, 4, 5, and 6 (in that order) into the B^+-tree of Figure 11.16.

11.13 Show the result of deleting the values 18, 19, and 20 (in that order) from the B$^+$-tree of Figure 11.20b.

11.14 You are given a series of records whose keys are letters. The records arrive in the following order: C, S, D, T, A, M, P, I, B, W, N, G, U, R, K, E, H, O, L, J. Show the B$^+$-tree of order four that results from inserting these records. Assume that the leaf nodes are capable of storing up to three records.

11.15 Assume that you have a B$^+$-tree whose internal nodes can store up to 100 children and whose leaf nodes can store up to 15 records. What are the minimum and maximum number of records that can be stored by the B$^+$-tree for 1, 2, 3, 4, and 5 levels?

11.16 Assume that you have a B$^+$-tree whose internal nodes can store up to 50 children and whose leaf nodes can store up to 50 records. What are the minimum and maximum number of records that can be stored by the B$^+$-tree for 1, 2, 3, 4, and 5 levels?

11.8 Projects

11.1 Implement a two-level linear index for variable length records as illustrated by Figures 11.1 and 11.2. Assume that disk blocks are 1024 bytes in length. Records in the database file should typically range between 20 and 200 bytes, including a 4-byte key value. Each record of the index file should store a key value and the byte offset in the database file for the first byte of the corresponding record. The top-level index (stored in memory) should be a simple array storing the lowest key value on the corresponding page in the index file.

11.2 Implement the 2-3$^+$ tree, that is, a 2-3 tree where the internal nodes act only as placeholders. You should modify the 2-3 tree node definition of Figure 11.10 as little as possible.

11.3 Implement the B$^+$-tree described in Section 11.5. Assume that disk blocks are 1024 bytes, and thus both leaf nodes and internal nodes are also 1024 bytes. Records should store a 4-byte (`int`) key value and a 60-byte data field. Internal nodes should store key value/pointer pairs where the "pointer" is actually the block number on disk for the child node. Both internal nodes and leaf nodes will need room to store various information such as a count of the records stored on that node, a pointer to the next node on that level, and so forth. Thus, leaf nodes will store 15 records, and internal nodes will have room to store about

120 to 125 children depending on how you implement them. Use the buffer pool library of Project 9.2 to manage access to the nodes stored on disk. Your implementation should support insert, delete, and search by exact key value or range of keys.

Part IV

Applications and Advanced Topics

12

Lists and Arrays Revisited

For many applications, simple lists and arrays are the right tool for the job. Other applications require support for operations that cannot be implemented efficiently by the standard list representations of Chapter 4. This chapter presents advanced implementations for lists and arrays that overcome some of the problems of simple linked list and contiguous array representations. The topics covered in this chapter should also serve to reinforce the concept of logical representation versus physical implementation, as some of the "list" implementations have quite different organizations internally.

Section 12.1 presents the Skip List, a probabilistic data structure for storing records ordered by key value, which allows efficient access and update with high probability despite its simplicity. Section 12.2 describes a series of representations for multilists, which are lists that may contain sublists. Section 12.3 discusses representations for implementing sparse matrices, large matrices where most of the elements have zero values. Section 12.4 discusses memory management techniques, which are essentially a way of allocating variable length sections of a large array.

12.1 Skip Lists

Skip Lists are designed to overcome a basic limitation of array-based and linked lists: Either search or update operations require linear time. The Skip List is an example of a **probabilistic data structure**, since it makes some of its decisions at random.

Skip Lists provide an alternative to the BST and related tree structures. The primary problem with the BST is that it may easily become unbalanced. The 2-3 tree of Chapter 11 is guaranteed to remain balanced regardless of the order in which data values are inserted, but it is rather complicated to implement. Chapter 13 presents the Splay Tree, which is also guaranteed to provide good performance, but again it adds complexity to the BST. The Skip List is not guaranteed to provide good performance (where good performance is defined as $\Theta(\log n)$ search, insertion, and deletion time), but it will provide good performance with extremely high probability. It is also easier to implement than known balanced tree structures. As such it represents a good compromise between difficulty of implementation and performance.

Figure 12.1 illustrates the concept behind the Skip List. Figure 12.1(a) shows a simple linked list whose nodes are ordered by node value. To search a sorted linked list requires that we move down the list one node at a time, visiting $O(n)$ nodes in the average case. Imagine that we add a pointer to every other node that lets us skip alternating nodes, as shown in Figure 12.1(b). Define nodes with only a single pointer as level 0 Skip List nodes, while nodes with two pointers are level 1 Skip List nodes.

To search, follow the level 1 pointers until a value greater than the search key has been found, then revert to a level 0 pointer to travel one more node if necessary. This effectively cuts the work in half. We can continue adding pointers in this way until we reach the ultimate of $\log n$ pointers in the first and middle nodes for a list of n nodes as illustrated in Figure 12.1(c). To search, start with the bottom row of pointers, going as far as possible and skipping many nodes at a time. Then, shift up to shorter and shorter steps as required. With this arrangement, the worst-case number of accesses is in $O(\log n)$.

Here is an implementation for searching in a Skip List. Each Skip List node contains an array named `forward` that stores the pointers as shown in Figure 12.1(c). Position `forward[0]` stores a level 0 pointer, `forward[1]` stores a level 1 pointer, and so on. The Skip List class definition includes data member `level` that stores the highest level for any node in the Skip List. The Skip List is assumed to store a header node named `head` with `level` pointers.

```
public Elem search(int searchKey) { // Skiplist Search
  SkipNode x = head;                 // Dummy header node
  for (int i=level; i>=0; i--)       // For each level...
    while ((x.forward[i] != null) && // go forward
           (x.forward[i].value().key() < searchKey))
      x = x.forward[i];              // Go one last step
  x = x.forward[0];  // Move to actual record, if it exists
  if ((x != null) && (x.value().key() == searchKey))
    return x.value();                // Got it
  else return null;                  // Its not there
}
```

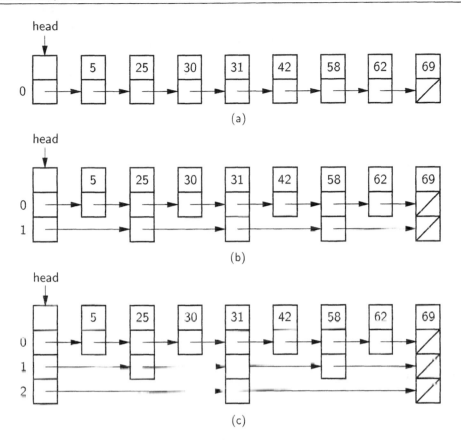

Figure 12.1 Illustration of the Skip List concept. (a) A simple linked list. (b) Augmenting the linked list with additional pointers at every other node. (c) The ideal Skip List, guaranteeing $O(\log n)$ search time.

Searching for a node with value 62 in the Skip List of Figure 12.1(c) begins at the header node. Follow the header node's pointer at `list.level`, which in this example is level 2. This points to the node with value 31. Since 31 is less than 62, we next try the pointer from `forward[2]` of 31's node to reach 69. Since 69 is greater than 62, we cannot go forward, but must instead decrement the current level counter to 1.

We next try to follow `forward[1]` of 31 to reach the node with value 58. Since 58 is smaller than 62, we follow 58's `forward[1]` pointer, to 69. Since 69 is too big, follow 58's level 0 pointer to 62. Since 62 is not less than 62, we fall out of the `while` loop, and move one step forward to the node with value 62.

The ideal Skip List of Figure 12.1(c) has been organized so that (if the first and last nodes are not counted) half of the nodes have only one pointer, one quarter have two, one eighth have three, and so on. The distances are equally spaced; in effect this is a "perfectly balanced" Skip List. Maintaining such balance would be expensive during the normal process of insertions and deletions. The key to Skip Lists is that we do not worry about any of this. Whenever inserting a node, we assign it a level (i.e., some number of pointers). The assignment is random, using an exponential distribution yielding a 50% probability that the node will have one pointer, a 25% probability that it will have two, and so on. The following function determines the level based on such a distribution:

```
int randomLevel() { // Pick a level on exponential distribution
   int lev;
   for (lev=0; DSutil.random(2) == 0; lev++); // Do nothing
   return lev;
}
```

Once the proper level for the node has been determined, the next step is to find where the node should be inserted, and link it in as appropriate at all of its levels. Here is an implementation for inserting a new value into the Skip List:

```
public void insert(Elem newValue) { // Insert into skiplist
   int newLevel = randomLevel();       // Select level for new node
   if (newLevel > level)               // New node will be deepest
     AdjustHead(newLevel);             // Add null pointers to header
   SkipNode[] update = new SkipNode[level+1]; // Track end of level
   SkipNode x = head;                  // Start at header node
   for (int i=level; i>=0; i--) {      // Search for insert position
     while((x.forward[i] != null) &&
           (x.forward[i].value().key() < newValue.key()))
       x = x.forward[i];
     update[i] = x;                     // Keep track of end at level i
   }
   x = new SkipNode(newValue, newLevel);  // Create new node
   for (int i=0; i<=newLevel; i++) {      // Splice into list
     x.forward[i] = update[i].forward[i]; // Who x points to
     update[i].forward[i] = x;            // Who y points to
   }
}
```

Figure 12.2 illustrates the Skip List insertion process. In this example, we begin by inserting a node with value 10 into an empty Skip List. Assume that **randomLevel** returns a value of 1 (i.e., the node is at level 1, with 2 pointers). Since the empty Skip List has no nodes, the level of the list

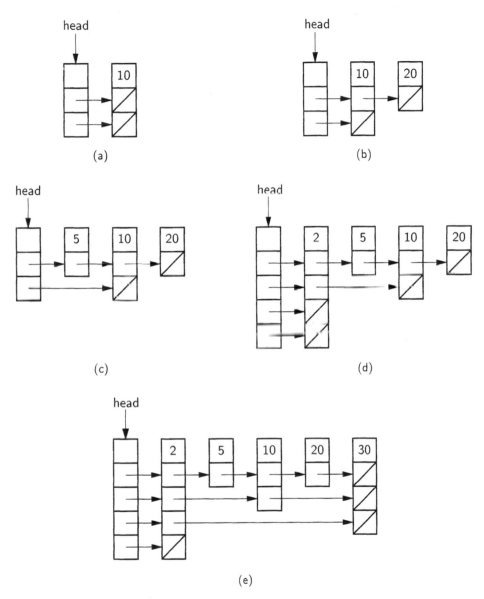

Figure 12.2 Illustration of Skip List insertion. (a) The Skip List after inserting initial value 10 at level 1. (b) The Skip List after inserting value 20 at level 0. (c) The Skip List after inserting value 5 at level 0. (d) The Skip List after inserting value 2 at level 3. (e) The final Skip List after inserting value 30 at level 2.

(and thus the level of the header node) must be set to 1. The new node is inserted, yielding the Skip List of Figure 12.2(a).

Next, insert the value 20. Assume this time that `randomLevel` returns 0. The search process goes to the node with value 10, and the new node is inserted after, as shown in Figure 12.2(b).

The third node inserted has value 5, and again assume that `randomLevel` return 0. This yields the Skip List of Figure 12.2.c.

The fourth node inserted has value 2, and assume that `randomLevel` returns 3. This means that the level of the Skip List must rise, causing the header node to gain an additional two (`null`) pointers. At this point, the new node is added to the front of the list, as shown in Figure 12.2(d).

Finally, insert a node with value 30 at level 2. This time, let us take a close look at what array `update` is used for. It stores the farthest node reached at each level during the search for the proper location of the new node. The search process begins in the header node at level 3, and proceeds to the node storing value 2. Since `forward[3]` for this node is `null`, we cannot go further at this level. Thus, `update[3]` stores a pointer to the node with value 2. Likewise, we cannot proceed at level 2, so `update[2]` also stores a pointer to the node with value 2. At level 1, we proceed to the node storing value 10. This is as far as we can go at level 1, so `update[1]` stores a pointer to the node with value 10. Finally, at level 0 we end up at the node with value 20. At this point, we can add in the new node with value 30. The new node's `forward[i]` pointers are set to `update[i]->forward[i]`, and the nodes stored in `update[i]` for indices 0 through 2 have their `forward[i]` pointers changed to point to the new node. This "splices" the new node into the Skip List at all levels.

The `remove` function is left as an exercise. It is similar to inserting in that the `update` array is built as part of searching for the record to be deleted, then those nodes specified by the update array have their forward pointers adjusted to point around the node being deleted.

A newly inserted node could have a high level generated by `randomLevel`, or a low level. It is possible that many nodes in the Skip List could have many pointers, leading to unnecessary insert cost and yielding poor ($\Theta(n)$) performance during search, since not many nodes will be skipped. Conversely, too many nodes could have a low level. In the worst case, all nodes could be at level 0, equivalent to a regular linked list. If so, search will again require $\Theta(n)$ time. However, the probability that performance will be poor is quite low. There is only once chance in 1024 that ten nodes in a row will be at level 0. The motto of probabilistic data structures such as the Skip List is "Don't worry, be happy." We simply accept the results of `randomLevel` and expect that probability will eventually work in our favor. The advantage of this approach is that the algorithms are simple, while requiring only $\Theta(\log n)$ time for all operations in the average case.

In practice, the Skip List will probably have better performance than a BST. The BST can have bad performance due to the order in which data are inserted. The Skip List's performance does not depend on the order in which values are inserted into the list. As the number of nodes in the Skip List increases, the probability of encountering the worst case decreases exponentially. Thus, the Skip List illustrates a tension between the theoretical worst case (in this case, $\Theta(n)$ for a Skip List operation), and a rapidly increasing probability of average-case performance of $\Theta(\log n)$, that characterizes probabilistic data structures.

12.2   Multilists

Recall from Chapter 4 that a list is a finite, ordered sequence of items of the form $(x_0, x_1, ..., x_{n-1})$ where $n \geq 0$. We can represent the empty list by `null` or `()`. In Chapter 4 we assumed that all list elements had the same data type. In this section, we extend the definition of lists to allow elements to be arbitrary in nature. In general, list elements are one of two types:

1. An **atom**, which is a data record of some type such as a number, symbol, or string.

2. Another list, which is called a **sublist**.

A list containing sublists will be written

$$(x1, (y1, (a1, a2), y3), (z1, z2), x4).$$

In this example, the list has four elements. The second element is the sublist $(y1, (a1, a2), y3)$ and the third is the sublist $(z1, z2)$. Note that sublist $(y1, (a1, a2), y3)$ also contains a sublist. If a list **L** has one or more sublists, we call **L** a **multilist**. Lists with no sublists are often referred to as **linear lists** or **chains**. Note that this definition for multilist fits well with our definition of sets from Definition 2.1, where a set's members can be either primitive elements or sets.

We can restrict the sublists of a multilist in various ways, depending on whether the multilist should have the form of a tree, a DAG, or a generic

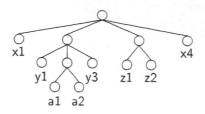

Figure 12.3 Example of a multilist represented by a tree.

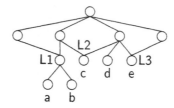

Figure 12.4 Example of a reentrant multilist. The shape of the structure is a DAG (all edges point downward).

graph. A **pure list** is a list structure whose graph corresponds to a tree, such as in Figure 12.3. In other words, there is exactly one path from the root to any node, which is equivalent to saying that no object may appear more than once in the list. In the pure list, each pair of parentheses corresponds to an internal node of the tree. The members of the list correspond to the children for the node. Atoms on the list correspond to leaf nodes.

A **reentrant list** is a list structure whose graph corresponds to a DAG. Nodes may be accessible from the root by more than one path, which is equivalent to saying that objects (including sublists) may appear multiple times in the list so long as no cycles are formed. All edges point downward, from the node representing a list or sublist to its elements. Figure 12.4 illustrates a reentrant list. To write out this list in parentheses notation, we can duplicate nodes as necessary. Thus, the parentheses notation for the list of Figure 12.4 could be written

$$(((a, b)), ((a, b), c), (c, d, e), (e)).$$

For convenience, we will adopt a convention of allowing sublists and atoms to be labeled, such as "L1:". Whenever a label is repeated, the element corresponding to that label will be substituted. Thus, the parentheses notation for the list of Figure 12.4 could be written

$$((L1 : (a, b)), (L1, L2 : c), (L2, d, L3 : e), (L3)).$$

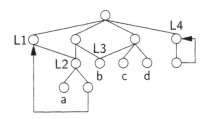

Figure 12.5 Example of a cyclic multilist. The shape of the structure is a directed graph.

| (| x1 | (| y1 | (| a1 | a2 |) | y3 |) | (| z1 | z2 |) | x4 |) |

Figure 12.6 List of nodes representation for the pure list of Figure 12.3.

A **cyclic list** is a list structure whose graph corresponds to any directed graph, possibly containing cycles. Figure 12.5 illustrates such a list. Labels are required to write this in parentheses notation. Here is the notation for the list of Figure 12.5:

$$(L1 : (L2 : (a, L1)), (L2, L3 : b), (L3, c, d), L4 ; (L4))$$

Multilists can be implemented in a number of ways. Most of these should be familiar from implementations suggested earlier in the book for list, tree, and graph data structures.

The simplest approach is to use an array representation. This works well for chains with fixed-length elements, equivalent to the simple list of Chapter 4. Implementations for chains with variable-length elements were briefly discussed in Chapter 4. We can view nested sublists as variable-length elements. To use this approach, we require some indication of the beginning and end of each sublist. We can use a variant of the sequential tree implementation discussed in Section 6.5. This should be no surprise, since the pure list is equivalent to a general tree structure. The simplest method is to store the parentheses of our written notation explicitly. In Figure 12.6, the parentheses can be stored as separate symbols. Unfortunately, as with any sequential representation, access to the nth sublist must be done sequentially from the beginning of the list.

Since pure lists are equivalent to trees, we can also use linked allocation methods to support direct access to the list of children. Simple linear lists are represented by linked lists. Pure lists can be represented as linked lists

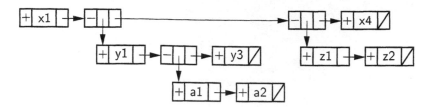

Figure 12.7 Linked representation for the pure list of Figure 12.3. The first field in each link node stores a tag bit. If the tag bit stores "+," then the data field stores an atom. If the tag bit stores "−," then the data field stores a pointer to a sublist.

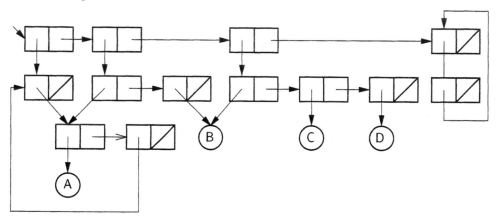

Figure 12.8 LISP-like linked representation for the cyclic multilist of Figure 12.5. Each link node stores two pointers. A pointer either points to an atom, or to another link node. Link nodes are represented by two boxes, and atoms by circles.

with an additional tag field to indicate whether the node is an atom or a sublist. If it is a sublist, the data field points to the first element on the sublist. This is illustrated by Figure 12.7.

Another approach is to represent all list elements with link nodes storing two pointer fields, except for atoms, which just contain data. This is the system used by the programming language LISP. Figure 12.8 illustrates this approach. Either the pointer contains a tag bit to identify what it points to, or the object being pointed to stores a tag bit to identify itself. Tags distinguish atoms from list nodes. This implementation can easily support reentrant and cyclic lists, since nodes can point to any other node.

$$
\begin{array}{|cccc|}
\hline
a_{00} & 0 & 0 & 0 \\
a_{10} & a_{11} & 0 & 0 \\
a_{20} & a_{21} & a_{22} & 0 \\
a_{30} & a_{31} & a_{32} & a_{33} \\
\hline
\end{array}
\qquad
\begin{array}{|cccc|}
\hline
a_{00} & a_{01} & a_{02} & a_{03} \\
0 & a_{11} & a_{12} & a_{13} \\
0 & 0 & a_{22} & a_{23} \\
0 & 0 & 0 & a_{33} \\
\hline
\end{array}
$$

(a) (b)

Figure 12.9 Triangular matrices. (a) A lower triangular matrix. (b) An upper triangular matrix.

12.3 Matrix Representations

Some applications require that a large, two-dimensional matrix be represented where many of the elements have a value of zero. One example is the lower triangular matrix that results from solving systems of simultaneous equations. A lower triangular matrix stores zero values at positions $[r, c]$ such that $r < c$, as shown in Figure 12.9(a). Thus, the upper-right triangle of the matrix is always zero. We can take advantage of this fact to save space. Instead of storing the required $n(n + 1)/2$ pieces of information in a $n \times n$ array, it would save space to use a list of length $n(n + 1)/2$. This is only practical if some means can be found to locate within the list the element that would correspond to position $[r, c]$ in the original matrix.

To derive such an equation, note that row 0 of the matrix has one non-zero value, row 1 has two non-zero values, and so on. Thus, row r is preceded by r rows with a total of $\sum_{k=1}^{r} k = (r^2 + r)/2$ non-zero elements. Adding c to reach the cth position in the rth row yields the the following equation to convert position $[r, c]$ in the original matrix to the correct position in the list:

$$\text{matrix}[r, c] = \text{list}[(r^2 + r)/2 + c].$$

A similar equation can be used to store an upper triangular matrix, that is, a matrix with zero values at positions $[r, c]$ such that $r > c$, as shown in Figure 12.9(b). In this case, for an $n \times n$ upper triangular matrix, the equation would be

$$\text{matrix}[r, c] = \text{list}[rn - (r^2 + r)/2 + c].$$

We now consider the more difficult situation where the vast majority of values stored in a $n \times n$ matrix are zero, but there is no restriction on which positions are zero and which are non-zero. This is known as a **sparse matrix**. One approach to representing a sparse matrix is to concatenate the two coordinates into a single value and use this as a key in a hash table.

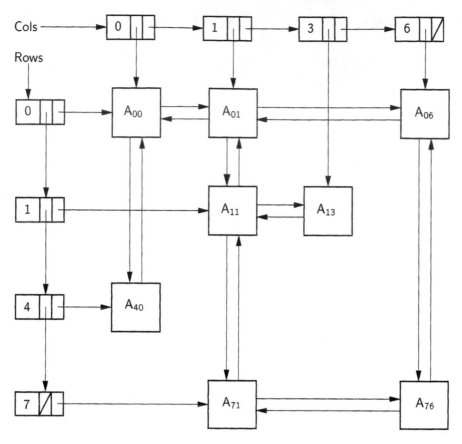

Figure 12.10 Example of a sparse matrix representation.

Thus, if we want to know the value of a particular position in the matrix, we search the hash table for the appropriate key. If a value for this position is not found, it is assumed to be zero. This is an ideal approach when all queries to the matrix are in terms of access by specified position. However, if we wish to find the first non-zero element in a given row, or the next non-zero element below the current one in a given column, then the hash table provides an unsatisfactory representation.

Another approach is to implement the matrix as an **orthogonal list**, as illustrated in Figure 12.10. Here we have a list of row headers, each of which contains a pointer to a list of matrix records. A second list of column headers also contains pointers to matrix records. Each non-zero matrix element stores pointers to its non-zero neighbors in the row, both following and preceding it. Each non-zero element also stores pointers to its non-zero neighbors following and preceding it in the column. Thus, each non-zero element stores its own value, its position within the matrix, and four pointers. Non-zero elements are found by traversing a row or column list. Note that the first non-zero element in a given row could be in any column; likewise, the neighboring non-zero element in any row or column list could be at any (higher) row or column in the array. Thus, each non-zero element must also store its row and column position explicitly.

To find if a particular position in the matrix contains a non-zero element, we traverse the appropriate row or column list. For example, when looking for the element at row 7 and column 1, we can traverse the list either for row 7 or for column 1. When traversing a row or column list, if we come to an element with the correct position, then its value is non-zero. If we encounter an element with a higher position, then the element we are looking for is not in the sparse matrix. In this case, the element's value is zero. For example, when traversing the list for row 7 in the matrix of Figure 12.10, we first reach the element at row 7 and column 1. If this is what we are looking for, then the search can stop. If we are looking for the element at row 7 and column 2, then the search proceeds along the row 7 list to next reach the element at column 6. At this point we know that no element at row 7 and column 2 is stored in the sparse matrix.

Insertion and deletion can be performed by working in a similar way to insert or delete elements within the appropriate row and column lists.

Each non-zero element stored in the sparse matrix representation takes much more space than an element stored in a simple $n \times n$ matrix. When is the sparse matrix more space efficient than the standard representation? To calculate this, we need to determine how much space the standard matrix requires, and how much the sparse matrix requires. The size of the sparse matrix depends on the number of non-zero elements, while the size of the standard matrix representation does not vary. We need to know the (relative) sizes of a pointer and a data value. For simplicity, our calculation will ignore the space taken up by the row and column pointers.

As an example, assume that a data value uses two bytes, a row or column index use two bytes, and a pointer uses four bytes. An $n \times m$ matrix requires $2nm$ bytes. The sparse matrix requires 22 bytes per non-zero element (four pointers, two array indices, and one data value). If we set X to be the percentage of non-zero elements, we can solve for the value of X below which the sparse matrix representation is more space efficient. Using the equation

$$22mnX = 2mn$$

and solving for X, we find that the sparse matrix using this implementation is more space efficient when $X < 1/11$, that is, when less than 9% of the elements are non-zero. Different values for the relative sizes of data values, pointers, or matrix indices can lead to a significantly different break-even point for the two implementations.

The time required to process a sparse matrix depends on the number of non-zero elements stored. When searching for an element, the cost is the number of elements preceding the desired element on its row or column list. The cost for operations such as adding two matrices should be $O(n + m)$ when the one matrix stores n non-zero elements and the other stores m non-zero elements.

12.4   Memory Management

Most of the data structure implementations described in this book store and access objects all of the same size, such as integers stored in a list or a tree. A few simple methods have been described for storing variable size records in an array or a stack. This section discusses memory management techniques for the general problem of handling space requests of variable size. The basic model for memory management is that we have a (large) block of contiguous memory locations, which we will call the **memory pool**. Periodically, memory requests are issued for some amount of space in the pool. The memory manager must find a contiguous block of locations of at least the requested size from somewhere within the memory pool. Honoring such a request is called a **memory allocation**. Previously allocated memory may be returned to the memory manager at some future time. This is called a **memory deallocation**.

If all requests and releases follow a simple pattern, such as last requested, first released (stack order), or first requested, first released (queue order), then memory management is fairly easy. We are concerned in this section with the general case where blocks of any size may be requested and released in any order. This is known as **dynamic storage allocation**. One example of dynamic storage allocation is managing free store for a compiler's runtime environment, such as the system `new` operation in Java. Another example is managing main memory in a multitasking operating system. Here, a program may require a certain amount of space, and the memory manager must

Figure 12.11 Dynamic storage allocation model. Memory is made up of a series of variable size blocks, some allocated and some free. In this example, shaded areas represent memory currently allocated and unshaded areas represent unused memory available for future allocation.

keep track of which programs are using which parts of the main memory. Yet another example is the file manager for a disk drive. When a disk file is created, expanded, or deleted, the file manager must allocate or deallocate disk space.

A block of memory or disk space managed in this way is sometimes referred to as a **heap**. In this context, the term "heap" is being used in a different way than the heap data structure discussed in other chapters. Here "heap" refers to the free memory accessed by a dynamic memory management scheme.

In the rest of this section, we first study techniques for dynamic memory management. We then tackle the issue of what to do when no single block of memory in the memory pool is large enough to honor a given request.

12.4.1 Dynamic Storage Allocation

For the purpose of dynamic storage allocation, we view memory as a single array broken into a series of variable size blocks, where some of the blocks are **free** and some are **reserved** or already allocated. The free blocks are linked together to form a freelist for servicing future memory requests. Figure 12.11 illustrates the situation that can arise after a series of memory allocations and deallocations.

When a memory request is received by the memory manager, some block on the freelist must be found that is large enough to service the request. If no such block is found, then the memory manager must resort to a **failure policy** such as discussed in Section 12.4.2.

If there is a request for m words, and no block exists of exactly size m, then a larger block must be used instead. One possibility in this case is that the entire block is given away to the memory allocation request. This may be desirable when the size of the block is only slightly larger than the request. Alternatively, for a free block of size k, with $k > m$, up to $k - m$

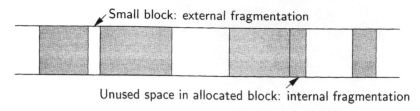

Figure 12.12 An illustration of internal and external fragmentation.

space may be retained by the memory manager to form a new free block, while the rest is used to service the request.

There are two types of fragmentation encountered in dynamic memory management. **External fragmentation** occurs when the memory requests create lots of small free blocks, no one of which is useful for servicing typical requests. **Internal fragmentation** occurs when more than m words are allocated to a request for m words, wasting free storage. This is equivalent to the internal fragmentation that occurs when files are allocated in multiples of the cluster size. The difference between internal and external fragmentation is illustrated by Figure 12.12.

Some memory management schemes sacrifice space to internal fragmentation to make memory management easier (and perhaps reduce external fragmentation). For example, external fragmentation does not happen in file management systems that allocate file space in clusters. Another example is the **buddy method** described in this section.

The process of searching them memory pool for a block large enough to service the request, possibly reserving the remaining space as a free block, are referred to as a **sequential fit** method.

Sequential Fit Methods

Sequential fit methods attempt to find a "good" block to service a storage request. The three sequential fit methods described here assume that the free blocks are organized into a doubly linked list, as illustrated by Figure 12.13. Since the free space is free, it can be used by the memory manager to help it do its job; that is, the memory manager temporarily "borrows" space within the free blocks to maintain its doubly linked list. To do so, each unallocated block must be large enough to hold these pointers. In addition, it is usually worthwhile to let the memory manager add a few bytes of space to a reserved block for its own purposes. In other words, a request for m bytes of space might result in slightly more than m bytes being allocated by the memory

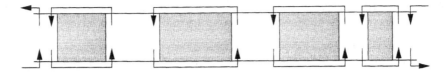

Figure 12.13 A doubly linked list of free blocks as seen by the memory manager. Shaded areas represent allocated memory. Unshaded areas are part of the freelist.

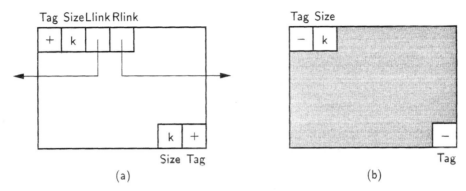

Figure 12.14 Blocks as seen by the memory manager. Each block includes additional information such as freelist link pointers, start and end tags, and a size field. (a) The layout for a free block. The beginning of the block contains the tag bit field, the block size field, and two pointers for the freelist. The end of the block contains a second tag field and a second block size field. (b) A reserved block of k bytes. The memory manager adds to these k bytes an additional tag bit field and block size field at the beginning of the block, and a second tag field at the end of the block.

manager, with the extra bytes used by the memory manager itself rather than the requester. We will assume that all memory blocks are organized as shown in Figure 12.14, with space for tags and linked list pointers. Here, free and reserved blocks are distinguished by a tag bit at both the beginning and the end of the block. In addition, both free and reserved blocks have a size indicator immediately after the tag bit at the beginning of the block to indicate how large the block is. Free blocks have a second size indicator immediately preceding the tag bit at the end of the block. Finally, free blocks have left and right pointers to their neighbors in the free block list.

The information fields associated with each block permit the memory manager to allocate and deallocate blocks as needed. When a request comes in for m words of storage, the memory manager searches the linked list of free blocks until it finds a "suitable" block for allocation. How it determines which block is suitable will be discussed below. If the block contains exactly m words (plus space for the tag and size fields), then it is removed from the freelist. If the block (of size k) is large enough, then the remaining $k - m$ words are reserved as a block on the freelist, in the current location. The appropriate tag, size, and link fields are set. Figure 12.15 shows a memory manager class to illustrate this process. Assume for simplicity that all fields (tag, size, and pointer) are a single integer in size.

The memory manager stores arrays of type int. It has three basic functions, as defined by the following interface.

```
interface MemManADT {
  public MemHandle request(int[] info);  // Request space
  public int[] getValue(MemHandle h);    // Retrieve data
  public void release(MemHandle h);      // Release space
} // interface MemManADT
```

Function **request** takes as input an integer array, and stores the contents of the array in the memory pool. It returns a MemHandle, which allows the MemManager class user to access the data just stored. Function **getValue** returns the integer array associated with h. Function **release** releases the memory taken up by the integer array associated with MemHandle h.

Note that the implementation of MemManager differs slightly from Figure 12.14 in that reserved blocks store two size fields: One is the actual amount of space reserved, and the other is the (possibly smaller) amount of space in the block that actually stores user data.

In function **request**, a block is split in two when its size is enough larger than m to be worth saving the remainder. If the block is split, the front part remains in the freelist while the back part is allocated. The bulk of function **request** is spent setting the various fields used by the memory manager.

When a block F is freed, it must be merged into the freelist. If we do not care about merging adjacent free blocks, then this is a simple insertion into the doubly linked list of free blocks. However, we would like to merge adjacent blocks, since this allows the memory manager to serve requests of the largest possible size. Merging is easily done due to the tag and size fields stored at the ends of each block, as illustrated by Figure 12.16. The memory manager first checks the unit of memory immediately preceding block F to see if the preceding block (call it P) is also free. If it is, then the unit before P's tag bit stores the size of P, thus indicating the position for the beginning of the block in memory. P can then simply have its size extended to include block F. If block P is not free, then we just add block F to the

```
class MemManager implements MemManADT{
  private static final int STARTTAG = 0;    // Start tag offset
  private static final int FULLSIZE = 1;    // Size field offset
  private static final int USERSIZE = 2;    // User size offset
  private static final int LPTR = 2;        // Left freelist pointer
  private static final int RPTR = 3;        // Right freelist pointer
  private static final int DATAPOS = 3;     // Start of data
  private static final int FREE = -1;       // Tag value
  private static final int RESERVED = -2;   // Tag value
  private static final int ENDSIZE = 4;     // Size field offset
  private static final int FREEENDTAG = 5;  // Tag field offset
  private static final int RESENDTAG = 3;   // Tag field offset
  private static final int MINEXTRA = -2;   // Extra space needed
  private static final int FREEOVERHEAD = 6; // Number free fields
  private static final int RESOVERHEAD = 4;  // Number of res fields
  private static final int MINREQUEST = 2; // Smallest data request

  int[] mempool;                 // The data space
  MemHandle freelist;            // Free memory access

  MemManager(int size) {         // Constructor
    mempool = new int[size];  // Allocate space
    freelist = new MemHandle(0); // Start of freelist
    mempool[STARTTAG] = mempool[size-1] = FREE;
    mempool[FULLSIZE] = mempool[size-2] = size - FREEOVERHEAD;
    mempool[LPTR] = mempool[RPTR] = 0; // Circ doubly-linked list
  }

  public int[] getValue(MemHandle h) { // Return data for h
    int startpos = h.getPos();
    int length = mempool[startpos + USERSIZE];
    int startdata = startpos + DATAPOS;
    int[] stuff = new int[length];
    for (int i=0; i<length; i++) stuff[i] = mempool[startdata + i];
    return stuff;
  }

  // Sample sequential fit implementation: First fit
  private int pickFreeBlock(int length) {
    if (freelist == null) return -1;  // No free block
    int freestart = freelist.getPos();
    for (int curr=freestart;;)
      if (mempool[curr + FULLSIZE] >= (length + MINEXTRA))
        return curr;
      else {
        curr = mempool[curr + RPTR];
        if (curr == freestart) return -1; // No block available
      }
  }
```

Figure 12.15 Class MemManager to illustrate memory management.

```java
    public MemHandle request(int[] info) {
      int datasize;
      if (info.length < MINREQUEST)     // Minimum necessary for
        datasize = MINREQUEST;          //    a sustainable block
      else datasize = info.length;
      int start= pickFreeBlock(info.length);
      if (start == -1) return null; // No block is big enough
      if (mempool[start + FULLSIZE] > (datasize + RESOVERHEAD)) {
        // Fix up the remaining free space
        int oldsize = mempool[start+FULLSIZE]-datasize-RESOVERHEAD;
        mempool[start + oldsize + FREEENDTAG] = FREE;
        mempool[start + oldsize + ENDSIZE] = oldsize;
        mempool[start + FULLSIZE] = oldsize;

        // Now, fix up the new block
        int newstart = start + mempool[start+FULLSIZE] + FREEOVERHEAD;
        mempool[newstart+STARTTAG] = RESERVED;
        mempool[newstart+FULLSIZE] = datasize;
        mempool[newstart+USERSIZE] = info.length;
        mempool[newstart+datasize+RESENDTAG] = RESERVED;
        for (int i=0; i<info.length; i++)
          mempool[newstart+DATAPOS+i] = info[i];
        return new MemHandle(newstart);
      }
      else { // Give over the whole block, remove from freelist
        // First, adjust the freelist
        if (mempool[start+RPTR] == start)
          freelist = null;  // This is the last block
        else {
          mempool[mempool[start+RPTR]+LPTR] = mempool[start+LPTR];
          mempool[mempool[start+LPTR]+RPTR] = mempool[start+RPTR];
        }
        // Now, fill in the block
        mempool[start+STARTTAG] = RESERVED;
        mempool[start+FULLSIZE] += FREEOVERHEAD - RESOVERHEAD;
        mempool[start+USERSIZE] = info.length;
        for (int i=0; i<info.length; i++)
          mempool[start+DATAPOS+i] = info[i];
        mempool[start+mempool[start+FULLSIZE]+RESENDTAG] = RESERVED;
        return new MemHandle(start);
      }
    }

    public void release(MemHandle h) {
      // Implementation is left as an exercise
    }

} // class MemManager
```

Figure 12.15 (continued)

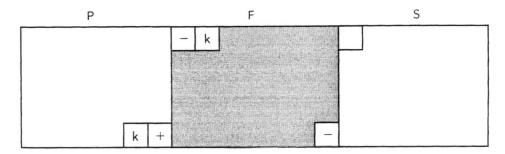

Figure 12.16 Adding block F to the freelist. The word immediately preceding the start of F in the memory pool stores the tag bit of the preceding block P. If P is free, merge F into P. We find the beginning of F by using F's size field. Likewise, the word following the end of F is the tag field for block S. If S is free, merge it into F.

freelist. Finally, we also check the bit following the end of block F. If this bit indicates that the following block (call it S) is free, then S is removed from the freelist and the size of F is extended appropriately. Coding Function **release** is left as an exercise.

We now consider how a "suitable" free block is selected to service a memory request. To illustrate the process, assume there are four blocks on the freelist of sizes 500, 700, 650, and 900 (in that order). Assume that a request is made for 600 units of storage. For our examples, we ignore the overhead imposed for the tag, link, and size fields discussed above.

The simplest method for selecting a block would be to move down the free block list until a block of size at least 600 is found. This is illustrated by Function **pickFreeBlock** in Figure 12.15. Any remaining space in this block is left on the freelist. If we begin at the beginning of the list and work down to the first free block at least as large as 600, we select the block of size 700. Since this approach selects the first block with enough space, it is called **first fit**. A simple variation that will improve performance is, instead of always beginning at the head of the freelist, remember the last position reached in the previous search and start from there. When the end of the freelist is reached, search begins again at the head of the freelist. This modification reduces the number of unnecessary searches through small blocks that were passed over by the last request.

There is a potential disadvantage to first fit: It may "waste" larger blocks and they will not be available for large requests later. A strategy that avoids using large blocks unnecessarily is called **best fit**. Best fit looks at the entire list, and picks the smallest block that is at least as large as the request (i.e., the "best" or closest fit to the request). Continuing with the preceding example, the best fit for a request of 600 units is the block of size 650, leaving a remainder of size 50. Best fit has the disadvantage that it requires that the entire list be searched. Another problem is that the remaining portion of the best-fit block is likely to be small, and thus useless for future requests. In other words, best fit tends to maximize problems of external fragmentation while it minimizes the chance of not being able to service an occasional large request.

A strategy contrary to best fit might make sense because it tends to minimize the effects of external fragmentation. This is called **worst fit**, which always allocates the largest block on the list hoping that the remainder of the block will be useful for servicing a future request. In the example, the worst fit is the block of size 900, leaving a remainder of size 300. If there are a few unusually large requests, this approach will have less chance of servicing them. If requests generally tend to be of the same size, then this may be an effective strategy. Like best fit, worst fit requires searching the entire freelist at each memory request to find the largest block. Alternatively, the freelist can be ordered from largest to smallest free block.

Which strategy is best? It depends on the expected types of memory requests. If the requests are of widely ranging size, best fit may work well. If they tend to be of similar size, with rare large and small requests, first or worst fit may work well. Unfortunately, there are always request patterns that one of the three sequential fit methods will service, but which the other two will not be able to service. For example, if the series of requests 600, 650, 900, 500, 100 is made to a freelist containing blocks (500, 700, 650, 900), the requests can all be serviced by first fit, but not by best fit. Alternatively, the series of requests 600, 500, 700, 900 can be serviced by best fit but not by first fit on this same freelist.

Buddy Methods

Sequential-fit methods rely on a linked list of free blocks, which must be searched for a suitable block at each memory request. Thus, the time to find a suitable free block would be $\Theta(n)$ in the worst case for a freelist containing n blocks. Merging adjacent free blocks is somewhat complicated. Finally, both free and reserved blocks require tag and size fields. Fields in free blocks do not cost any space (since they are stored in memory that is not otherwise being used), but fields in reserved blocks create additional overhead.

The buddy system solves most of these problems. Search for a block of proper size is efficient, merging adjacent free blocks is simple, and no tag or other information fields need be stored within reserved blocks. The buddy system assumes that memory is of size 2^N for some integer N. Both free and reserved blocks will always be of size 2^k for $k \leq N$. At any given time, there may be both free and reserved blocks of various sizes. The buddy system keeps a separate list for free blocks of each size. There can be at most N such lists, since there can only be N distinct sizes.

When a request comes in for m words, we first determine the smallest value of k such that $2^k \geq m$. A block of size 2^k is selected from the free list for that block size if one exists. The buddy system does not worry about internal fragmentation: the entire block of size 2^k is allocated.

If no block of size 2^k exists, the next larger block is located. This block is split in half (repeatedly if necessary) until the desired block of size 2^k is created. Any other blocks generated as a by-product of this splitting process are placed on the appropriate freelists.

The disadvantage of the buddy system is that it allows internal fragmentation. For example, a request for 257 words will require a block of size 512. The primary advantages of the buddy system are that there is less external fragmentation; search for a block of the right size is cheaper than, say, best fit since we need only find the first available block on the block list for blocks of size 2^k; and merging of adjacent free blocks is easy.

The reason why this method is called the buddy system is because of the way that merging takes place. The **buddy** for any block of size 2^k is another block of the same size, and with the same address except that the kth bit is reversed. For example, the block of size 8 with beginning address 0000 in Figure 12.17(a) has buddy with address 1000. Likewise, in Figure 12.17(b), the block of size 4 with address 0000 has buddy 0100. If free blocks are sorted by address value, the buddy can be found by searching the correct block size list. Merging simply requires that the combined buddies be moved to the freelist for the next larger block.

Other Memory Allocation Methods

In addition to sequential fit and buddy methods, there are many ad hoc approaches to memory management. In particular, if the application is sufficiently complex, it may be desirable to break available memory into several memory **zones**, each with a different memory management scheme. This is known as a **segregated storage method**. For example, some zones

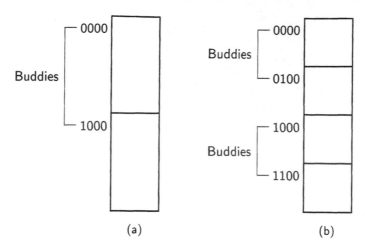

(a)   (b)

Figure 12.17 Example of the buddy system.

may have a simple memory access pattern of first-in, first-out for fixed-size records. This zone can therefore be managed efficiently by using a simple stack. Other zones may need one of the general purpose memory allocation methods discussed in this section. The advantage of zones is that some portions of memory can be managed more efficiently. The disadvantage is that one zone may fill up while other zones have excess memory if the zone sizes are chosen poorly.

Another approach to memory management is to impose a standard size on all memory requests. We have seen an example of this concept already in disk file management, where all files are allocated in multiples of the cluster size. This approach leads to internal fragmentation, but managing files composed of clusters is easier than managing arbitrarily sized files. The cluster scheme also allows us to relax the restriction that the memory request be serviced by a contiguous block of memory. Most disk file managers and operating system main memory managers work on a cluster or page system. Page management is usually done with a buffer pool to allocate available pages in main memory efficiently.

12.4.2 Failure Policies and Garbage Collection

At some point during processing, a memory manager may encounter a request for memory that it cannot satisfy. In some situations, there may be nothing that can be done: There simply may not be enough free memory to service the request, and the application may require that the request be

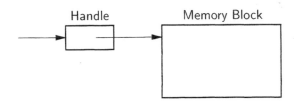

Figure 12.18 Using handles for dynamic memory management. The memory manager returns the address of the handle in response to a memory request. The handle stores the address of the actual memory block. In this way, the memory block may be moved (with its address updated in the handle) without disrupting the application program.

serviced immediately. In this case, the memory manager has no option but to return an error, which may in turn lead to a failure of the application program. However, in many cases there are alternatives to simply returning an error. The possible options are referred to collectively as **failure policies**.

In some cases, there may be sufficient free memory to satisfy the request, but it is scattered among small blocks. This can happen when using a sequential-fit memory allocation method, where external fragmentation has lead to a series of small blocks that collectively could service the request. In this case, it may be possible to **compact** memory by moving the reserved blocks around so that the free space is collected into a single block. A problem with this approach is that the application must somehow be able to deal with the fact that all of its data have now been moved to different locations. If the application program relies on the absolute positions of the data in any way, this would be disastrous. One approach for dealing with this problem is the use of **handles**. A handle is a second level of indirection to a memory location. The memory allocation routine does not return a pointer to the block of storage, but rather a pointer to a variable that in turn points to the storage. This variable is the handle. The handle never moves its position, but the position of the block may be moved and the value of the handle updated. Figure 12.18 illustrates the concept.

Another failure policy that may work in some applications is to defer the memory request until sufficient memory becomes available. For example, a multitasking operating system could adopt the strategy of not allowing a process to run until there is sufficient memory available. While such a delay may be annoying to the user, it is better than halting the entire system. The assumption here is that other processes will eventually terminate, freeing memory.

Another option may be to allocate more memory to the memory manager. In a zoned memory allocation system where the memory manager is part of a larger system, this may be a viable option. In a Java program that implements its own memory manager, it may be possible to get more memory using the **new** operator, such as is done by the freelist of Chapter 4.

The last failure policy that we will consider is **garbage collection**. Consider the following series of statements:

```
p = new int [i];
q = new int [j];
p = q;
```

In some languages, such as **C++**, this would be considered bad form since the original space allocated to p is lost as a result of the third assignment. This space cannot be used again by the program. Such lost memory is referred to as **garbage**, also known as a **memory leak**. When no program variable points to a block of space, no future access to that space is possible. Note that if another variable had first been assigned to point to p's space, then reassigning p would not create garbage.

Java treats garbage differently. Java programs may allocate space using **new**, and later drop all pointers to that space. Thus, garbage is normal in Java, and in fact cannot be avoided during normal processing. When Java runs out of memory, it resorts to a failure policy known as **garbage collection** to recover the space tied up in garbage. Garbage collection consists of examining the managed memory pool to determine which parts are still being used and which parts are garbage. In particular, a list is kept of all program variables, and any memory locations not reachable from one of these variables are considered garbage. When the garbage collector executes, all unused memory locations are placed in free store for future access. This approach has the advantage that it allows for easy collection of garbage. It has the disadvantage, from a user's point of view, that every so often the system must halt while it performs garbage collection. For example, garbage collection is noticeable in the Emacs text editor, which is normally implemented in LISP, another language that implements garbage collection. Occasionally the user must wait for a moment while the memory management system performs garbage collection.

Several algorithms have traditionally been used for garbage collection. The first is the **reference count** algorithm. Every memory block includes space for a count field. Whenever a pointer is directed to a link node, the reference count is increased. Whenever a pointer is directed away from a

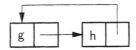

Figure 12.19 Garbage cycle example. All memory elements in the cycle have non-zero reference counts since each element has one pointer to it, even though the entire cycle is garbage.

link node, the reference count is decreased. If the count ever becomes zero, then the link node is considered garbage and is immediately placed in free store. This approach has the advantage that it does not require an explicit garbage collection phase, since information is put in free store immediately when it becomes garbage.

The reference count algorithm is used by the UNIX file system. Files can have multiple names, called links. The file system keeps a count of the number of links to each file. Whenever a file is "deleted," in actuality its link field is simply reduced by one. If there is another link to the file, then no space is recovered by the file system. Whenever the number of links goes to zero, the file's space becomes available for reuse.

Reference counts have several major disadvantages. First, a reference count must be maintained for each memory object. This works well when the objects are large, such as a file. However, it will not work well in a system such as LISP where the memory objects typically consist of two pointers or a value (an atom). Another major problem occurs when garbage contains cycles. Consider Figure 12.19. Here each memory object is pointed to once, but the collection of objects is still garbage since no pointer points to the collection. Thus, reference counts only work when the memory objects are linked together without cycles, such as the UNIX file system where files can only be organized as a DAG.

Another approach to garbage collection is the **mark/sweep** strategy. Here, each memory object needs only a single mark bit rather than a reference counter field. When free store is exhausted, a separate garbage collection phase takes place as follows:

1. Clear all mark bits.

2. Perform depth-first search following pointers from each variable on the variable list. Each memory element encountered during the DFS has its mark bit turned on.

3. A "sweep" is made through the memory pool, visiting all elements. Unmarked elements are considered garbage and placed in free store.

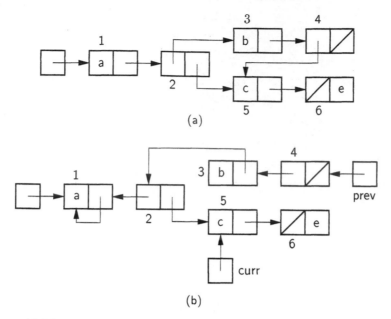

Figure 12.20 Example of the Deutsch-Schorr-Waite garbage collection algorithm. (a) The initial multilist structure. (b) The multilist structure of (a) at the instant when link node 5 is being processed by the garbage collection algorithm. A chain of pointers stretching from variable **prev** to the head node of the structure has been (temporarily) created by the garbage collection algorithm.

The advantages of the mark/sweep approach are that it needs less space than is necessary for reference counts, and it works for cycles. However, there is a major disadvantage. This is a "hidden" space requirement needed to do the processing. DFS is a recursive algorithm: Either it must be implemented recursively, in which case the compiler's runtime system maintains a stack, or else the memory manager can maintain its own stack. What happens if all of memory is contained in a single linked list? Then the depth of the recursion (or the size of the stack) is the number of memory cells! Unfortunately, the space for the DFS stack must be available at the worst conceivable instant, when free memory has been exhausted.

Fortunately, a clever technique allows DFS to be performed without requiring additional space for a stack. Instead, the structure being traversed is used to hold the stack. At each step deeper into the traversal, instead of storing a pointer on the stack, we "borrow" the pointer being followed. This pointer is set to point back to the node we just came from in the previous step, as illustrated by Figure 12.20. Each borrowed pointer stores an additional bit to tell us whether we came down the left branch or the right branch of the link node being pointed to. At any given instant we have passed down only one path from the root, and we can follow the trail of pointers back up. As we return (equivalent to popping the recursion stack), we set the pointer back to its original position so as not to disturb the structure. This is known as the Deutsch-Schorr-Waite garbage collection algorithm.

12.5 Further Reading

For further information on Skip Lists, see "Skip Lists: A Probabilistic Alternative to Balanced Trees" by William Pugh [Pug90].

An introductory text on operating systems covers many topics relating to memory management issues, including layout of files on disk and caching of information in main memory. All of the topics covered here on memory management, buffer pools, and paging are relevant to operating system implementation. For example, see *Operating Systems* by Harvey M. Deitel [Dei90]. For a discussion on memory management in the Apple Toolbox system, see the *Inside Macintosh* series from Apple Computer [App85].

For information on LISP, see *The Little LISPer* by Friedman and Felleisen [FF89]. Another good lisp reference is *Common Lisp: The Language* by Guy L. Steele [Ste84]. For information on Emacs, which is both an excellent text editor and a fully developed programming environment, see the *GNU Emacs Manual* by Richard M. Stallman [Sta94].

12.6 Exercises

12.1 Show the Skip List that results from inserting the following values. Draw the Skip List after each insert. With each value, assume the depth of its corresponding node is as given in the following list:

value	depth
5	2
20	0
30	0
2	0
25	1
26	3
31	0

12.2 If we had a list that would never be modified, we can use a simpler approach than the Skip List. The concept would remain the same in that we add additional pointers to list nodes for efficient access to the ith element. How can we add a second pointer to each element of a singly linked list to allow access to the ith element in $O(\log n)$ time?

12.3 What is the expected level (i.e., the average number of pointers) for a Skip List node?

12.4 Write a function to remove a node with given value from a Skip List.

12.5 Write a function to find the ith node on a Skip List.

12.6 What fraction of the values in a matrix must be zero for the sparse matrix representation of Section 12.3 to be more space efficient than the standard two-dimensional matrix representation when data values require eight bytes, array indices require two bytes, and pointers require four bytes?

12.7 Given the linked representation of a pure list such as

$$(x_1, (y_1, y_2, (z_1, z_2), y_4), (w_1, w_2), x_4),$$

write an in-place reversal algorithm to reverse the sublists at all levels including the topmost level. For this example, the result would be a linked representation corresponding to

$$(x_4, (w_2, w_1), (y_4, (z_2, z_1), y_2, y_1), x_1).$$

12.8 Write a function to add an element at a given position to the sparse matrix representation of Section 12.3.

12.9 Write a function to delete an element from a given position in the sparse matrix representation of Section 12.3.

12.10 Write a function to transpose a sparse matrix as represented in Section 12.3.

12.11 Write a function to add two sparse matrices as represented in Section 12.3.

12.12 Write memory manager allocation and deallocation routines for the situation where all requests and releases follow a last-requested, first-released (stack) order.

12.13 Write memory manager allocation and deallocation routines for the situation where all requests and releases follow a last-requested, last-released (queue) order.

12.14 Write a function to return a block to a sequential-fit memory management system.

12.15 Assume that the memory pool contains three blocks of free storage. Their sizes are 1300, 2000, and 1000. Give examples of storage requests for which:

    (a) first-fit allocation will work, but not best fit or worst fit.

    (b) best-fit allocation will work, but not first fit or worst fit.

    (c) worst-fit allocation will work, but not first fit or best fit.

12.7 Projects

12.1 Implement the Skip List of Section 12.1. The Skip List class ADT should be as similar as possible to the BST class ADT.

12.2 Implement the sparse matrix representation of Section 12.3. Your implementation should do the following.

    • insert into a matrix an element with given position,

    • delete from a matrix an element with given position,

    • search a matrix for an element with given position,

    • take the transpose of a matrix, and

    • add two matrices.

12.3 Complete implementation of the `MemManager` class of Figure 12.15. Your implementation should work for any of the three sequential-fit methods: first fit, best fit, and worst fit. Test your system empirically to determine under what conditions each method performs well.

12.4 Write a memory management system based on the buddy method of Section 12.4.1. Your system should support requests for blocks of a specified size and release of previously requested blocks.

12.5 Implement the Deutsch-Schorr-Waite garbage collection algorithm illustrated by Figure 12.20.

13

Advanced Tree Structures

This chapter introduces several tree structures designed for use in specialized applications. The trie of Section 13.1 is commonly used to store strings, and is suitable for storing and searching dictionaries. It also serves to illustrate the concept of a key space decomposition. The Splay Tree of Section 13.2 is a variant on the BST. The Splay Tree is an example of a self-balancing search tree, and has guaranteed good performance regardless of the insertion order for records. An introduction to several spatial data structures used to organize point data by xy-coordinate is presented in Section 13.3.

For each data structure, descriptions of its fundamental operations are given. The actual implementations are left as project suggestions for the reader.

13.1 Tries

The shape of a BST depends on the order in which its data records are inserted. One permutation of the records might yield a balanced tree while another might yield an unbalanced tree in the shape of a linked list. The reason is that the value of the key stored in the root node splits the key range into two parts: those key values less than the root's key value, and those key values greater than the root's key value. Depending on the relationship between the root node's key value and the distribution of the key values for the other records in the the tree, the resulting BST might be balanced or unbalanced. Thus, the BST is an example of a data structure whose organization is based on an **object space** decomposition, so called because the decomposition of the key range is driven by the objects (i.e., the key values of the data records) stored in the tree.

The alternative to object space decomposition is to predefine the splitting position within the key range for each node in the tree. In other words, the root could be predefined to split the key range into two equal halves, regardless of the particular values or order of insertion for the data records. Those records with keys in the lower half of the key range will be stored in the left subtree, while those records with keys in the upper half of the key range will be stored in the right subtree.

While such a decomposition rule will not necessarily result in a balanced tree (the tree will be unbalanced if the records are not well-distributed within the key range), at least the shape of the tree will not depend on the order of key insertion. Furthermore, the depth of the tree will be limited by the resolution of the key range; that is, the depth of the tree can never be greater than the number of bits required to store a key value. For example, if the keys are integers in the range 0 to 1023, then the resolution for the key is ten bits. Thus, two keys may be identical only until the tenth bit. In the worst case, two keys will follow the same path in the tree only until the tenth branch. As a result, the tree will never be more than ten levels deep.

Decomposition based on equal subdivision of the key range is called **key space** decomposition. In computer graphics, a related technique is known as **image space** decomposition, and this term is sometimes applied to data structures based on key space decomposition as well. Any data structure based on key space decomposition is called a **trie**. Folklore has it that "trie" comes from "retrieval." Unfortunately, that would imply that the word is pronounced "tree," which would lead to confusion with regular use of the word "tree." "Trie" is actually pronounced as "try."

Like the B$^+$-tree, a trie stores data records only in leaf nodes. Internal nodes serve as placeholders to direct the search process.

Figure 13.1 illustrates the trie concept. So that we may compute the middle of the key range, upper and lower bounds must be imposed on the key values. Since the largest value inserted in this example is 120, a range from 0 to 127 is assumed, as 128 is the smallest power of two greater than 120. The binary value of the key determines whether to select the left or right branch at any given point during the search. The most significant bit determines the branch direction at the root. Figure 13.1 shows a **binary trie**, so called because in this example the trie structure is based on the value of the key interpreted as a binary number, which results in a binary tree.

The Huffman coding tree of Section 5.4 is another example of a binary trie. All data values in the Huffman tree are at the leaves, and each branch

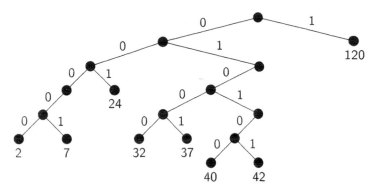

Figure 13.1 The binary trie for the set of values (2, 7, 24, 31, 37, 40, 42, 120). All data values are stored in the leaf nodes. Edges are labeled with the value of the bit used to determine the branching direction of each node. The binary form of the key value determines the path to the record, assuming that each key is represented as a 7-bit value representing a number in the range 0 to 127.

splits the range of possible letter codes in half. The Huffman codes are actually derived from the letter positions within the trie.

While these are examples of binary tries, in fact tries can be built with any branching factor. Normally the branching factor is determined by the alphabet used. For binary numbers, the alphabet is {0, 1} and a binary trie results. Other alphabets lead to other branching factors.

One application for tries is storing a dictionary of words. Such a trie will be referred to as an **alphabet trie**. For simplicity, our examples will ignore case in letters. The alphabet consists of the 26 standard English letters, plus one special character ($) used to represent the end of a string. Thus, the branching factor for each node is (up to) 27. Once constructed, the alphabet trie is used to determine if a given word is in the dictionary. Consider searching for a word in the alphabet trie of Figure 13.2. The first letter of the search word determines which branch to take from the root, the second letter determines which branch to take at the next level, and so on. Only the letters that lead to a word are shown as branches. In Figure 13.2(b) the leaf nodes of the trie store a copy of the actual words, while in Figure 13.2(a) the word is built up from the letters associated with each branch.

One way to implement a node of the alphabet trie is as an array of 27 pointers indexed by letter. Since most nodes have branches to only a small fraction of the possible letters in the alphabet, an alternate implementation is to use a linked list of pointers to the child nodes, as in Figure 6.9.

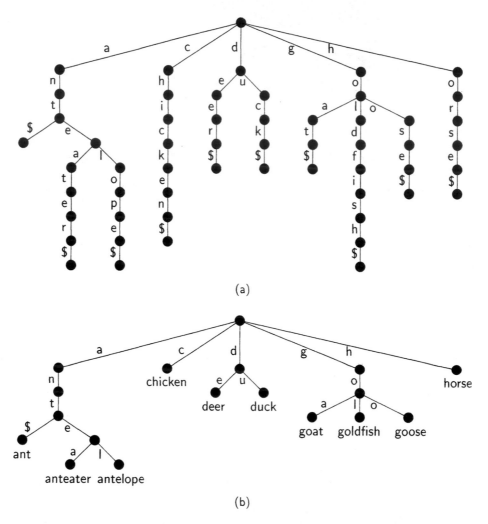

Figure 13.2 Two variations on the Alphabet Trie representation for a set of ten words. (a) Each node contains a set of links corresponding to single letters, and each letter in the set of words has a corresponding link. "$" is used to indicate the end of a word. Internal nodes direct the search and also spell out the word one letter per link. The word need not be stored explicitly. (b) Here the trie extends only far enough to discriminate between the words. Leaf nodes of the trie each store a complete word; internal nodes merely direct the search.

The depth of a leaf node in the alphabet trie of Figure 13.2(b) has little to do with the number of nodes in the trie. Rather, a node's depth depends on the number of characters required to distinguish this node's word from any other. For example, if the words "anteater" and "antelope" are both stored in the trie, it is not until the fifth letter that the two words can be distinguished. Thus, these words must be stored at least as deep as level five. In general, the limiting factor on the depth of nodes in the alphabet trie is the length of the words stored.

Poor balance and clumping can result when certain prefixes are heavily used. For example, an alphabet trie storing the common words in the English language would have many words in the "th" branch of the tree, but not many in the "zq" branch.

Any multiway branching trie can be replaced with a binary trie by replacing the original trie's alphabet with an equivalent binary code. Alternatively, we can use the techniques of Section 6.3.4 for converting a general tree to a binary tree without modifying the alphabet.

The trie implementations illustrated by Figures 13.1 and 13.2 are potentially quite inefficient as certain key sets may lead to a large number of nodes with only a single child. A variant on trie implementation invented by D. Morrison is known as PATRICIA, which stands for "Practical Algorithm To Retrieve Information Coded In Alphanumeric." In the case of a binary alphabet, a PATRICIA trie (refered to hereafter as a PAT trie) is a full binary tree that stores data records in the leaf nodes and uses the internal nodes only to store the position within the key's bit pattern that is used to decide on the branching. A PAT trie corresponding to the values of Figure 13.1 is shown in Figure 13.3.

For example, when searching for the value 7 (0000111 in binary) in the PAT trie of Figure 13.3, the root node indicates that bit position 0 (the leftmost bit) is checked first. Since the 0th bit for value 7 is 0, take the left branch. At level 1, branch depending on the value of bit 1, which again is 0. At level 2, branch depending on the value of bit 2, which again is 0. At level 3, the index stored in the node is 4. This means that bit 4 of the key is checked next (the value of bit 3 is irrelevant, since all values stored in that subtree have the same value at bit position 3). For key value 7, bit 4 has value 1, so the rightmost branch is taken. Since this leads to a leaf node, the search key is compared against the key stored in that node. If they match, then the desired record has been found.

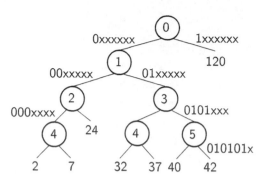

Figure 13.3 The PAT trie for the set of values (2, 7, 24, 31, 37, 40, 42, 120). All data values are stored in the leaf nodes, while internal nodes store the bit position used to determine the branching decision, assuming that each key is represented as a 7-bit value representing a number in the range 0 to 127. Some of the branches in this PAT trie have been labeled to indicate the binary representation for all values in that subtree. For example, all values in the left subtree of the node labeled 0 must have value 0xxxxxx (where x means that bit can be either a 0 or a 1). All nodes in the right subtree of the node labeled 3 must have value 0101xxx.

Note that during the search process, only a single bit of the search key is compared at each internal node. This is significant, because the search key could be quite large. Search in the PAT trie requires only a single full-key comparison, which takes place once a leaf node has been reached.

13.2   Splay Trees

As has been noted several times, the BST has a high risk of becoming un-balanced, resulting in excessively expensive search and update operations. One solution to this problem is to adopt another search tree structure such as the 2-3 tree. An alternative is to modify the BST access functions in some way to guarantee that the tree performs well. This is an appealing concept, and it works well for heaps, whose access functions maintain the heap in the shape of a complete binary tree. Unfortunately, requiring that the BST always be in the shape of a complete binary tree requires excessive modification to the tree during update, as discussed in Section 11.3. A different approach to improving the performance of the BST is to not require that the tree always be balanced, but rather to expend some effort toward making the BST more balanced every time it is accessed. One example of such a compromise is called the **Splay Tree**.

The Splay Tree is not actually a data structure per se, but rather is a collection of rules for improving the performance of a BST. These rules govern modifications made to the BST whenever a search, insert, or delete operation is performed. Their purpose is to provide guarantees on the time required by a series of operations, thereby avoiding the worst-case linear time behavior of standard BST operations. No single operation in the Splay Tree is guaranteed to be efficient. Instead, the Splay Tree access rules guarantee that a series of m operations will take $O(m \log n)$ time for a tree of n nodes whenever $m \geq n$. Thus, a single insert or search operation could take $O(n)$ time. However, m such operations are guaranteed to require a total of $O(m \log n)$ time, for an average cost of $O(\log n)$ per access operation. This is a desirable performance guarantee for any search-tree structure.

The Splay Tree access functions operate in a manner reminiscent of the move-to-front rule for self-organizing lists from Section 10.2, and of the path compression technique for managing parent-pointer trees from Section 6.2. These access functions tend to make the tree more balanced, but an individual access will not necessarily result in a more balanced tree.

Whenever a node S is accessed (e.g., when S is inserted, deleted, or is the goal of a search), the Splay Tree performs a process called **splaying**. Splaying moves S to the root of the BST. When S is being deleted, splaying moves the parent of S to the root. A splay of node S consists of a series of **rotations**. A rotation moves S higher in the tree by adjusting its position with respect to its parent and grandparent. There are three types of rotation.

A **single rotation** is performed only if S is a child of the root node. The single rotation is illustrated by Figure 13.4. It basically switches S with its parent in a way that retains the BST property.

There are two types of **double rotation**. Double rotations involve S, its parent (call it P), and S's grandparent (call it G). The effect of a double rotation is to move S up two levels in the tree.

The first double rotation is called a **zigzag rotation**. It takes place when either of the following two conditions are met:

1. S is the left child of P, and P is the right child of G.
2. S is the right child of P, and P is the left child of G.

In other words, a zigzag rotation is used when G, P, and S form a zigzag. The zigzag rotation is illustrated by Figure 13.5.

The other double rotation is known as a **zigzig** rotation. A zigzig rotation takes place when either of the following two conditions are met:

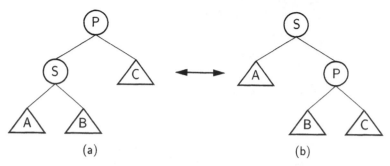

Figure 13.4 Splay Tree single rotation. This rotation takes place only when the node being splayed is a child of the root. Here, node S is promoted to the root, rotating with node P. Since the value of S is less than the value of P, P must become S's right child. The positions of subtrees A, B, and C are altered as appropriate to maintain the BST property, but the contents of these subtrees remains unchanged. (a) The original tree with P as the parent. (b) The tree after a rotation takes place. Performing a single rotation twice will return the tree to its original shape. Equivalently, if (b) is the initial configuration of the tree (i.e., S is at the root and P is its right child), then (a) shows the result of a single rotation.

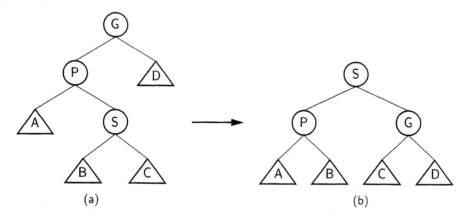

Figure 13.5 Splay Tree zigzag rotation. (a) The original tree with S, P, and G in zigzag formation. (b) The tree after the rotation takes place. The positions of subtrees A, B, C, and D are altered as appropriate to maintain the BST property.

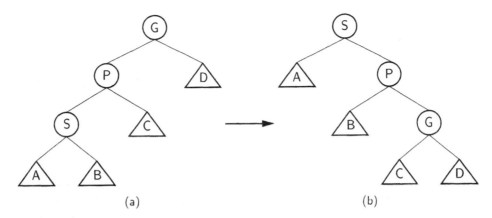

Figure 13.6 Splay Tree zigzig rotation. (a) The original tree with S, P, and G in zigzig formation. (b) The tree after the rotation takes place. The positions of subtrees A, B, C, and D are altered as appropriate to maintain the BST property.

1. S is the left child of P, which is in turn the left child of G.

2. S is the right child of P, which is in turn the right child of G.

Thus, a zigzig rotation takes place in those situations where a zigzag rotation is not appropriate. The zigzig rotation is illustrated by Figure 13.6.

Note that zigzag rotations tend to make the tree more balanced, since they bring subtrees B and C up one level while moving subtree D down one level. The result is often a reduction of the tree's height by one. Zigzig promotions do not typically reduce the height of the tree, they merely bring the newly accessed record toward the root.

Splaying node S involves a series of double rotations until S reaches either the root or the child of the root. Then, if necessary, a single rotation makes S the root. This process tends to rebalance the tree. In any case, it will make frequently accessed nodes stay near the top of the tree, resulting in reduced access cost. Proof that the Splay Tree does in fact meet the guarantee of $O(m \log n)$ is beyond the scope of this book. For more information see the references in Section 13.4.

To illustrate how the Splay Tree operates, consider a search for value 89 in the Splay Tree of Figure 13.7(a). Searching for value 89 in the Splay Tree is identical to searching in a BST. However, once the value has been found, it is splayed to the root. Three rotations are required in this example. The first is a zigzig rotation, whose result is shown in Figure 13.7(b). The second is a zigzag rotation, whose result is shown in Figure 13.7(c). The final step is a single rotation resulting in the tree of Figure 13.7(d). Notice that the splaying process has made the tree shallower.

The Splay Tree's insert operation is the same as for the BST, except that once the node has been inserted it is splayed to the root. Likewise, deleting a node from the Splay Tree is identical to deleting it from the equivalent BST, except that the parent of the node deleted is then splayed to the root.

13.3 Spatial Data Structures

All of the search trees discussed so far – BSTs, Splay Trees, B-trees, and tries – are designed for searching on a one-dimensional key. A typical example is an integer key, whose one-dimensional range can be visualized as a number line. Some databases require support for multiple keys, that is, records can be searched based on any one of several keys. Typically, each such key has its own index or hash table, and any given search query searches one or more of these independent indices as appropriate.

A multi-dimensional search key presents a rather different concept. Imagine that we have a database of city records, where each city has a name and an xy-coordinate. A BST or Splay Tree provides good performance for searches on city name. Separate BSTs could be used to index the x and y coordinates. This would allow you to insert and delete cities, and locate them by name or by one coordinate. However, search on one of the two coordinates is not a natural way to view search in a two-dimensional space. Another option is to combine the xy-coordinates into a single key, say by concatenating the two coordinates, and index cities by the resulting key in a BST. That would allow search by coordinate, but would not allow for efficient two-dimensional **range queries** such as searching for all cities within a given distance of a specified point. The problem is that the BST only works well for one-dimensional keys, while a coordinate is a two-dimensional key where neither dimension is more important than the other.

Multi-dimensional range queries are the defining feature of a **spatial application**. Since a coordinate gives a position in space, it is called a **spatial attribute**. To implement spatial applications efficiently requires the use of **spatial data structures**. Spatial data structures store data objects organized by position, and are an important class of data structures used in geographic information systems, computer graphics, robotics, and many other applications.

This section presents two spatial data structures for storing point data in two or more dimensions. They are the **k-d tree** and the **PR quadtree**.

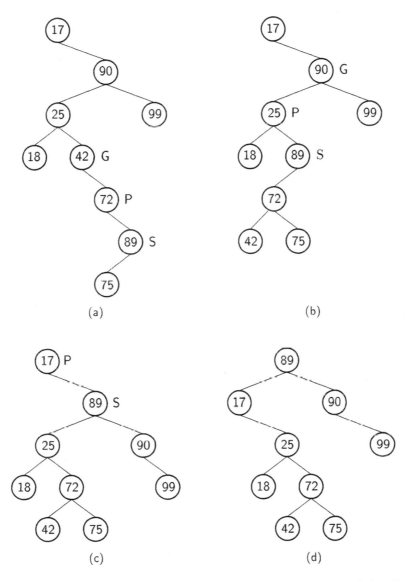

Figure 13.7 Example of splaying after performing a search in a Splay Tree. After finding the node with value 89, that node is splayed to the root by performing three rotations. (a) The original Splay Tree. (b) The result of performing a zigzig rotation on the node with value 89 in the tree of (a). (c) The result of performing a zigzag rotation on the node with value 89 in the tree of (b). (d) The result of performing a single rotation on the node with value 89 in the tree of (c).

The k-d tree is a natural extension of the BST to multiple dimensions. It is a binary tree whose splitting decisions alternate among the key dimensions. Like the BST, the k-d tree uses object space decomposition. The PR quadtree uses key space decomposition and so is a form of trie. It is a binary tree only for one-dimensional keys (in which case it is a trie with a binary alphabet). For d dimensions it has 2^d branches. Thus, in two dimensions, the PR quadtree has four branches (hence the name "quadtree"), essentially splitting space into four equal-sized quadrants at each branch.

13.3.1 The K-D Tree

The k-d tree is a modification to the BST that allows for efficient processing of multi-dimensional keys. The k-d tree differs from the BST in that each level of the k-d tree makes branching decisions based on a particular search key for that level, called the **discriminator**. We define the discriminator at level i to be $i \bmod k$ for k dimensions. For example, assume that we store data organized by xy-coordinates. In this case, k is 2 (there are two coordinates), with the x coordinate field arbitrarily designated key 0, and the y coordinate field designated key 1. At each level, the discriminator alternates between x and y. Thus, a node N at level 0 (the root) would have in its left subtree only nodes whose x values are less than N_x (since x is search key 0, and $0 \bmod 2 = 0$). The right subtree would contain nodes whose x values are greater than N_x. A node M at level 1 would have in its left subtree only nodes whose y values are less than M_y. There is no restriction on the relative values of M_x and the x values of M's descendants, since branching decisions made at M are based solely on the y coordinate. Figure 13.8 shows an example of how a collection of two-dimensional points would be stored in a k-d tree.

In Figure 13.8 the region containing the points is (arbitrarily) restricted to a 100×100 square, and each internal node splits the search space. Each split is shown by a line, vertical for nodes with x discriminators and horizontal for nodes with y discriminators. The root node splits the space into two parts; its children further subdivide the space into smaller parts. The childrens' split lines do not cross the root's split line. Thus, each node in the k-d tree helps to decompose the space into rectangles that show the extent of where nodes may fall in the various subtrees.

Searching a k-d tree for the record with a specified xy-coordinate is like searching a BST, except that each level of the k-d tree is associated with a particular descriminator. Consider searching the k-d tree for a record located

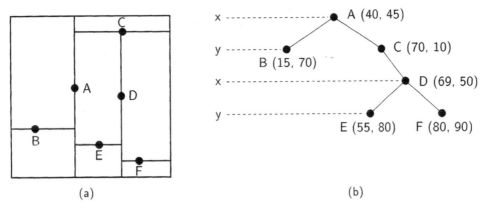

Figure 13.8 Example of a k-d tree. (a) The k-d tree decomposition for a 100×100 unit region containing seven data points. (b) The k-d tree for the region of (a).

at $P = (69, 50)$. First compare P with the point stored at the root (record A in Figure 13.8). If P matches the location of A, then the search is successful. In this example the positions do not match (A's location $(40, 45)$ is not the same as $(69, 50)$), so the search must continue. The x value of A is compared with that of P to determine in which direction to branch. Since A_x's value of 40 is less than P's value of 69, we branch to the right subtree (all cities with x value greater than or equal to 40 are in the right subtree). A_y does not affect the decision on which way to branch at this level. At the second level P does not match record C's position, so another branch must be taken. However, at this level we branch based on the relative y values of point P and record C (since 1 mod 2 = 1, which corresponds to the y coordinate). Since C_y's value of 10 is less than P_y's value of 50, we branch to the right. At this point, P is compared against the position of D. A match is made and the search is successful. As with a BST, if the search process reaches a null pointer, then the search point is not contained in the tree. Here is an implementation for k-d tree search, equivalent to the **findhelp** function of the BST class. Note that variable D stores the key's dimension.

```
private DElem findhelp(BinNode rt, int[] key, int level) {
  if (rt == null) return null;
  DElem it = (DElem)rt.element();
  if (it.equalKey(key)) return (DElem)rt.element();
  if (it.key(level) > key[level])
    return findhelp(rt.left(), key, (level+1)%D);
  else
    return findhelp(rt.right(), key, (level+1)%D);
}
```

Inserting a new node into the k-d tree is similar to BST insertion. The k-d tree search procedure is followed until a `null` pointer is found, indicating the proper place to insert the new node. For example, inserting a record at location (10, 50) in the k-d tree of Figure 13.8 first requires a search to the node containing record B. At this point, the new record is inserted into B's left subtree.

Deleting a node from a k-d tree is similar to deleting from a BST, but slightly harder. As with deleting from a BST, the first step is to find the node (call it N) to be deleted. It is then necessary to find a descendant of N which can be used to replace N in the tree. If N has no children, then N is replaced with a `null` pointer. Note that if N has one child that in turn has children, we cannot simply assign N's parent to point to N's child as would be done in the BST. To do so would change the level of all nodes in the subtree, and thus the discriminator used for a search would also change. The result is that the subtree would no longer be a k-d tree since a node's children might now violate the BST property for that discriminator.

Similar to BST deletion, the record stored in N should be replaced either by the record in N's right subtree with the least value of N's discriminator, or by the record in N's left subtree with the greatest value for this discriminator. Assume that N was at an odd level and therefore y is the discriminator. N could then be replaced by the record in its right subtree with the least y value (call it $Y_{\min}$). The problem is that $Y_{\min}$ is not necessarily the leftmost node, as it would be in the BST. A modified search procedure to find the least y value in the left subtree must be used to find it instead. This find-minimum search can be implemented as follows.

```
private DElem findmin(BinNode rt, int descrim, int level) {
  DElem temp1, temp2;
  if (rt == null) return null;
  temp1 = findmin(rt.left(), descrim, (level+1)%D);
  if (descrim != level) {
    temp2 = findmin(rt.right(), descrim, (level+1)%D);
    if ((temp1 == null) || ((temp2 != null) &&
                  (temp1.key(descrim) > temp2.key(descrim))))
      temp1 = temp2;
  } // Now, temp1 has the smaller value
  if ((temp1 == null) || (temp1.key(descrim) >
                        ((DElem)rt.element()).key(descrim)))
    return (DElem) rt.element();
  else
    return temp1;
}
```

A recursive call to the delete routine will then remove Y_{min} from the tree. Finally, Y_{min}'s record is substituted for the record in node N.

Note that we can replace the node to be deleted with the least valued node from the right subtree only if the right subtree exists. If it does not, then a suitable replacement must be found in the left subtree. Unfortunately, it is not satisfactory to replace N's record with the record having the greatest value for the discriminator in the left subtree, because this new value might be duplicated. If so, then we would have equal values for the discriminator in N's left subtree, which violates the ordering rules for the k-d tree. Fortunately, there is a simple solution to the problem. We first move the left subtree of node N to become the right subtree (i.e., we simply swap the values of N's left and right child pointers). At this point, we proceed with the normal deletion process, replacing the record of N to be deleted with the record containing the *least* value of the discriminator from what is now N's right subtree.

Assume that we want to print out a list of all records that are within a certain distance d of a given point P. We will use Euclidian distance, that is, point P is defined to be within distance d of point N if

$$\sqrt{(P_x - N_x)^2 + (P_y - N_y)^2} \le d.$$

If the search process reaches a node whose key value for the discriminator is more than d above the corresponding value in the search key, then it is not possible that any record in the right subtree can be within distance d of the search key since all key values in that dimension are always too great. Similarly, if the current node's key value in the discriminator is d less than that for the search key value, than no record in the left subtree can be within the radius. In such cases, the subtree in question need not be searched, potentially saving much time. In general, the number of nodes that must be visited during a range query is related to the number of data records that fall within the query circle.

For example, assume that a search will be made to find all cities in the k-d tree of Figure 13.8 within 25 units of the point (25, 65). The search begins with the root node, which contains record A. Since (40, 45) is exactly 25 units from the search point, it should be reported. The search procedure then determines which branches of the tree to take. The search circle extends to both the left and the right of A's (vertical) dividing line, so both branches of the tree must be searched. The left subtree is processed first. Here, record B is checked and found to fall within the search circle. Since the

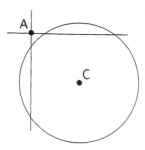

Figure 13.9 Function InCircle must check the Euclidean distance between a record and the query point. It is possible for a record A to have x and y coordinates each within the query distance of the query point C, yet have A itself lie outside the query circle.

node storing B has no children, processing of the left subtree is complete. Processing of A's right subtree now begins. The coordinates of record C are checked, and found not to fall within the circle. Thus, it should not be reported. However, it is possible that cities within C's subtrees could fall within the search circle even if C does not. As C is at level 1, the discriminator at this level is the y coordinate. Since $65 - 25 > 10$, no record in C's left subtree (i.e., records above C) could possibly be in the search circle. Thus, C's left subtree (if it had one) need not be searched. However, cities in C's right subtree could fall within the circle. Thus, search proceeds to the node containing record D. Again, D is outside the search circle. Since $25 + 25 < 69$, no record in D's right subtree could be within the search circle. Thus, only D's left subtree need be searched. This leads to comparing record E's coordinates against the search circle. Record E falls outside the search circle, and processing is complete. Here is an implementation for the region search function.

```
private void rshelp(BinNode rt, int[] point, int radius, int lev) {
  if (rt == null) return;
  if (InCircle(point, radius, ((DElem)rt.element()).coord()))
    System.out.println(rt.element());
  if (((DElem)rt.element()).key(lev) > (point[lev] - radius))
    rshelp(rt.left(), point, radius, (lev+1)%D);
  if (((DElem)rt.element()).key(lev) < (point[lev] + radius))
    rshelp(rt.right(), point, radius, (lev+1)%D);
}
```

When a node is visited, function InCircle is used to check the Euclidean distance between the node's record and the query point. It is not enough to simply check that the differences between the x and y coordinates are less than the query distances because the the record could still be outside the search circle, as illustrated by Figure 13.9.

13.3.2 The PR quadtree

The Point-Region Quadtree (hereafter referred to as the PR quadtree) is a tree structure where each node either has exactly four children or is a leaf (i.e., it is a full four-way branching [4-ary] tree in shape). The PR quadtree represents a collection of data points in two dimensions by decomposing the region containing the data points into four equal quadrants, subquadrants, and so on, until no leaf node contains more than a single point. In other words, if a region contains zero or one data points, then it is represented by a PR quadtree consisting of a single leaf node. If the region contains more than a single data point, then the region is split into four equal quadrants. The corresponding PR quadtree then contains an internal node and four subtrees, each subtree representing a single quadrant of the region, which may in turn be split into subquadrants. Each internal node of a PR quadtree represents a single split of the two dimensional region. The four quadrants of the region (or equivalently, the corresponding subtrees) are designated (in order) NW, NE, SW, and SE. Each quadrant containing more than a single point would in turn be recursively divided into subquadrants until each leaf of the corresponding PR quadtree contains at most one point.

For example, consider the region of Figure 13.10(a) and the corresponding PR quadtree in Figure 13.10(b). The decomposition process demands a fixed key range. In this example, the region is assumed to be of size 128×128. Note that the internal nodes of the PR quadtree are used solely to indicate decomposition of the region; internal nodes do not store data records.

Search for a record matching point Q in the PR quadtree is straightforward. Beginning at the root, we continuously branch to the quadrant that contains Q until it reaches a leaf node. If the root is a leaf, then just check to see if the node's data record matches point Q. If the root is an internal node, proceed to the child that contains the search coordinate. For example, the NW quadrant contains points whose x and y values each fall in the range 0 to 63. The NE quadrant contains points whose x value falls in the range 64 to 127, and whose y value falls in the range 0 to 63. If the root's child is a leaf node, then that child is checked to see if Q has been found. If the leaf is another internal node, the search process continues through the tree until a leaf node is found. If this leaf node stores a record whose position matches Q then the query is successful; otherwise Q is not in the tree.

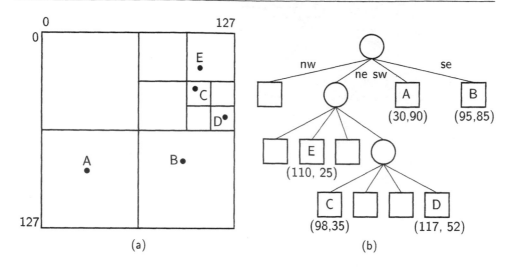

Figure 13.10 Example of a PR quadtree. (a) A map of data points. We define the region to be square with origin at the upper left-hand corner and sides of length 1024. (b) The PR quadtree for the points in (a). (a) also shows the block decomposition imposed by the PR quadtree for this region.

Inserting record P into the PR quadtree is performed by first locating the leaf node that contains the location of P. If this leaf node is empty, then P is stored at this leaf. If the leaf already contains P (or a record with P's coordinates), then a duplicate record should be reported. If the leaf node already contains another record, then the node must be repeatedly decomposed until the existing record and P fall into different leaf nodes. Figure 13.11 shows an example of such an insertion.

Deleting a record P is performed by first locating the node N of the PR quadtree that contains P. Node N is then changed to be empty. The next step is to look at N's three siblings. N and its siblings must be merged together to form a single node N' if only one point is contained among them. This merging process continues until some level is reached at which at least two points are contained in the subtrees represented by node N' and its siblings. For example, if point C is to be deleted from the PR quadtree representing Figure 13.11(b), the resulting node must be merged with its siblings, and that larger node again merged with its siblings to restore the PR quadtree to the decomposition of Figure 13.11(a).

Region search is easily performed with the PR quadtree. To locate all points within radius r of query point Q, begin at the root. If the root is an empty leaf node, then no data points are found. If the root is a leaf

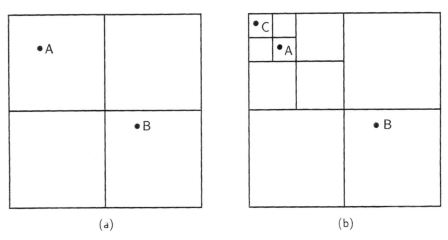

(a)   (b)

Figure 13.11 PR quadtree insertion example. (a) The initial PR quadtree containing two data points. (b) The result of inserting point C. The block containing A must be decomposed into four subblocks. Points A and C would still be in the same block if only one subdivision takes place, so a second decomposition is required to separate them.

containing a data record, then the location of the data point is examined to determine if it falls within the circle. If the root is an internal node, then the process is performed recursively, but *only* on those subtrees containing some part of the search circle.

13.3.3   Other Spatial Data Structures

The differences between the k-d tree and the PR quadtree illustrate many of the issues encountered when implementing spatial data structures. The k-d tree provides an object space decomposition of the region, while the PR quadtree provides a key space decomposition. The k-d tree stores records at all nodes, while the PR quadtree stores records only at the leaf nodes. Finally, the two tree structures are distinct in their structure. The k-d tree is a binary tree, while the PR quadtree has 2^d branches (in the two-dimensional case, $2^2 = 4$). Consider the extension of this concept to three dimensions. A k-d tree for three dimensions would alternate the discriminator through the x, y, and z dimensions. The three-dimensional equivalent of the PR quadtree would be a tree with 2^3 or eight branches. Such a tree is called an **octree**.

   Following on these concepts, it is also possible to devise a binary trie based on a key space decomposition in each dimension, or a quadtree that uses the two-dimensional equivalent to an object space decomposition. The

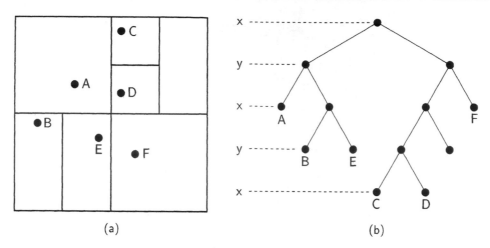

(a)   (b)

Figure 13.12 An example of the Bintree, a binary tree using key space decomposition and discriminators rotating among the dimensions. Compare this with the k-d tree of Figure 13.8.

Bintree is a binary trie that alternates discriminators at each level in a manner similar to the k-d tree. The Bintree for the points of Figure 13.8 is shown in Figure 13.12. Alternatively, we can use a four-way decomposition of space centered on the data points. The tree resulting from such a decomposition is called a **Point quadtree**. The Point quadtree for the data points of Figure 13.10 is shown in Figure 13.13.

This section has only scratched the surface of the field of spatial data structures. By now dozens of distinct spatial data structures have been invented, many with variations and alternate implementations. Some of the most interesting developments have to do with adapting spatial data structures for disk-based applications. It is important to note that all such disk-based implementations boil down to variants on either B-trees or hashing.

13.4   Further Reading

PATRICIA tries and other trie implementations are discussed in *Information Retrieval: Data Structures & Algorithms*, Frakes and Baeza-Yates, eds. [FBY92].

For further reading on Splay Trees, see "Self-adjusting Binary Search" by Sleator and Tarjan [ST85]. An alternative to the Splay Tree is the AVL tree. The AVL tree uses an alternate set of rotations to guarantee a balanced BST at all times. See Knuth [Knu73] for a discussion of the AVL tree.

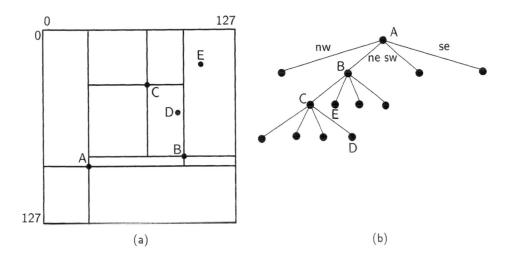

Figure 13.13 An example of the Point quadtree, a 4-ary tree using object space decomposition. Compare this with the PR quadtree of Figure 13.10.

The world of spatial data structures is rich and rapidly evolving. For a good introduction, see the two books by Hanan Samet, *Applications of Spatial Data Structures* and *Design and Analysis of Spatial Data Structures* [Sam90a, Sam90b]. The best reference for more information on the PR quadtree is also [Sam90b]. The k-d tree was invented by John Louis Bentley. For further information on the k-d tree, in addition to [Sam90b], see [Ben75].

For a discussion on the relative space requirements for two-way versus multiway branching, see "A Generalized Comparison of Quadtree and Bintree Storage Requirements" by Shaffer, Juvvadi, and Heath [SJH93].

13.5 Exercises

13.1 Show the binary trie (as illustrated by Figure 13.1) for the following collection of values: 42, 12, 100, 10, 50, 31, 7, 11, 99.

13.2 Show the PAT trie (as illustrated by Figure 13.3) for the following collection of values: 42, 12, 100, 10, 50, 31, 7, 11, 99.

13.3 Write the insertion routine for a trie.

13.4 Write the deletion routine for a trie.

13.5 Show the Splay Tree that results from searching for value 75 in the Splay Tree of Figure 13.7(d).

13.6 Show the Splay Tree that results from searching for value 18 in the Splay Tree of Figure 13.7(d).

13.7 Show the k-d tree for the points of Figure 13.10, inserted in alphabetical order.

13.8 Show the PR quadtree for the points of Figure 13.8, inserted in alphabetical order.

13.9 When performing a region search on a PR quadtree, we need only search those subtrees of an internal node whose corresponding square falls within the query circle. This is most easily computed by comparing the x and y ranges of the query circle against the x and y ranges of the square corresponding to the subtree. However, as illustrated by Figure 13.9, the x and y ranges may overlap without the circle actually intersecting the square. Write a function that accurately determines if a circle and a square intersect.

13.10 Show the Bintree for the points of Figure 13.10, inserted in alphabetical order.

13.11 Show the Point quadtree for the points of Figure 13.8, inserted in alphabetical order.

13.6 Projects

13.1 Use the trie data structure to devise a program to sort variable length strings that does work proportional to the total number of letters in all of the strings. Note that some strings may be very long while most are short.

13.2 Call the set of **suffix strings** for a string to be the string, the string without its first character, the string without its first two characters, and so on. For example, the complete set of suffix strings for "HELLO" would be

$$\{HELLO, ELLO, LLO, LO, O\}.$$

A **Suffix Tree** is a PAT trie that contains all of the suffix strings for a given string. The advantage of a Suffix Tree is that it allows a search for strings using "wildcards." For example, the search key "TH*" means to find all strings with "TH" as the first two characters. This can easily be done with a regular trie. Searching for "*TH" is not efficient in a regular trie, but it is efficient in a Suffix Tree. Implement the Suffix Tree for a dictionary of words or phrases.

13.3 Revise the BST class of Section 5.5 to use the Splay Tree rotations. Your new implementation should not modify the original BST class ADT.

13.4 Compare an implementation of the standard BST against the Splay Tree over a wide variety of input data. Under what conditions does the Splay Tree actually save time?

13.5 Implement a city database using the k-d tree. Each database record contains the name of the city (a string of arbitrary length) and the coordinates of the city expressed as integer x and y coordinates. Your database should allow records to be inserted, deleted by name or coordinate, and searched by name or coordinate. You should also support region queries, that is, a request to print all records within a given distance of a specified point.

13.6 Implement a city database using the PR quadtree. Each database record contains the name of the city (a string of arbitrary length) and the coordinates of the city expressed as integer x and y coordinates. Your database should allow records to be inserted, deleted by name or coordinate, and searched by name or coordinate. You should also support region queries, that is, a request to print all records within a given distance of a specified point.

13.7 Implement a city database using the Bintree. Each database record contains the name of the city (a string of arbitrary length) and the coordinates of the city expressed as integer x and y coordinates. Your database should allow records to be inserted, deleted by name or coordinate, and searched by name or coordinate. You should also support region queries, that is, a request to print all records within a given distance of a specified point.

13.8 Implement a city database using the Point quadtree. Each database record contains the name of the city (a string of arbitrary length) and the coordinates of the city expressed as integer x and y coordinates. Your database should allow records to be inserted, deleted by name or coordinate, and searched by name or coordinate. You should also support region queries, that is, a request to print all records within a given distance of a specified point.

13.9 Use the PR quadtree to implement an efficient solution to Problem 6.5. That is, store the set of points in a PR quadtree. For each point, use the PR quadtree to find those points within distance D that should be equivalenced. What is the asymptotic complexity of this solution?

13.10 Select any two of the point representations described in this chapter (i.e., the k-d tree, the PR quadtree, the Bintree, and the Point quadtree). Implement your two choices and compare them over a wide range of data sets. Describe which is easier to implement, which appears to be more space efficient, and which appears to be more time efficient.

14

Analysis Techniques

This book contains many examples of asymptotic analysis of the time requirements for algorithms and the space requirements for data structures. Often it is a simple matter to invent an equation to model the behavior of the algorithm or data structure in question, and then to derive a closed form solution for the equation should it contain a recurrence or summation. Sometimes an analysis proves more difficult. It may take a clever insight to derive the right model, such as the snowplow argument for analyzing the average run length resulting from Replacement Selection (Section 9.7).

The equations resulting from the Snowplow argument are quite simple. In other cases, developing the model is straightforward, but analyzing the resulting equations is not. An example is the average-case analysis for Quicksort. The equation given in Section 8.4 simply enumerates all possible cases for the pivot position, summing corresponding costs for the recursive calls to Quicksort. However, deriving a closed form solution for the resulting recurrence relation is not so easy.

Many iterative algorithms require that we compute a summation to determine the cost of a loop. Techniques for finding closed form solutions to summations are presented in Section 14.1. Time requirements for many algorithms based on recursion are best modeled by recurrence relations. A brief introduction to techniques for solving recurrences is provided in Section 14.2.

Section 14.3 provides an introduction to the topic of **amortized analysis**. Amortized analysis deals with the cost of a series of operations. Perhaps a single operation in the series has high cost, but as a result the cost of the remaining operations are limited in such a way that the entire series can be done efficiently. Amortized analysis has been used successfully to analyze several of the algorithms presented in this book, including the cost of a series of UNION/FIND operations (Section 6.2), the cost of a series of Splay Tree operations (Section 13.2), and the cost of a series of operations on self-organizing lists (Section 10.2). Section 14.3 discusses the topic in more detail.

14.1 Summation Techniques

This section presents some basic techniques for deriving closed form solutions for summations (also referred to as "solving" the summation). Our first approach is the "guess and test" method, appropriate for summations whose closed form solution is a polynomial expression.

> **Example 14.1** Consider the familiar summation $\sum_{i=0}^{n} i$. Clearly, this is less than $\sum_{i=0}^{n} n$, which is simply $n^2 + n$. Thus, it is reasonable to guess that the closed form solution for this summation is a polynomial of the form $c_1 n^2 + c_2 n + c_3$ for some constants c_1, c_2, and c_3. If this is the case, we can plug in the answers to small cases of the summation to solve for the coefficients. For this example, substituting 0, 1, and 2 for n leads to three simultaneous equations. Since the summation when $n = 0$ is just 0, c_3 must be 0. For $n = 1$ and $n = 2$ we get the two equations
>
> $$\begin{aligned} c_1 + c_2 &= 1 \\ 4c_1 + 2c_2 &= 3, \end{aligned}$$
>
> which in turn yield $c_1 = 1/2$ and $c_2 = 1/2$. If the closed form for the summation is a polynomial, it can only be
>
> $$1/2n^2 + 1/2n + 0$$
>
> which is more commonly written
>
> $$\frac{n(n+1)}{2}.$$

Now that we have a candidate closed form solution, we can use mathematical induction to verify whether it is correct. In this case it is indeed correct, as shown by Example 2.2.

The approach of "guess and test" is useful whenever the solution is a polynomial expression. In particular, similar reasoning can be used to solve for $\sum_{i=1}^{n} i^2$, or more generally $\sum_{i=1}^{n} i^c$ for c any positive integer.

A more general approach to solving summations is known as the **shifting method**. The shifting method subtracts the summation from a variation on the summation. The variation to be selected is one that makes most of the terms cancel out.

Example 14.2 Our first example of shifting sums solves the summation

$$F(n) = \sum_{i=0}^{n} ar^i = a + ar + ar^2 + \cdots + ar^n.$$

This is called a geometric series. Our goal is to find some variation for $F(n)$ such that subtracting one from the other leaves us with an easily manipulated equation. Since the difference between consecutive terms of the summation is a factor of r, we can shift terms if we multiply the entire expression by r.

$$rF(n) = r \sum_{i=0}^{n} ar^i = ar + ar^2 + ar^3 + \cdots + ar^{n+1}.$$

We can now subtract the one equation from the other, as follows.

$$
\begin{aligned}
F(n) - rF(n) = \quad a \quad &+ \quad ar + ar^2 + ar^3 + \cdots + ar^n \\
&- \quad (ar + ar^2 + ar^3 + \cdots + ar^n) - ar^{n+1}.
\end{aligned}
$$

The result leaves only the end terms:

$$
\begin{aligned}
F(n) - rF(n) &= \sum_{i=0}^{n} ar^i - r \sum_{i=0}^{n} ar^i. \\
(1 - r)F(n) &= a - ar^{n+1}.
\end{aligned}
$$

Thus, we get the result

$$F(n) = \frac{a - ar^{n+1}}{1 - r}$$

where $r \neq 1$.

Example 14.3 For our second example of the shifting method, we solve

$$F(n) = \sum_{i=1}^{n} i2^i = 1 \cdot 2^1 + 2 \cdot 2^2 + 3 \cdot 2^3 + \cdots + n \cdot 2^n.$$

We can collapse terms if we multiply by two:

$$2F(n) = 2\sum_{i=1}^{n} i2^i = 1 \cdot 2^2 + 2 \cdot 2^3 + 3 \cdot 2^4 + \cdots + (n-1) \cdot 2^n + n \cdot 2^{n+1}.$$

The ith term of $2F(n)$ is $i \cdot 2^{i+1}$, while the $(i+1)$th term of $F(n)$ is $(i+1) \cdot 2^{i+1}$. Subtracting one expression from the other yields the summation of 2^i and a few non-canceled terms.

$$
\begin{aligned}
2F(n) - F(n) &= 2\sum_{i=1}^{n} i2^i - \sum_{i=1}^{n} i2^i \\
&= \sum_{i=1}^{n} i2^{i+1} - \sum_{i=1}^{n} i2^i.
\end{aligned}
$$

Shift i's value in the second summation, substituting $(i+1)$ for i:

$$= n2^{n+1} + \sum_{i=0}^{n-1} i2^{i+1} - \sum_{i=0}^{n-1} (i+1)2^{i+1}.$$

Break the second summation into two parts:

$$= n2^{n+1} + \sum_{i=0}^{n-1} i2^{i+1} - \sum_{i=0}^{n-1} i2^{i+1} - \sum_{i=0}^{n-1} 2^{i+1}.$$

Cancel like terms:

$$= n2^{n+1} - \sum_{i=0}^{n-1} 2^{i+1}.$$

Again shift i's value in the summation, substituting i for $(i+1)$:

$$= n2^{n+1} - \sum_{i=1}^{n} 2^i.$$

Replace the new summation with a solution that we already know:

$$= n2^{n+1} - \left(2^{n+1} - 2\right).$$

Finally, reorganize the equation:

$$= (n-1)2^{n+1} + 2.$$

14.2 Recurrence Relations

Recurrence relations are often used to model the cost of recursive functions. For example, the standard Mergesort (Section 8.5) takes a list of size n, splits it in half, performs Mergesort on each half, and finally merges the two sublists in n steps. The cost for this can be modeled as

$$\mathbf{T}(n) = 2\mathbf{T}(n/2) + n.$$

In other words, the cost of the algorithm on input of size n is two times the cost for input of size $n/2$ (the recursive calls to Mergesort) plus n (the time to merge the sublists together again).

There are many approaches to solving recurrence relations, and we briefly consider three here. The first is an estimation technique: Guess the upper and lower bounds for the recurrence, use induction to prove the bounds, and tighten as required. The second approach is to expand the recurrence to convert it to a summation and then use summation techniques. The third approach is to take advantage of already proven theorems when the recurrence is of a suitable form. In particular, typical divide and conquer algorithms such as Mergesort yield recurrences of a form that fits a pattern for which we have a ready solution.

14.2.1 Estimating Upper and Lower Bounds

The first approach to solving recurrences is to guess the answer, and then attempt to prove it correct. If a correct upper or lower bound estimate is given, an easy induction proof will verify this fact. If the proof is successful, then try to tighten the bound. If the induction proof fails, then loosen the bound and try again. Once the upper and lower bounds match, you are finished. This is a useful technique when you are only looking for asymptotic complexities. When seeking a precise closed form solution (i.e., you seek the constants for the expression), this method will not be appropriate.

Example 14.4 Use the guessing technique to find the asymptotic bounds for Mergesort, whose running time is described by the equation

$$\mathbf{T}(n) = 2\mathbf{T}(n/2) + n; \quad \mathbf{T}(2) = 1.$$

We begin by guessing that this recurrence has an upper bound in $O(n^2)$. To be more precise, assume that

$$\mathbf{T}(n) \leq n^2.$$

We prove this guess is correct by induction. In this proof, we assume that n is a power of two, to make the calculations easy. For the base case, $\mathbf{T}(2) = 1 \leq 2^2$. For the induction step, we need to show that $\mathbf{T}(n) \leq n^2$ implies that $\mathbf{T}(2n) \leq (2n)^2$ for $n = 2^N, N \geq 1$. The induction hypothesis is

$$\mathbf{T}(i) \leq i^2, \text{for all } i \leq n.$$

It follows that

$$\mathbf{T}(2n) = 2\mathbf{T}(n) + 2n \leq 2n^2 + 2n \leq 4n^2 \leq (2n)^2$$

which is what we wanted to prove. Thus, $\mathbf{T}(n)$ is in $O(n^2)$.

Is $O(n^2)$ a good estimate? In the next-to-last step we went from $n^2 + 2n$ to the much larger $4n^2$. This suggests that $O(n^2)$ is a high estimate. If we guess something smaller, such as $\mathbf{T}(n) \leq cn$ for some constant c, it should be clear that this cannot work since $c2n = 2cn$ and there is no room for the extra n cost to join the two pieces together. Thus, the true cost must be somewhere between cn and n^2.

Let us now try $\mathbf{T}(n) \leq n \log n$. For the base case, the definition of the recurrence sets $\mathbf{T}(2) = 1 \leq (2 \cdot \log 2) = 2$. Assume (induction hypothesis) that $\mathbf{T}(n) \leq n \log n$. Then,

$$\mathbf{T}(2n) = 2\mathbf{T}(n) + 2n \leq 2n \log n + 2n \leq 2n(\log n + 1) \leq 2n \log 2n$$

which is what we seek to prove. In similar fashion, we can prove that $\mathbf{T}(n)$ is in $\Omega(n \log n)$. Thus, $\mathbf{T}(n)$ is also $\Theta(n \log n)$.

14.2.2 Expanding Recurrences

Estimating bounds is effective if you only need an approximation to the answer. More precise techniques are required to find an exact solution. One such technique is called **expanding** the recurrence. In this method, the smaller terms on the right side of the equation are in turn replaced by their definition. This is the expanding step. These terms are again expanded, and so on, until a full series with no recurrence results. This yields a summation, and techniques for solving summations can then be used.

Example 14.5 Find the solution for

$$\mathbf{T}(n) = 2\mathbf{T}(n/2) + 5n^2; \quad \mathbf{T}(1) = 7.$$

For simplicity we assume that n is a power of two, so we will rewrite it as $n = 2^k$. This recurrence can be expanded as follows:

$$
\begin{aligned}
\mathbf{T}(n) &= 2\mathbf{T}(n/2) + 5n^2 \\
&= 2(2\mathbf{T}(n/4) + 5(n/2)^2) + 5n^2 \\
&= 2(2(2\mathbf{T}(n/8) + 5(n/4)^2) + 5(n/2)^2) + 5n^2 \\
&= 2^k\mathbf{T}(1) + 2^{k-1} \cdot 5 \left(\frac{n}{2^{k-1}} \right)^2 + \cdots + 2 \cdot 5 \left(\frac{n}{2} \right)^2 + 5n^2.
\end{aligned}
$$

This last expression can best be represented by a summation as follows:

$$
7n + 5 \sum_{i=0}^{k-1} n^2/2^i
$$

$$
= 7n + 5n^2 \sum_{i=0}^{k-1} 1/2^i.
$$

From Equation 2.5, we have:

$$
\begin{aligned}
&= 7n + 5n^2 \left(2 - 1/2^{k-1} \right) \\
&= 7n + 5n^2 (2 - 2/n) \\
&= 7n + 10n^2 - 10n \\
&= 10n^2 - 3n.
\end{aligned}
$$

This is the *exact* solution to the recurrence for n a power of two.

14.2.3   Divide and Conquer Recurrences

The third approach to solving recurrences is to take advantage of known theorems that describe the solution for classes of recurrences. One useful example is a theorem that gives the answer for a class known as **divide and conquer** recurrences. These have the form

$$\mathbf{T}(n) = a\mathbf{T}(n/b) + cn^k; \quad \mathbf{T}(1) = c$$

where a, b, c, and k are constants. In general, this recurrence describes a problem of size n divided into a subproblems of size n/b, while cn^k is the amount of work necessary to combine the partial solutions. Mergesort is an example of a divide and conquer algorithm, and its recurrence fits this form. So does binary search. We use the method of expanding recurrences to derive the general solution for any divide and conquer recurrence, assuming that $n = b^m$.

$$
\begin{aligned}
\mathbf{T}(n) &= a(a\mathbf{T}(n/b^2) + c(n/b)^k) + cn^k \\
&= a^m\mathbf{T}(1) + a^{m-1}c(n/b^{m-1})^k + \cdots + ac(n/b)^k + cn^k \\
&= c\sum_{i=0}^{m} a^{m-i}b^{ik} \\
&= ca^m\sum_{i=0}^{m}(b^k/a)^i.
\end{aligned}
$$

Note that

$$a^m = a^{\log_b n} = n^{\log_b a}. \tag{14.1}$$

The summation is a geometric series whose sum depends on the ratio $r = b^k/a$. There are three cases.

1. $r < 1$. From Equation 2.4,

$$\sum_{i=0}^{m} r^i < 1/(1-r), \text{a constant.}$$

Thus,

$$\mathbf{T}(n) = \Theta(a^m) = \Theta(n^{\log_b a}).$$

2. $r = 1$. Since $r = b^k/a$, we know that $a = b^k$. From the definition of logarithms it follows immediately that $k = \log_b a$. We also note from Equation 14.1 that $m = \log_b n$. Thus,

$$\sum_{i=0}^{m} r = m + 1 = \log_b n + 1.$$

Since $a^m = n\log_b a = n^k$, we have

$$\mathbf{T}(n) = \Theta(n^{\log_b a}\log n) = \Theta(n^k\log n).$$

3. $r > 1$. From Equation 2.6,

$$\sum_{i=0}^{m} r = \frac{r^{m+1} - 1}{r - 1} = \Theta(r^m).$$

Thus,

$$\mathbf{T}(n) = \Theta(a^m r^m) = \Theta(a^m (b^k/a)^m) = \Theta(b^{km}) = \Theta(n^k).$$

We can summarize the above derivation as the following theorem.

Theorem 14.1

$$\mathbf{T}(n) = \begin{cases} \Theta(n^{\log_b a}) & \text{if } a > b^k \\ \Theta(n^k \log n) & \text{if } a = b^k \\ \Theta(n^k) & \text{if } a < b^k. \end{cases}$$

This theorem may be applied whenever appropriate, rather than re-deriving the solution for the recurrence. For example, apply the theorem to solve

$$\mathbf{T}(n) = 3\mathbf{T}(n/5) + 8n^2.$$

Since $a = 3$, $b = 5$, $c = 8$, and $k = 2$, we find that $3 < 5^2$. Applying case (3) of the theorem, $\mathbf{T}(n) = \Theta(n^2)$.

As another example, use the theorem to solve the recurrence relation for Mergesort:

$$\mathbf{T}(n) = 2\mathbf{T}(n/2) + n; \quad \mathbf{T}(1) = 1.$$

Since $a = 2$, $b = 2$, $c = 1$, and $k = 1$, we find that $2 = 2^1$. Applying case (2) of the theorem, $\mathbf{T}(n) = \Theta(n \log n)$.

14.2.4 Average-Case Analysis of Quicksort

In Section 8.4, we determined that the average case analysis of Quicksort had the following recurrence:

$$\mathbf{T}(n) = cn + \frac{1}{n}\sum_{k=0}^{n-1}[\mathbf{T}(k) + \mathbf{T}(n-1-k)], \qquad \mathbf{T}(0) = \mathbf{T}(1) = c.$$

The cn term is an upper bound on the `findpivot` and `partition` steps. This equation comes from observing that each element k is equally likely to be the partitioning element. It can be simplified by observing that the two recurrence terms $\mathbf{T}(k)$ and $\mathbf{T}(n-1-k)$ are equivalent, since one simply counts up from $T(0)$ to $T(n-1)$ while the other counts down from $T(n-1)$ to $T(0)$. This yields

$$\mathbf{T}(n) = cn + \frac{2}{n}\sum_{k=0}^{n-1}\mathbf{T}(k).$$

The shifting method for summations provides the closed form solution. Multiply both sides by n and subtract the result from the formula for $n\mathbf{T}(n+1)$.

$$n\mathbf{T}(n) = cn^2 + 2\sum_{k=1}^{n-1}\mathbf{T}(k)$$

$$(n+1)\mathbf{T}(n+1) = c(n+1)^2 + 2\sum_{k=1}^{n}\mathbf{T}(k)$$

Subtracting $n\mathbf{T}(n)$ from both sides yields:

$$
\begin{aligned}
(n+1)\mathbf{T}(n+1) - n\mathbf{T}(n) &= c(n+1)^2 - cn^2 + 2\mathbf{T}(n) \\
(n+1)\mathbf{T}(n+1) - n\mathbf{T}(n) &= c(2n+1) + 2\mathbf{T}(n) \\
(n+1)\mathbf{T}(n+1) &= c(2n+1) + (n+2)\mathbf{T}(n) \\
\mathbf{T}(n+1) &= \frac{c(2n+1)}{n+1} + \frac{n+2}{n+1}\mathbf{T}(n).
\end{aligned}
$$

Note that $\frac{c(2n+1)}{n+1} < 2c$. Expanding the recurrence, we get

$$
\begin{aligned}
\mathbf{T}(n+1) &\le 2c + \frac{n+2}{n+1}\mathbf{T}(n) \\
&= 2c + \frac{n+2}{n+1}\left(2c + \frac{n+1}{n}\mathbf{T}(n-1)\right) \\
&= 2c + \frac{n+2}{n+1}\left(2c + \frac{n+1}{n}\left(2c + \frac{n}{n-1}\mathbf{T}(n-2)\right)\right) \\
&= 2c + \frac{n+2}{n+1}\left(2c + \cdots + \frac{4}{3}\left(2c + \frac{3}{2}\mathbf{T}(1)\right)\right) \\
&= 2c\left(1 + \frac{n+2}{n+1} + \frac{n+2}{n+1}\frac{n+1}{n} + \cdots + \frac{n+2}{n+1}\frac{n+1}{n}\cdots\frac{3}{2}\right) \\
&= 2c\left(1 + (n+2)\left(\frac{1}{n+1} + \frac{1}{n} + \cdots + \frac{1}{2}\right)\right) \\
&= 2c + 2c(n+2)\left(\mathcal{H}_{n+1} - 1\right)
\end{aligned}
$$

for $\mathcal{H}_{n+1}$ the Harmonic series. From Equation 2.10, $\mathcal{H}_{n+1} = \Theta(\log n)$, so this summation is $\Theta(n \log n)$.

14.3   Amortized Analysis

This section presents the concept of **amortized analysis**, which is the analysis for a series of operations. In particular, amortized analysis allows us to deal with the situation where the worst-case cost for n operations is less than n times the worst-case cost of any one operation. Rather than focusing on the individual cost of each operation and summing them up, amortized analysis looks at the cost of the entire series and "charges" each individual operation with a share of the total cost.

A simple example of amortized analysis applies to a series of sequential searches in a unsorted array. For n random searches, the average-case cost for each search is $n/2$, and so the *expected* total cost for the series is $n^2/2$. Unfortunately, in the worst-case all of the searches would be to the last item in the array. In this case, each search costs n for a total worst-case cost of n^2. Compare this to the cost for a series of n searches such that each item in the array is searched for precisely once. In this situation, some of the searches *must* be expensive, but also some searches *must* be cheap. The total number of searches, in the best, average, and worst-case, for this problem must be $\sum_{i=1}^{n} i \approx n^2/2$. This is a factor of two better than the more pessimistic analysis that charges each operation in the series with its worst-case cost.

As another example of amortized analysis, consider the process of incrementing a binary counter. The algorithm is to move from the lower-order (rightmost) bit toward the high-order (leftmost) bit, changing 1s to 0s until the first 0 is encountered. This 0 is changed to a 1, and the increment operation is done. Below is Java code to implement the increment operation, assuming that a binary number of length n is stored in array A of length n.

```
for (i=0; ((i<A.length) && (A[i] == 1)); i++)
  A[i] = 0;
if (i < A.length)
  A[i] = 1;
```

If we count from 0 through $2^n - 1$, (requiring a counter with at least n bits), what is the average cost for an increment operation in terms of the number of bits processed? Naive worst-case analysis says that if all n bits are 1 (except for the high-order bit), then n bits need to be processed. Thus, if there are 2^n increments, then the cost is $n2^n$. However, this is much too

high, since it is rare for so many bits to be processed. In fact, half of the
time the low-order bit is 0, and so only that bit is processed. One quarter of
the time, the low-order two bits are 01, and so only the low-order two bits
are processed. Another way to view this is that the low-order bit is always
flipped, the bit to its left is flipped half the time, the next bit one quarter
of the time, and so on. We can capture this with the summation (charging
costs to bits going from right to left)

$$\sum_{i=0}^{n-1} \frac{1}{2^i} < 2.$$

In other words, the average number of bits flipped on each increment is 2,
leading to a total cost of only $2 \cdot 2^n$ for a series of 2^n increments.

A useful concept for amortized analysis is illustrated by a simple variation on the stack data structure, where the pop function is slightly modified
to take a second parameter k indicating that k pop operations are to be performed. This revised pop function, called multipop, might look as follows:

```
void multipop(int k) { ... } // pop k elements from stack
```

The "local" worst-case analysis for multipop is $\Theta(n)$ for n elements in the
stack. Thus, if there are m_1 calls to push and m_2 calls to multipop, then the
naive worst-case cost for the series of operation is $m_1 + m_2 \cdot n = m_1 + m_2 \cdot m_1$.
This analysis is unreasonably pessimistic. Clearly it is not really possible
to pop m_1 elements each time multipop is called. Analysis that focuses
on single operations cannot deal with this global limit, and so we turn to
amortized analysis to model the entire series of operations.

The key to an amortized analysis of this problem lies in the concept of
potential. At any given time, a certain number of items may be on the
stack. The cost for multipop can be no more than this number of items.
Each call to push places another item on the stack, which can be removed
by only a single multipop operation. Thus, each call to push raises the
potential of the stack by one item. The sum of all calls to multipop can
never cost more than the total potential of the stack (aside from a constant
time cost associated with each call to multipop itself).

The amortized cost for any series of push and multipop operations is
the sum of three costs. First, each of the push operations takes constant
time. Second, each multipop operation takes a constant time in overhead,
regardless of the number of items popped on that call. Finally, we count

the sum of the potentials expended by all `multipop` operations, which is at most m_1, the number of `push` operations. This total cost can therefore be expressed as

$$m_1 + (m_2 + m_1) = \Theta(m_1 + m_2).$$

Our final example uses amortized analysis to prove a relationship between the cost of the move-to-front self-organizing list heuristic from Section 10.2 and the cost for the optimal static ordering of the list.

Recall that, for a series of search operations, the minimum cost for a static list results when the list is sorted by frequency of access to its records. This is the optimal ordering for the records if we never allow the positions of records to change, since the most frequently accessed record is first (and thus has least cost), followed by the next most frequently accessed record, and so on.

Theorem 14.2 *The total number of comparisons required by any series S of n or more searches on a self-organizing list of length n using the move-to-front heuristic is never more than twice the total number of comparisons required when series S is applied to the list stored in its optimal static order.*

Proof: Each comparison of the search key with a record in the list is either successful or unsuccessful. For m searches, there must be exactly m successful comparisons for both the self-organizing list and the static list. The total number of unsuccessful comparisons in the self-organizing list is the sum over all pairs of distinct keys for the number of comparisons between the pair.

Consider a particular pair of keys A and B. For any sequence of searches S, the total number of (unsuccessful) comparisons between A and B is identical to the number of comparisons between A and B required for the subsequence of S made up only of searches for A or B. Call this subsequence S_{AB}. In other words, including searches for other keys does not affect the relative position of A and B, and so does not affect the relative contribution to the total cost of the unsuccessful comparisons between A and B.

The number of unsuccessful comparisons between A and B made by the move-to-front heuristic on subsequence S_{AB} is at most twice the number of unsuccessful comparisons between A and B required when S_{AB} is applied to the optimal static ordering for the list. To see this, assume that S_{AB} contains i As and j Bs, with $i \leq j$. Under the optimal static ordering, i unsuccessful comparisons are required since B must appear before A in the list (its access frequency is higher). Move-to-front will yield an unsuccessful comparison whenever the request sequence changes from A to B or from B to A. The total number of such changes possible is $2i$ since each change involves an A and each A can be part of at most two changes.

Since the total number of unsuccessful comparisons required by move-to-front for any given pair of keys is at most twice that required by the optimal static ordering, the total number of unsuccessful comparisons required by move-to-front for all pairs of keys is also at most twice as high. Since the number of successful comparisons is the same for both methods, the total number of comparisons required by move-to-front is less than twice the number of comparisons required by the optimal static ordering.   □

14.4   Further Reading

A good introduction to solving recurrence relations is *Applied Combinatorics* by Fred S. Roberts [Rob84]. For a more advanced treatment, see *Concrete Mathematics* by Graham, Knuth, and Patashnik [GKP89].

Cormen, Leiserson, and Rivest provide a good discussion on various methods of performing amortized analysis in *Introduction to Algorithms* [CLR90]. For an amortized analysis that the Splay Tree requires $m \log n$ time to perform a series of m operations on n nodes when $m > n$, see "Self-Adjusting Binary Search Trees" by Sleator and Tarjan [ST85]. The proof for Theorem 14.2 comes from "Amortized Analysis of Self-Organizing Sequential Search Heuristics" by Bentley and McGeoch [BM85].

14.5   Exercises

14.1 Use the technique of guessing a polynomial and deriving the coefficients to solve the summation

$$\sum_{i=1}^{n} i^2.$$

14.2 Use the technique of guessing a polynomial and deriving the coefficients to solve the summation

$$\sum_{i=1}^{n} i^3.$$

14.3 Find a closed form solution for

$$\sum_{i=a}^{b} i^2.$$

14.4 Use the shifting method to solve the summation

$$\sum_{i=1}^{n} i.$$

14.5 Use the shifting method to solve the summation

$$\sum_{i=1}^{n} 2^i.$$

14.6 Use the shifting method to solve the summation

$$\sum_{i=1}^{n} i2^{n-i}.$$

14.7 Prove that the number of moves required for function TOH from Section 2.4 is $2^n - 1$.

14.8 Give and prove the closed form solution for the recurrence relation $\mathbf{T}(n) = \mathbf{T}(n-1) + c$, $\mathbf{T}(1) = c$.

14.9 Prove by induction that the closed form solution for the recurrence relation

$$\mathbf{T}(n) = 2\mathbf{T}(n/2) + n; \quad \mathbf{T}(2) = 1$$

is in $\Omega(n \log n)$.

14.10 Find the solution (in asymptotic terms, not precise constants) for the recurrence relation

$$\mathbf{T}(n) = \mathbf{T}(n/2) + \sqrt{n}; \quad \mathbf{T}(1) = 1.$$

14.11 Find the exact closed form solution for the following recurrence relation by expanding the recurrence:

$$\mathbf{T}(n) = 2\mathbf{T}(n/2) + n; \quad \mathbf{T}(2) = 2.$$

14.12 Use Theorem 14.1 to prove that binary search requires $\Theta(\log n)$ time.

14.13 Recall that when a hash table gets to be more than about one half full, its performance quickly degrades. One solution to this problem is to reinsert all elements of the hash table into a new hash table that is twice as large. Assuming that the (expected) average case cost to insert into a hash table is $\Theta(1)$, prove that the average cost to insert is still $\Theta(1)$ when this re-insertion policy is used.

14.14 The standard algorithm for multiplying two $n \times n$ matrices requires $\Theta(n^3)$ time. It is possible to do better than this by rearranging and grouping the multiplications in various ways. One example of this is known as Strassen's matrix multiplication algorithm. Assume that n is a power of two. In the following, A and B are $n \times n$ arrays, while A_{ij} and B_{ij} refer to arrays of size $n/2 \times n/2$. Strassen's algorithm is to multiply the subarrays together in a particular order, as expressed by the following equation:

$$\begin{bmatrix} A_{11} & A_{12} \\ A_{21} & A_{22} \end{bmatrix} \begin{bmatrix} B_{11} & B_{12} \\ B_{21} & B_{22} \end{bmatrix} = \begin{bmatrix} s_1 + s_2 - s_4 + s6 & s_4 + s_5 \\ s_6 + s_7 & s_2 - s_3 + s_5 - s_7 \end{bmatrix}$$

In other words, the result of the multiplication for an $n \times n$ array is obtained by a series of matrix multiplications and additions for $n/2 \times n/2$ arrays. Multiplications between subarrays also use Strassen's algorithm, and the addition of two subarrays requires $\Theta(n^2)$ time. The subfactors are defined as follows:

$$\begin{aligned} s_1 &= (A_{12} - A_{22}) \cdot (B_{21} + B_{22}) \\ s_2 &= (A_{11} + A_{22}) \cdot (B_{11} + B_{22}) \\ s_3 &= (A_{11} - A_{21}) \cdot (B_{11} + B_{12}) \\ s_4 &= (A_{11} + A_{12}) \cdot B_{22} \\ s_5 &= A_{11} \cdot (B_{12} - B_{22}) \\ s_6 &= A_{22} \cdot (B_{21} - B_{11}) \\ s_7 &= (A_{21} + A_{22}) \cdot B_{11} \end{aligned}$$

(a) Show that Strassen's algorithm is correct.

(b) How many multiplications of subarrays and how many additions are required by Strassen's algorithm? How many would be required by normal matrix multiplication if it were defined in terms of subarrays in the same manner? Show the recurrence relations for both Strassen's algorithm and the normal matrix multiplication algorithm.

(c) Derive the closed form solution for the recurrence relation you derived for Strassen's algorithm (use Theorem 14.1).

(d) Give your opinion on the practicality of Strassen's algorithm.

14.15 Given a 2-3 tree with N nodes, prove that inserting M additional nodes requires $\mathrm{O}(M + N)$ node splits.

14.16 One approach to implementing an array-based list where the list size is unknown is to let the array grow and shrink. This is known as a **dynamic array**. (Java's `vector` class implements a dynamic array.)

   (a) What is the amortized cost of inserting elements into the list if the array is initially of size 0 and we double the array size whenever the number of elements in the array exceeds the size of the array?

   (b) Consider an underflow strategy that cuts the array size in half whenever the array falls below half full. Give an example where this strategy leads to a bad amortized cost.

   (c) Give a better underflow strategy than that suggested in part (b). Your goal is to find a strategy whose amortized analysis shows that deletion is in $O(n)$ time.

14.17 Recall that two vertices in an undirected graph are in the same connected component if there is a path connecting them. A good algorithm to find the connected components of an undirected graph begins by calling a DFS on the first vertex. All vertices reached by the DFS are in the same connected component, and are so marked. We then look through the vertex `mark` array until an unmarked vertex i is found. Again calling the DFS on i, all vertices reachable from i are in a second connected component. We continue working through the `mark` array until all vertices have been assigned to some connected component. A sketch of the algorithm is as follows:

```
for (i=0; i<G.n(); i++) // Assume n vertices in the graph
   G.setMark(i, 0);      // Vertices start in no component
int compcount = 1;       // Counter for current component
for (i=0; i<G.n(); i++)
   if (G.getMark(i) == 0) // Start a new component
     DFS_component(G, i, compcount++);

void DFS_component(Graph G, int v, int compcount) {
  G.setMark(v, compcount);
  for (Edge w = G.first(v); G.isEdge(w); w = G.next(w))
    if (G.getMark(G.v2(w)) == 0)
      DFS_component(G, G.v2(w));
}
```

Use the concept of potential from amortized analysis to explain why the total cost of this algorithm is $\Theta(|V| + |E|)$. (Note that this will not be a true amortized analysis since this algorithm does not allow an arbitrary series of DFS operations, but rather is fixed to do a single call to DFS from each vertex.)

14.18 Give a proof similar to that used for Theorem 14.2 to show that the total number of comparisons required by any series of n or more searches S on a self-organizing list of length n using the count heuristic is never more than twice the total number of comparisons required when series S is applied to the list stored in its optimal static order.

14.6   Projects

14.1 Implement the UNION/FIND algorithm of Section 6.2 using both path compression and the weighted union rule. Count the total number of node accesses required for various series of equivalences to determine if the actual performance of the algorithm matches the expected cost of $\Theta(n \log^* n)$.

14.2 Implement both a standard $\Theta(n^3)$ matrix multiplication algorithm and Strassen's matrix multiplication algorithm (see Exercise 14.14). Using empirical testing, try to estimate the constant factors for the run-time equations of the two algorithms. How big must n be before Strassen's algorithm becomes more efficient than the standard algorithm?

15

Limits to Computation

15.1 Introduction

This book contains many examples of data structures used to solve a wide variety of problems. There are also many examples of efficient algorithms. In general, our search algorithms strive to be at worst in $O(\log n)$, while our sorting algorithms strive to be in $O(n \log n)$. A few algorithms, such as the all-pairs shortest-paths algorithms, have higher asymptotic complexity, with Floyd's all-pairs shortest-paths algorithm being $\Theta(n^3)$.

Part of the reason why we can solve many problems efficiently has to do with the fact that we use efficient algorithms. Given any problem for which you know *some* algorithm, it is always possible to write an inefficient algorithm to "solve" the problem. For example, consider a sorting algorithm that tests every possible permutation of its input until it finds the correct permutation that provides a sorted list. The running time for this algorithm would be unacceptably high, since it is proportional to the number of permutations which is $n!$ for n inputs. When solving the minimum-cost spanning tree problem, if we were to test every possible subset of edges to see which forms the shortest minimum spanning tree, the amount of work would be proportional to $2^{|E|}$ for a graph with $|E|$ edges. Fortunately, for both of these problems we have more clever algorithms that allow us to find answers (relatively) quickly.

Unfortunately, in real life there are many computing problems that must be solved for which the best possible algorithm takes a long time. A simple example is the Towers of Hanoi problem, which requires 2^n moves to "solve" a tower with n disks. It is not possible for any computer program that solves the Towers of Hanoi problem to run in less than $\Omega(2^n)$ time, since that many moves must be printed out.

Besides those problems whose solutions *must* take a long time to run, there are also many problems for which we simply do not know if there are efficient algorithms or not. The best algorithms that we know for such problems are very slow, but perhaps there are better ones waiting to be discovered. Yet, while having a problem with high running time is bad, it is even worse to have a problem that cannot be solved at all! Such problems do exist, and we will study some in this chapter. This chapter presents a brief introduction to the theory of expensive and impossible problems.

15.2   Reductions

We begin with an important concept for understanding the relationships between problems, called **reduction**. Reduction allows us to solve one problem in terms of another. Equally importantly, when we wish to understand the difficulty of a problem, reduction allows us to make relative statements about upper and lower bounds on the cost of a problem (as opposed to an algorithm or program).

Since the concept of problems is discussed extensively in this chapter, we begin with notation to simplify problem descriptions. Throughout this chapter, a problem will be defined in terms of a mapping between inputs and outputs, and the name of the problem will be given in all capital letters. Thus, a complete definition of the sorting problem could appear as follows.

Definition 15.1 SORTING:
  Input: A sequence of integers x_0, x_1, x_2, ..., x_{n-1}.
  Output: A permutation y_0, y_1, y_2, ..., y_{n-1} of the sequence such that $y_i \leq y_j$ whenever $i < j$.

Once you have bought or written a program to solve one problem, such as sorting, you may be able to use it as a tool to solve a different problem. This is known in software engineering as **software reuse**. To illustrate this, let us consider another problem.

Definition 15.2 PAIRING:
  Input: Two sequences of integers $X = (x_0, x_1, ..., x_{n-1})$ and $Y = (y_0, y_1, ..., y_{n-1})$.
  Output: A pairing of the elements in the two sequences such that the least value in X is paired with the least value in Y, the next least value in X is paired with the next least value in Y, and so on.

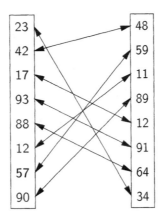

Figure 15.1 An illustration of PAIRING. The two lists of numbers are paired up so that the least value in each list makes a pair, the next smallest values in each list makes a pair, and so on.

Figure 15.1 illustrates PAIRING. One way to solve PAIRING is to use an existing sorting program by sorting each of the two sequences, and then pairing-off items based on their position in sorted order. Technically, we say that PAIRING is **reduced** to SORTING, since SORTING is used to solve PAIRING.

Notice that reduction is a three-step process. The first step is to convert an instance of PAIRING into two instances of SORTING. The conversion step is not very interesting; it simply takes each sequence and assigns it to an array to be passed to SORTING. The second step is to sort the two arrays (i.e., apply SORTING to each array). The third step is to convert the output of SORTING to the output for PAIRING. This is done by pairing the first elements in the sorted arrays, the second elements, and so on.

The reduction of PAIRING to SORTING helps to establish an upper bound on the cost of PAIRING. In terms of asymptotic notation, assuming that we can find one method to convert the inputs to PAIRING into inputs to SORTING "fast enough," and a second method to convert the result of SORTING back to the correct result for PAIRING "fast enough," then the asymptotic cost of PAIRING cannot be more than the cost of SORTING. In this case, there is little work to be done to convert from PAIRING to SORTING, or to convert the answer from SORTING back to the answer for PAIRING, so the dominant cost of this solution is performing the sort operation. Thus, an upper bound for PAIRING is in $O(n \log n)$.

There is another use of reductions besides solving a new problem (and coincidentally establishing an upper bound for that problem). Assume we can go the other way and convert SORTING to PAIRING "fast enough." What does this say about the minimum cost of PAIRING? We know from Section 8.9 that the cost of SORTING is in $\Omega(n \log n)$. Assume that PAIRING could be done in $O(n)$ time. Then, one way to create a sorting algorithm would be to convert SORTING into PAIRING, run the algorithm for PAIRING, and finally convert the answer back to the answer for SORTING. Provided that we can convert SORTING to/from PAIRING "fast enough," this process would yield an $O(n)$ algorithm for sorting! Since this contradicts what we know about the lower bound for SORTING, and the only flaw in the reasoning is the initial assumption that PAIRING can be done in $O(n)$ time, we can conclude that there is no $O(n)$ time algorithm for PAIRING. In fact, we know that PAIRING must be at least as expensive as SORTING, and so must itself have a lower bound in $\Omega(n \log n)$.

To complete this proof regarding the lower bound for PAIRING, we need now to find a way to reduce SORTING to PAIRING. This is easily done. Take an instance of SORTING (i.e., an array A of n elements). A second array B is generated that simply stores i in position i for $0 \leq i < n$. Pass the two arrays to PAIRING. Take the resulting set of pairs, and use the value from the B half of the pair to tell which position in the sorted array the A half should take; that is, we can now reorder the records in the A array using the corresponding value in the B array as the sort key, and running a simple $\Theta(n)$ Binsort. The conversion of SORTING to PAIRING can be done in $O(n)$ time, and likewise the conversion of the output of PAIRING can be converted to the correct output for SORTING in $O(n)$ time. Thus, the cost of this "sorting algorithm" is dominated by the cost for PAIRING.

Consider any two problems for which a suitable reduction from one to the other can be found. The first problem takes an arbitrary instance of its input, which we will call **I**, and transforms **I** to a solution, which we will call **SOL**. The second problem takes an arbitrary instance of its input, which we will call **I′**, and transforms **I′** to a solution, which we will call **SOL′**. We can define reduction more formally as a three-step process:

1. Transform an arbitrary instance of the first problem to an instance of the second problem. In other words, there must be a transformation from any instance **I** of the first problem to an instance **I′** of the second problem.

2. Apply an algorithm for the second problem to the instance **I′**, yielding a solution **SOL′**.

3. Transform **SOL′** to the solution of **I**, known as **SOL**. Note that **SOL** must in fact be the correct solution for **I** for the reduction to be acceptable.

It is important to note that the reduction process does not give us an algorithm for solving either problem by itself. It merely gives us a method for solving the first problem given that we already have a solution to the second. More importantly for the topics to be discussed in the remainder of this chapter, reduction gives us a way to understand the bounds of one problem in terms of another. Specifically, given efficient transformations, the upper bound of the first problem is at most the upper bound of the second. Conversely, the lower bound of the second problem is at least the lower bound of the first.

As a second example of reduction, consider the simple problem of multiplying two n-digit numbers. The standard long-hand method for multiplication is to multiply the last digit of the first number by the second number (taking $\Theta(n)$ time), multiply the second digit of the first number by the second number (again taking $\Theta(n)$ time), and so on for each of the n digits of the first number. Finally, the intermediate results are added together. Note that adding two numbers of length M and N can easily be done in $\Theta(M + N)$ time. Since each digit of the first number is multiplied against each digit of the second, this algorithm requires $\Theta(n^2)$ time. Asymptotically faster (but more complicated) algorithms are known, but none is so fast as to be in $O(n)$.

Next we ask the question: Is squaring an n-digit number as difficult as multiplying two n-digit numbers? We might hope that something about this special case will allow for a faster algorithm than is required by the more general multiplication problem. However, a simple reduction proof serves to show that squaring is "as hard" as multiplying.

The key to the reduction is the following formula:

$$X \times Y = \frac{(X + Y)^2 - (X - Y)^2}{4}.$$

The significance of this formula is that it allows us to convert an arbitrary instance of multiplication to a series of operations involving three addition/subtractions (each of which can be done in linear time), two squarings, and a division by 4. Note that the division by 4 can be done in linear time (simply convert to binary, shift by two digits, and convert back).

This reduction shows that, if a linear time algorithm for squaring can be found, it can be used to construct a linear time algorithm for multiplication.

An example of a useful reduction is multiplication through the use of logarithms. Multiplication is considerably more difficult than addition, since the cost to multiply two n-bit numbers directly is $O(n^2)$, while addition of two n-bit numbers is $O(n)$. Recall from Section 2.3 that one property of logarithms is

$$\log nm = \log n + \log m.$$

Thus, if taking logarithms and anti-logarithms were cheap, then we could reduce multiplication to addition by taking the log of the two operands, adding, and then taking the anti-log of the sum.

Under normal circumstances, taking logarithms and anti-logarithms is expensive, and so this reduction would not be considered practical. However, this reduction is precisely the basis for the sliderule. The sliderule uses a logarithmic scale to measure the lengths of two numbers, in effect doing the conversion to logarithms automatically. These two lengths are then added together, and the inverse logarithm of the sum is read off of another logarithmic scale. The part normally considered expensive (taking logarithms and anti-logarithms) is cheap since it is a physical part of the sliderule. Thus, the entire multiplication process can be done cheaply via a reduction to addition.

Our next example of reduction concerns the multiplication of two $n \times n$ matrices. For this problem, we will assume that the values stored in the matrices are simple integers and that multiplying two simple integers takes constant time. The standard algorithm for multiplying two matrices is to multiply each element of the first matrix's first row by the corresponding element of the second matrix's first column, then adding the numbers. This takes $\Theta(n)$ time. Each of the n^2 elements of the solution are computed in similar fashion, requiring a total of $\Theta(n^3)$ time. Faster algorithms are known, but none are so fast as to be in $O(n^2)$.

Now, consider the case of multiplying two **symmetric** matrices. A symmetric matrix is one in which entry ij is equal to entry ji; that is, the upper right triangle of the matrix is a mirror image of the lower left triangle. Is there something about this restricted case that allows us to multiply two symmetric matrices faster than in the general case? The answer is no, as can be seen by the following reduction. Assume that we have been given two $n \times n$ matrices A and B. We can construct a $2n \times 2n$ symmetric matrix from an arbitrary matrix A as follows:

$$\begin{bmatrix} 0 & A \\ A^{\mathrm{T}} & 0 \end{bmatrix}$$

Here 0 stands for a $n \times n$ matrix composed of zero values, A is the original array, and A^{T} stands for the transpose of matrix A.[1] Note that the resulting matrix is now symmetric. We can convert matrix B to a symmetric matrix in a similar manner. If symmetric matrices could be multiplied "quickly" (in particular, if they could be multiplied together in $\Theta(n^2)$ time), then we could find the result of multiplying two arbitrary $n \times n$ matrices in $\Theta(n^2)$ time by taking advantage of the following observation:

$$\begin{bmatrix} 0 & A \\ A^{\mathrm{T}} & 0 \end{bmatrix} \begin{bmatrix} 0 & B^{\mathrm{T}} \\ B & 0 \end{bmatrix} = \begin{bmatrix} AB & 0 \\ 0 & A^{\mathrm{T}}B^{\mathrm{T}} \end{bmatrix}.$$

In the above formula, AB is the result of multiplying matrices A and B together.

15.3 Hard Problems

This section discusses some really "hard" problems. There are several ways that a problem could be considered hard. First, we might have trouble understanding the definition of the problem itself. Second, we might have trouble finding or understanding an algorithm to solve a problem. Neither of these is what is commonly meant when a computer theoretician uses the word "hard." Throughout this section, "hard" means that the best-known algorithm for the problem is expensive in its running time. One example of a hard problem is Towers of Hanoi. It is simple to understand this problem and its solution. It is also simple to write a program to solve this problem. But, it takes an extremely long time to run for any "reasonably" large value of n. Try running a program to solve Towers of Hanoi for only 30 disks!

The Towers of Hanoi problem takes exponential time, that is, its running time is $\Theta(2^n)$. This is radically different than an algorithm that takes $\Theta(n \log n)$ time or $\Theta(n^2)$ time. It is even radically different from a problem that takes $\Theta(n^4)$time. These are all examples of polynomial running time, since the exponents for all terms of these equations are constants. Recall from Chapter 3 that if we buy a new computer that runs twice as fast, the

---

[1] The transpose operation takes position ij of the original matrix and places it in position ji of the transpose matrix.

size of problem with complexity $\Theta(n^4)$ that we can solve in a certain amount of time is increased by the fourth root of two. In other words, there is a multiplicative factor increase, even if it is a rather small one. This is true for any algorithm whose running time can be represented by a polynomial.

Consider what happens if you buy a computer that is twice as fast and try to solve a bigger Towers of Hanoi problem in a given amount of time. Since its complexity is $\Theta(2^n)$, we can solve a problem only one disk bigger! There is no multiplicative factor, and this is true for any exponential algorithm: A constant factor increase in processing power results in only a fixed addition in problem-solving power.

For the rest of this chapter, we define a **hard algorithm** to be one that runs in exponential time, that is, in $\Omega(c^n)$ for some constant $c > 1$. A definition for a hard *problem* will be presented in the next section.

15.3.1 $\mathcal{NP}$-Completeness

Imagine a magical computer that works by guessing the correct solution from among all of the possible solutions to a problem. Another way to look at this is to imagine a super parallel computer that could test all possible solutions simultaneously. Certainly this magical computer can do anything a normal computer can do. It might also solve some problems more quickly than a normal computer can. Consider some problem where, given a guess for a solution, checking the solution to see if it is correct can be done in polynomial time. Even if the number of possible solutions is exponential, any given guess can be checked in polynomial time (equivalently, all possible solutions are checked simultaneously in polynomial time), and thus the problem can be solved in polynomial time. Conversely, if you cannot get the answer to a problem in polynomial time by guessing the right answer and then checking it, you cannot do it in polynomial time in any other way.

The idea of "guessing" the right answer to a problem – or checking all possible solutions in parallel to determine which is correct – is called **nondeterminism**. An algorithm that works in this manner is called a **nondeterministic algorithm**, and any problem with an algorithm that runs on a nondeterministic machine in polynomial time is given a special name: It is said to be a problem in $\mathcal{NP}$. Thus, problems in $\mathcal{NP}$ are those problems that can be solved in polynomial time on a nondeterministic machine.

Not all problems requiring exponential time on a regular computer are in $\mathcal{NP}$. For example, Towers of Hanoi is *not* in $\mathcal{NP}$, since it must print out

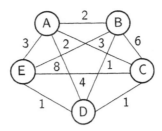

Figure 15.2 An illustration of the TRAVELING SALESMAN problem. Five vertices are shown, with edges between each pair of cities. The problem is to visit all of the cities exactly once, returning to the start city, with the least total cost.

$O(2^n)$ moves for n disks. A nondeterministic machine cannot "guess" and print the correct answer in polynomial time.

On the other hand, consider a problem that is commonly known as the Traveling Salesman Problem.

Definition 15.3 TRAVELING SALESMAN (1)

Input: A complete, directed graph **G** with distances assigned to each edge in the graph.

Output: The shortest simple cycle that includes every vertex.

Figure 15.2 illustrates this problem. Five vertices are shown, with edges and associated costs between each pair of edges. (For simplicity, we assume that the cost is the same in both directions, though this need not be the case.) If the salesman visits the cities in the order ABCDEA, he will travel a total distance of 13. A better route would be ABDCEA, with cost 11. The best route for this particular graph would be ABEDCA, with cost 9.

We cannot solve this problem in polynomial time with a nondeterministic computer. The problem is that, given a candidate cycle, while we can quickly check that the answer is a cycle of the appropriate form, we have no easy way of knowing if it is in fact the *shortest* such cycle. However, we can solve a variant of this problem, which is in the form of a **decision problem**. A decision problem is simply one whose answer is either YES or NO. The decision problem form of TRAVELING SALESMAN is as follows.

Definition 15.4 TRAVELING SALESMAN (2)

Input: A complete, directed graph **G** with distances assigned to each edge in the graph, and an integer K.

Output: YES if there is a simple cycle with total distance $\leq K$ containing every vertex in **G**, and NO otherwise.

We can solve this version of the problem in polynomial time with a nondeterministic computer. The nondeterministic algorithm simply checks all of the possible subsets of edges in the graph, in parallel. If any subset of the edges is an appropriate cycle of total length less than or equal to K, the answer is YES; otherwise the answer is NO. Note that it is only necessary that *some* subset meet the requirement; it does not matter how many subsets fail. Checking a particular subset is done in polynomial time by adding the distances of the edges and verifying that the edges form a cycle that visits each vertex exactly once. Thus, the checking algorithm runs in polynomial time. Unfortunately, there are $|E|!$ subsets to check, so this algorithm cannot be converted to a polynomial time algorithm on a regular computer. Nor does anybody in the world know of any other polynomial time algorithm to solve TRAVELING SALESMAN on a regular computer, despite the fact that the problem has been studied extensively by many computer scientists for many years.

It turns out that there is a large collection of problems with this property: We know efficient nondeterministic algorithms, but we do not know if there are efficient deterministic algorithms. At the same time, we cannot prove that any of these problems do *not* have efficient deterministic algorithms. This class of problems is called $\mathcal{NP}$-**complete**. What is truly strange and fascinating about $\mathcal{NP}$-complete problems is that if anybody ever finds the solution to any one of them that runs in polynomial time on a regular computer, then by a series of reductions, every other problem that is in $\mathcal{NP}$ can also be solved in polynomial time on a regular computer!

A problem X is defined to be $\mathcal{NP}$-complete if

1. X is in $\mathcal{NP}$, and

2. Every other problem in $\mathcal{NP}$ can be reduced to X in polynomial time.

This second requirement may seem to be impossible, but in fact there are hundreds of such problems, including TRAVELING SALESMAN. Another such problem is called K-CLIQUE. K-CLIQUE asks, given an arbitrary undirected graph $\mathbf{G}$, if there is a complete subgraph of at least k vertices. Nobody knows whether there is a polynomial time solution for K-CLIQUE, but if such an algorithm is found for K-CLIQUE *or* for TRAVELING SALESMAN, then that solution can be modified to solve the other, or any other problem in $\mathcal{NP}$, in polynomial time.

The primary theoretical advantage of knowing that a problem P1 is $\mathcal{NP}$-complete is that it can be used to show that another problem P2 is $\mathcal{NP}$-

complete. This is done by finding a polynomial time reduction of P1 to P2. Since we already know that all problems in $\mathcal{NP}$ can be reduced to P1 in polynomial time (by the definition of $\mathcal{NP}$-complete), we now know that all problems can be reduced to P2 as well by the simple algorithm of reducing to P1 and then from there reducing to P2.

There is an extremely practical advantage to knowing that a problem is $\mathcal{NP}$-complete. It relates to knowing that if a polynomial time solution can be found for *any* problem that is $\mathcal{NP}$-complete, then a polynomial solution can be found for *all* such problems. The implication is that,

1. Since no one has yet found such a solution, it must be difficult or impossible to do; and

2. Effort expended to find a polynomial time solution for one $\mathcal{NP}$-complete problem can be considered to have been expended for all $\mathcal{NP}$-complete problems.

How is $\mathcal{NP}$-completeness of practical significance for typical programmers? Well, if your boss demands that you provide a fast algorithm to solve a problem, she will not be happy if you come back saying that the best you could do was an exponential time algorithm. But, if you can find that the problem is $\mathcal{NP}$-complete, while she still won't be happy, at least she should not be mad at you! By showing that your problem is $\mathcal{NP}$-complete, you are in effect saying that the most brilliant computer scientists for the last 30 years have been trying and failing to find a polynomial time algorithm for your problem.

Problems that are solvable in polynomial time on a regular computer are said to be in class $\mathcal{P}$. Clearly, all problems in $\mathcal{P}$ are solvable in polynomial time on a nondeterministic computer simply by neglecting to use the nondeterministic capability. Some problems in $\mathcal{NP}$ are $\mathcal{NP}$-complete. We can consider all problems solvable in exponential time or better as an even bigger class of problems since all problems solvable in polynomial time are solvable in exponential time. Thus, we can view the world of exponential-time-or-better problems in terms of Figure 15.3.

The most important unanswered question in theoretical computer science is whether $\mathcal{P} = \mathcal{NP}$. If they are equal, this means that there is a polynomial time algorithm for TRAVELING SALESMAN and all related problems. Since TRAVELING SALESMAN is known to be $\mathcal{NP}$-complete, if a polynomial time algorithm were to be found for this problem, then *all* problems in $\mathcal{NP}$ would also be solvable in polynomial time. Conversely, if

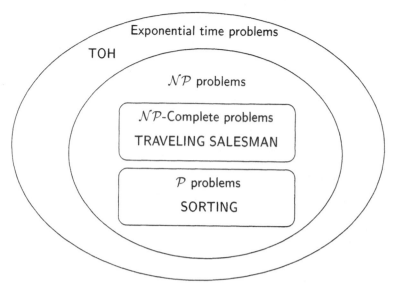

Figure 15.3 Our knowledge regarding the world of problems requiring exponential time or less. Some of these problems are solvable in polynomial time by a nondeterministic computer. Of these, some are known to be $\mathcal{NP}$-complete, and some are known to be solvable in polynomial time on a regular computer.

we were able to prove that TRAVELING SALESMAN has an exponential time lower bound, then we would know that $\mathcal{P} \neq \mathcal{NP}$.

15.3.2 Getting Around $\mathcal{NP}$-Complete Problems

Unfortunately, finding that your problem is $\mathcal{NP}$-complete may not mean that you can just forget about it. Traveling salesmen need to find a reasonable sales route regardless of the complexity of the problem. What do you do when faced with an $\mathcal{NP}$-complete problem that you must solve?

There are several techniques to try. One approach is to run only small instances of the problem. For some problems, this is not acceptable. For example, TRAVELING SALESMAN grows so quickly that it cannot be run on modern computers for problem sizes much over 20 cities. However, some other problems in $\mathcal{NP}$, while requiring exponential time, do not grow so quickly that they do not allow solutions for useful size problems. One such example is the KNAPSACK problem. Given a set of items each with given size and each with given value, and a knapsack of size k, is there a subset of the items whose total size is less than or equal to k and whose total value is greater than or equal to v? While this problem is $\mathcal{NP}$-complete, and so the best-known solution requires exponential running time, it is still solvable for dozens of items with k and v in the thousands.

A second approach to handling $\mathcal{NP}$-complete problems is to solve a special instance of the problem that is not so hard. For example, many problems on graphs are $\mathcal{NP}$-complete, but the same problem on certain restricted types of graphs is not so difficult. For example, the VERTEX COVER problem asks if there is a subset of vertices of size k or less such that every edge in the graph has at least one of its ends in the subset. This is $\mathcal{NP}$-complete in general, but there is a polynomial time solution for bipartite graphs (i.e., graphs whose vertices can be separated into two subsets such that no pair of vertices within one of the subsets has an edge between them).

A third approach is to find an approximate solution to the problem. There are a number of approaches to finding approximate solutions. One way is to use a heuristic to solve the problem, that is, an algorithm based on a "rule of thumb" that does not always give the correct answer. For example, the TRAVELING SALESMAN problem can be solved approximately by using the heuristic that we start at an arbitrary city, and then always proceed to the next unvisited city that is closest. This rarely gives the shortest path, but the solution may be good enough. There are many other heuristics for TRAVELING SALESMAN that do a better job. For some problems, an approximation algorithm can give guaranteed performance, perhaps that the answer will be within a certain percentage of the best possible answer.

15.4 Impossible Problems

Every day professional programmers write programs that go into an infinite loop. Of course, when a program is in an infinite loop, you do not know for sure if it is just a slow program or a program in an infinite loop. After "enough time," you shut it down. Wouldn't it be great if your compiler could look at your program and tell you before you run it that it might get into an infinite loop? Alternatively, given a program and a particular input, it would be useful to know if executing the program on that input will result in an infinite loop without actually running the program.

Unfortunately, the **Halting Problem**, as this is called, cannot be solved. There will never be a computer program that can positively determine if another computer program will halt for all input. Nor will there ever be a computer program that can positively determine if another computer program will halt for a specified input. How can this be? Programmers look at programs regularly to determine if they will halt. Surely this can be programmed. As a warning to those who believe any program can be analyzed, carefully examine the following code fragment before reading on:

```
while (n > 1)
  if (ODD(n))
    n = 3 * n + 1;
  else
    n = n / 2;
```

This is a famous piece of code. The sequence of values that is assigned to n by this code is sometimes called the **Collatz sequence** for input value n. Does this code fragment halt for all values of n? Nobody knows the answer. Every input that has been tried halts. But does it always halt? Note that for this code fragment, since we do not know if it halts, we also do not know an upper bound for its running time. As for the lower bound, we can easily show $\Omega(\log n)$ (see Exercise 3.11).

Personally, I have faith that someday some smart person will completely analyze this program, and prove once and for all that the code fragment halts for all values of n. Doing so may well give us techniques that advance our ability to analyze programs in general. Unfortunately, proofs from **computability** – the branch of computer science that studies what is impossible to do with a computer – compel us to believe that there will always be another program that we cannot analyze. This comes as a result of the fact that the Halting Problem is unsolvable.

15.4.1 Uncountability

Before proving that the Halting Problem is unsolvable, we first prove that not all functions can be programmed. This is so because the number of programs is much smaller than the number of possible functions.

> **Definition 15.5** A set is said to be **countable** if every member of the set can be uniquely assigned to a positive integer. A set is said to be **uncountable** if it is not possible to assign every member of the set to a positive integer.

To understand what is meant when we say "assigned to a positive integer," imagine that there is an infinite row of bins, labeled 1, 2, 3, and so on. Take a set and start placing members of the set into bins, with at most one member per bin. If we can find a way to assign all of the members to bins, then the set is countable. For example, consider the set of positive even integers 2, 4, and so on. We can assign an integer i to bin $i/2$ (or, if we don't mind skipping some bins, then we can assign even number i to bin i). Thus, the set of even integers is countable. This should be no surprise, since there seems to be "fewer" positive even integers than there are positive integers. Interestingly, there are not really any more positive integers than there are positive even integers, since we can uniquely assign every positive integer to some positive even integer by simply assigning positive integer i to positive even integer $2i$.

Are the number of programs countable or uncountable? A program can be viewed as simply a string of characters (including special punctuation, spaces, and line breaks). Let us assume that the number of different characters that can appear in a program is P. (In the ASCII character set, P must be less than 128, but the actual number does not matter). If the number of strings is countable, then surely the number of programs is also countable. We can assign strings to the bins as follows. Assign the null string to the first bin. Now, take all strings of one character, and assign them to the next P bins in "alphabetic" or ASCII code order. Next, take all strings of two characters, and assign them to the next P^2 bins, again in ASCII code order working from left to right. Strings of three characters are likewise assigned to bins, then strings of length four, and so on. In this way, a string of any given length can be assigned to some bin.

By this process, any string of finite length is assigned to some bin. Thus, any program, which is merely a string of finite length, is assigned to some bin. All programs are assigned to some bin, and so the set of all programs is countable. Naturally most of the strings in the bins are not legal programs, but this is irrelevant. All that matters is that the strings that *do* correspond to programs are also in the bins.

Now we consider the number of possible functions. To keep things simple, assume that all functions take a single positive integer as input, and yield a single positive integer as output. We will call such functions **integer functions**. A function is simply a mapping from input values to output values. Of course, not all computer programs literally take integers as input and yield integers as output. However, everything that computers read and write is essentially a series of numbers, which may be interpreted as letters or something else. Any useful computer program's input and output can be coded as integer values, so our simple model of computer input and output is sufficiently general to cover all possible computer programs.

1		2		3		4		5
x	$f_1(x)$	x	$f_2(x)$	x	$f_3(x)$	x	$f_4(x)$	
1	1	1	1	1	7	1	15	
2	1	2	2	2	9	2	1	
3	1	3	3	3	11	3	7	
4	1	4	4	4	13	4	13	
5	1	5	5	5	15	5	2	
6	1	6	6	6	17	6	7	
⋮	⋮	⋮	⋮	⋮	⋮	⋮	⋮	

Figure 15.4 An illustration of assigning functions to bins.

We now wish to see if it is possible to assign all of the integer functions to the infinite set of bins. If so, then the number of functions is countable, and it might then be possible to assign every integer function to a program. If the set of integer functions cannot be assigned to bins, then there will be integer functions that must have no corresponding program.

Imagine each integer function as a table with two columns and an infinite number of rows. The first column lists the positive integers starting at 1. The second column lists the output of the function when given the value in the first column as input. Thus, the table explicitly describes the mapping from input to output for each function. Call this a **function table**.

Next we will try to assign function tables to bins. To do so we must order the functions, but it does not matter what order we choose. For example, bin 1 could store the function that always returns 1 regardless of the input value. Bin 2 could store the function that returns its input. Bin 3 could store the function that doubles its input and adds 5. Bin 4 could store a function for which we can see no simple relationship between input and output. These four functions as assigned to the first four bins are shown in Figure 15.4.

Can we assign every function to a bin? The answer is no, because there is always a way to create a new function that is not in any of the bins. Suppose that somebody presents a way of assigning functions to bins that they claim includes all of the functions. We can build a new function that has not been assigned to any bin, as follows. Take the output value for input 1 from the function in the first bin. Call this value $F_1(1)$. Add 1 to it, and assign the result as the output of a new function for input value 1. Regardless of the remaining values assigned to our new function, it must be different

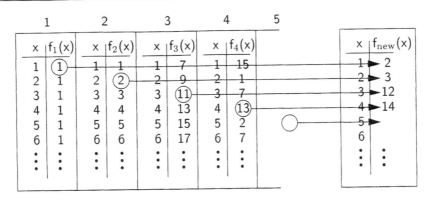

Figure 15.5 Illustration for the argument that the number of integer functions is uncountable.

from the first function in the table, since the two give different outputs for input 1. Now take the output value for 2 from the second function in the table (known as $F_2(2)$). Add 1 to this value and assign it as the output for 2 in our new function. Thus, our new function must be different from function 2, since they will differ at least at the second value. Continue in this manner, assigning $F_{new}(i) = F_i(i) + 1$ for all values i. Thus, the new function must be different from any function F_i at least at position i. Since the new function is different from every other function, it must not already be in the table. This is true no matter how we try to assign functions to bins, and so the number of integer functions is uncountable. The significance of this is that not all functions can possibly be assigned to programs; there *must* be functions with no corresponding program. Figure 15.5 illustrates this argument.

15.4.2   The Halting Problem is Unsolvable

While it is theoretically interesting to know that there exists *some* function that cannot be computed by a computer program, does this mean that there is any *useful* problem that cannot be computed? Now we will prove that the Halting Problem cannot be computed by any computer program. The proof is by contradiction.

We begin by assuming that there is a function named `halt` that can solve the Halting Problem. Obviously, it is not possible to write out something that does not exist, but here is a plausible sketch of what a function to solve the Halting Problem might look like if it did exist. Function `halt` takes two inputs: a string representing the source code for a Java program or function, and another string representing the input that we wish to determine if the input program or function halts on. Function **halt** returns **true** if the input program or function does halt on the given input, and **false** otherwise.

```
bool halt(char[] prog, char[] input)
{
  Code to solve halting problem
  if (prog does halt on input) then
    return(true);
  else
    return(false);
}
```

We now will examine two simple functions, that clearly can exist since the complete Java code for them is presented here:

```
boolean selfhalt(char[] prog) {
  // Return TRUE if program halts when given itself as input.
  if (halt(prog, prog))
    return(true);
  else
    return(false);
}
```

```
void contrary(char[] prog) {
  if (selfhalt(prog))
    while(true); // Go into an infinite loop
}
```

What happens when function **contrary** is run on itself? One possibility is that the call to **selfhalt** returns **true**; that is, **selfhalt** claims that **contrary** will halt when run on itself. In that case, **contrary** goes into an infinite loop (and thus does not halt). On the other hand, if **selfhalt** returns **false**, then **halt** is proclaiming that **contrary** does not halt on itself, and **contrary** then returns, that is, it halts. Thus, **contrary** does the contrary of what **halt** says that it will do.

The action of **contrary** is logically inconsistent with the assumption that **halt** solves the Halting Problem correctly. There are no other assumptions we made that might cause this inconsistency. Thus, by contradiction, we have proved that **halt** cannot solve the Halting Problem correctly, and thus there is no program that can solve the Halting Problem.

Now that we have proved that the Halting Problem is unsolvable, we can use reduction arguments to prove that other problems are also unsolvable. The strategy is to assume the existence of a computer program that solves the problem in question, and use that program to solve another problem that is already known to be unsolvable.

For example, consider the following variation on the Halting Problem. Given a computer program, will it halt when its input is the empty string (i.e., will it halt when it is given no input)? To prove that this problem is unsolvable, we will employ a standard technique for computability proofs: Use a computer program to modify another computer program.

Assume that there is a function `Ehalt` that determines whether a given program halts when given no input. Recall that our proof for the Halting Problem involved functions that took as parameters a string representing a program and another string representing an input. Consider another function `combine` that takes a program P and an input string I as parameters. Function `combine` modifies P to store I as a static variable S, and further modifies all calls to input functions within P to instead get its input from S. Call the resulting program P'. It should take no stretch of the imagination to believe that any decent compiler could be modified to take computer programs and input strings, and produce a new computer program that has been modified in this way. Now, take P' and feed it to `Ehalt`. If `Ehalt` says that P' will halt, then we know that P would halt on input I. In other words, we now have a procedure for solving the original Halting Problem. The only assumption that we made was the existence of `Ehalt`. Thus, the problem of determining if a program will halt on no input must be unsolvable.

15.4.3 Determining Program Behavior is Unsolvable

There are many things that we would like to have a computer do that are unsolvable. Many of these have to do with program behavior. For example, proving that a program is "correct," that is, proving that a program computes a particular function, is a proof regarding program behavior. As such, what can be accomplished is severely limited. In particular, it is not possible to reliably determine if a particular program computes a particular function. Nor is it possible to determine whether a particular line of code in a particular program will ever be executed.

This does *not* mean that a computer program cannot be written that works on special cases, possibly even on most programs that we would be interested in checking. For example, some **C** compilers will check if the control expression for a `while` loop is a constant expression that evaluates to `false`. If it is, the compiler will issue a warning that the `while` loop code will never be executed. However, it is not possible to write a computer program that can check for *all* input programs whether a specified line of code will be executed when the program is given some specified input.

Another unsolvable problem is whether a program contains a computer virus. The property "contains a computer virus" is a matter of behavior. Thus, it is not possible to determine positively whether an arbitrary program contains a computer virus. Fortunately, there are many good heuristics for determining if a program is likely to contain a virus, and it is usually possible to determine if a program contains a particular virus, at least for the ones that are now known. Real virus checkers do a pretty good job. But, it will always be possible for malicious people to invent new viruses that no existing virus checker can recognize.

15.5 Further Reading

The classic text on the theory of $\mathcal{NP}$-completeness is *Computers and Intractability: A Guide to the Theory of $\mathcal{NP}$-completeness* by Garey and Johnston [GJ79]. *The Traveling Salesman Problem*, edited by Lawler et al. [LLKS85], discusses many approaches to finding an acceptable solution to this particular $\mathcal{NP}$-complete problem in a reasonable amount of time.

For more information about the Collatz function see "On the ups and downs of hailstone numbers" by B. Hayes, "Computer Recreations" in Scientific American, Jan. 1984, and "The $3x + 1$ problem and its generalizations" by J.C. Lagarias in American Mathematical Monthly, Jan. 1985.

For an introduction to the field of computability and impossible problems, see *Discrete Structures, Logic, and Computability* by James L. Hein [Hei95].

15.6 Exercises

15.1 Consider this algorithm for finding the maximum element in an array: Find the maximum element by first sorting the array and then selecting the last (maximum) element. What (if anything) does this reduction tell us about the upper and lower bounds to the problem of finding the maximum element in a sequence? Why can we not reduce SORTING to finding the maximum element?

15.2 Use a reduction to prove that squaring a $n \times n$ matrix is just as expensive as multiplying two $n \times n$ matrices.

15.3 Use a reduction to prove that multiplying two upper triangular $n \times n$ matrices is just as expensive as multiplying two arbitrary $n \times n$ matrices.

15.4 **(a)** Explain why computing the factorial of n by multiplying all values from 1 to n together is an exponential time algorithm.

     (b) Explain why computing an approximation to the factorial of n by making use of Stirling's formula (see Section 2.2) is a polynomial time algorithm.

15.5 A **Hamiltonian cycle** in graph G is a cycle that visits every vertex in the graph exactly once before returning to the start vertex. The problem HAMILTONIAN CYCLE asks whether graph G does in fact contain a Hamiltonian cycle. Assuming that HAMILTONIAN CYCLE is $\mathcal{NP}$-complete, prove that TRAVELING SALESMAN is $\mathcal{NP}$-complete.

15.6 Assuming that VERTEX COVER is $\mathcal{NP}$-complete, prove that K-CLIQUE is $\mathcal{NP}$-complete by finding a polynomial time reduction from VERTEX COVER to K-CLIQUE.

15.7 Assuming that K-CLIQUE is $\mathcal{NP}$-complete, prove that VERTEX COVER is $\mathcal{NP}$-complete by finding a polynomial time reduction from K-CLIQUE to VERTEX COVER.

15.8 Prove that the set of real numbers is uncountable. Use a proof similar to the one used in Section 15.4.1 to prove that the set of integer functions is uncountable.

15.9 Here is another version of the knapsack problem, which we will call EXACT KNAPSACK. Given a set of items each with given integer size, and a knapsack of size integer k, is there a subset of the items which fits exactly within the knapsack?

Assuming that EXACT KNAPSACK is $\mathcal{NP}$-complete, use a reduction argument to prove that KNAPSACK is $\mathcal{NP}$-complete.

15.10 Prove, using a reduction argument such as given in Section 15.4.2, that the problem of determining if a program will print any output is unsolvable.

15.11 Prove, using a reduction argument such as given in Section 15.4.2, that the problem of determining if a program executes a particular statement within that program is unsolvable.

15.12 Prove, using a reduction argument such as given in Section 15.4.2, that the problem of determining if two programs halt on the same inputs is unsolvable.

15.13 Prove, using a reduction argument such as given in Section 15.4.2, that the problem of determining whether there is some input on which two programs will both halt is unsolvable.

15.7 Projects

15.1 Implement VERTEX COVER; that is, given graph **G** and integer K, answer the question of whether or not there is a vertex cover of size K or less. Begin by using a brute-force algorithm of checking all possible sets of vertices of size K to find an acceptable vertex cover, and measure the running time on a number of input graphs. Then try to reduce the running time through the use of any heuristics you can think of. Next, try to find approximate solutions to the problem in the sense of finding the smallest set of vertices that forms a vertex cover.

15.2 Implement KNAPSACK. Measure its running time on a number of inputs. What is the largest practical input size for this problem?

15.3 Implement an approximation of TRAVELING SALESMAN; that is, given a graph **G** with costs for all edges, find the cheapest cycle that visits all vertices in **G**. Try various heuristics to find the best approximations for a wide variety of input graphs.

15.4 Write a program that, given a positive integer n as input, prints out the Collatz sequence for that number. What can you say about the types of integers that have long Collatz sequences? What can you say about the length of the Collatz sequence for various groups of integers?

Part V

Appendix

A

Java Tutorial for C and Pascal Programmers

This appendix offers a brief tutorial introduction to Java for **C** and Pascal programmers. This tutorial will not teach you how to program in Java. It merely attempts to provide enough background so that you can understand the code examples in the book.

The tutorial consists of three examples taken from Chapter 4. Each section begins with the code, followed by a description of the new Java syntax introduced. Once you understand the Java syntax embodied in these examples, you should be able to understand all of the Java code used in this book.

The first example presents the `List` interface. A Java interface can be used to describe an ADT. No implementation for lists is presented at this point. Example 2 shows part of the array-based implementation for lists. Example 3 contains the `Link` class and selected member functions from the linked list implementation.

Before getting started with the code examples, we should begin with a few words about Java and classes. Java is an object-oriented programming language. Readers familiar with **C++** will find Java easy to learn, since Java is a "purer" object-oriented programming language than **C++**. Java is also a fairly small language. Most of the syntax is taken from **C**, though Java is by no means a superset or a subset of **C**. Most of what a **C** programmer needs to learn to read Java programs is the syntax for classes.

On the surface, a class is something like a **C** structure or a Pascal record. However, a class is more than this. A class contains **members**. There are two types of members: data members (variables) and member functions. The member functions perform the operations associated with the class. Every function in Java is a member of some class – there are no "free" functions unassociated with any class. Java programs are simply a collection of classes, with the "main" routine a member function of some class. Nearly all of the code examples contained in this book are implementations for classes, or member functions of classes.

A.1   Example 1: Interface for Lists

```
1     public interface List {           // List ADT
2        public void clear();           // Remove all Objects
3        public void insert(Object item); // Insert Object at curr
4        public void append(Object item); // Insert Object at tail
5        public Object remove();        // Remove/return Object
6        public void setFirst();        // Set current to first pos
7        public void next();            // Move current to next pos
8        public void prev();            // Move current to prev pos
9        public int length();           // Return current length
10       public void setPos(int pos);   // Set current to pos
11       public void setValue(Object val); // Set current Object
12       public Object currValue();     // Return value of Object
13       public boolean isEmpty();      // True if list is empty
14       public boolean isInList();     // True if within list
15       public void print();           // Print list elements
16    } // interface List
```

Our first example shows an interface. An interface does not actually implement a Java class. Instead, it specifies some functions and associated parameter types that a class claiming to implement the interface must have. Here we use an interface to define the list ADT.

Line 1 specifies that this is an interface whose name is List, and that this interface is public, that is, all parts of the Java program know about the existence of the List interface. Line 1 also illustrates the syntax for a Java comment. Any text to the right of the // symbol is a comment, and so is ignored by the compiler.

Lines 2–15 present a series of member functions that must be implemented by any class claiming to implement the List interface. Each of these functions is also declared public, meaning that they are all available for use by users of a List object. Function clear on line 2 is declared to have void as its return type. This means that it does not return any value. Function clear also has no input parameters.

Function insert also has no return value, but it has one parameter. This parameter is of type Object. An Object is the most generic type in Java. This means that the parameter can actually be of any class, since all classes are subclasses of Object, and since an actual parameter may be a subclass of the formal parameter type.

Function isEmpty on line 13 has a return value of type boolean, which is Java's Boolean type.

A.2   Example 2: Array-Based List Implementation

```
1     class AList implements List {    // Array-based list
2       private static final int defaultSize = 10;
3       private int msize;               // Maximum size of list
4       private int numInList;           // Actual number in list
5       private int curr;                // Position of current Object
6       private Object[] listArray;      // Array holding list Objects
7
8       AList() { setup(defaultSize); } // Constructor: fixed size
9
10      AList(int sz) { setup(sz); }     // Constructor: default size
11
12      private void setup(int sz) {     // Do actual initializations
13        msize = sz;
14        numInList = curr = 0;
15        listArray = new Object[sz];    // Create listArray
16      }
17
18      public void clear()              // Remove Objects from list
19      { numInList = curr = 0; }        //    Reinitialize values
20
21      public void insert(Object it) { // Insert Object
22        Assert.notFalse(numInList < msize, "List is full");
23        Assert.notFalse((curr >=0) && (curr <= numInList),
24                        "Bad value for curr");
25        for (int i=numInList; i>curr; i--) // Shift Objects
26          listArray[i] = listArray[i-1];
27        listArray[curr] = it;
28        numInList++;                   // Increment current size
29      }
30
31      public Object currValue() {      // Return current value
32        Assert.notFalse(isInList(), "No current element");
33        return listArray[curr];
34      }
35
36      public void print() {            // Print all list's Objects
37        if (isEmpty()) System.out.println("()");
38        else {
39          System.out.print("( ");
40          for (setFirst(); isInList(); next())
41            System.out.print(currValue() + " ");
42          System.out.println(")");
43        }
44      }
45    } // class Alist
```

This example presents selected parts of the array-based list implementation. It comes in the form of a Java class named `Alist`.

Line 1 indicates that we are defining a class named `Alist`. This class implements an interface named `List`. By "implements" we mean that `Alist` contains functions with the correct parameters and return type as specified by interface `List`.

Lines 2–6 declare the private data members of this class. Private members are used by the class, but are not available for use by other classes. Thus, their contents are protected from inappropriate access from other parts of the program.

Line 3 shows the declaration of a constant value. The keyword `static` indicates that there is only one copy of this variable shared among all `Alist` objects. Normally, each `Alist` object will get its own copy of each data member. However, member `defaultSize` will be created only once and then be shared by the various instances of `Alist` variables. The keyword `final` indicates that the value for this variable cannot be changed later in the program.

Lines 2-6 declare the four regular data members for the class. Each `Alist` object will have its own copy of each data member. The first three data members are integers; the fourth one is an array of type `Object`. Note that the variable declaration of line 6 does not actually declare any space for `listArray`. This will be done later.

Lines 8 and 10 show two **constructors** for the class. You can tell that these are constructors because they have the name of the class, and they have no return type. A constructor for an object is called whenever a new instance of the object is created. An object is created dynamically from free store using the `new` operator (we will see an example of this further on). In this example, the constructors cause an array to be allocated each time an `Alist` object is created.

Note that there are two versions of the the constructor. This is an example of **overloading**. Any member function can be overloaded in this way, so long as each version has a distinct set of parameter types. The distinct parameter types allow the compiler to distinguish which version is being referenced in a function call.

One version of the constructor takes an integer parameter and the other does not. In the version with the parameter, the parameter specifies the size of the array to be allocated. The version with no parameter sets the size of the array to be `defaultSize`. Both versions of the the constructor call a private member function **setup**, shown on lines 12–16. Function **setup** is not accessible except by other member functions of class **Alist**. It does the actual work of initializing a new **Alist** object.

Line 15 allocates space for array **listArray** using the **new** operator. This line says that the array will be given space for **sz** references to type **Object**. References are similar to pointers in a language such as **C** or Pascal. Note that this line *does not* allocate an array of **Object** variables, but merely an array of pointers to **Object** variables. Initially, these pointers are set to **null**. As the list is filled with data elements, these pointers will point to real data. By making the type be **Object**, we are using the most generic type possible. The actual data elements may be of any subclass of **Object**, which means any class at all.

Note that line 13 of function **setup** assigns a value to variable **msize**. Variable **msize** has not been declared in this function. Thus, it is referring to **Alist**'s data member **msize**.

Lines 22 and 23 of function **insert** show the syntax for calling a member function for some class. The normal syntax is "**object.funcname(params)**" where **object** is some variable of the class type. Lines 22 and 23 show a special case of this general syntax. Java has no concept of a function separate from the member functions of a particular class. In this case, the class is **Assert** and the member function is **notFalse**. **Assert** is the class, not an instance of an object of that class (i.e., not a variable). It would be rather silly to be required to allocate a "variable" of class **Assert** to make a call to one of its member functions. So, Java allows programmers to declare a member function to be of type **static**, which means in this case that it may be accessed using the class name rather than a variable of that class.

Note that the calls to member **setup** on lines 8 and 10 appear to violate the syntax for calling a class member function just discussed. Just as the use of variable **msize** on line 13 is assumed to refer to a member of class **Alist**, so does the reference to **setup** on lines 8 and 10.

The **print** function of lines 36 to 44 illustrates the syntax for writing output. The calls on lines 37, 41, and 42 to functions **System.out.print()** and **System.out.println()** are further examples of calling a static member function from some class (in this case, the **out** class of Java standard package **System**). These functions both take a parameter of type **String**. **System.out.println()** appends a newline character to the end of the string. Line 41 illustrates use of both type conversion and string concatenation. Function **currValue** returns a reference to an object of type **Object**. It is assumed that the object has some string representation for itself. Those objects that have none defined will be given a default string representation by the compiler. The "+" symbol in line 41 indicates that a space will be concatenated onto the string generated for currValue.

A.3   Example 3: Linked List Implementation

```
1     class Link {                    // A singly linked list node
2       private Object element;    // Object for this node
3       private Link next;          // Pointer to next node in list
4       Link(Object it, Link nextval)        // Constructor 1
5         { element = it;  next = nextval; }  //  Given Object
6       Link(Link nextval) { next = nextval; } // Constructor 2
7       Link next() { return next; }
8       Link setNext(Link nextval) { return next = nextval; }
9       Object element() { return element; }
10      Object setElement(Object it) { return element = it; }
11    } // class Link
12
13    ///////////////////////////////////////////////////////////////
14
15    public class LList implements List { // Linked list class
16      private Link head;                // Pointer to list header
17      private Link tail;                // Pointer to last Object
18      protected Link curr;              // Position of current Object
19
20      LList(int sz) { setup(); }        // Constructor -- Ignore sz
21      LList() { setup(); }              // Constructor
22
23      private void setup()
24      { tail = head = curr = new Link(null); } // Create header
25
26      public void clear() {             // Remove all Objects
27        head.setNext(null);
28        curr = tail = head;             // Reinitialize
29      }
30
31      // Insert Object at current position
32      public void insert(Object it) {
33        Assert.notNull(curr, "No current element");
34        curr.setNext(new Link(it, curr.next()));
35        if (tail == curr)               // Appended new Object
36          tail = curr.next();
37      }
38
39      public Object remove() {          // Remove and return Object
40        if (!isInList()) return null;
41        Object it = curr.next().element();   // Remember value
42        if (tail == curr.next()) tail = curr; // Set tail
43        curr.setNext(curr.next().next());    // Remove from list
44        return it;                      // Return value
45      }
46    } // class LList
```

This example shows two classes: The Link class for linked list nodes, and part of the LList class to implement linked lists. This example presents only a few new instances of Java syntax.

Note that class LList is declared **public** while class Link is not. The idea is that users of the linked list need access to class LList, while class Link is only a helper for class LList and not meant to be public. Depending on how the classes are organized into files, the Java **package** facility can be used to hide the existence of the Link class from outside users. The details for doing such hiding are beyond the scope of this tutorial.

Line 18 shows a data member declared as **protected**. Protected members have a status between public and private. In particular, only members of classes derived from class LList can use this variable. Variable **curr** has been declared **protected** because an extension of the linked list class, named **GraphList**, is used by the adjacency list graph implementation of Chapter 7.

Line 24 shows a typical allocation of space for an object using the **new** operator. Note again that declaring a variable of some class type does not actually allocate space of that type. Rather, the variable is merely a reference to the object. A call to **new** is required to make the necessary space. In line 24, a new Link object is created (using the Link class constructor of line 6), and the three references named tail, head, and curr are each assigned to point to this new Link object.

Line 27 shows a typical access to an object's member function. Here the Link class member function setNext is being called. The syntax is object.funcname(params). Here, the object is the Link variable named head. The parameter in this example is the "null" pointer value.

Line 41 again shows a call to a class member function, but here a series of calls is being made. The term curr.next().element() has two instances of the "." operator. This is processed from left to right. Thus, curr.next() is invoked to return a Link reference. The element function of this returned Link reference is then called.

Bibliography

[Ada79]   James L. Adams. *Conceptual Blockbusting*. Norton, New York, second edition, 1979.

[AHU74]   Alfred V. Aho, John E. Hopcroft, and Jeffrey D. Ullman. *The Design and Analysis of Computer Algorithms*. Addison-Wesley, Reading, MA, 1974.

[AHU83]   Alfred V. Aho, John E. Hopcroft, and Jeffrey D. Ullman. *Data Structures and Algorithms*. Addison Wesley, Reading, MA, 1983.

[App85]   Apple Computer, Inc. *Inside Macintosh*, volume I. Addison-Wesley, Reading, MA, 1985.

[BB88]   G. Brassard and P. Bratley. *Algorithmics: Theory and Practice*. Prentice Hall, Englewood Cliffs, NJ, 1988.

[Ben75]   John Louis Bentley. Multidimensional binary search trees used for associative searching. *Communications of the ACM*, 18(9):509–517, September 1975. ISSN: 0001-0782.

[Ben82]   John Louis Bentley. *Writing Efficient Programs*. Prentice Hall, Englewood Cliffs, NJ, 1982.

[Ben84]   John Louis Bentley. Programming pearls: The back of the envelope. *Communications of the ACM*, 27(3):180–184, March 1984.

[Ben85]   John Louis Bentley. Programming pearls: Thanks, heaps. *Communications of the ACM*, 28(3):245–250, March 1985.

[Ben86a]   John Bentley. *Programming Pearls*. Addison-Wesley, Reading, MA, 1986.

[Ben86b]   John Louis Bentley. Programming pearls: The envelope is back. *Communications of the ACM*, 29(3):176–182, March 1986.

473

[Ben88]   John Bentley. *More Programming Pearls: Confessions of a Coder.* Addison-Wesley, Reading, MA, 1988.

[BM85]   John Louis Bentley and Catherine C. McGeoch. Amortized analysis of self-organizing sequential search heuristics. *Communications of the ACM*, 28(4):404–411, April 1985.

[Bro75]   Frederick P. Brooks. *The Mythical Man-Month: Essays on Software Engineering.* Addison-Wesley, Reading, MA, 1975.

[BSTW86]   John Louis Bentley, Daniel D. Sleator, Robert E. Tarjan, and Victor K. Wei. A locally adaptive data compression scheme. *Communications of the ACM*, 29(4):320–330, April 1986.

[CLR90]   Thomas H. Cormen, Charles E. Leiserson, and Ronald L. Rivest. *Introduction to Algorithms.* The MIT Press, Cambridge, MA, 1990.

[Com79]   Douglas Comer. The ubiquitous b-tree. *Computing Surveys*, 11(2):121–137, June 1979.

[Dei90]   Harvey M. Deitel. *Operating Systems.* Addison-Wesley, Reading, MA, second edition, 1990.

[ECW92]   Vladimir Estivill-Castro and Derick Wood. A survey of adaptive sorting algorithms. *Computing Surveys*, 24(4):441–476, December 1992.

[ED88]   R.J. Enbody and H.C. Du. Dynamic hashing schemes. *Computing Surveys*, 20(2):85–113, June 1988.

[Epp95]   Susanna S. Epp. *Discrete Mathematics with Applications.* Wadsworth Publishing Company, Belmont, CA, second edition, 1995.

[FBY92]   W.B. Frakes and R. Baeza-Yates, editors. *Information Retrieval: Data Structures & Algorithms.* Prentice Hall, Englewood Cliffs, NJ, 1992.

[FF89]   Daniel P. Friedman and Matthias Felleisen. *The Little LISPer.* Macmillan Publishing Company, New York, 1989.

[FHCD92]   Edward A. Fox, Lenwood S. Heath, Q. F. Chen, and Amjad M. Daoud. Practical minimal perfect hash functions for large databases. *Communications of the ACM*, 35(1):105–121, January 1992.

[Fla96]   David Flanagan. *Java in a Nutshell.* O'Reilly & Associates, Inc., Sebatopol, CA, 1996.

[FZ92]   M.J. Folk and B. Zoellick. *File Structures: A Conceptual Toolkit.* Addison-Wesley, Reading, MA, second edition, 1992.

[GI91]   Zvi Galil and Giuseppe F. Italiano. Data structures and algorithms for disjoint set union problems. *Computing Surveys,* 23(3):319–344, September 1991.

[GJ79]   Michael R. Garey and David S. Johnson. *Computers and Intractability: A Guide to the Theory of NP-Completeness.* W.H. Freeman, New York, 1979.

[GKP89]   Ronald L. Graham, Donald E. Knuth, and Oren Patashnik. *Concrete Mathematics: A Foundation for Computer Science.* Addison-Wesley, Reading, MA, 1989.

[Gla93]   Graham Glass. *UNIX for Programmers and Users.* Prentice Hall, Englewood Cliffs, NJ, 1993.

[Gle92]   James Gleick. *Genius: The Life and Science of Richard Feynman.* Vintage, New York, 1992.

[Hei95]   James L. Hein. *Discrete Structures, Logic, and Computability.* Jones and Bartlett, Sudbury, MA, 1995.

[Jay90]   Julian Jaynes. *The Origin of Consciousness in the Breakdown of the Bicameral Mind.* Houghton Mifflin, Boston, MA, 1990.

[Knu73]   Donald E. Knuth. *The Art of Computer Programming: Fundamental Algorithms,* volume 1. Addison-Wesley, Reading, MA, second edition, 1973.

[Knu81]   Donald E. Knuth. *The Art of Computer Programming: Sorting and Searching,* volume 3. Addison-Wesley, Reading, MA, second edition, 1981.

[Knu94]   Donald E. Knuth. *The Stanford GraphBase.* Addison-Wesley, Reading, MA, 1994.

[KP78]   Brian W. Kernighan and P.J. Plauger. *The Elements of Programming Style.* McGraw-Hill, New York, second edition, 1978.

[Lam93]   Leslie Lamport. How to write a proof. Technical Report 94, DEC Systems Research Center, February 1993.

[LLKS85]   E.L. Lawler, J.K. Lenstra, A.H.G. Rinnooy Kan, and D.B. Shmoys, editors. *The Traveling Salesman Problem: A Guided Tour of Combinatorial Optimization.* John Wiley & Sons, New York, 1985.

[LP81]   Harry R. Lewis and Christos H. Papadimitriou. *Elements of the Theory of Computation*. Prentice Hall, Englewood Cliffs, NJ, 1981.

[Man89]   Udi Manber. *Introduction to Algorithms: A Creative Approach*. Addision-Wesley, Reading, MA, 1989.

[Pól57]   George Pólya. *How To Solve It*. Princeton University Press, Princeton, NJ, second edition, 1957.

[Pug90]   W. Pugh. Skip lists: A probabilistic alternative to balanced trees. *Communications of the ACM*, 33(6):668–676, June 1990.

[Raw92]   Gregory J.E. Rawlins. *Compared to What? An Introduction to the Analysis of Algorithms*. Computer Science Press, New York, 1992.

[Rob84]   Fred S. Roberts. *Applied Combinatorics*. Prentice Hall, Englewood Cliffs, NJ, 1984.

[Rob86]   Eric S. Roberts. *Thinking Recursively*. John Wiley & Sons, New York, 1986.

[RW94]   Chris Ruemmler and John Wilkes. An introduction to disk drive modeling. *IEEE Computer*, 27(3):17–28, March 1994.

[Sal88]   Betty Salzberg. *File Structures: An Analytic Approach*. Prentice Hall, Englewood Cliffs, NJ, 1988.

[Sam90a]   Hanan Samet. *Applications of Spatial Data Structures*. Addison-Wesley, Reading, MA, 1990.

[Sam90b]   Hanan Samet. *Design and Analysis of Spatial Data Structures*. Addison-Wesley, Reading, MA, 1990.

[SB93]   Clifford A. Shaffer and Patrick R. Brown. A paging scheme for pointer-based quadtrees. In D. Abel and B-C. Ooi, editors, *Advances in Spatial Databases*, pages 89–104, Springer Verlag, Berlin, June 1993.

[Sed80]   Robert Sedgewick. *Quicksort*. Garland Publishing, Inc., New York, 1980.

[Sed88]   Robert Sedgewick. *Algorithms*. Addison-Wesley, Reading, MA, second edition, 1988.

[Sel95]   Kevin Self. Technically speaking. *IEEE Spectrum*, 32(2):59, February 1995.

[SJH93]   Clifford A. Shaffer, Ramana Juvvadi, and Lenwood S. Heath. A generalized comparison of quadtree and bintree storage requirements. *Image and Vision Computing*, 11(7):402–412, September 1993.

[SM83]   Gerard Salton and Michael J. McGill. *Introduction to Modern Information Retrieval*. McGraw Hill, New York, 1983.

[Sol90]   Daniel Solow. *How to Read and Do Proofs*. John Wiley & Sons, New York, second edition, 1990.

[ST85]   D.D. Sleator and Robert E. Tarjan. Self-adjusting binary search trees. *Journal of the ACM*, 32:652–686, 1985.

[Sta94]   Richard M. Stallman. *GNU Emacs Manual*. Free Software Foundation, Cambridge, MA, tenth edition, July 1994.

[Ste84]   Guy L. Steele. *Common Lisp: The Language*. Digital Press, Bedford, MA, 1984.

[Sto88]   James A. Storer. *Data Compression: Methods and Theory*. Computer Science Press, Rockville, MD, 1988.

[Tan90]   Andrew S. Tanenbaum. *Structured Computer Organization*. Prentice Hall, Englewood Cliffs, NJ, third edition, 1990.

[Tar75]   Robert E. Tarjan. Efficiency of a good but not linear set merging algorithm. *Journal of the ACM*, 22(2):215–225, April 1975.

[TRE88]   Pete Thomas, Hugh Robinson, and Judy Emms. *Abstract Data Types: Their Specification, Representation, and Use*. Clarendon Press, Oxford, 1988.

[Wel88]   Dominic Welsh. *Codes and Cryptography*. Oxford University Press, Oxford, 1988.

[WN96]   Patrick Henry Winston and Sundar Narasimhan. *On to Java*. Addison-Wesley, Reading, MA, 1996.

Index

abstract data type (ADT), 7–10, 14, 16, 463, 465
accounting, 103, 110
Ackermann's function, 185
activation record, *see* compiler, activation record
adjacency list, 192, 220
adjacency matrix, 192, 220
algorithm analysis, xi, 14, 41–74, 225
    amortized, *see* amortized analysis
    asymptotic, 51–57, 421
    empirical comparison, 41–42, 69, 226
    for program statements, 57–62
    multiple parameters, 63–64
    running time measures, 43
    space requirements, 42, 64–67
algorithm, definition of, 11–13
all-pairs shortest paths, 211–214, 221, 222, 439
amortized analysis, 60, 96, 306, 421, 431–434, 437
array
    dynamic, 96, 437
    implementation, 7, 8, 16

artificial intelligence, 189
assert, xiv, 25
asymptotic analysis, *see* algorithm analysis, asymptotic
average-case analysis, 47–48
AVL tree, 161, 416

back of the envelope, napkin, *see* estimating
basic operation, 4, 5, 15, 16, 43, 50
best-case analysis, 47–48
big-Oh notation, *see* O notation
binary search, *see* search, binary
binary search tree, *see* BST
binary tree, 121–167
    BST, *see* BST
    complete, 122, 123, 134, 154, 247
    element, 126
    full, 122–125, 131, 133, 137, 161, 184
    implementation, 121, 124, 161
    node, 121, 126, 128–131
    notation, 121–123
    null pointers, 125
    overhead, 131
    parent pointer, 128